ROBERT BRIDGES

ROBERT BRIDGES

A Biography

CATHERINE PHILLIPS

Oxford New York
OXFORD UNIVERSITY PRESS
1992

Oxford University Press, Walton Street, Oxford OX2 6DP
Oxford New York Toronto
Delhi Bombay Calcutta Madras Karachi
Petaling Jaya Singapore Hong Kong Tokyo
Nairobi Dar es Salaam Cape Town
Melbourne Auckland
and associated companies in
Berlin Ibadan

Oxford is a trade mark of Oxford University Press

British Library Cataloguing in Publication Data
Data available

Library of Congress Cataloging in Publication Data
Phillips, Catherine.
Robert Bridges: a biography / Catherine Phillips.
p. cm.
Includes bibliographical references.
1. Bridges, Robert Seymour, 1844–1930—Biography. 2. Poets, English—19th century—Biography. 3. Poets, English—20th century—Biography. I. Title.
PR4161.B6Z82 1992 821'.8—dc20 91–32948
ISBN 0–19–212251–7

Typeset by Cambridge Composing (UK) Ltd
Printed in Hong Kong

CONTENTS

LIST OF ILLUSTRATIONS

Between pages 146 and 147

(Numbers 1, 2, 3, 4, 5, 7, 8, 9, 12, 13, 14, 16, 17 reproduced courtesy of the Hon. R. O. Bridges; nos. 11 and 15 reproduced courtesy of the Lord Bridges and Professor Donald Stanford; no. 6 reproduced courtesy of Corpus Christi College, Oxford; no. 10 reproduced courtesy of Mr David Waterhouse)

INTRODUCTION

Robert Bridges is best known today for his editing of the *Poems of Gerard Manley Hopkins*. While it is undoubtedly to Bridges that we owe much of our knowledge of Hopkins, Bridges' own work and life are also of interest and importance. Like Hardy, Bridges wrote very fine poetry but of a sort that is not densely allusive. This does not mean that either poet wrote only simple verse but that the difficulties of many of their best lyrics require most attention to the subtleties of the way in which ideas and emotions are being conveyed. Hardy's poetry has found its admirers, but Bridges', which is similarly in an English rather than Modernist tradition, is not at present given the recognition it deserves.

Bridges' long and active life, from 1844 to 1930, is of interest to the cultural historian because it illustrates vividly a number of the problems experienced by those who lived through the transition from the Victorian age to the modern world. While Bridges' reactions to some of the changing attitudes and beliefs were characteristic of his class and time, others were thoughtfully independent. The range of his interests, from medicine to literature and music, gave him a wide circle of friends that included the Royal physician Sir Thomas Barlow, the architect Alfred Waterhouse, the philosopher George Santayana, the artist Roger Fry, the musician Hubert Parry, and the poets Gerard Manley Hopkins and W. B. Yeats.

Deciding that he did not want a biography to be written of him, Bridges destroyed a great deal of material that would have been useful in such an undertaking. Unfortunately, that avoidance of scrutiny has left him the victim of misunderstanding and anachronistic judgements. Hopkins' letters are well known and Bridges is most often seen through them. But Hopkins' perspective was a somewhat unusual one. He also made comments that were deliberately exaggerated, sometimes for comic effect, sometimes as part of an argument. Many of those he made about Bridges' actions, motivation, and critical opinions need Bridges' rejoinders before a true picture can be established. Because Bridges destroyed most of his side of the correspondence this cannot always be provided specifically, but it is possible to build up a general idea of his attitudes and values and his epistolary style. This provides greater comprehension, not only of Bridges but of the issues with which Hopkins was concerned. It is also necessary for a deeper understanding of Hopkins that he be seen in a wider perspective than that of his own letters and Bridges' life contributes significantly to this.

Although in recent years Bridges has received comparatively little attention, there have been some notable exceptions to the rule: Edward Thompson's book of 1944 provided a critical survey of his work and a vivid account of Bridges as Thompson knew him in his last years. Thompson, who was Bridges' junior by forty years, lived in India until 1923 when he became lecturer in Bengali at Oxford to Indian Civil Service probationers. He was a neighbour of the Bridges on Boars Hill. But Thompson either knew no more of the sorrows and difficulties of the older man's life than had been published or drew a discreet veil over them, perpetuating the myth that Bridges had led an almost completely happy, healthy, and uneventful existence.[1]

There have been several specifically literary studies of Bridges' writing: Albert Guérard's *Study of Traditionalism in Poetry* contains a more comprehensive and sophisticated interpretation of his work than Thompson undertook,[2] and John Sparrow's *Robert Bridges* is a brief, concise, and appreciative account.[3] The largest contribution to Bridges studies has undoubtedly been made by Donald Stanford, who has published a series of important articles on topics ranging from Bridges' relation with both English and Modernist poets to his interest in prosody, drama, and printing.[4] Stanford has edited a selection of Bridges' poems, written a critical book on him,[5] and produced two large volumes of his letters with an enormous amount of information in notes and prefaces. These argue for the importance of Bridges' work and make available much of the material necessary for a complete revaluation of his life.

Bridges' destruction of material especially from his early life has of course caused me problems. There are sections of this book where deductions have had to be made from scraps of information, where it has been possible to provide only a general picture of what a place or a 'typical experience' at the time was like. The material kept by the family relates largely to Bridges' later life and most of it is now in the Bodleian Library. It was devotedly prepared for the family's descendants by Bridges' son, Edward, who bound many of the important manuscripts and letters on particular subjects and wrote introductions to them. He followed his father's wish that his life remain private, with the result that it was only in 1977 that the vast majority of what is extant became accessible to scholars. The staff of the Bodleian Library have also contributed to sorting the papers and there is a useful catalogue prepared by Mrs Elizabeth Turner. I have been helped by a great many people during the writing of this book. First by the executors of Katharine, Lady Bridges, who have been extremely generous, patient and hospitable. David Waterhouse and Maurice and Rowan Waterhouse have also been most kind in finding, reproducing, and lending me family photographs and documents. Local historians such as Mr Les Cozens of Walmer and Mr Tony Arnold of the *East Kent Mercury* were extremely helpful. I am grateful to the verger of St Mary's, Walmer, to the librarians of the Public Libraries of Deal, Dover, and Maidstone, and staff of Canterbury Cathedral Library. I was helped considerably by Mr Patrick Strong and Mr Paul Quarrie, Librarian of Eton College, and by the archivists of St Bartholomew's Hospital and the Royal College of Physicians. Special thanks must go to Mr Colin Harris and his staff of the Bodleian Library for retrieving, time and again, trolley-loads of papers for me, and to the librarians of the British Library and the University libraries of Oxford, Cambridge, and Exeter. I greatly appreciated the knowledgeable assistance given me by Mrs Christine Butler, Assistant Archivist of Corpus Christi College, and by the archivists of New College and Pusey House, Oxford, and Trinity College and King's College, Cambridge. The staff of the Public Records offices at Somerset House and Chancery Lane were also very helpful. Dr Donald Stanford has been for many years a most stimulating and generous fellow-worker on Bridges. I am also grateful for information provided by Dr John Leigh and Dr John Kelly on Pound and W. B. Yeats, and by Dr Ann Thwaite on Edmund Gosse. In its rather different form as a doctoral dissertation I was encouraged and guided by Dr John Rathmell, Dr Philip Gaskell, and Dr Carl Baron, who kindly continued to assist me by suggesting sources of information at various later stages. I could not have done the work without the financial assistance of a Canada Council Doctoral Research Fellowship and a 'Thank-offering-to-Britain' Research Fellowship provided by the British Academy. Similarly, an Honorary Fellowship at the University of Exeter and a generous Visiting Scholarship at St John's College, Oxford, were very important in enabling me to carry out the research. I am grateful to Downing College, Cambridge, for a sabbatical term and to Lincoln College, Oxford, for hospitality. Thanks are due to Oxford University Press for allowing quotation from Hopkins' published volumes and to Professors Eugene Hollahan and Betty Crump, editors of *Gerard Manley Hopkins: The Centenary Revaluation* (1988) and a *Festschrift in Honour of Donald Stanford* for permitting the information originally contained in articles to be included here. I am very grateful for the advice given me by Lord Bridges and the readers at Oxford University Press, who assisted considerably in the shaping of the book. I would like finally to express thanks for the support and practical assistance that have been given to me unstintingly over the years by my husband and my parents.

AUTHOR'S NOTE

Readers may wonder at Bridges' spelling and punctuation. He developed a 'simplified' spelling that was closer to pronunciation and distinguished one or two parts of speech. Although this can be distracting initially, it never diverges from standard English to the extent of leaving a reader in any doubt about the intended word. In his letters Bridges used various abbreviations, mostly common ones. He also departed from standard punctuation by using a full stop in two ways, one conventional, but the second as a pause rather like the Greek high stop usually transliterated as a semicolon. He would also use the sign '=' as a hyphen, and two dots '..' to mark a pause. Since his letters are not so much prose compositions as the rapid transcriptions of his flow of thought, his punctuation and abbreviations have generally not been regularized.

1

Childhood in Roseland

(1844–1854)

The Bridges family had been yeoman farmers in the Isle of Thanet, Kent since the sixteenth century. They had prospered, and in 1810 their holdings were considerably enlarged when John Bridges purchased St Nicholas Court and took a long lease on the attached farm. Their principal crop was wheat and the rise in the family's fortunes was related to the escalation in the price of wheat at this time. John Bridges' only son, John Thomas Bridges (1805–53) inherited the family property. He took his degree from Oxford in 1827, and having no taste for farming, especially at a time when the price of wheat was plummeting, soon decided to settle elsewhere. He married Harriett Affleck, the third daughter of the Revd Sir Robert Affleck of Dalham in Suffolk, and in 1832 the couple and their 2-year-old daughter, Maria Elizabeth, took up residence at Upper Walmer in Kent.[1] They bought Roseland, a large and rather ugly house built in the latter part of the eighteenth century by Admiral Sir Henry Harvey and owned by his son, Admiral Sir Thomas Harvey.[2] Here five sons and three more daughters were born: John Affleck in 1832, Frances Caroline in 1834, George Lovibond in 1835, Harriett Louisa in 1837, Thomas Walker in 1839, Julia Mary in 1841, Robert Seymour on 23 October 1844, and Edward in 1846.

Although Robert's earliest memories were of having pneumonia when he was between 3 and 4, and he remembered nothing else, he said, until he 'got a bad fright', much of what he has left on record of the later stages of his childhood is happy. He had a particularly kind nurse, Catharine Ashby, whom he described as 'a saint, a nurse and mate of . . . loving devotion patience and full trust'. In 1924 he had a brass memorial tablet installed in Mongeham Church, reading:

Neither thy loving kindness nor thy piety saved thee Nurse when
Among the living from grievous suffering
But if among the blessed there is compensation for good deeds
Thou wilt be in greater honour than the poet
Who (having been nurtured the 8th of 9) to repay the dues of rearing
Has set up this memorial of enduring love.[3]

Under her watchful eye he was able to adventure beyond Roseland. The house was situated in the heart of the small village, on the east side of High Street, nearly opposite the village forge, which was flanked by grocery shops and the post office.

Walmer when Robert knew it was essentially two communities, Upper and Lower Walmer, totalling some two thousand inhabitants.[4] Upper Walmer was perched fifty feet above and half a mile from the sea. Nearby there were the remains of ancient earthworks and tumuli. As at so many places along the south-east coast, it was said that Julius Caesar had first landed in Britain close by, and the numerous Roman remains suggested that at some point there had been a sizeable Roman settlement. St Mary's, the local church, had been built and bequeathed to Langdon Abbey in 1192 by the D'Auberville family, whose castellated mansion had stood adjacent to it. The abbey had been the first to be dissolved by Henry VIII, who granted St Mary's to Archbishop Cranmer. The other main historical building in the area was Walmer Castle, which Henry VIII had built as one of five forts to protect the coast against the French, and it still maintained a garrison for that purpose. It was the residence of the Warden of the Cinque Ports, a position held from 1806 to 1852 by the Duke of Wellington, who usually spent August living there and sometimes invited the Bridges to his receptions. He feared that Britain would no longer be able to withstand an attack by the French and sought to increase the size of the armed forces. They were very much in evidence in Walmer, which had a large barracks housing several hundred naval personnel, cavalry, and infantry, and there were many officers living in the neighbourhood. The Royal Naval Hospital was also situated in Walmer. Although in peace it became a coastguard station, during the Crimean War it was fully operational.

As a child Robert was taken to hear concerts given regularly by military bands in the village. These delighted him, gifted as he was with acute hearing and a love of music. Escaping from Kate, he would, he later recalled,

> steal between the legs of the performers into the magic circle, where I could stand close under the instruments and drink in their peculiar sonorities to my heart's content. The spectacle of my innocent delight must have amused the bandsmen and lightened the monotony of their routine; but I fancy that the bassoon-player may have been annoyingly rallied by his comrades for the special attention that his particular performance won from me; for the low notes of his register amazed me as much as anything of the kind ever has since, and I do not know that I have now quite lost my original feeling towards them.[5]

Behind Roseland and to the north there were six acres of land, some of it garden, some grazing meadow. A poem, 'Elegy: The Summer-House on the Mound', written decades later shows Robert's childhood pleasure in it:

> How well my eyes remember the dim path . . .
> Its leafy walls, beneath its arching green . . .
>   There grew two fellow limes, two rising trees,
> Shadowing the lawn, the summer haunt of bees,
> Whose stems, engraved with many a russet scar
> From the spear-hurlings of our mimic war,
> Pillar'd the portico to that wide walk,
> A mossy terrace of the native chalk
> Fashion'd, that led thro' the dark shades around
> Straight to the wooden temple on the mound. . . .
>   High on the mound the ivied arbour stood,
> A dome of straw upheld on rustic wood:
> Hidden in fern the steps of the ascent,
> Whereby unto the southern front we went,
> And from the dark plantation climbing free,
> Over a valley look'd out on the sea.

The ground sloped steeply from the edge of the garden into a valley running down to Walmer Castle on the sea-front. From the upper windows of Roseland, as from the summer-house in the grounds, it was possible to look out to the Downs, a broad stretch of sea in which hundreds of vessels waited for the right winds to begin their voyages. At low tide the treacherous Goodwin Sands could be seen littered with the stumps of wrecks; the danger was advertised by warning-lights and buoys and, except in the calmest weather, by an ominous line of tossing white surf. Many local men were known for their bravery in rescuing shipwrecked sailors. Beyond the Goodwins, on a clear day, it was possible to see the coast of France and, through a telescope, the fields, houses, and windmills on the cliffs of Boulogne and Calais. The beach too was steep, and under the care of his nurse Robert played by the hour with a child's insatiable interest in sea and shore. Writing of a similar coast visited as an adult, he recalled his earlier experience:

> On such a stony, breaking beach
> My childhood chanced and chose to be:
> 'Twas here I played, and musing made
> My friend the melancholy sea.
>   He from his dim enchanted caves
> With shuddering roar and onrush wild
> Fell down in sacrificial waves
> At feet of his exulting child.

In summer, on birthdays and other special occasions, family excursions would be made to Pegwell Bay, where the Stour feeds into the sea in a wet marsh and the children prized the wide range of sea shells. Robert's love of the sea was the many-sided attachment of someone raised beside it rather than the city child's memories of summer holidays. Images of it pervade his poetry, and when in later years he sought to escape from the pressures he faced in London it was to this coast that he most often fled.

The Bridges children were taught at home by a governess until the sons reached the age of 10, when they were sent away to school, while the daughters remained at home until they married. The first of the governesses that Robert would have known was a middle-aged Scottish spinster by the name of Mansfield R. Bradfoot. Her successor, a Miss Strutt, made a deeper impression on his mind. As an adult he once dreamt that he was again a 7-year-old staring up into her 'wizened and unsympathetic' face framed with 'curious dark black ringlets',[6] a contrast with his sisters' simple arrangements of their straight, brown hair. Since Tom, the brother nearest in age to Robert, was five years his senior, there was a period of five years during which for much of the year Julia would have been his closest playmate. In a poem of 1924 he recorded an expedition undertaken with her and their nurse when they were allowed to accompany Catharine on her weekly visit to her mother, who lived across the downs in the next combe, a round trip of several miles. This rolling, open land, swept by the sea breezes, was another of Robert's favourite haunts, later recalling for him a sense of freedom and leisure that appears in such poems as 'The Downs'. Although he could not have been more than 8 or 9 at the time, he absorbed impressions of the route that he wrote about seventy years later. He and Julia pretended to be Israelites crossing the treeless plain, a game abandoned to forage for flowers.

> . . . with such posies in hand
> we ran bragging to Kate who plodded on the track
> and now with skilful words beguiled us in her train
> warning how far off yet the promised land, and how
> journey so great required our full strength husbanded
> for the return: 'twere wise today to prove our strength
> and walk like men. Whereat we wished most to be wise
> and keeping near beside her heeded closely our steps
> so that our thoughts now wander'd no more from the way
> (O how interminable to me seem'd that way!)
> till it fell sloping downwards and we saw the green
> of great elms that uplifted their heads in the combe

The old lady's thatched cottage in its sweet-smelling garden and her mantelpiece ornaments made a deep impression on him, as did the symptoms of her condition, which he was later to recognize as shaking palsy:

> . . . I saw
> how her right foot in the air was all a-tremble and jerked
> in little restless kicks: so when we sat to feast
> about the table spredd with tea and cottage cakes
> whenever her eye was off me I watched her furtively
> to make myself assured of all the manner and truth
> of this new thing

Fatigue must then have set in, for he notes that 'what follow'd is lost, | how I chew'd mint-leaves waiting there in the garden | is my latest remembrance of that July day, | all after is blank'.

During the absence of his elder brothers, Robert's world would have been dominated by women. None of his sisters married before he was sent away to school and most of the half-dozen servants in the household were women. Photographs of three of his elder sisters show them well-dressed with their hair identically arranged: parted in the middle and drawn back loosely into a net. One photograph shows the youngest of the boys, Edward, sitting on one sister's lap, her hand closed protectively on his arm while his hand rests in a relaxed, confident way on a second of his sisters. As is clear in the photograph, Edward was the family favourite. His health was fragile and yet the photograph shows a merry, even cheeky face. Robert became devoted to him, and by the time he left school intended to set up house looking after him. Both boys were fond of music and, unlike the elder brothers, learned to read and write it. Their sisters were all taught to play the piano, and although Robert does not seem to have achieved the proficiency to perform on the instrument, he knew enough later to write hymns with accompaniments. The Bridges frequently had musical evenings with friends, and Sunday evenings customarily ended with the family gathered round the piano singing hymns. While at Oxford, Mr Bridges, who seems to have written some music himself, had purchased 'basshorns, trombones, saxhorns' and various other instruments for the use of himself and his friends. One day during his childhood Robert came across these while playing in the cellar at Roseland and, captivated by the possibility of producing the sounds he heard from the military bands, he proceeded to blow and puff, in vain; the disappointment was intensely remembered even in his old age.[7]

Mrs Bridges was the pious daughter of a clergyman, but her personality was not chilled by her belief. Histories of the Walmer area mention her as the founder of St Saviour's, a chapel in Lower Walmer which she endowed in 1848. Local people recorded appreciatively the generous dinner she gave for the parish after the consecration in July 1849. Robert and John both wrote about her with great affection. Robert was clearly both very proud of and deeply attached to her. In his memoir of his cousin, Digby Mackworth Dolben, he wrote:

> I was related through my mother with both Dolbens and Mackworths, indeed my mother's great-grandmother in the direct male line was a

Dolben, so that, I myself am in some fractional part a Dolben; and the names of Dolben, Mackworth, and Finedon [the home of the Mackworth Dolbens] were familiar to me as far back as nursery days, when my mother used to amuse us younger children with tales of her own childhood. A merry, gamesome spirit was not the least of her charms, and that she had been so universal a favourite in her girlhood may have been greatly due to the original pranks with which she would enliven any society whose dulness or gravity provoked her. Among the various scenes of her fund of stories Finedon was one. Her grandfather had once been rector of the parish, and the family associations were continued by occasional visits to Hall or Rectory, in days that seemed to the younger generation to have been unusually supplied with a dignified and long-lived aristocracy of generals, baronets and divines, whose features were familiar to me among the many miniatures, silhouettes and other little portraits, mementos of personal affection, that hung in my mother's rooms, and in their eighteenth-century fashions, kindled our imaginations of a strange and remote world.

A story which I well remember will exhibit the keeping of these associations—though I can not truly locate it at Finedon,—how my mother espying one of these old-fashioned gentlemen taking a nap by the open window of a garden-room, drew his pigtail through to the outside, and shut the sash down upon it. Her freak, inspired by simple delight in the prospect of the mighty anger and fuss that would ensue when the hero awoke, was fully successful, and the consequent disturbance went on rippling with amusement in her memory for at least seventy-five years.[8]

She tried hard to make the annual Christmas parties fun, on one occasion replacing the usual Christmas tree with a model of a Swiss scene. Mountains, a valley, and even a small lake were constructed from barrow-loads of soil, with cuttings for forests and brown paper moulded into mountain peaks and valleys. Her letters suggest that she was a practical and humane person, unobtrusively charitable and close to her children.

On Sundays the family would attend services in St Mary's. The church path led between graves and ancient yew trees to a beautiful Norman entrance at the end of the side wall. In 1826 the wall on the other side of the nave was knocked down and a transept built on the higher ground at the back of the church in an attempt to seat the congregation of the growing village. From the transept the altar could not be seen, but the tall pulpit could. Many of the wealthier families had their own pews, decorated at Christmas with sprigs of holly. The Bridges' pew was across the aisle from the Duke of Wellington's, which was just in front of the pulpit, and the children had the satisfaction of seeing the elderly general dozing through the sermon. There were other reminders that the area was of military and naval importance. Memorial tablets on the walls commemorated generations of officers, and the congregation usually included military and naval personnel. Wellington died at Walmer, and as a 7-year-old Robert watched the flag dropped at the Castle announcing the Duke's death.

When his brothers were at home Robert spent most time with George, who was fascinated by ships. Together they would spend hours staring through the telescope kept in the summer-house on the mound. George drew the boats and their flags, and Robert later included his own acute impressions in 'The Summer-House on the Mound'.

> The brazen disc is cold against my brow,
> And in my sight a circle of the sea
> Enlarged to swiftness, where the salt waves flee,
> And ships in stately motion pass so near
> That what I see is speaking to my ear:
> I hear the waves dash and the tackle strain,
> The canvas flap, the rattle of the chain
> That runs out thro' the hawse, the clank of the winch
> Winding the rusty cable inch by inch,
> Till half I wonder if they have no care,
> Those sailors, that my glass is brought to bear
> On all their doings, if I vex them not
> On every petty task of their rough lot
> Prying and spying, searching every craft
> From painted truck to gunnel, fore and aft,—
> Thro' idle Sundays as I have watch'd them lean
> Long hours upon the rail, or neath its screen
> Prone on the deck to lie outstretch'd at length,
> Sunk in renewal of their wearied strength.

As soon as he left school George joined the navy, becoming a midshipman on the *Phaeton*, one of the last and fastest sailing frigates to be built without auxiliary steam power. During the Crimean War he served on the *Duke of Wellington*, the flagship of Napier's Baltic Fleet. Robert remembered watching him being rowed out to the ship in a dinghy flying a flag made by their sisters. Throughout his time in the navy George drew ships and scenes as far afield as the Gulf of Mexico, the Mediterranean, and the Baltic. Later, when he served aboard the Royal Yacht, his book of paintings was sometimes called for to be shown to Royal visitors. A photograph of George, probably taken when he was in his early twenties, shows a generous mouth and direct gaze. His clothes are made of heavy cloth, warm rather than elegant, the collar is slightly awry, his hair uncombed. His pose suggests that he found having his photograph taken an uncomfortably vain thing to do, though one with which he was determined to go through. It may perhaps have been taken to give to his family and wife Harriet Butler, Samuel Butler's elder sister whom he married in 1859.

At home the children were encouraged to read. The eldest son John disparagingly compared the obvious didacticism of many of their books with the imaginative stories of Kipling and Lewis Carroll available to later generations. However, he noted,

> yet what our literature lacked in quality was made up to us in quantity. For our behoof on Sundays and weekdays, Messrs Crossman, Magnall and Co asked sacred and profane riddles, to which they were so obliging as to supply answers. To the query in the former as to why Ash Wednesday was so called, the reply was appended: 'Because the ancient Christians used on that day to sprinkle ashes on their heads, or sit in embers or ashes.' We hoped they preferred the latter.

'Our literature,' he said, 'was divided into two parts, sacred and profane.' The younger children had copies of Lear's *Book of Nonsense*, carefully bowdlerized by their governess of anything 'vulgar', while the older children had *Elegant Extracts*, two big volumes of poetry and prose. They had a distinct preference for the poetry volume, which included many of the most familiar extracts from Shakespeare, Cotton's 'Visions', samples from Young, Thomson, Collins, Crabbe and Gray, and Dryden's 'Religio Laici', which John considered to have 'very rude' versification but matter 'fine and quite above us children'; Robert was never an admirer of Dryden. John recalled:

> For week-day prose we had 'Robinson Crusoe', which is not a children's book; the priggish 'Sandford and Merton'; 'Parents' Assistant'; Miss

Edgeworth's tales—these must still have some measure of popularity, Simple Susan's advice to 'take a spoon pig' being to some extent a household word . . .

Chief among the books reserved for Sunday reading was the 'Pilgrim's Progress', with its funny little engravings . . . Samuel Wilberforce's 'Agathos', 'The Spring Morning', and other allegories, for which Bunyan no doubt supplied the inspiration. We spent Sunday evening reading or reciting sacred poetry, of which we had numerous collections, each of them with some arresting favourites. Indeed, a book of sacred poetry was quite an acceptable present on one of our numerous birthdays.[9]

Robert later thought that Keble's *Christian Year*, one of the books given to him to memorize on Sunday evenings, had substantially influenced him towards Puseyism. The children compiled their own newspaper, the 'St Margaret's News', to which all except the very youngest contributed. It was largely devoted to comic versions of local events, often written in verse.

In May 1853 the children's father, whose health does not seem to have been particularly good, fell ill and died a few weeks later. Robert was 9. The only allusions to his father among his papers mention his irrepressible sense of humour and a journal that his father had kept when in Italy and which Robert later wanted to read before visiting the country. The latter comment, made in a letter to his mother, shows an affectionate memory of him evident too in John's idea of him as a kindly and moderate man who, 'while objecting to our "making fun" of our neighbours' in the 'St Margaret's News', generally ended by laughing. Mr Bridges was buried in the Isle of Thanet.

In 1854 the eldest daughter, Maria, married Guilford Molesworth and settled in a small house in Bexley. Guilford, one of the younger sons of the Revd Dr John Edward Nassau Molesworth, was an engineer who was to become important in the construction of railways and other engineering projects in Ceylon and was later knighted for his contribution. The marriage evidently brought the two families together, for in October 1854 the widowed Mrs Bridges married Guilford's father, who had been widowed in 1851.[10] She was doubtless lonely and faced with daunting responsibility. Molesworth had been made vicar of Minster-in-Thanet in 1839, and early in 1840 had been presented to the living of Rochdale in Lancashire. Mrs Bridges sold the family property in the Isle of Thanet and Roseland, and moved with her daughters and Edward to the rectory in Rochdale. Robert was old enough to go to Eton. Molesworth was by this time 64 years old, wealthy and an eminent churchman. He had been curate of Millbrook, Hampshire, then rector of Wirksworth, Derbyshire, and St Martin's, Canterbury, and one of the Six Preachers of Canterbury Cathedral. At Canterbury his energy and enthusiasm led to his becoming one of the leaders in Church matters there and—his other main interest being education—he helped in establishing a girls' school to which he sent his own daughters. In 1835 he started the *Penny Sunday Reader*, the first of the cheap Church Sunday periodicals, which proved so popular that he produced it for five years. He followed a similar pattern in Rochdale where he used money from development on church land to finance the building of new churches in the parish and the conversion of chapels of ease into churches, and he was industrious in providing the grammar school with new buildings. An elderly inhabitant remarked, 'What surprised me most that has happened during my lifetime, is the resurrection of the Church in Rochdale. When Dr Molesworth came it seemed to be quite dead,' (*A Life*, 105). By 1855, when the vicarage in Rochdale became Robert's home, Dr Molesworth would have been well established in the area.

Two incidents related by Guilford Molesworth show other sides of his character: 'That artistic tastes did not appeal to his eminently practical mind may be gathered from the fact that, whenever his [first] wife, who was both a good musician and vocalist, sat down to the piano, he was wont to observe: "Don't you think you could do something more useful, my Queen?"' The second occurred when his eldest daughter from his first marriage had been given money by an aunt to buy an evening-dress in which to attend a dinner-party with her father. When she came downstairs ready to go out, 'instead of being pleased with her appearance, he simply said he was sorry to see the daughter of a clergyman dressing in a style above her station' (*A Life*, xi). These anecdotes suggest that life in the vicarage would have been much less carefree for Robert than in his early childhood. John, who was in his twenties, would have been too old to have been much affected by the new environment. George and Tom were both already at school and intending to enter the navy and army. However, the influence of religion on the children still at home clearly increased. Robert's elder sisters, Frances and Harriett, both married clergymen and Julia entered a Mission House. Robert seriously considered entering the Church himself. It would seem that although, guided by his mother, he was respectful of Dr Molesworth, he did not grow fond of him. There is no extant correspondence between them, and what allusions to him there are in Robert's later letters do not suggest a bond. It is perhaps fortunate that the new and liberating world of Eton was opened up to him at this time.

2

Eton

(1854–1863)

Robert entered Eton on 23 September 1854. Among the brothers only John and Robert went to Eton, and John left the school before Robert arrived. John's ability at sport had been given free reign there, but his account of classes suggests that there was too little discipline for much to be learnt. John and Robert were both considerable athletes—both were to be over six feet tall. John rowed in the Eton eight and, although Robert did not achieve this while at school, he developed into a very good oarsman at Oxford and also played football and cricket. With his talent for sport and the arts and a certain readiness to undertake mild pranks, Robert fitted into the school easily. He was straightforward and kindly and rapidly made friends, with some of whom he was to remain close throughout his life.

Eton College has traditionally been divided into two communities: collegers, students awarded scholarships 'on the foundation' who do not pay fees, and oppidans, by far the larger number, whose parents pay considerable fees.[1] The living conditions of the collegers had been appalling, as numerous memoirs recall, but during the 1850s and 1860s some efforts were made to try and improve these. The oppidans lived in twenty-nine houses, some run by masters, others simply by householders called 'Dames' or Dominie. Some of these contributed very little to the boys' development: John noted that his Dominie confiscated any books not on the curriculum which he found the boys reading, regardless of their quality. By contrast, Dominie Thomas H. Stevens, who ran Westons—the house in which Robert spent most of his years at Eton—was kindly and less rigid towards the twenty-three boys in his care. Robert was fond of him and sufficiently convinced of his interest in what he would achieve to send him a copy of his first published volume of poems. Westons, which is still standing, is an attractive brick building of great character built largely in the seventeenth century. Some of the boys' rooms were small and at least one of those that Robert had was later described by a friend of his as 'appallingly sordid',[2] but each boy did have the privilege of privacy and quiet. From the upper floors it was possible to see the main college buildings and, above their crenellated walls, the Gothic spires of the chapel. The north side of Westons lies along the Slough Road and to the east the windows overlook a large sports field called 'Little Britain'.

The rooms were heated by open fires, which were made each morning and raked out each evening by the women servants who also washed and mended the boys' clothes. The first lessons of the day were at 7.00 or 7.30 before breakfast, although Robert doubtless followed the custom of fortifying himself for them with rolls or cooked provisions from the 'sock' shops in the town. In his early years he would have had to fetch such provisions for the older boys to whom he served as a fag. At 9.15 there was a half-hour service in chapel. Further lessons were from 9.45 to 10.30, 11.15 to noon, 2.45 to 3.30 and 5.00 to 6.00, except on Tuesdays, Thursdays, and Saturdays, which were half-holidays. Dinner and supper were communal meals, with Mr Stevens presiding at Westons. The sense of community was also enhanced by the various games competitions between houses. Except for special classes the boys were not allowed out after 6.00 p.m. in winter or 8.45 p.m. in summer. After 'lock-up' they could work together and chat or play music. Bedtime, when the servants removed candles and cleared out fires, was at 10.00 p.m. for Fourth Form and Lower School boys, 10.30 for those in Remove (between Fourth and Fifth Form), and, in some houses, 11.00 p.m. for the Fifth Form.

Robert entered Eton before the sweeping changes of the 1860s were made to its curriculum in response to criticism about poor academic standards. Eton traditionally took all its tutors from its sister foundation, King's College, Cambridge, and most were clerics. Masters teaching subjects such as French, arithmetic, or drawing were relegated to inferior status in a number of petty and annoying ways. Dr Goodford, headmaster from 1853 to 1862, hired two masters from Oxford, a step towards decreasing the inbreeding, and he accorded the arithmetic masters the right to wear gowns in school and chapel as the classics masters did. Care for the oppidans was shared by their housemasters and their tutors. To the latter Robert would have rehearsed Latin and Greek verses before submitting them in school. He would also have learned from his tutor passages of scripture in Greek, ancient and modern history and geography, and written for him an essay in Latin once a week. The Lower School boys were given three lessons a week in handwriting until they wrote well. Mr Harris, who would have taught Robert, passed on to him a preference for quills rather than steel pens and a lifelong interest in calligraphy. The absent-minded Mr Harris had the habit of sticking a quill behind his ear, and on occasion was observed to go out with his hat on and 'a pair of fresh-mended quills sticking out underneath'.

It was still firmly believed that to master Latin and Greek was 'to lay the surest, broadest foundation on which to build up other knowledge subsequently'.[3] One of Bridges' contemporaries records that in the Third Form, 'when not piecing dactyls and spondees together, we droned through the pages of the Eton Latin grammar. Oh, most foggy of books, in which the study of the simplest among languages was so obscured as to become mysterious and hard.' The boys retaliated with rowdiness. Robert noted that 'our behaviour to the Masters in those days was none of the best: we found pleasure in provoking them by constant petty annoyances. I look back with only regret and shame to my share in it, and have welcomed the gentler relations that now obtain.'[4] But he was critical of the way in which Latin had been taught and of the length of time it took in such a heavily classical curriculum before there was an intellectual reward for the labour involved, a stage that some never reached. He said later that he would also have had plenty of time to have learned additional subjects such as science.[5] Once the basics of Latin and Greek were sufficiently grasped, the boys moved gradually through Horace, Ovid, Livy, Cicero, Catullus, Propertius, Caesar, Greek lyric and elegiac writers, Virgil, Homer, some Thucydides, Herodotus, Demosthenes, Pindar, Plato's *Republic*, and a selection of Greek tragedies and comedies. The examinations which Robert took in 1863 show clearly the emphasis on parsing, on translation, and on being able to write in Greek and Latin. Some of the questions, however, suggest both the teachers' understanding of what might well catch the boys' fancy, and the patriotism and moral virtues that were being inculcated. For example, Latin lyrics were asked for in praise of Captains Speke and Grant for their discovery of the source of the Nile, and another question asked for Greek iambics translating the following:

> She heard, and bid him pause, to let the sound
> Of his sweet accents find a settled home,
> Not playfully disport in mazy run,
> Like notes of sacred harmony beneath
> The fretted vault of some high masonry.
> Then through the clear blue eye of him who spoke,
> Which gleam'd with soft delight to look on her,
> She threw a piercing shaft from her own ken,
> To hit the scope and purpose of his heart.
> 'Yes,' thought she, 'thou art true as crystal rock;
> No flaw, no dullness there, no crevice left
> For foul deceit to enter, and deface
> By secret working virtue's purity.
> Thou shalt be mine!'[6]

In addition the boys did some geometry and algebra, subjects in which Robert earned respectable but not top marks. He also learnt French. Although such 'extra' classes were often badly attended and unruly, he must have applied himself to the language for he acquired a sufficient grasp to read and comment on French writers, and a friend later recalled having tea with him in his room one afternoon while they quoted Molière to each other.[7]

Besides the classics, the other major ingredient of the curriculum at Eton was Christianity. The examinations show that the boys were trained to be orthodox and knowledgeable Anglicans: the final paper on the Bible which Robert sat, for example, required a number of translations of passages from the Greek New Testament accompanied by such questions as: 'Explain the allusions to errors, which obstructed the progress of the Gospel. Enumerate other difficulties, against which the first preachers of Christianity had to contend; stating the sources from which they took their origin. Support your answer by quotations from the Acts. What argument for the truth of Christianity is deduced therefrom?' and 'Give an analysis of St Paul's argument in the Epistle to the Hebrews. Quote what is said of Melchizedec in the Old Testament. State the several points of comparison, in which St Paul proves that our Lord's Priesthood, as being after the order of Melchizedec, is superior to that of the Levitical priesthood'. Once a week they prepared 'Sunday Questions', essays on passages assigned on Saturday and marked on Monday by their tutors. The books from which the passages came varied according to the tutor's taste. Although Robert deprecated the fact that in his final year he had to work at Bishop Wordsworth's *Notes on the Greek Testament* while one of his friends was assigned parts of *Paradise Lost*, the examinations on biblical and doctrinal knowledge for 1862 and 1863 suggest that Bishop Wordsworth would have been the more useful.

There were compulsory chapel services on three afternoons a week, and a tradition, prescribed in the statutes, of singing a polyphonic antiphon to the Virgin every evening. A collection of these, called the *Eton Choirbook*, was housed in the College Library. It is the most important collection of English church music of the late fifteenth century and Robert developed a deep love of the style. The 'Eton' choir at this time was that of St George's, the chapel at Windsor Castle, and in order to be on time for the service at St George's it had to file out in the middle of the service at Eton. Robert liked their singing and often slipped away during the afternoon break to listen to it at Windsor.[8] George Elvey, the organist, was a composer of oratorios, religious services, and anthems, who was later knighted in 1871. Robert became friendly with him, and in St George's would perch himself in the organ loft or the north aisle and creep out during the service in order to be back for a class at 5.00 p.m. St George's was out of bounds but such contravention of unimportant rules was condoned. Robert spent a lot of time making music with friends; Hubert Parry, four years Robert's junior and with whom he was later to collaborate in writing oratorios, remembered trying out the new school organ in his company, and Robert wrote music himself. He set a poem, 'O earlier shall the rose buds blow', written by William Johnson Cory, a master at Eton, of which Gerard Manley Hopkins later said, 'I feel sure you have a genius in music—on the strength of the only piece I know "O earlier": it is an inspiration of melody, but somewhat "sicklied o'er", as indeed the words are.'[9] Hopkins' statement suggests that this was not the only music Robert wrote during his school and university days, though he later destroyed it all.

Although the school was of broad Anglican persuasion, there were small groups with more High Church tendencies, to one of which Bridges belonged. At school, he said later, he had been a Puseyite, indirectly influenced by Newman's advocacy of the ideals of the Oxford Movement. He had not read any 'controversial' books and described himself as impatient of controversy, but his serious attitude to religion drew him to men who took religious orders; some became converts to Roman Catholicism, a course which met with disapproval; a number of the school sermons were outspoken against the Roman Catholic Church, and there was some alarm when John Walford, one of the masters at Eton became a Catholic convert. Later, when Digby Mackworth Dolben, one of Robert's 'cousins', seemed inclined to conversion, his family and the school authorities made concerted efforts to prevent it. The Puseyites at Eton did not form a clique but a 'free masonry' who met as a group so seldom that Robert knew well less than half of the dozen members.[10] By the end of Robert's time at Eton these included Wentworth Beaumont Hankey, Robert Bickersteth, Frederick Wood, Dolben, and V. S. S. Coles. Hankey, Bickersteth, and Dolben had all been at a private school at Cheam together and were considerably younger than Robert. The leader of the 'group' was Coles, the son of a minister at Shepton Beauchamp, who later became the Principal of Pusey House at Oxford. As a schoolboy his knowledge of Church doctrine was already somewhat more sophisticated than that of most of the others, and his well-balanced personality made him a favourite confidant. Robert's religious attitudes were reinforced by vacations spent at the rectory at Rochdale which exposed him to the influence of Dr Molesworth, who had been in sympathy with the Oxford Movement in its early stages for its reinvigorating effect on the Church of England. Although outspoken against Catholicism he always advocated tolerance in factional in-fighting within the Church of England, afraid that fanatical opposition would lead to more extreme positions and secessions to Rome.[11]

Digby Mackworth Dolben, whose personality in his short life

was to influence both Bridges and Hopkins profoundly, entered Eton when Robert was in his final year and became a member of Westons. Robert said later,

> Of our first meeting I have no recollection; but I remember him very well as a lower-boy in his broad collar and jacket. He was tall, pale, and of delicate appearance, and though his face was thoughtful and his features intellectual, he would not at that time have been thought good-looking. Indeed he was persistently teased by the little boys for his appearance, his neglectful dress, his abstracted manner, and his incapacity for games at ball. Not that he was inactive; he had his own pony at home and was fond of riding; he also became a good swimmer and delighted in open-air bathing; but his short sight excluded him from the common school-games; and though the dreaminess which it gave to his expression came to be a characteristic and genuine charm, it was, until it won romantic interpretation, only an awkwardness.[12]

Robert recorded, 'I had never myself met any of his family until Digby came to Eton, but our sisters were intimate, and we could call each other cousin. As I happened to be captain of the house, I was able without inconvenience to discharge those duties of elder relative which are so specially obnoxious to Eton boys. I enrolled Dolben among my fags, and looked after him.'[13] Although 'fagging' is clearly open to abuse, it was intended to provide younger boys with someone to defend and advise them. Digby indulged in a number of religious escapades that were strictly against the rules—attending Catholic services, spending the night at Catholic religious houses, and the like—which would have given Robert no little worry in his advisory role, but he was very fond of Digby and went out of his way to spend time with him: 'he was a boy who evidently needed both protection and sympathy, and I could not have talked to him without discovering the attraction of our similar inclinations and outlook on life.'[14] Their paths did not cross in class or in sport. Instead, they tended to meet in the evenings when Digby would go to Robert's room, or, more frequently, Robert take his work to Digby's small and narrow room, overlooking the Slough road. Tilting his chair back, Digby would balance by pressing his fingers against two of the walls, and by the light of his tallow dip they would spend a large part of the time talking.

We may very often have spoken on religious matters, but when I try to recall those evenings, it is only of poetry that I think, of our equal enthusiasm for it, and mutual divergence of taste: the conversations themselves perished no doubt of sheer immaturity. I was then reading Shakespeare for the first time, and my imperfect understanding hindered neither my enjoyment nor admiration. I also studied Milton, and carried Keats in my pocket.

These were the writers critics were later to see as most influential on Robert's style in his poems in traditional metres. On the other hand,

Dolben, though I cannot remember that he had any enthusiasm for Shakespeare, was more widely read in poetry than I, as he was also more abreast with the taste of the day. Browning, Mrs Browning, Tennyson and Ruskin were the authors of whom he would talk; and among the poets he ranked Faber, a Romanized clergyman, of whose works I have nothing to say, except that a maudlin hymn of his, when Digby showed it me, provoked my disgust.

a reaction Bridges also had to many Anglican hymns. But the disapproval had other effects in his relationship with Digby:

I used to think that he had written a good many hymns in imitation of Faber, and that it was partly my dislike of that sort of thing which made him unwilling to show me his verses. My own boyish muse was being silenced by my reading of the great poets, and we were mutually coy of exposing our secret productions, which were so antipathetically bad. My last serious poem at school was a sentimental imitation of Spenser, and I remember his reading that. I was also abhorrent towards Ruskin, for I thought him affected, and was too ignorant of painting to understand his sermonizing; nor could I imagine how another could presume to tell me what I should like or dislike: and well as I loved some of Tennyson's early lyrics, and had them by heart, yet when I heard *The Idylls of the King* praised as if they were the final attainment of all poetry, then I drew into my shell, contented to think that I might be too stupid to understand, but that I could never expect as good a pleasure from following another's taste as I got from my own. I remember how I submissively concluded that it must be my own dulness which prevented my admiring Tennyson as much as William Johnson [Cory] did,—and this no doubt was a very proper conclusion; and I yielded to the vogue enough to choose from the *Idylls* my speech on the 4th of June, wherewith I indulged the ears of his late majesty K. Edward VII on the year of his marriage; and I even purchased as gifts to my friends the fashionable volumes which I had never read through.[15]

Interestingly, Gerard Manley Hopkins reacted somewhat similarly, enjoying much of early Tennyson but objecting to *The Idylls* as 'Charades from the Middle Ages'.[16] Bridges continued

As for Browning, I had no leaning towards him; but when Digby read me extracts from *Saul*, I responded fairly well, and remember the novelty of the impression to this day. Of Dolben's own verse of this date no scrap remains. One evening when I was sitting in his room and moved to pull out the drawer where he kept his poems, the usual protest was not made. The drawer was empty; and he told me that he had burned them, every one. I was shocked, and felt some remorse in thinking that it was partly his dislike of my reading them that had led him to destroy them; and I always regretted their destruction until the other day [in 1911], when having to consider all his poems in the order of their composition, I realized for the first time that there is nothing of merit dating so far back even as a year after this holocaust. The poetry began suddenly in 1865, when, after a few poems of uncertain quality, the true vein was struck, and yielded more and more richly till the end.[17]

Bridges later discovered that some in fact of the poems of 1863 were preserved through copies made by Dolben's friends, but they did not change his opinion.

Digby's school poems were outpourings of his emotions over two subjects—religion and a fellow student on whom he doted. Bridges later criticized much of his early verse for encouraging in him a distortion of feeling, an exaggerated intensity, and a prizing of these emotions, although he acknowledged this impetus as one of the apprentices' approaches to the writing of poetry. He was himself taking what he thought of as the other approach, one which concentrated on finding which forms could most successfully express his various thoughts and feelings, although this too, as he recognized, did not guarantee escape from sentimentality. An interest in technical experimentation using the sort of analysis taught for classical verse was inevitably widespread among well-educated Victorian poets and their critics. Many modern critics have quoted Bridges' description of the two approaches, but nearly all of them have omitted the statement at the end of the passage, that with poetic maturity he believed that sincere emotion and technical mastery had both to be present. He praised Digby warmly for achieving this fusion in poems written between 1865 and his death in 1867.[18] Of Robert's poems only one is extant from this period, 'Love is up at break of day', and that was heavily revised in 1873.[19] He included it in his first published volume of poetry but not in any subsequent collection.

This enjoyment of the arts was balanced by another and equally typical Victorian preoccupation of the great public schools—patriotism. In 1859 Eton became the first of the schools to be caught up in the Rifle Volunteer Movement, which soon spread to the universities and throughout the country. The Duke of Wellington had given the movement new life some years previously by expressing fears that England would soon be at war with Napoleon III's France and that this time her regular forces would be too weak to repel invasion. By the summer of 1860 nearly half the upper-school boys at Eton (some 300) were enrolled in the Corps, among them Robert and his friend Lionel Muirhead. Robert would already have been familiar with the spectacle and purposes of military drill as marching troops had been a familiar sight at Lower Walmer with its large barracks, and his family had military connections: of his brothers, George had been in the navy, Tom was in the army, and John had belonged to the Kent Volunteers sent to the Crimean War, although he never saw action because peace was declared as he reached Malta.

These connections would have given Robert additional commitment to participating in the defence of the country. Drill at Eton was regular; the

> whole corps used to drill from 8.15 to 9.15 on Monday mornings, prayers in the houses being retarded a quarter of an hour for this purpose; and again on Fridays at 4 p.m. In addition to this, there were parades of the different companies singly for drill by their own officers. So long as the volunteer movement was in its freshness all this worked very well; there was a full muster at parades in the school yard; the masters and their families, officers from Windsor, a concourse of ladies and gentlemen from the neighbourhood used to assemble to admire the spectacle, and there was also a fife and drum band of one of the battalions of Guards in attendance to discourse music and speed up the corps on its march to the playing fields.[20]

Drill was initially supervised by sergeants from the Grenadier Guards; shooting practice was held less frequently because it involved a journey to the Windsor practice butts. The Corps probably reached its greatest popularity in 1861 when it was reviewed by the Queen and was invited to dine at Windsor afterwards.

Enthusiasm after that waned, although Robert attended a Volunteer dinner at Marlow in 1873 for members of the First Buckinghamshire Regiment and the Eton Rifle Volunteers presided over by his friend Owen Wethered, a contemporary of John Affleck's and a captain in the Bucks.

Patriotism was probably accentuated at Eton by the proximity of Windsor Castle and the Royal Family; the castle was not out of bounds and the boys regularly mingled with tourists there. The Prince of Wales frequently came to Eton to watch games or listen to lectures. Many of the court pages were Etonians and the school participated in the celebrations of the Prince of Wales's wedding with an enthusiasm that bordered on the riotous.

Robert left Eton in the summer of 1863, staying on after the end of term for a few days in order to entertain his brother Edward to trips on the river and, since he had developed into a keen musician, to introduce him to the early music at St George's; Dr Elvey allowed Robert to choose the anthems to be sung during Edward's stay. Edward's health was so delicate that, instead of experiencing the rough and tumble of school, he was studying with a tutor in Yorkshire. It must have been a poignant visit for Robert. In 1860 he had lost his brother George, who had caught a cold in the Baltic which had turned to pneumonia from which he had died at the age of 24. Having already lost this more robust brother and his father, Robert found that time spent with Edward, who could never enjoy the school life he had experienced, had a large element of sadness.

On his way home he spent a few days with Digby and his family at Finedon, their home in Northamptonshire, a large Elizabethan mansion with over twenty bedrooms. Although Robert disliked the sentimentality of Digby's father's manner, he was charmed by his mother and had happy memories of the visit: 'hot sunshine, the gay garden, the avenue in the summer night, the early rambles before breakfast, the fruit and the flowers and the family prayers.'[21] Asked to write a commemorative sonnet, he sent instead some comic rhymes, legacy of 'St Margaret's News'.

3

Oxford

(1863–1867)

Oxford was still a small town in September 1863 when Robert entered Corpus Christi College. It extended as far north as the newly constructed Museum of Science, as far east as Magdalen Bridge, west to the station, and south to Folly Bridge. The society at the university was exclusively male; the tutors were all, by regulation, unmarried, and although the President of Corpus, Dr Norris, had a family, they lived at Leamington and had nothing to do with the college. Corpus was the smallest of the colleges, with about sixty members, and ranked second academically behind Balliol. Situated between Merton and Christ Church, to which John had belonged, it backed on to the meadows that stretched down to the Thames with their college boat-houses. The small size of Corpus tended to work against the formation of cliques and the college was known for its friendly atmosphere.[1] A number of Bridges' contemporaries were the sons of British civil servants working in India.[2]

The daily routine of Corpus students was a simple one. Breakfast was taken in the students' rooms and breakfast parties with several courses were common.[3] Lectures were held in the college from 10.00 to 1.00 p.m., either in the tutors' rooms or the Hall and professors, whose lectures were open to the University, lectured from 1.00 to 2.00 p.m. A light lunch of bread, cheese, and beer was followed by recreation, which Robert generally spent rowing or playing football. In college he was known as one of the boating fraternity.

The Corpus Boat Club had only been established in 1858. Robert rowed during his first term in the college and by his second term the Captain's Book records that 'there was much more dash about the boat than previously, for which the crew were in a great measure indebted to the excellent stroke of Robert Bridges'.[4] Rowing took a considerable amount of time since the training included not only outings in the boat but also a daily run, and after his first year Bridges usually only rowed in the summer term, when he was invariably stroke. He served successively as treasurer, secretary, and captain (1865) of the Boat Club. Francis Chavasse, who sometimes rowed in 'R.B.'s' boats, noted in his journal the occasion in May 1866, when Corpus was for one day head of the river and Bridges was carried along the crowded bank on the shoulders of the crew.[5] They lost the position the following day, and although Bridges was still technically entitled to have a dinner held in his and the crew's honour, he refused to put the college to the expense. He also played football for Oxford, sometimes returning to Eton for games between the university and school teams. These games kept alive his contacts with the school, although the number of his friends there had obviously dwindled. He wrote to Muirhead in November 1865:

> I was at Eton yesterday. We had a firstrate game of football. But I saw very few people that I cared to. Gosselin [Dolben's friend and idol] was in London, which I knew beforehand. Walford [who became a Catholic in March 1866 and later as a Jesuit looked after Hopkins when he entered the novitiate] ditto—James [probably Charles Caldecott James, an assistant master] has grown a beard. Dom Stevens a moustache. Stephen Hawtrey [the head mathematics master] a beard. The Head [Edward Balston] was very gracious. We had a pleasant day on the whole, though it was a miserable way to spend best of All Saints in . . . Dolben as you know is ill though it is time he was well again now.[6]

Robert also entertained various members of his family in college. His brother Tom, who was at Woolwich, and John, Edward, and his mother all came at one time or another but there is no mention of his having played host to Dr Molesworth.

Bridges had friends too in several other colleges, especially Balliol; V. S. S. Coles was there, as was Lionel Muirhead until he had to give up his degree because of eye-trouble. Muirhead, who was to lead the life of a country gentleman and amateur artist, later became Bridges' closest friend. Bridges kept in contact with other former schoolfellows through the Old Etonians Club. It may have been Coles, or perhaps their mutual friend William

Sanday, with whom he later went to Germany, who introduced him to Gerard Manley Hopkins. Sanday was a year Bridges' senior, having spent his first year at Balliol before entering Corpus as a scholar in 1863. Hopkins described him as a 'Cosmopolite belonging equally to Balliol and Corpus . . . probably the most popular man known to the college' [Balliol], and 'the most charming'.[7] Hopkins' journals and letters of 1863–4 make little mention of Bridges; instead, it was Muirhead whom he was eager to get to know because of his reputation, thoroughly deserved, of being able to draw beautifully, a talent of special interest to Hopkins who was intending to emulate Dante Gabriel Rossetti's career of poet-artist. The friendship between Hopkins and Bridges seems to have started in 1865, when the first mentions of it occur in Hopkins' confession notes. On 30 April he wrote, 'nothing read, not very culpable perhaps, but chiefly through going to Bridges in the evening' and on 10 December, 'Foolish gossipy way with Bridges'.[8] Bridges admired Hopkins' poems and later praised them for their Keatsian sweetness; Keats was his favourite poet during his undergraduate days. Although Bridges almost certainly wrote poetry himself at this time there is no record of his having shown it to others, certainly not to Hopkins, who until 1874 thought of him as someone who wrote music.

The evening meal, Hall, was at 5.30. The Hall had three tables. The meals were liberal—a joint of meat which the students carved for themselves, bread, and beer. Dinner parties were discouraged and students allowed to eat the meal in their rooms if they wanted to work, and it was one of the principal times in the day for work. However, for those who wanted to relax for an hour or so, the Oxford Union had journals, newspapers, and letter-writing materials, and on Thursdays there was a debate in the Union open to members of the university. There were, too, smaller essay societies such as Hexameron, to which Hopkins and Coles belonged, where papers on such subjects as 'The Relation of Science to History' and 'Democracy: its nature and effects' were read, and discussion groups in which dons like Liddon and Pater gave papers.[9] 'Wines'—after-dinner parties at which desserts and drinks were served—were popular. Whist was a favourite pastime; Bridges was a life-long devotee and sometimes organized games in his rooms; but he liked too just to sit and chat by the light of candles or the fire in the grate.

Although it may not yet have been clear to undergraduates at the time, the university was on the road to changes that were to revolutionize its role. Was Oxford to be primarily an Anglican institution fostering the national religion, with its teaching-fellows unmarried clerics who would teach only until a living became vacant somewhere in the country? Or were the dons to be professional, lifelong academics with the right to marry? Such large questions surfaced in smaller issues, such as the recurrent debate over whether students and staff need declare an adherence to the Thirty-Nine Articles, or the associated long-running dispute over raising Benjamin Jowett's salary in line with that for other chairs despite his 'too liberal' religious views.

At the time the most widespread controversies among the students at Oxford were about religion. Morning chapel at 8.00 was compulsory, and until 1866–7, when Corpus became the first of the colleges to be allowed to use a shortened service, the whole of Morning Prayer was said. Afternoon chapel at 5.00 was optional or used as a punishment for venial offences. Except with special dispensation, it was still necessary to pass in divinity in both of the two public examinations required for a degree. In Moderations, the first of these examinations for *Literae Humaniores*, knowledge of the four gospels in Greek was tested, and in Greats, the second classical examination, the gospels, Acts in Greek, biblical history, the Thirty-Nine Articles and 'Evidences of Religion'. Although the Oxford Commission of 1853 had concluded that in many cases students signed the list of 'believers' as a mere formality of university entrance, there were many ardent and knowledgeable adherents to various sects.[10] At one end were the Catholic converts, who saw Newman as their example, and the High Churchmen, who looked to Pusey and Liddon, both of whom lectured regularly on Sunday evenings. In 1864 there was quite a stir when it was rumoured that Newman was moving back to Oxford to look after Roman Catholic students,[11] who were being allowed into certain colleges under rules that admitted dissenters in the hope that they might be persuaded to join the Church of England. At the other end of the spectrum were the sincere near-atheists such as Walter Pater, and T. H. Green who, in a paper widely circulated in the colleges, suggested that 'Faith rests not on the facts recorded in the Bible, but on their spiritual significance', and appealed to students who had lost their faith not to become indifferent to religion or separate themselves from the devout.[12] Inevitably, most of the university fitted between these poles into various Broad Church groups (which were predominant at Corpus). There were factions here too, probably aggravated by Benjamin Jowett, who was influential but also unintentionally divisive.

The strongest force in moving the university away from being primarily a religious institution was the rise of science. The famous debate between Thomas Huxley and Bishop Wilberforce in 1860 was held in the new Museum building, which the British Association for the Advancement of Science had wanted and which Henry Acland had seen as a way of bringing together all the groups of scientists in the University.[13] It was Acland—later to examine Bridges for his degree in medicine—who had persuaded the university in 1850 to allow students who obtained Honours in Classics or Mathematics to take examinations in Mechanical Philosophy, Chemistry, and Physiology. But the refusal of Acland and others to establish schools of medicine and engineering at Oxford and their insistence that science students first pass Moderations—much more rigorous demands than were made at Cambridge—meant that while Oxford initially had led in founding science courses, it was to fall behind by the 1880s through appealing to too few students.[14] When Hopkins and Bridges graduated there were only about twenty students a year obtaining BAs in science as opposed to some 300 taking *Literae Humaniores*. However, many more students attended the classes than attempted the examinations, and while Bridges was at Oxford the number increased steadily. In 1871 Acland, who was the Radcliffe Librarian, reported 'fully 150 persons habitually use the Museum', indicating that 'the subjects included under the head of Physical Science have become attractive here as a branch of general education'.[15] Although it is impossible to tell whether Bridges attended science classes, at least one of his tutors for Greats, John Wilson, did, and his influence seems to have had an effect in pushing Bridges towards a more scientific view of the world.

Literae Humaniores was in many ways a continuation for Bridges of his school training. Responsions, the initial examination commonly known as Smalls or Little-go, and taken within a term or two of entry, checked that students could write with good classical style in prose and verse, understand grammatical structure, and translate. They also had to manage basic Euclid or Algebra.

After that, work began for Moderations, which Robert took in Trinity, 1865. This examination covered several topics: divinity, logic, once again Greek and Latin grammar and literature, and at least one poet and one orator. One of Robert's contemporaries later wrote of Moderations, 'I remember no instruction on authenticity of books, no criticising of their trustworthiness, no discussion of the literary political or religious problems they presented'[16], although notebooks kept by Bridges' contemporaries show that even if the examinations were dry—and the compulsory viva voce may not have been—there was much fascinating detailed analysis of the texts.[17]

Among the professors in Corpus was John Conington, the Professor of Latin, nicknamed 'the sick vulture' for his stooped posture and pallor, whose translation of Virgil's *Aeneid* was standard. He lectured once a week on Virgil, translating with running commentary, and once a week on Latin lyric verse, reading out and criticizing the most proficient of the students' translations of specific poems, and ending the class by giving his own version. The best of the other tutors in the college was generally acknowledged to be Henry Furneaux, a gentlemanly Cornishman who was said to have 'boiled down Mods Logic so effectually that it was . . . believed that no examiner could floor the pupils who had had the benefit of one term's teaching from him'.[18] He also taught Latin authors and his translations of Horace and Tacitus in lectures twice a week were greatly admired by the students, whose own translations of passages he marked carefully, sparing in his praise and pungent in rebuke of idleness.

Only Conington and Furneaux lectured in the Hall. All the other classes were held in the tutors' rooms, the students sitting on whatever chairs the tutor could provide and making notes in books on their laps. In addition to Virgil, Horace, and Tacitus, undergraduates also studied Thucydides, Demosthenes, Cicero, Aeschylus, Sophocles, Aristophanes, and Aristotle. Francis Chavasse noted the common view that Sophocles was the best of the Greek dramatists: 'Both in the changes he introduced and in modifying the pomp and occasional roughness of Aeschylus and in the temperate grandeur which he diffuses over his whole plays he was the type of that sobriety and moderation which was so marked a trait in Greek character and the secret of their good taste.'[19] The ascription to the Greeks of sobriety, moderation, and good taste was commonly used prescriptively for English literature of the day. Writing in 1870, F. T. Palgrave declared of Greek art: 'A certain high pleasure, as the end of all art, is uniformly kept in view; hence the last impression left is always beauty; never the grotesque, or the piquant, or the baldly natural, or the repulsively powerful, as in modern art. It is unfantastic; it is moderate; it is sane; it rejects what goes no further than mere suggestion; it hates the vague and the introspective.'[20] Although this is not a full description of Bridges' literary values, these widely held views form an important part of what he tried initially to achieve in his own writing, and some of their assumptions lie behind his criticism of others' work.

Students at Corpus were under some pressure not simply to pass but to obtain first, second, or third-class honours in Moderations. This meant being prepared to 'answer deeper questions in Philology and Criticism, and to translate from English into Greek as well as Latin'.[21] In April 1865 Bridges wrote to Lionel Muirhead,

> as I am very much behindhand in my books, not having even read them all yet, I cannot make up my mind whether I shall be able to go in for a class or not. I want very much to get thro' this term, & do not care at all abt. honours myself, (epec[iall]y as they prob[ably] would be such inferior ones) but the dons, and several other people, among whom of course Coles, urge me on provokingly . . . You must conclude from my saying so much about the schools that I am anxious about them.

When he had been forced to leave Oxford, Muirhead had given him his decorative list of 'Books to be Read and Lectures' as an ornament for his room, but Bridges reported,

> my conscience wd not allow me to leave [it] up . . . for my reading reputation wd not at all match such pretensions to work. I hope that you will soon come back to Oxford to claim it, when you shall also have the notes wh I hope I shall read before 'Mods'. unfortunately in the Vacation my sister [probably Julia] was ill at home. 2ndly we had an election, of which you must have heard the disgraceful result. [the candidate of Dr Molesworth's opponent John Bright had won] 3rdly, I was getting up a petition—4thly my brother [Edward?] was at home, from wh premises naturally follows the conclusion that I did not open a book.[22]

His later displeasure at the class of his degree suggests that he was being overly modest about his academic work and goals, but it is also clear that he had a number of non-academic interests: he ended his letter to Muirhead by saying, 'I will write again soon but ought to be retiring now for the benefit of our eight oar'.

Just as religion had provided a bond with others for Bridges at Eton so it did at Oxford. He was one of the few High Church adherents in Corpus. Bridges, Hopkins, and Hopkins' friend, William Addis, were among the half-dozen nominated for election to Pusey's Brotherhood of the Most Holy Trinity (BHT) on 8 December 1863. Hopkins decided against joining, but Bridges and Addis were admitted at a meeting of 1 March 1864.[23] The BHT had been formed late in 1844 as the Brotherhood of Saint Mary the Virgin to study ecclesiastical art, but by the 1860s its name had been changed and its main objects were 'communion in prayer and works of charity, and mutual encouragement in regularity of life'. It called its members to live 'lives at variance with the world', to set forth 'simplicity against the world's luxury, love against the world's censoriousness, self-denial against the world's boundless indulgence, reverence against the world's irreverence, strictness against the world's laxity'.[24] The rules to be aimed at included rising an hour before Morning Chapel for private prayers and theological reading, simplicity in dress and food, observing the fasts of the Church 'as health shall permit', avoiding 'attendance at the theatre and opera [except where offence would be given to relatives by declining invitations], as well as all places and practices in any way connected with the promotion of known and deliberate sin', 'to keep careful guard over the eyes, when in the streets or elsewhere, so as not to look at anything hurtful unless it is a duty', to contribute a tenth of one's income to the Church except when 'the claims of any near and dependent relative or the smallness of the income itself prevent it', to receive Holy Communion once a week, and make use of confession when troubled.[25] Membership increased steadily during the 1860s with over 150 participants on the rolls in 1864.[26]. Many of the Puseyite group Bridges had known at Eton joined, including Coles, Hankey, Bickersteth, and Muirhead. Hopkins was again nominated in October 1864, and it is easy to see why he would have found the group congenial to his own practices, but again he did not join although most of his friends who became Catholic converts when he did in 1866 were members.

Henry Parry Liddon, whose Sunday evening lectures and social gatherings Hopkins attended, was one of the leaders of the BHT. Bridges became friendly with him, calling on him in his rooms in Christ Church when he could, and subsequently turning to him for help in finding an appropriate tutor for Dolben in 1865. It is also suggestive of Bridges' esteem for Liddon's opinion that the tutor was someone to whom he was eager to introduce Monica shortly after their marriage in 1884.[27] The BHT had several committee-meetings each term at which Office was sung, new members nominated, elected, or admitted, an address given, and decisions made as to policy and allocation of funds; the society helped to staff a night-school for boys and money was sent to missions in Nassau and Delhi. Bridges did not attend more than half the committee-meetings, but was evidently sufficiently active in the society's other activities to be allowed to remain a member; those who were too little in evidence were asked to resign. Commenting on a mutual acquaintance, Henry Challis, who belonged to the BHT, Hopkins once said to Bridges, 'he never used the same strictness in practices (such as fasting) as most of our acquaintance would', suggesting that they both belonged to a group that did follow such practice.[28] George Saintsbury, Bridges' exact contemporary and a member of Merton, the college adjacent to Corpus, also belonged to the BHT, and records that he and Mandell Creighton (who was to become a friend of Bridges) and other 'Merton Popes', as they were called, caused such resentment within their college by having 'eggy teas' instead of dinner in Hall on Wednesdays and Fridays during Lent, 1865, that some of them had their windows broken.[29]

Although Bridges was at no point close to Roman Catholicism, it is clear that Anglicanism of this sort could become a 'half-way house' to Rome. The BHT was not just an Oxford society but participated in some of the events of the English Church Union; a letter Bridges sent Muirhead shows his involvement in the High Church community beyond Oxford and the controversy about the use of Catholic practices in Anglican churches:

I write now waiting for a Captain's Meeting in the Barge Club, & the arrival of the president may at any moment put an end to my letter. You were in right in thinking [Brother] Nihill belonged to the BHT . . . I was at the service at St Stephen's Manchester wh was the ultimate cause of the row . . . last vac[ation] the Engl Ch[urch] Union went to Manchester & a certain well disposed Rector lent his ch[urch]. High mass was very ritualistic certainly, but neither lights vestments nor incense used. The elevation [by Nihill of the cup above his head while the congregation bowed their heads] was wh[at] offended the B[isho]p tho' really it was fear that Nihill [who belonged to a supposedly secret ritualistic Society of the Holy Cross] was about to establish a monastery in Manchester for wh there was fair foundation.[30]

In February 1865 Dolben was Bridges' guest in Oxford. He was seeing old friends such as Coles and looking round the university, where he hoped to become a student. Bridges introduced him to Hopkins and, finding that Hopkins and Dolben had considerable shared interests, invited them and Coles to stay at Rochdale. However, Hopkins was unable to come and Coles and Dolben could not come at the same time. It was Dolben's only visit to Rochdale and Bridges wrote of it, 'in his delightful companionship the few days passed quickly, and as we were alone I had much talk with him.' The visit was a significant one for Robert's religious belief. Dolben had been drifting towards Roman Catholicism, but Constantine Prichard, the private tutor with whom he had begun to study a few months previously, had won his esteem and started to challenge his belief, forcing him to question the literal truths of the Bible in the light of the discoveries of modern science and criticism. 'For minds nurtured from childhood in unquestioning submission to a system of religious dogma', Bridges said,

it is very difficult to break sufficiently away from their position to see the full bearing and breadth of the philosophic objections; and this step Prichard had led Digby to take . . . in those talks with him I made also the same step that he had made; and if I might not perceive the full significance at the time, yet I know the very spot in the garden where we were walking when I saw certain familiar ideas in a new light. The exact tone seems to me to be perfectly caught and fixed in the magical simplicity of his half-suppressed utterance

Suppose it but a fancy that it groaned,
This dear Creation.[31]

Dolben was keen to establish a monastic group associated with the Catholic Father Ignatius [the Revd Joseph Leycester Lyne], and planned to have Bridges in charge and Muirhead as a participant. Of this idea Bridges wrote,

the essence of this brotherhood was, of course, nothing more than the natural projection into the future of the present conditions of friendship and religious conviction already binding us together. In so far as it was in any sense a deliberate scheme or plan, it no doubt appealed with different force to each one of us. It was, I suppose, the same sort of idea that had grown up between Wm Morris and his friends, ten years earlier, at Oxford. For myself I can say that the only definite plan of the kind which had seriously influenced me, was an understanding between my younger brother and myself that we would always live together.[32]

Dolben's scheme, his 'monastery in the air', was never to come to fruition, and Bridges' plan too was destroyed within months when, in 1866, Edward's health, always delicate, took a sudden turn for the worse. Robert was shocked when, shortly after having returned to Oxford for the Trinity term 1866 he was summoned home. He wrote to Lionel,

we never expected that he wd be overcome by such a short illness, as his complaint is wht usually ends in decline & gradual loss of strength, & he himself, till 6 or 7 hours before his death, had no idea, or rather could not believe that he wd not recover. it was very fortunate that all of us who were in England were in time to be with him at the last & we have every comfort that we possibly could have, as he was very nervous & sensitive, & a long illness wh always seemed inevitable (unless he had quite overcome his weakness & disease wh was almost impossible) wd have been a great trial to him.[33]

But the loss was a bitter one: Edward's death 'plunged me into deep sorrow at the time, and considerably altered the hopes and prospects of my life.'[34] His grief can still be seen in a letter to his sister Frances written thirteen years later, when he had become a doctor:

I am this evening in a state of dejection—and filled with old family melancholies. I have today destroyed all the correspondence I have ever kept except that of Edward and Julia, who both wrote to me as they wrote to no one else=and their history is very sad to read—They both possessed in an extraordinary degree the beauty of singlemindedness, and both united with it that irrepressible humour that our father gave more or less to all his children, and most I think to John. I am surprised at reading

Edward's letters to find that he had a much greater command of language than I remembered. greater I think than any of us but John, and then he was so young when he died that it was no doubt a sign of high promise—And to think that [with] a little more knowledge, or even tact he might have been with us still! At least I always think that the means taken to guard against his disease were sadly insufficient. I hope I may never make such a mistake: the thought makes one's profession a real care.[35]

With term in full swing Bridges had, however, despite his sorrow, to continue his preparation for Greats. This second public examination in the classics dealt with ancient history and political and moral philosophy. The papers for Michaelmas term 1867, which he would have taken, included many questions on matters of fact for which one can easily imagine that answers would have been well-rehearsed: 'Sketch concisely the extent of Greek commerce in the period before 400 B.C.'—but those on logic and philosophy would have required more wide-ranging thought—for example, '"Science is the coordination of verified facts". Discuss the validity and universal applicability of this definition, and compare it with any other conception of science'. 'How far and in what form may the elements which are combined in our ideas of moral obligation be recognized in Greek thought?'—while others would have prompted application of general principles to contemporary life—'Compare Plato's Communism with modern schemes' and 'Institutions are stable in proportion to the area over which they extend', an idea that may well have influenced Bridges' attitude to democracy, since one of the objections he made to it in 1916 was that Great Britain was too large for such a political system.

W. A. Spooner, a friend of Hopkins', and Bridges' exact contemporary at New College,[36] gives an idea of the range of reading required at this time:

Herodotus and Thucydides, the *Republic* and the *Ethics*, Livy and Tacitus, Aristotle's *Logic*, and Bacon [*Novum Organum*], and . . . the great Commentaries on them, Grote's *History of Greece*, Mommsen's and Merivale's *Histories of Rome*, Stallbaum on Plato and Sir Alexander Grant on the *Ethics* . . . To them we added a rather careful study of the Pre-Socratic Philsophers (Jowett's great hobby at the time), a knowledge of the general *History of Philosophy* as set forth by Schwegler as well as a speaking acquaintance with Kant's *Critique* and Hegel's *Philosophy of History*. Our

Logic we worked at principally in Mill [*Inductive Logic*] which many of us knew with great thoroughness, supplementing it on the critical side by reading his work on Hamilton, Mansel's *Prolegomena Logica* and his appendix on Aldridge's *Logic*; and Ferrier's *Institutes of Metaphysics*. On Ethics we read besides Butler's *Sermons*, which we knew well, [Sir James] Mackintosh, Mill's *Utilitarianism* and a few of the earlier English moralists, such as [Richard] Price and Adam Smith, and [Théodore] Jouffroy . . . Our Political Philosophy we studied in Hobbes, in Locke, in Maine's *Ancient Law*, and to some extent in [François] Guizot. Very few of us were specialists according to the modern standard either in History or Philosophy, but we gained from our reading an exceedingly complete view of ancient thought and civilisation.[37]

The historical approach to classical scholarship, instilled by the influence of German criticism in the late 1850s, also made the retention of a literal belief in the Bible more difficult. The effect on Bridges can be seen in a remark he made later comparing the Bible with Herodotus' history: 'Our Bible', he remarked, 'matching the Greek book in its legendary matter and excursions into old-world history, is much more poetic and varied than Herodotus; and its sources being more original, the documents which it collects are far richer in mental attitudes and literary forms, and have escaped the tincture of one mind.'[38]

Bridges did some of the preparation for Greats in the company of Hopkins, whom he invited to stay with him at Rochdale in August 1866. They began to read Herodotus together but Robert found that Hopkins 'so enjoyed loitering over the difficulties' that he despaired of finishing the reading list and began to study by himself.[39] But getting a First, as Hopkins did, depended on being able to answer questions requiring very close knowledge of texts and being able to translate the most difficult parts. Bridges' more rapid reading contributed to the second that Hopkins predicted for him.

It was common at the time for students preparing for Greats to be given extra tutorials with specialist tutors. Robert was sent to Henry William Chandler, Waynflete Professor of Moral and Metaphysical Philosophy, for weekly tutorials on Aristotle. 'Chandler', he noted, 'was a little sallow man with chronic diabetes . . . He was most pleasant to deal with, but I was quite unworthy of his wisdom.'[40] He was also tutored by John Wilson, Whyte's Professor of Moral Philosophy, whom he liked. Wilson was dean in the college and a fierce opponent of Pusey on the Hebdomadal Council, as one of the principal advocates of the abolition of religious tests and the practical, if not nominal, leader of the Liberal Party at Oxford. He had regularly attended Acland's practical classes on Histology and Embryology, and Pusey said of him that he 'did not mean to be skeptical; but he balanced things so that he landed his pupils in skepticism'.[41] He does seem to have contributed towards leaving Bridges in this state. When Robert left Oxford in 1867 he was, he said, as a result of the philosophy he had studied, 'drifting fast away from . . . my old religious sympathies'.[42] (He had resigned from the BHT during his last term at Oxford.) Knox commented that divinity was frequently taught by men who were followers of Strauss, Renan, and Colenso,[43] in other words, by those affected by the interest of German Higher Criticism in the historical context of the Bible, and study of German philosophers (Wilson was responsible for teaching Kant and Hegel) could have extended further a critical historical attitude to religion which was leading Bridges, if not to atheism, then at least towards a less literal Christian belief. The death of Edward, too, had helped impel this revision of his ideas and plans. Then, in July 1867, another of the links with the religious world of his youth was snapped when Dolben was drowned in the Welland river. Bridges was committed to taking part in a race on the Seine and, reluctantly, missed Digby's funeral. 'I was spared, it is true,' he wrote later, 'the distress of witnessing the inconsolable grief of his home, but it was an added distress not to be able to take one's share in it, and to be absent from the last scene.'[44]

Hopkins, too, was modifying his belief in the religious ideas in which he had been raised. During the time that he spent with Bridges at Rochdale in 1866, he was waiting to hear whether Newman would see him about admitting him to the Roman Catholic communion. Staying in the Anglican rectory, Hopkins kept this news from Bridges until afterwards. The objections of Bridges and his family to Catholicism were certainly deep-seated, but Robert seems to have been most hurt by the fact that Hopkins had not confided in him. Hopkins received a second invitation to stay at Rochdale the following year but, perhaps fearing awkward moments, he declined it. He was also keen not to mar the pleasant memories he had of his first visit; he told his mother that, despite the anxiety, it had probably been the happiest fortnight of his life,[45] and he remained grateful to Robert for the tolerant attitude he had taken to his inevitable moodiness. In June 1867 Bridges gave him his copy of Henry Vaughan's *Sacred Poems & Pious Ejaculations*, perhaps as a leaving present since Hopkins graduated that term. In September, Bridges wrote to him:

> I wish that I had time to write you a decent letter. my mother is very ill indeed, & has been now for some time. it is a nervous illness wh is very distressing to her & to us, but the doctors all assure us that it is not dangerous tho' tedious and that we shall only have gt difficulty in keeping [?mamma] quiet eno' after she gets well . . . I have consequently a good deal to do besides my Greats work . . . not the least tiresome of all being the playing of backgammon every evening with the Dr—in the little oven called the breakfast room. This with the time taken up by the exercise, wh you know is necessary to keep me from deteriorating into some outlandish animal & upsetting all the received theories of species etc. completely absorbs my letter-writing moments—I wish I cd give you a good report of my work . . . I have got thro' almost all my Grecian history . . . & hope to do the Latin before the term . . . I feel to be a good deal in your society for every now & then I look into one of your notebooks wh thanks to your style recall you very vividly. I had a curious dream the other night in wh your Dr Newman, Dolben, & a strange Roman Cath priest & myself had the most wonderful discussion possible.[46]

The letter ends, 'Remember you *stay with* me next term when you come up. if you do not get rooms in college, & mine are to spare', but it also contains what sounds like a religious jibe: 'Please write when you feel the least inclined, & even sometimes when you don't, if you think that a little self mortification wd be timely.' But rather than an objection to Catholicism this was more probably prompted by the lingering hurt at the way in which the honesty of his friend's response to him had been modified by religious considerations; in other words, a reference back to the deception Hopkins had practised at Rochdale.

Bridges described himself as 'of a plain blurting disposition',[47] although Hopkins noted that he was quite capable of tactful reticence. During his life he had a number of friends who were Catholics, and there is no evidence that he ever broke off a friendship because of religious or political differences. However, he certainly disliked the Catholic religion, although the nature of his objections to it altered as he developed his own unorthodox faith. Initially, he would presumably have been influenced by the views with which he was raised and, as was common in England at the time, they had been anti-Catholic: in November 1850, for example, there had been a long meeting of the congregation of St Mary's, Walmer, in order to draw up a petition against the proposed restoration of the Catholic hierarchy in Britain. Fanning the widespread fear at the time of a French invasion, it was urged that recognition of Catholicism was also political submission to such Catholic nations as France and Austria. The 'illogicalities' of Catholic belief were stressed, and the people urged, in conclusion to 'present as bold a front against error, as their magnificent beach did against the sea'.[48] Clearly Robert would have been too young to have known the details of the protest, but the popular fears it reveals might well have affected his view of Catholics.

When Dolben was looking for a tutor to coach him for entrance to Balliol he asked whether he could be taught with Edward, but Dolben's Catholic tendencies, shown, for example, in his custom of crossing himself, made Bridges' mother reject his request in case he might influence her son who, she felt, was already predisposed towards Catholicism.[49] The grief of Hopkins' family at his conversion was not atypical, and it is interesting to see the reaction to Catholic converts of Bridges' contemporary at Corpus Christi Francis Chavasse (an Evangelical who was later to become Bishop of Liverpool):

> Was much startled and deeply moved to hear from Lock that Addis, Hopkins and Garret of Balliol and Wood of Trinity had gone over to Rome. For the first time in my life the reality of a perversion came home with stunning violence to my heart. I could scarcely believe it . . . Only yesterday I saw Hopkins's wan face. Oh what a terrible thought to leave light for darkness, and reformed for an apostate Church; to brand all their friends and relatives as schismatics and heretics. To join the Roman Church only to be overwhelmed in her certain and fast approaching ruin . . . Ritualism! Ritualism! if a man of clear and logical mind be ensnared by thy splendours, thy gaudy flowers will not satisfy his hungering soul.—He will know no rest, until, e'er he himself suspects it he is borne into the full blaze of Roman Ritual and Roman superstition.—Oh Jesus keep me and all dear to me safe from the tempter. Succour thy Church—

her foes are numberless, and even her own sons are proving traitors and her destroyers.[50]

Although this is expressed with an extravagance alien to Bridges, it reflects attitudes common at the time; there were 'anti-Popery' riots in Rochdale in 1868.

In his final year Bridges, like all Corpus undergraduates, had to find rooms out of college, although he would have continued to take his main meals in Hall. He had been living in what he described as 'luxurious' rooms on the ground floor of staircase 12 and moved into a 'poky little house but convenient and cheap'.[51] He was also pleased that he had been able to arrange to share the house with Montagu George Knight, whom he had known at Eton.

Despite his approaching finals Bridges spent considerable time coaching the Corpus boat crew during his final twelve months at Oxford. He developed a dangerous habit of standing in the stern to coach, and on one occasion, when the river was very full and the crew about to turn just above Iffley Lock, Bridges, who had been standing in the stern, steering and coaching, overbalanced and fell into the torrent. He seized the gunwale close to the rudder, but the end of the bow side came away in his hands. Six of the crew promptly jumped overboard and they and Bridges swam to shore. The eighth member of the crew, declining the soaking, was able to paddle the lightened boat to shore and, after a struggle, tie it up.[52] As soon as the university races were over in July 1867, the Corpus crew began training for a race to be rowed on the Seine. Bridges was not particularly keen on the trip but was needed to stroke the boat. The crew generally spent the morning visiting the Paris Exhibition, rowing the course twice in the late afternoon. There were three other boats against which they raced, all English: an Old Etonian Crew, one from the London Rowing Club, and Worcester College. Corpus lost the race to Eton by a quarter of a length.[53] In 1868, after Bridges had left Oxford, Corpus finally managed to become head of the river, a success to which he had contributed by improving the crew's technique and leaving them placed second.

Bridges took Greats in November 1867. He was dismayed when

he obtained a second, but for the Michaelmas 1867 examinations that he sat there were only twelve firsts awarded, eighteen seconds, and nineteen thirds, with 110 unclassed passes, so it was not an insignificant achievement, especially given his other interests. However, even as the examinations began his thoughts had already begun to turn to the future. He wrote to Muirhead:

> I was very sorry to miss you when you were in Oxford I can scarcely say a *few* days ago as I wanted particularly to see you.—I have not time to write a long letter, but want to know whether you will be able to have an evening with me some day soon. The schools begin on Thursday. any day after that day I will entertain you at dinner and get up a whist party, or what I would rather do have some conversation. I have a good deal to talk about generally—at least so it appears to me at present. and in particular I want to ask you if you are disposed for a good long excursion abroad next summer—with me the only difficulties are funds and a companion. the first I think that I can get over. and if it is at all what you are inclined to do I shd like a regular good and not hurried trip . . .[54]

The trip they decided on was to the Middle East.

4

A Period of Uncertainty

(1868–1869)

Before setting out for Egypt with Lionel Muirhead, Bridges tried to see all the remaining, scattered members of his family and various friends, including Hopkins. The latter was delayed by an aunt and missed the one time when they could have met.[1] Bridges and Muirhead sailed from Southampton on 10 January 1868. The books Bridges packed for the trip give some idea of his intellectual interests at the time, and add to the impression that he may have made the trip partly to test the strength of his religious faith. He asked Muirhead to bring Gibbon's *Decline and Fall of the Roman Empire*, and packed 'Shakespeare—Browning-selections—Milman's Latin Churches—Max Muller's languages—[Palgrave's] Golden Treasury—Ellicott's notes to S. Paul—Riddle's Plato i Apol[ogy]—Soph[ocles] Ajax (this for your benefit)—Stanley's Sinai—Grk Test[ament]—Bible'.[2] No doubt a copy of Keats's poems went too.

The most popular method for visitors of travelling to Egypt at the time was to take a boat up the Nile. From the speed with which Lionel and Robert travelled, it seems that they took a steamer, which had only relatively recently been introduced on the route—with more time it was possible to take a leisurely sailing *dahabieh*. Muirhead, whose eye was now giving him less trouble, sketched some of these graceful boats with their slanted masts on 13 and 14 February and drew Bridges with a brimmed cap pulled firmly down as he sat 'composing an ode' which has not survived.[3] From the boat, which provided the travellers' accommodation, expeditions on camel or donkey could be made to nearby sites. By 16 February they reached Assiut, once a centre for worship of Wepwawa, the jackal god, and said to have been a resting place for

Joseph and Mary on their flight from Egypt. By the middle of the nineteenth century it was one of the largest cities on the Nile above Cairo, with wide streets, well-built houses, and numerous minarets.

It took a further three weeks for Bridges and Muirhead to reach Philae, 'sharing the delights of that idle strange life, and that perfect sky. One never enjoys a drink of water in England as one can hourly in the East'.[4] Bridges took to smoking narghiles, the Arab hookah, a habit he taught Muirhead. At Philae Lionel painted a watercolour of Robert sitting writing in the doorway of a tent dwarfed by huge pillars with ornate capitals. Dedicated to Osiris, Isis, and Horus, Philae was the most sacred place in Egypt, and to reach it tourists had to travel from Aswan, just above the First Cataract, by donkey or camel to the other side of the cataract and then take a boat. Like most nineteenth-century travellers, Bridges and Muirhead turned back at this point.

Lionel seems to have done rather more drawing on the journey back to Cairo, including a sketch described by its title: 'RB stalking a crocodile. Exiit Crocodile'. On 13 March they reached Edfoo, a town whose inhabitants, like those of many of the towns along the Nile, were suffering by the 1860s from the popularity of the trip with European visitors, who would anchor their boats, sometimes for several months, in one spot and hunt the local birds for food. Bridges and Muirhead appear to have been caught in the reaction to such a practice. The results of their attempt to hunt wild geese near the village were evidently sufficiently unpleasant to make Muirhead avoid any further 'wild-goose' chases during his extended travels in the Middle East.[5] One of Muirhead's drawings here is noted as being 'fr. R. B.'s book', suggesting that Bridges may also have done some sketching although nothing of his from this trip seems to have survived.

They stopped at Karnak, where Lionel drew details of friezes and the heads of two gigantic statues of Rameses, then visited the most recent of Egyptian temples, dedicated by Cleopatra to Isis at Dendera. By Easter they were back in Cairo, four hundred miles to the north of Dendera, from where they embarked for Syria, arriving at Jaffa in early May. Their goal was Jerusalem, forty-five miles south-east of Jaffa, a journey they made on horseback, travelling by way of Lydda and Horan. By 10 May they were settled in Jerusalem where they appear to have spent the rest of the month. Muirhead's sketches show that they visited the Hospital of the Knights of St John, King Solomon's tomb, and the Church of the Holy Sepulchre, which he drew on two occasions.

Jerusalem may have clarified for Bridges the problem of his future. He was not rich enough to dispense with a profession, and of the three gentlemen's professions of the day does not seem to have contemplated law. The Church, which he had originally thought would suit him, would seem from a sonnet he wrote about Jerusalem to have become practically impossible:

O weary pilgrims, chanting of your woe,
That turn your eyes to all the peaks that shine,
Hailing in each the citadel divine
The which ye thought to have enter'd long ago;
Until at length your feeble steps and slow
Falter upon the threshold of the shrine,
And your hearts overburden'd doubt in fine
Whether it be Jerusalem or no:

Dishearten'd pilgrims, I am one of you;
For, having worshipp'd many a barren face,
I scarce now greet the goal I journey'd to:
I stand a pagan in the holy place;
Beneath the lamp of truth I am found untrue,
And question with the God that I embrace.

A letter Muirhead sent him in 1869 asking whether he had made up his mind to take orders suggests that he hid these doubts from his friend.[6] At the end of the month Bridges made his way back to Jaffa where he took a boat for England. Hopkins recorded on 24 June 1868 receiving a letter on his return.[7] Meanwhile, Muirhead travelled north to Tyre, remaining in the Middle East until July 1870. His letters to Bridges recount many adventures including a spell of solitary confinement in a Turkish jail, painting a Pasha's portrait, for which he was rewarded with a magnificent stallion, and a race across the desert pursued by soldiers determined to take him prisoner.[8]

When Bridges returned home it was to find that tragedy had struck his family again, this time of a more bizarre kind. The victims were his sister, Harriett Louisa, and her family. Harriett had married the Revd Henry Plow, vicar of Todmorden, near Rochdale in Lancashire, in 1864. On 2 March 1868 the Plows were attacked with pistols and a hatchet by the lover of a 16-year-old servant-girl whom they had dismissed and sent home to get her away from the liaison for which they considered her too young. The servant who had told the Plows of the relationship, was shot dead then partially dismembered, Henry was savagely attacked with the hatchet, and Harriett, who had recently given birth, was attacked in bed, shot at, and beaten about the head with a poker.[9] Henry and the baby died a few days later and Harriett never fully recovered. Robert evidently planned to make a home for his sister at Wantage, near Newbury, but her condition deteriorated and in March of the following year she died. Her one surviving child, Mary, was brought up by Mrs Molesworth.

Bridges' grief over his family, probably accentuated by realizing that another of his relations was dying, is clear in one of the few poems extant from this period. 'In my most serious thoughts' was started in 1868 and expanded in 1873, when the first four and the last four lines were added.

In my most serious thoughts o' wakeful nights,
When my sad spirit in a solemn trance
Views herself stripped of earthly circumstance,
And severed from the round of day delights:
When the blank silence of night invites
The dreamy ghosts, with faded countenance,
And noiseless movement, round my bed to dance,
Till their weird company no more affrights:

Then in the presence of the long-departed,
Aghast in wonder at my well-known sorrow,
Oft to my sleepless eyes the tears have started;
Nor know I whence my secret hope I borrow,
That I should care to rise as if light-hearted,
And deck my soul and body for the morrow.

The original lines, which would seem to refer to the loss of his father and two closest brothers, are especially weird and imaginative. They were evidently also too personal since, although Bridges included the sonnet in the volume of 1873, it did not appear in any subsequent collection. In many of the poems in which he described himself as grieving, Bridges attempted to confine the picture of his sorrow and reduce its intensity by suggesting that it was only a passing mood. To a certain extent this is true of the way in which the physically fit and especially the young experience grief: in intense surges of sorrow eased by periods of comparative happiness, and he acknowledged the contribution of his generally good health in this respite from grief in another early sonnet:

In that dark time, when joys that now delight
This pampered sense shall vanish and be lost;
And without rival shall appear of cost
The subtler powers our mortal passions slight:

In the first hour of that eventful night
Shall I encounter many a well-known ghost,
And face to face those enemies accost
I scatter now and banish from my sight.

Now but in waking dreams, on filmy wings,
Or when the body is sick, they harass me:
Ill-feeding flies, coward, of puny stings:

But then resistless, unmistakeably,
Immortal captains of potential things,
Will they torment me with their devilry.[10]

This poem is of course not just about grief. Besides a sinking into melancholy from loss there are also suggestions of regret; those 'things ill done and done to others' harm' that T. S. Eliot called the 'gifts reserved for age'. The element almost of guilt at being melancholy is evident in a number of Bridges' poems. When he was growing up he experienced the grief of losing close relatives again and again, but met these as a member of a large and Christian family and he would have been encouraged not to allow his sorrow to show for too long. The habitual and determined effort to suppress his melancholy while in good health is important in understanding his sometimes impatient response to friends such as Hopkins and Wooldridge, who were frequently depressed with rather less obvious cause. As Bridges made successive collections of his poems, he omitted more and more of those poems that might have been seen as referring to his grief, with the result that he is thought of as having indulged, when young, in almost adolescent melancholy and of having had a life with few sorrows. This is far from true.

When Hopkins heard of Harriett's death, he wrote to Bridges:

> It is nearly a fortnight since my mother gave me the sad news of Mrs Plow's death but I have not till today had an opportunity of writing to you, as I wished to do. I cannot help thinking that perhaps for her own sake she could not have much wished to live longer with such dreadful grief upon her memory but it is different with you and with your mother: I have wondered with myself how Mrs Molesworth would bear all these things. I know nothing but the fact of your sister's death, so that I can only speak generally. No doubt her health never really recovered the first shock. What suffering she had! Even during Mr Plow's life she had troubles, you told me, and it appeared in her face. But sufferings falling on such a person as your sister was are to be looked on as the marks of God's particular love and this is truer the more exceptional they are. I wonder what will become of her child: she had not more than one living, I think.[11]

Bridges' reply is not extant. He would have appreciated Hopkins' kindness and the affection he expressed for his sister, but may have been rather less certain that her repeated suffering was a mark of 'particular love'. The shock to religious faith of seemingly undeserved human pain certainly lies behind the later disagreement between Hopkins and Bridges over the latter's poem, 'On a Dead Child', though the few details that we have of the friendship in 1868 suggest that at that time religious controversy was not straining the relationship. In August 1868 Bridges had visited Hopkins at his home. Hopkins noted in his Journal: 'Rover [the family's dog] bit him. After this we went down to town together and talked in Hyde Park' and walked along Oxford Street. Hopkins entered the Jesuit Novitiate in September, and sometime between then and probably the end of the year Bridges tried again to see him, but the Community was in a three-day retreat.

Bridges' interest in science, begun in Oxford, had developed to the point where he decided that he needed to become more proficient at German, the language in which much scientific literature was written. After working at the grammar, he arranged to visit Germany with William Sanday, his friend from Oxford.

They spent eight months living in Dresden, probably the German town most popular at the time with English intellectuals (George Eliot had written most of *Adam Bede* while staying there in 1857), perhaps at the suggestion of Bridges' friend Mandell Creighton, who had taken a group of students there for a vacation reading party the previous year. Some idea of the effort that Bridges invested in learning German may be deduced from advice he later gave to Laurence Binyon. Using a textbook, it was, he said, a matter of committing rules to memory and doing exercises, and in three months of five or six hours a day, 'a clever student' should have learnt its basics, although he would not have an extensive vocabulary.[12]

From Urfa in Syria Muirhead wrote to Bridges in July 1869:

> Your letter from Dresden turned up this morning covered with German postmarks which are refreshing in this sultry atmosphere. I am truly sorry it contains so much bad news, at least you have done your best not to give way to melancholy thoughts by going to Germany and studying the uncooth but fine language. I shall feel horribly afraid of you when you are perfect in German grammar, as hitherto I have regarded it with distant awe. You ought to come back tolerably perfect after so long a series of lessons, and I envy you the power of reading Goethe in the original.[13]

Bridges evidently kept up his command of German. A letter of February 1875 from Hopkins reveals that Bridges was at that time reading Hegel in the original, and beginning to feel that he was getting nearer 'the top than the bottom' of the philosopher's 'bottomless pit'.[14] But literature and philosophy were the attractive by-products and not the most serious reason for Bridges' battle with the language. That lay in his decision to become a doctor, and on his return from Dresden he lost no time in starting on his career. Passing through London on his way back home to Rochdale he entered his name as a medical student at St Bartholomew's Hospital.[15]

5

Medical Training (1869–1874)

St Bartholomew's was a charity hospital established in 1123. In Bridges' day it consisted of four large blocks built around a central square. Three of the buildings contained hospital wards with some 700 beds, and the fourth administrative offices and the banqueting hall. In an outer circle around the central block and the other side of narrower courtyards were the library, the dispensary, the casualty department, and buildings devoted to teaching the students.

During the second half of the nineteenth century there was in England a significant increase in the scientific nature of medical practice, in part as a result of the growth in general scientific training, and partly through the influence of developments in France and Germany.[1] This led to a change in the notion of what the product of a medical school should be. In place of the old idea that a newly fledged doctor should be a Christian gentleman with a broad training in the humanities, who would spend the rest of his life becoming increasingly adept at the technical skills of his profession, there developed the idea that the public needed protection from men under-qualified to treat them; the emergent student must be a 'safe' doctor from his first days in practice. The amount of technical information which the student had to acquire was growing rapidly; Bridges later recalled that it had been 'the era of cellular pathology and of the microscope', when 'numberless books on the use of the microscope' were written and 'every student was cutting and staining thin sections of the tissues'.[2] Recognition was growing, too, of the importance of chemical analysis. In 1867 the Medical Council decided to institute a curriculum organized into a logically cumulative syllabus taking four years to complete. The prime instigator of this reform was Sir Henry Acland, who had done so much to foster interest in science at Oxford.

During the first winter term Bridges studied physiology, chemistry, and anatomy, all subjects considered necessary preliminaries to medicine. Hopkins reported to his mother on 20 October 1869 that Bridges was hard at work and declining dinner invitations.[3] Three mornings a week he would have had chemistry lectures at 9.15, on four days there were physiology lectures at 10.15, and immediately afterwards lectures on the skeleton and dissection classes. The Calendar urged that:

> All students of the first year should be diligent in their attendance in the Dissecting Rooms, immediately after the morning lectures, where parts for dissection will be allotted to them after they have been instructed in the subject of the bones by the Demonstrators, who will arrange them in classes for this purpose.
>
> The time from 12.30 to 1.30 should be occupied, when the Student is not engaged in dissection, in attendance on the Post-mortem Examinations and the Surgical Out-patients.
>
> At 1.30 he should attend in the Wards; and especially, in this his first Winter Session, in the Surgical Wards.
>
> On Wednesdays and Saturdays he should attend in the Operating Theatre, at half-past 1, to watch the various surgical operations performed; and in the same theatre, and in the wards, at half-past 1 on Thursdays, he will attend the Surgical Consultations.[4]

Attendance at post-mortems and medical and surgical out-patients' clinics continued in the second, summer session. There were classes on analysis of tissue using microscopes on Monday and Thursday afternoons from 2.00 to 4.00, and since there was a problem in preserving bodies in hot weather, in the summer the dissection classes were replaced for first-year students by work in the chemical laboratories. The lectures on clinical medicine and surgery that had been recommended but considered optional for students in their first term became compulsory as the emphasis shifted closer to medical practice. The morning lectures were devoted to 'the consideration of all the officinal substances employed in the cure of disease'. Since many doctors working outside hospitals had to prepare their own medicines, the schedule included lectures three mornings a week on botany, sometimes supplemented by 'herbonizing excursions' into the less urbanized areas of London, when one of the hospital's apothecaries would guide the students and check their identification of the plants they had gathered. These added botanical knowledge to Bridges' already keen admiration for the colours of flowers. When he was an elderly man living near Oxford his knowledge of local plants was 'legendary'.[5] He also incorporated into a number of his poems botanical catalogues or detailed descriptions of particular plants' habits. The museum at St Bartholomew's contained a general herbarium and collection of officinal plants and fruits which students were urged to study.

Bridges evidently also spent time in the museum of the Royal College of Surgeons, which included among its exhibits fossils collected by Darwin in Patagonia. These were, of course, important at the time in the controversy between a Biblical and scientific explanation of creation, and might have caused Bridges to think about this issue; in 'Wintry Delights', a poem written after the turn of the century, he mentions these fossils and speaks of the geological and fossil record as 'the only commandments | By God's finger of old inscribed on tablet of earth-stone'.

The books that Bridges would have used in his medical training also seem to have had a profound effect on his religious belief. Written at a time when the relation between scientific and theological thought was controversial, they reflect this by, even if somewhat perfunctorily, placing science within a larger metaphysical context. J. P. Cooke in *Elements of Chemical Physics*, for instance, defined scientific law as 'the thoughts of God manifested in nature' and force as 'the constant action of his infinite will'. Cooke then distinguished between these unifying metaphysical explanations and those of physical science. The latter were only able to point towards such conclusions and, hampered by the 'unavoidable imperfections of scientific language', could merely imply 'the existence of separate and distinct forces'.[6] Similarly, W. B. Carpenter's *Principles of Physiology* eased the sting of his observation that 'there is nothing in Man's present condition which removes him from the pale of the Animal kingdom . . . his reasoning powers differ rather in degree than in kind from those of the inferior animals', by suggesting that man is distinguished by his 'innate tendency . . . to believe in some unseen Existence'. 'By this immortal Soul', said Carpenter, 'Man is connected with beings of a higher order, amongst whom intelligence exists, unrestrained in its exercise by the imperfections of that corporeal mechanism by which it here operates.'[7] Although the acknowledgement of religion was sometimes little more than recognition of the strength of public opinion, it none the less gave to these books the suggestion of a unified view of the world. This was to become very important to Bridges, who was unable either to accept a faith that simply ignored convincing scientific explanations of phenomena or to silence what appeared to someone brought up within Christian belief to be an 'innate tendency' to believe in an 'unseen Existence'.

It must have been an exciting but difficult time in which to be a medical student, not only because of the questions which the advance of science was raising about religion but because of the radical way in which medical training was changing. The older doctors made much use in diagnosis of 'facies', the identification of disease from an accumulation of almost subconsciously noticed visual symptoms. This was largely dismissed by the medical students, who valued the continental practice of diagnosis through the tabulating of symptoms. Bridges, with an open-mindedness and independence of thought that is admirable, saw that 'facies' made use of man's intuition, a resource worth harnessing. He set himself to learn the technique from Dr Patrick Black, who was renowned for his skill. He later explained that it was similar to the way in which we daily recognize the handwriting and appearance of friends without being able to cite the specific characteristics by which we make the identification.[8] Conversely, he pointed out, we would be equally incapable of making the identification from tabulated characteristics. The appreciation of the older method did not lead Bridges simply to ally himself with the older men nor to restrict himself to their techniques. Like the other students he valued chemical and microscopical analysis, and was diligent in learning these too.

A second area in which there was a conflict in approach was the use of antiseptic practices, especially in surgery. Bridges later recalled watching one of the older surgeons in the hospital perform an abdominal operation:

> So short-sighted was he (no doubt he saw more accurately for that) that he seemed to be working as much with his face as with his hands—like a dog at a rabbit hole—all that he did seemed to be a confused groping—

and when he had done there was no more attempt at cleanliness than what seemed a casual mopping up with odds and ends of sponges, before the walls were stitched together.[9]

He was one of the dirtiest doctors at Bart's, and yet he had the best statistics for the recovery of his patients. This cast doubt on the validity of Lister's theories. Even the famous Sir James Paget, whom Bridges evidently considered better at the social graces than at surgery, taught that inflammation and suppuration were, as Bridges records

nature's beneficent device for the cure of wounds and he would draw pictures (from the microscope) of the network of new blood vessels which Nature at once creates and multiplies to promote the necessary inflammation and secretion of pus—Traumatic fever was the rule . . . Lacerated wounds were treated with hot poultices—and I shall never forget seeing (in hot weather) maggots breeding in the proud flesh under the poultice . . . I doubt if in that department of surgery the practice [as regards disinfection] was as good as it was in the school of Hippocrates,[10]

though he added that the doctors were excellent anatomists. Reluctance to use scientific techniques was to draw scathing lines from him in 'Wintry Delights' (1903):

With what wildly directed attack, what an armory illjudged,
Has he, (alas, poor man,) with what cumbrous machination
Sought to defend himself . . .
His simples, compounds, specifics, chemical therapeutics,
Juice of plants, whatever was nam'd in lordly Salerno's
Herbaries and gardens, vipers, snails, all animal filth,
Incredible quackeries, the pretentious jugglery of knaves,
Green electricities, saints' bones and priestly anointings.
Fools! that oppose his one scientific intelligent hope!

It was while he was at St Bartholomew's that antiseptic practice became accepted.

Bridges took lodgings at 35 Great Ormond Street, a few blocks away from the British Museum and a short walk to the west of the hospital. Another of the lodgers in the house was Willoughby Furner, who finished his training as a surgeon a couple of years before Bridges completed the course for physicians. He was a close friend, the son of the leading surgeon at Brighton and one of the prizemen at Bart's. After working in London he returned in 1876 to Brighton to take over his father's practice, and in his turn became the area's leading surgeon. The other medical student with whom Bridges became good friends was Lonsdale Holden, son of the headmaster of Durham School. He later emigrated to Australia, marrying and settling for many years in Sydney before returning to England. Coincidentally, Bridges, Furner, and Holden all had the same birthday. Despite living in different places and following different careers, they were to remain friends.

Muirhead returned to England in July 1870, and Bridges, whose medical term ended on 22 July and who intended to spend August to October in France, was eager to see him before he left. He wrote urging Muirhead to visit London:

> if you wd come down for a day even to town this week or the few first days of next week—Sunday or any other day, I can put you up in my diggings, and make you comfortable I think. I know that you will be fast bound at home. but really it will not take you many hours, and you *must* want to do some London shopping soon. & I shall be away after next week—besides the National Gallery has been so very much & worthily replenished since you last saw it.—Think of an express train up in the afternoon. a comfortable supper. chat—late retirement, proper & suitable breakfast. necessary shopping. luxurious & well adjusted express—dinner again at home—[11]

It is far from certain that Bridges was able to go to France that autumn; certainly it seems unlikely that he went to Paris. Provoked by Prussia, France had declared war on 19 July, and by the end of August Paris was fortified for a siege. However, at some point before his marriage in 1884, Bridges made a visit during which he managed to go to 'all the literary and some of the classical lectures at the Sorbonne', as well as lectures at the Collège de France and 'of course Theatre *every night*.'[12]

The medical course for the second winter term consisted of anatomy, dissections, and physiology and ended with examinations in anatomy, physiology, chemistry, pharmacy etc. But this heavy programme does not seem to have dampened Bridges' spirits. He wrote to Muirhead:

> Unto Abracadabra, the much travelled and magnificent . . . With much more deferential greeting and in the name of the prophet he wd therefore suggest to the aforesaid muchtobeepitheted Abracadabra esquire that the

following questions arising in the light of his mind lead to the inextricable labyrinth of the shadow of darkness

1) Where *is* Abraca[da]bra?

2) Has he visited the exhibition of old Masters?

3) If he has not done so, does he know how good it is? . . . Shd doubts concerning the sanity of the writer arise in the soul of the addressed let him take the wings of a vehicle and hasten to the relief of the imbecile—

who is only at home in the evenings.[13]

The Old Masters exhibition, held in the Royal Academy, opened in January 1871 and contained 426 pictures, most of them acknowledged masterpieces drawn from numerous private collections.

At the end of February Bridges went to Margate. He was under the weather, and although he had brought his 'solid' works with him, he was more inclined to read lighter literature and asked his landlady to lend him a selection of her books. Among these was John Cumming's popular *The Great Tribulation: On the Things Coming on the Earth*, about which he remarked,

really I think that Dr Cumming has some eloquence—on dipping into his book I don't wonder at all at his popularity, & I am convinced more & more that the one thing which must be taught before all others in religious education is the right estimation of the 'letter'—without the implicit faith which people have in the text of the Bible, & its inspired authority no such nonsense as this of Cumming's wd be possible.[14]

It is easy to see why Bridges should have responded in this way. Cumming regarded the period from 1848 to 1867 as the period of the Great Tribulation as described in the Book of Revelation. He ascribes 'diseases of various types, from the consuming fever of Lisbon in 1857 down to less marked degeneracy of physical health' to 'a fulfilment of the effects of the seventh apocalyptic vial' (p. iv), a risible idea to an Anglican trying to ease human physical suffering with the best that current scientific treatment could provide.

Bridges' brother-in-law, Samuel Butler, may have had less orthodox views at this time. Bridges had first met Butler early in 1859 when the latter, who was 23, had visited Dr Molesworth. This was the year in which George Bridges had married Butler's sister, Harriett, and contact between the families would have been frequent. Butler had taken the opportunity of discussing his religious beliefs with Dr Molesworth because he was unsure whether they were too unorthodox for him to enter the Church, one of the careers that he was considering at the time. Bridges said later,

> I well remember the expression of S. B.'s face as he came up the stairs from his long interview to where I was installing a huge aquarium. We had at least one day's ramble together on the moors, and I found him a very pleasant companion and talker—no doubt he had been warned not to communicate his heresies to me—and we parted on terms of sympathetic mutual friendship.[15]

They met again in 1871 when Butler had established himself in rooms at Clifford's Inn. Bridges noted, 'I visited him, but we never had a meal together, and I do not remember his visiting me in my lodgings in Great Ormond St. I would occasionally go and sit with him of late afternoons and chat chiefly about his new book Erewhon, of which he would read me extracts.' Finding that Butler did not have the money to publish the book, Bridges offered to help but the offer was refused, Butler asserting that he had a friend on whom he could 'draw without compunction if need were'. The friendship continued, said Bridges, 'through the series of his Darwinian books, all of which he sent to me, and we had many talks about them'. But their intimacy faded as Bridges came to think that Butler was 'vain and ugly in mind', with 'a meanness in his general mental attitude towards humanity' and a venomous attitude to his family. Nevertheless, as Bridges recognized, he was capable of sympathizing with individuals very different in temperament from himself and of being extremely generous, as, for example, when their mutual friend, W. S. Rockstro, fell off an omnibus and lay dying in hospital. Butler sent him money regularly, concealing his charity lest Rockstro refuse to take the gift from someone who could, as Bridges said, 'so ill afford to spare it'.[16] There was no open break between Butler and Bridges; they greeted each other as friends whenever they met, as they frequently did in the British Museum, corresponded with each other about their published volumes, and Bridges continued to praise *Erewhon* warmly, recommending it and the evolutionary books as 'the best possible reading'.[17]

During the Easter vacation Bridges stayed at Seymour Court near Marlow, the home of his friend Owen Wethered who belonged to a brewing firm, was an officer in the Bucks Volunteers, and MP for Greater Marlow. In the area, Bridges told Muirhead, he had 'many more indefinite relatives . . . than it is possible for the most sanguine man ever either to desire or to deserve—& their friendliness is equally beyond & above the merit & expectation of so ornary a mortal as i'. He spent his time rowing, learning archery, walking, 'lunching and loitering', and felt 'much better for the change of habit'.[18]

After a summer term at St Bartholomew's spent in hospital practice, with initiatory clinical instruction in medicine and surgery, Bridges retired to Seaford on the south coast for a few days. Longing for outdoor exercise he avoided his friends, and, as he reported to Muirhead, 'went where a preponderance of water is normal. The first day I had a splendid sail, & got drenched with salt water. the second day I walked 25 miles & got wet to the skin with aerial showers. the third day, today, I lay & basked in the sun on the beach: & I came home by the evening train.'[19] Bridges' need for regular exercise led him to join 'The Tramps', which he described as 'a sort of walking club of Londoners who took long walks in the country on Sundays, and intended talking'. On one occasion he found himself accompanying Leslie Stephen, of whom he was somewhat in awe, and discussed with him a new machine for measuring the speed of thought; but Stephen, who admired the machine, ridiculed Bridges for his reservations, and the latter was not eager to repeat the experience.[20]

In August 1872, Hopkins sent Bridges what has become known as his 'Red Letter', in which he condoned violent revolution by the working class on the grounds that they should have received fair reward for their contribution to the increase in Britain's wealth and had not done so.[21] Bridges did not reply, and Hopkins suggested that he had been offended by his political remarks. Although this has been uncritically accepted as the explanation for the break in communication, the breach seems to have started in October 1869 when Bridges visited Hopkins at Roehampton. The latter concluded that he must have 'behaved unkindly' then, since Bridges did not write for nearly eighteen months.[22] What probably happened was that Hopkins tried to influence Bridges' religious or political views and evidently ruffled his friend, who made a quip in his letter of May 1871 about Hopkins thinking badly of him.

Republicanism was at a high-point in Britain, and the Paris Commune dominated the English newspapers in May. As with the French Revolution, it was seen by political factions in Britain either as a hopeful sign of greater democracy or as a dreadful warning. Although Bridges and Hopkins were encountering urban poverty for the first time, neither believed that socialism was a desirable solution. Bridges was more class-conscious than Hopkins and he would have been horrified at the idea of revolution, but, by itself, the expression of such views is unlikely to have led him to make a deliberate break. As with Hopkins' conversion, he was probably more concerned about Hopkins' attitude to him than with his opinions, and may have felt that he was being unfairly criticized for his way of life; until 1888 Hopkins was strikingly unsympathetic to the strain placed on medical students and physicians.[23] Conversely, Bridges was now openly sceptical about certain elements of orthodox religion, especially Catholicism. He also objected to his letters being read by Hopkins' superiors, who could censor his mail, and Hopkins was slow to reassure him that they seldom did so.[24] Finally, the mutual interest in poetry, so vital to the friendship, was not yet evident. It seems most likely that Bridges did not so much decide on a break as give answering the letter low priority because there were no pressing reasons for wanting to continue the exchange. It was not the first, and would not be the last, time that one or other of these friends was a tardy correspondent.

Bridges' medical course for 1871–2 combined further hospital practice with lectures on medicine and surgery in the winter term, while in the summer therapeutics, pathological anatomy, and operative surgery were added to the hospital practice and clinical lectures. Much of the practice was still somewhat barbaric. James Verco, one of Bridges' fellow students at Bart's, described his first experience of extracting teeth without local anaesthetic; with the patient's head tucked under his arm, he wrenched and twisted with a pair of forceps for all he was worth.[25] The eight extractions he made that day left him with aching muscles.

In the final year there was forensic medicine, midwifery, and diseases of women and children, vaccination, diseases of the eye, ear, and teeth, and mental illness to be learnt. Some of these branches of medicine had, in the early 1870s, acquired sufficient bodies of knowledge to become specialisms for which separate wards were established at St Bartholomew's, among them the Aural Department, the Dermatological Department and the Orthopaedic Department, in each of which Bridges would have worked for several months. He later told one story of his experience when 'clerking' as a senior student for the out-patient physician which gives an idea of the formality of the relations among the staff:

> The Out Patient physician held a morning clinique chiefly of the patients which had been filtered out for him from the Casualty Department . . . and he sat in a room with two tables; he and his clinique at one, and at the other his 'clerk', an advanced student, who took an equal share of the patients (independently of him) but after seeing them, passed them on to his senior for sanction or correction. I was clerking for Dr Jones (that was not his name at all). He was a magnificent person, an Oxford graduate and country gentleman, who came to the highest professional honours. Baronet and Member of the College of Physicians and he is still living, much my senior. On this occasion he had been puzzled to tell his class what was the matter with a greatly swollen hand which a patient had offered him for cure and he had been talking to the students of gout and rheumatism. The patient was a big heavy full-blooded man of 35 or 40. Dr Jones was always a pattern of courtesy and for some reason he said, 'Let us ask Dr Bridges'. So he walked the patient across the room to me. 'What's the matter with this hand, Bridges?' and the man held his hand towards me. Without touching it or examining it, I said, 'He's broken his 3rd metacarpal Dr Jones'—and to the man, 'Did you hit him in the face?' The man's smile betrayed him and Dr Jones said, 'Broken his 3rd metacarpal you say? Well I'll take him to the surgeon'. So he then walked him out into the next room where the surgeon had a corresponding surgical clinique, and returning in a few minutes said, 'Yes, Bridges, Langton says it is a fracture of the 3rd metacarpal' . . . But how did I know it? When I was at school, aged 12, this accident happened to a schoolfellow in a fight and the appearance of his hand, and the queer nature of the injury had been stamped on my mind indelibly.[26]

Although Bridges' visual memory served him well in this case, the amount of information students were expected to memorize and have to hand was becoming more than any individual could manage. This had not yet been realized, and Bridges' career was one of those on which it was to have a drastic effect.

During 1871–2 Bridges moved to 50 Maddox Street, a house he

shared with the painter and musician Harry Ellis Wooldridge just off Hanover Square, in the centre of London and a few blocks south of Oxford Circus. Bridges described Wooldridge as the 'most intimate friend of my younger days'. He had a 'well-formed, thick-set frame, massive bust and noble head which early baldness forced on the attention; blue eyes in wide orbits, fine and muscular features, ruddy auburn beard trimmed like a Frenchman's.'[27] Bridges said of him, 'In dress and manners punctilious, in character brave and generous, of philosophical conviction and strict morality, he was gentle-hearted and indulgent towards others, genial in conventional chatter but intolerant of pretence, especially in the talk of artists, to whom his undisguised amusement and devastating irony were obnoxious'; he was 'a good raconteur and mimic, and a loud laugher', all qualities that Bridges would have enjoyed. A year younger than Bridges, Wooldridge did not come from a wealthy family. His father had held a 'literary post' in the publishing house Smith, Elder, but the business failed. He had articled Harry to Lloyd's Bank, but when Bridges met him, Wooldridge had left the bank and, having attended the Royal Academy School, was painting under the influence of Burne-Jones, with whom he had long been friendly. In her *Memoir* of her husband, Georgiana Burne-Jones records that in the 1860s Wooldridge had introduced the family

> to a new world of beauty in Italian songs of the seventeenth century—then almost entirely unknown—and his singing of Carissimi and Stradella gave us the keenest pleasure . . . Most of these treasures Mr Wooldridge had discovered for himself among manuscripts in the British Museum, and others he brought afterwards from the Bodleian and Christ Church Libraries and from Rome.[28]

Wooldridge did not have Bridges' classical training but he was fluent in French and Italian. 'From his youth an accomplished singer', he was now becoming 'an expert contrapuntist', having been taught Palestrinal counterpoint by W. S. Rockstro, to whom he introduced both Butler and Bridges. Rockstro, a church-organist who wrote most of the articles on plainsong for *Grove's Dictionary*, and edited Mozart's operas, had, according to Bridges, 'distinguished intellectual features' and an 'impressive personality which he consciously though quite naturally conformed to and lived on'. His 'suave manners', 'noble kind of courtesy', and 'sweet temper which appeared plainly in his sensitive features', endeared him to Bridges, whose friendship with him continued for the rest of Rockstro's life.[29]

Bridges had other friends who were involved in the arts. Among these was the composer John Stainer, four years Bridges' senior, who had been University organist at Oxford while Bridges was an undergraduate, and a fellow-member of the BHT. Hopkins obtained his textbook on the *Theory of Harmony* (1871) in 1880, hoping to learn to write accompaniments for the tunes he so readily thought of, but it was evidently a struggle. The third edition of Stainer's *Primer* was printed in 1876, and Hopkins, who obtained it in 1884, wrote to Bridges:

> Stainer has written a capital Treatise on harmony which has earned him the heartfelt thanks of people as ignorant as myself (I cannot say his Novello-Primer of the same earned them) and of others, I believe, not ignorant at all. For instance Sir Robert Stewart, learned musician of this city [Dublin], much given to Purcell, Handel, and Bach, says it is the most scientific treatment he has seen. Though his theory is not final, it is a great step forward and has quite a daylight, a *grand jour*, of sense. I am sure Stainer must be very nice to know and meet.[30]

Hopkins later tried to persuade Bridges to pass on to Stainer compositions with which he felt he could make no further progress, explaining that he felt drawn to him since they had been contemporaries at Oxford and he knew him by sight, but Bridges suggested showing them to another friend, probably Hubert Parry whom he had known at Eton.[31] Bridges spent many evenings making music with friends, especially after Stainer moved to St Paul's late in 1874, and went to a number of concerts, thoroughly enjoying for example a performance in the Albert Hall in November 1873 of Handel's *Theodora*.[32] He may also have written some music. Hopkins, referring to an evening Robert had spent with his family, wrote:

> It was embarrassment made Grace [his musical sister] odd that night, I have no doubt: you think she only cares for learned music and she thinks so of you. No question she admires Handel. She stands in dread of your judgment probably.
>
> I sent her your hymn. I mentioned it and she begged to see it. She said

it was not original-sounding but it was very sweet: she wd not be pleased if she knew I repeated her criticism.[33]

In 1872 Bridges' circle of friends was further extended when he joined the Savile Club, which had been formed in 1868 with the aim of allowing middle-class men from a variety of backgrounds to meet.[34] Membership fees were deliberately kept low, and companionship was fostered by having the members dine together at a single sitting rather than providing restaurant service at small tables as in most other London clubs. Bridges was a member from 1872 to 1907, and was then re-elected in 1915. He served on the committee for three years from 1879 along with Basil Champneys, Professor Thomas Fowler, Edmund Gosse, and Charles Kegan Paul. Among Bridges' many friends and acquaintances who belonged to the Savile during the period of his first membership were Mandel Creighton, Henry Woods, Andrew Lang, Wooldridge, Alfred Waterhouse, Muirhead, Philip Rathbone, Coventry Patmore, and George Saintsbury. Some of these friends from the literary world may have influenced him towards a more serious interest in writing.

Bridges' first published volume appeared in 1873. It was elegantly printed with beautiful decorative headings and dedicated to Wooldridge. The title-page identifies the poet as 'Robert Bridges, Bachelor of Arts in the University of Oxford', and the table of contents, classified in part by subject and partly by verse-forms such as sonnet, rondeau, and the fashionable triolet, suggests the work of a young man wanting to show the range of which he is capable. Although five of the fifty-three poems date from 1868 or 1869, almost all the rest were written during the summers of 1872 and 1873, a number of them during a two-week holiday at Seaford in August 1873.[35] Only eighteen pieces from the collection can be found in the *Poetical Works* (1953), which is not arranged to show Bridges' poetic development and through its extensive omissions hides much of his personality. The subjects tackled in the 1873 volume, for instance, included, as well as the elegies and descriptions of nature usually associated with him, two poems classified as 'philosophical' and several ballads. Of the philosophical poems, 'Capital Punishment' treats its subject with a dispassionate thoughtfulness that is striking, given the associations it must have had for him after 1868 when the murderer of his brother-in-law was hanged. Bridges pictures the final night of someone—clearly not meant to be the man who had attacked the Plows—condemned to death, and leaves the reader with the question whether eternal punishment is not yet more repulsive than capital punishment. It is the earliest expression extant of the abhorrence of eternal punishment that was a crucial element of Bridges' religious belief.

It seems an irresponsive force
Urged him to sin with such slow course
He cannot breed a quick remorse,

Now retribution, so long time
Asleep, has met him at his prime,
To match his final crime with crime.

His penalty seems too akin
Unto his fault, as welded in
To clench the horror of his sin . . .

And there one bitter stroke of pain
Will sever head and trunk in twain,
Body and soul,—to meet again?

He knows not, and his past is such
He hopes not;—at the fatal touch
All will be nothing or too much.

No grief in this world has perplext
His mind, nor pain his being vext,
As this old terror of the next.

A number of the other serious poems in the volume, such as 'Beatus Ille', treat the theme of rigorous striving for a virtuous life, self-discipline, and independence of judgement, while several warn against abandoning duty to love, suggestive perhaps of some of the strain of his life as a medical student.

The 1873 collection shows a gift for narrative sufficient to hold a reader's attention despite an uneven command of rhythm and some banal phrasing. While the whole of *Poetical Works* contains two ballads, 'Screaming Tarn' and the Wordsworthian 'A Villager', *Poems* (1873) has four ballads and a 'romance' that together deal with such diverse topics as Zopyrus and the Seige of Babylon, a Frenchwoman's search for her lost son, twenty would-be robbers of an abbot's feast, and, in 'The Two Rings', a sentimental tale about unfortunate love. One reason why Bridges did not write more narrative poems of this sort may have been the sheer number of successful ones written by Wordsworth, whom he found himself copying only too readily. In time he was to develop his own narrative style, one that was crisply anecdotal, strengthened by his writing of memoirs of friends.

Some of the lyrics in the volume bear the marks of having been written hurriedly—lines are padded, as frequently in 'A Boy and a Girl' for instance, archaic words such as 'trow' and 'mayhap' are used without proper integration, and several poems, such as 'The Temptation', are little more than doggerel. On the other hand, the triolet, 'When first we met we did not guess', with its stringent requirements of form, was called 'perfect of its kind' by Francis Heuffer in a review in *Macmillan's Magazine* in 1880,[36] and the three rondeaux are equally strict. 'I will not let thee go' deftly upsets the expectations established by its chorus, and 'Long are the hours the sun is above' has a similarly neat reversal in its ending:

Long are the hours the sun is above,
But when evening comes I go home to my love . . .

She does not meet me upon the stair,—
She sits in my chamber and waits for me there . . .

And she lets me take my wonted place
At her side, and gaze in her dear dear face.

There as I sit, from her head thrown back
Her hair falls straight in a shadow black.

Aching and hot as my tired eyes be,
She is all that I wish to see . . .

And so I sit here night by night,
In rest and enjoyment of love's delight.

But a knock at the door, a step on the stair
Will startle, alas, my love from her chair . . .

And he wonders, my guest, usurping her throne,
That I sit so much by myself alone.

The identity of the beloved is unknown. Perhaps she was the same woman about whom one of the book's two elegies was written. This has the ring of experience about it. Beginning 'The wood is bare', it is a beautiful poem, although occasionally attention is distracted by inversion and obvious alliteration. As in some of Hardy's poems, a bleak winter scene is used as the setting of an encounter between a lover and the ghost of his beloved. In the best stanzas, the grief becomes a tribute to the lost woman:

> The wood is bare: a river-mist is steeping
> The trees that winter's chill of life bereaves:
> Only their stiffened boughs break silence, weeping
> Over their fallen leaves . . .
>
> For on this path, at every turn and corner,
> The fancy of her figure on me falls:
> Yet walks she with the slow step of a mourner,
> Nor hears my voice that calls.
>
> So through my heart there winds a track of feeling,
> A path of memory, that is all her own:
> Whereto her ghostly figure ever stealing
> Haunts the sad spot alone.

He later changed 'figure' in the penultimate line to 'beauty'.

In the lyric, 'Poor withered rose and dry', Bridges experimented with a mild version of the sprung rhythm which Hopkins had used in 'For a Picture of Saint Dorothea'. Although Bridges was later to use the metre's possibilities to aid the creation of mood, even in this early poem he shows that he understood its two principal features: he placed two adjacent stresses in 'That of jóy pást', and evidently appreciated the freedom to have several unstressed syllables running in 'Skeleton of a rose'. Yeats later gave qualified praise to 'I heard a linnet courting' in which a slightly arch sophistication is reinforced rhythmically by ending each stanza with an unsettlingly short line.[37] His final assessment of Bridges was really based on this volume. In the introduction to the *Oxford Book of Modern Verse*, he wrote:

> His influence—practice, not theory, was never deadening; he gave to lyric poetry a new cadence, a distinction as deliberate as that of Whistler's

painting, an impulse moulded and checked like that in certain poems of Landor, but different, more in the nerves, less in the blood, more birdlike, less human; words often commonplace made unforgettable by some trick of speeding and slowing,

> A glitter of pleasure
> And a dark tomb,

or by some trick of simplicity, not the impulsive simplicity of youth but that of age, much impulse examined and rejected:

> I heard a linnet courting
> His lady in the spring! His mates were idly sporting,
> Nor stayed to hear him sing
> His song of love.—I fear my speech distorting
> His tender love.

Every metaphor, every thought a commonplace, emptiness everywhere, the whole magnificent

(pp. xvii–xviii)

This is couched as praise but, given that it was published in 1936, it is a somewhat backhanded compliment. The phrase, 'the simplicity . . . of age', for example, does not state but certainly suggests that the poem belongs to Bridges' old age, whereas, written in 1869, it is one of the earliest of his poems extant. It would be no more appropriate to 'sum up' Yeats with a poem of equivalent youth and lightness, such as 'To an Isle in the Water'. Bridges published poems of much greater seriousness and technical excellence than 'I heard a linnet courting', even in *Poems* (1873), but Yeats did not read very much of Bridges' later verse, and did not do him justice by selecting this part of a review originally written in 1897 for inclusion in his later assessment.

Although initially Bridges did what he could to have the book noticed by sending out complimentary copies, he subsequently had the unsold copies destroyed, saying that it contained some things that he did not want to get about.[38] The second edition of 1880 was to contain only nineteen of the forty-six poems. Andrew Lang wrote a review of the volume which appeared in the *Academy* in January 1874. He praised the Romantic 'Elegy on a Lady' as the best poem, and concluded: 'a fancy that can be strange when it chooses, and has always a power of delicate surprise, simplicity, courtliness, feeling, music of no vulgar order,—these are Mr

Bridges' qualities. His defect is to exaggerate the antique roughness of his models . . . We think he is unsuccessful in a few pieces which aim at being humorous.' Hopkins saw the review and realized for the first time that Bridges was interested in writing poetry. He wrote, protesting over the lapsed correspondence, but Bridges was out of the country and when he returned and replied, inviting Hopkins to Maddox Street, the Jesuit had been moved to north Wales.

Shortly after Christmas, 1873, Bridges had to go to Oxford to take his final examinations in therapeutics, medicine, surgery, midwifery, forensic medicine, and hygiene. They consisted of a week of written tests, a viva voce, and clinical examinations. He failed the written tests, and therefore the entire examination, largely because his answers were considered too brief.[39] It was a severe blow but may have caused him to extend a trip to Italy that he had planned. He travelled with Muirhead and Philip Rathbone, president of the Liverpool Chamber of Commerce, and an art-collector who enriched the Walker Gallery's collection with gifts of Rossetti's paintings, among others; he was well-known in the artistic circles in which Bridges moved at the time. Mrs Rathbone, their daughter and a friend of hers went too, and Wooldridge intended to join them when he could earn enough money. In January 1874 they went to Nice by train, and by coach from there to Genoa where they again took the train to Pisa.[40] The Rathbones evidently found that they enjoyed the company of Robert and Lionel rather more than they had anticipated and, catching the young men's enthusiasm for exploration, decided to join them on their more leisurely trip instead of going straight to Rome. They spent three days in Siena and a day exploring Orvieto, before taking the Florence train to Rome.

Although the Rathbones were booked into a different hotel from Bridges and Muirhead, they all met frequently and by the end of the month had taken three coach trips of some forty miles together. Bridges had mixed feelings about Rome—delight, admiration, and irritation. Staying in his rooms until 11 a.m. he spent the crisp, sunny afternoons exploring, dining in a café and not returning until 6 o'clock, except on the two afternoons a week when he had an hour's Italian lesson. He had been looking forward to learning

Italian and expected to be able to start reading it late in February. He then tried to give it an hour a day, but had so many other things to do that he confessed that he was not getting on very fast. One of the things to which he gave attention was learning about Italian art. This he did in Muirhead's knowledgeable company, spending many afternoons in the Vatican Museum, whose art treasures he described as 'inexhaustible'.[41] In February, thanks to money sent by his mother, he hired a strong, spirited horse and revelled in daily exercise on it; it also allowed him to participate in group excursions with the wealthier Rathbones.

Wooldridge arrived in March and he and Muirhead started spending whole days sketching and painting. Just before Easter the Rathbones left to make their way home by a direct route, while Bridges and Muirhead went first to Naples for a few days over Easter before heading north to Florence. Bridges liked the city and browsed in the bookshops, purchasing a volume of Boccaccio and a sixteenth-century copy of Petrarch, which he lost shortly afterwards but which Muirhead miraculously recovered on a subsequent visit. At Bologna, Bridges decided to curtail his sightseeing; having seen new things for five months, he told his mother, he felt 'like a man who won't take any more plumpudding'. Wooldridge and Muirhead wanted to visit Venice and Ravenna, but Bridges, although he was tempted, left them, travelling back by train to arrive early in June. The others returned shortly afterwards, and Bridges wrote to Muirhead:

I write to tell you that I am coming North tomorrow, so that if you are in the neighbourhood of Rochdale you can pay me a visit. There will be very good cricket & that will be my amusement: I am afraid it will not be the same attraction to you, but you can read Dr Molesworth's manuscript sermons if you like when I am playing. He is an eminent divine—the sermons are not very interesting but on the other hand they are nearly illegible so that they wouldn't bore you much. Wooldridge & I are very comfortable here . . . my Boccaccio is certainly a forgery. an Italian one, but still a good book. I find the edition was also reprinted in London, in French type with a facsimile title. It is a sell. but the book is worth nearly what I gave for it in the English market . . . I have taken down from my walls your picture of Friebourg or Freibourg, or Freiberg or Frieberg.—and elevated the Nile. Meredith Brown suggested the other day that the latter would do as well upside down. I saw Stainer today he is very well.

I miss a private music evening at his house next week, with string quartett etc. by coming north, a great bore.

I wish that Wooldridge hadn't worn out this pen by writing music, but he has, and I fear my writing is illegible. It doesn't much matter. W. sends his kindest remembrances to the Rathbones, & hopes that when he finds time to pay his promised visit to Manchester he may come on and make them a visit, *& please ask R from me if he will make arrangements for me to see the collection of Rosetti's pictures in Liverpool* if I may come and see him in about a weeks time. a line to Rochdale Vicarage will 'oblige'—in ten days I must be back in town. Remember the cricket.[42]

Hopkins was working in Liverpool at the time and Bridges, knowing that he would like to see the Rossetti paintings, wrote to Philip Rathbone mentioning that an invitation to Hopkins would be appreciated but no response seems to have been forthcoming.[43]

Late in July 1874 Bridges went to Dublin, where for nearly a month he studied the methods of 'physic and surgery' there; 'I never saw such a lot of doctors', he declared, 'the place is wholly given to the healing art'. He had 'excellent lodgings in the best part of the town' and intended to see something of the country before returning to England, but thought Dublin 'a very dull place', as indeed Hopkins was to find it ten years later.[44] It is strange that Hopkins does not seem to have known of this visit. He described Dublin to Bridges as one would to someone who had never seen it.

By October Bridges was expressing his frustration that he could have no regular medical work until he passed his examinations, which he was scheduled to resit in December. He would have liked to have taken a house with a couple of friends, but could not afford to do so. While Bridges was not poor, he was also not particularly wealthy; Willoughby Furner had enabled him to go to Italy by taking over his room in Maddox Street and paying two-thirds of its rent; his mother too had helped, and Bridges kept very careful accounts on his trips to the Middle East and Italy. He found a house that he wanted to share with Wooldridge and Furner and asked if Dr Molesworth would be interested as a business venture in helping with the cost of the lease and premium, but the plan had to be dropped when Furner's plans became too unsettled.[45] Over the winter Bridges hoped that he would be able to live in the hospital.

Early in December he was summoned to Oxford for his medical examination and was then asked to postpone it because Dr Acland had been bitten by a dog. Bridges, who was the only candidate, refused to withdraw and was tested by four doctors for four days. Despite having a fever, he felt he had done well and this time was successful, receiving his degree the following week (17 December 1874).[46]

6

House Physician

(1875–1876)

In 1875 Bridges began work as house physician to Dr Patrick Black, the Senior Physician at St Bartholomew's. House physicians were paid £25 a year but had to pay 25 guineas to the physician to whom they were apprenticed, leaving them 25 shillings out of pocket.[1] The hospital provided them with a room but not food. Patrick Black was a 'tall and handsome man' with 'an open countenance', who had been appointed in 1852 as the first anaesthetist at St Bartholomew's, some five years after the discovery of chloroform and its immediate purchase for the hospital. Black was a sceptical man, who 'regarded his own prescriptions as a ceremonial observance rather than as a practical measure'.[2] He was a doctor of the old school, scarcely using even the wooden monaural stethoscope of the day as a diagnostic tool, but he showed how much could be accomplished by 'facies', with observational powers so highly developed that they verged on instinct. Bridges had great admiration for his skill and the highest respect for his integrity and character. Black was a generous and conscientious teacher and often, as he leisurely washed up after visiting the wards, he discussed carefully all the critical cases with Bridges, trying to answer the latter's questions as to his reasons for arriving at diagnoses, though he could not always explain these, and passing on to him tips from his experience. Bridges gave an example:

'I see, Dr Bridges,' he said, 'that you are anxious about the patient in bed so and so. You really need not be troubled about him. He will recover.' I begged him to tell me why he was so confident. It was a case of double pneumonia from which the lungs did not clear up—both bases remained solid for weeks after the active symptoms had ceased—and I pointed out that there had been no physical signs of improvement whatever.

'It is true,' he said, 'there are yet no signs of improvement—but tell me this: is the patient any worse than he was 3 weeks ago?'—'No,' I said, 'he is no worse.' 'Well,' said he, 'if he had not been going to recover he wd have been worse'.—From such simple axioms as this I was always learning from him.[3]

Bridges was keen to do what he could for his patients and, working hard at developing his skills in 'facies' as well as the new analytical methods, soon showed a flair for the work. Just as Dr Black was able to arrive at diagnoses that initially surprised Bridges so, says Bridges,

my modern methods sometimes got the better of him and I am proud to think that he came to have as much respect for my opinion as I had for his and so friendly a feeling towards me that he liked my opposition and was honestly pleased at my skill when he found himself beaten. It is natural that I shd remember some of these cases . . . He had been, as must sometimes happen, constrained by private personal obligations to admit an improper case into his wards.—a woman who was in the last stage of consumption. He apologised for it and said, 'she has only a few days to live: but I wish you to make careful clinical examination and exact statement of her condition for the students' use. It is the only thing that we can do—' At his next clinique I read my exhaustive report at the bedside and among my items stated that the patient had tubercle also in the kidney. Dr B thanked me, but said I might leave the kidney out.—and certainly there was eno[ugh] without it. but when she died a few days after, I boldly asked Dr B that there might be a p[ost] m[ortem] to examine the kidneys. He looked grave, and said it wd be an extremely difficult thing to manage becos the kinsfolk would resent it especially as there was no reason for it. But, he said, it shall be done if possible becos I think it will be a good lesson for you. He duly obtained permission and at his next visit he asked me with a pleasant smile, 'and how about that tubercular kidney?' 'Oh (I replied) the pathologists thought it so typical a specimen that they have put it up in spirits. It is in the Museum'—He stared a little, and then consumed with good-natured amusement said, 'Well Bridges, if you live to be 100 you'll never beat that.'[4]

Black's faith in Bridges was so great that he once left him in charge while he was away, an unheard-of transgression of the rules that brought down on Bridges the resentment of the other staff.[5] On the first day of Black's absence, Bridges recalled later in a lecture to medical students,

I admitted into the wards a boy who was brought to the hospital wrapped in blankets and in great pain.—I supposed it was a case of rheumatic fever, and sent him up to bed, and then leaving him to be settled in, I visited him about half an hour after.—I had not been two minutes at the bedside when I saw that he had hydrophobia.—I had never seen a case—and I suppose but few of you hav ever seen one. But if they are all like that boy I can tell you that there is no difficulty in the diagnosis. The most peculiar symptoms were the terror and the extreme sensibility to any sort of impact, however indirectly conveyed—I had him put into an isolated room; and, as a matter of courtesy, acquainted all the physicians of the fact, that they might see the case if they wished. Of course they all visited him and not a single one of them confirmed my diagnosis, and some repudiated it strongly. The boy was dead in a few days. Pasteur's treatment then in its infancy was not possible—and [before the post-mortem examination] I gave evidence at the Coroner's inquest of the cause of death. history confirmed me—there was a scar on the ball of the thumb, and the story of a cat's bite. As I came out from the inquest Dr Black's carriage drove up—he had returned—'Oh, Dr Black,' I said, 'you were away at an unfortunate time—I have had a case of hydrophobia and am just come out from the Coroner's Inquest where I gave evidence of the cause of death. All the physicians examined the case and repudiated or doubted my diagnosis, and they are now all of them collecting in the p[ost]m[ortem] room to discover a lesion of the brain.[6]

On several occasions Bridges was prompted by the suffering of his patients to write papers on treatment which he believed might ease pain for others. For instance, he contributed an article on 'A Severe Case of Rheumatic Fever Treated Successfully by Splints' to the *St Bartholomew's Hospital Reports*. It begins:

The inflammation of joints, which is the characteristic and constant symptom of rheumatic fever, is the cause of such intense suffering to the patient, that even were it possible to believe that this might in all cases be neglected without danger or fear of bad consequences, yet the physician would hardly be the less bound to do all in his power to alleviate it. Unfortunately the remedies that have been tried bear witness by their number to their inefficiency; and it is common in clinical teaching to see the special assaults of this disease considered in themselves as unimportant so long as they spare the viscera, while attention is mainly directed to the heart and pericardium; and the state of the patient in whom these continue sound is held to be so satisfactory that he is merely encouraged to support his agonies, in expectation of a future and uncertain day when they will probably take their leave.

This method of treatment, if treatment it may be called, has found support in the tendency of a therapeutic fashion, that by the watchword of expectancy has not only taught prudence, but has often excused indolence and spared judgment; so that it is not a matter of wonder to the student to see some patients waiting for their pain to pass off as others do for their fever, while the knowledge that inflammation of the heart is more serious than that of the knee is sufficient erudition to divert their attention and defer their efforts.

Such considerations, coupled with the common agreement of surgeons concerning the treatment of inflamed joints, led me to ask leave to publish in this volume the account of a case of rheumatic fever of unusual severity treated by splints. The method is not a new one, and I shall be able to give some account of its history; but since during five years at our Hospital I had never seen it put in practice, nor even heard it mentioned, so it was not till I became responsible for the treatment of a patient who seemed to be dying of sheer pain, that being myself compelled to seek some such resource, I had an opportunity of witnessing its effects. I make no apology for having only one case to report; it is more likely to be read, and is, in my opinion, of more value than a table of figures, and whatever experience I have persuades me that it is worth reporting.[7]

These are the sentences of an articulate person made angry by concern; recognizably the writing of a dedicated young reformer. The detailed record of the patient's treatment, with visits at all times of day, testifies to Bridges' worry and compassion. Then, as now, young doctors worked long hours. Bridges was responsible for looking after two wards and he frequently had to go on duty at 3 or 4 a.m. and might still be at work after 11 p.m.

In July 1875 Robert's sister Frances, known as Carry, scolded him for playing croquet on a Sunday. Bridges' reply shows something of his attitudes and life:

Dearest Carry,
3 p.m. Sunday July 11 1875. I am quite tired of pulling my ox out of the pit, especially as I can't tell whether he's any further from the bottom yet though I began this figurative entertainment at 3 a.m. this morning. You will conclude rightly from this parable of the ox that it is my week on duty, & that I have had a busy morning & that I wish I was playing croquet on Mr Lynch's lawn in the country, or spending my time in some equally unexhausting amusement. I don't like your having found out that I played croquet with Mr Lynch on Sunday, & I don't think, considering

how much you dislike knowing it, and know how much I should dislike your disliking knowing it, that it was kind of you to upbraid me with my very harmless recreation. If I had got drunk at the Rose and Crown, & thrown stones in at the window of the Church while Mr Molyneux was preaching . . . then I might have felt your rebuke—but really the muscular effort involved in playing croquet does not much exceed that expended in turning over the leaves of a volume of Mr Jones' sermons, while granting the intellectual effort to be about the same in the 2 cases, & moral heroism to be absent from either occupation, there remains a balance of propriety in favour of the one that one likes best—& I was much the better for it.

However you may rest in peace of mind for my Sunday occupation today,—I am doing penance we will suppose for my croquet.

I can't writ you a longer letter as I am too tired & have to go and see a patient who has endangered his life by drinking too much bad beer on Saturday night—now if he had only waited till Sunday. and played croquet then instead of drinking beer, how much better wd it have been for him. & for me. & for you. if you wd like my letter to go on. Now I never drink beer on Saturday night—nor on any other night.

It was very fine at 3 a.m. this morning, but it has been showery ever since & is cloudy now.[8]

During 1875 Bridges wrote a number of sonnets. He sent these to Lionel Muirhead on 5 October, asking him to

take a pencil and mark at the side any thing that you like—or dislike, or don't understand—any thing especially which *grates* in the *wording*—And I want you to read them in this manner. 1st *neglect all the prose*. & see if you can make any thing of the verse. I mean if you see enough argument in it to induce you to go on rather than leave off. don't even read the suggestive headings. This you can do by always doubling the book back on itself. Then having followed my instructions so far go back & read all the prose. and see if that gives you a notion. a new notion, or none at all—Then read the verse again & send it me back . . . If they *do*, I shall print them, but only a few copies . . . please do all this to oblige your extravagantly demanding friend.[9]

This manuscript notebook is unfortunately no longer extant. In 1883 Hopkins wrote, 'you speak of writing the sonnet in prose first. I read the other day that Virgil wrote the Aeneid in prose. Do you often do so? Is it a good plan? If it is I will try it; it may help on my flagging and almost spent powers.'[10]

Bridges' response to Muirhead's criticisms suggests that he did not take overly much notice of them. He had already pressed ahead with new work: 'I wrote a poem of 300 lines last night! & I have a swelled face today. I don't know whether this is cause and effect— I need not tell you that the 300 verses want a good deal doing to them—I think it will amuse you. It is *very* serious.' About the sonnets he had sent he asked, 'whether the whole had an effect as whole—on the *mind*—Do they seem to be about anything in particular?'[11] He published the series as *The Growth of Love: A Poem in Twenty-Four Sonnets* in 1876, but the sonnets scarcely attain the unity that 'a poem' suggests. Edward Thompson states that some of the sonnets were written with a particular woman in mind:

> Bridges left it on record that *The Growth of Love* [1876] is autobiographical. This is clear enough; a moving and beautiful love-story casts its shadow. Yet, if with this key Bridges unlocked his heart, the lock has clashed to, and the key is lost. He kept his personal secrets, and throughout life and in especial just before he died was at pains to destroy all that told more than he chose should be told of him. The lady abides in eternal anonymity, which is what her lover desired.[12]

The opening sonnet says that the lady died unwon and several of the sonnets suggest various stages in a courtship: ecstasy of love, fear of proposing, a retrospective glance at the growth of feeling. There are several on loss, including one that movingly alludes to such feelings in the course of telling the story of Orpheus and Eurydice:

> Sound flute and viol, hautboy, clarionet!
> Since in dispelling sorrow lies your fame,
> Sound now, I cried, and put my grief to shame!—
> . . . .
> Vain hope, and ill-instructed, to forget
> When Orpheus singing before Pluto came
> To win his bride from Hell, and won his claim,
> How plain a clause his triumph overset.

The sequence also deals with a number of other types of love. Several sonnets praise artistic or poetic creation, suggesting that by this man advances his likeness to God the Creator and helps to perfect Nature. The octave of Sonnet XIX alludes to the problems of artistic creation: the inevitable discontent with the gap between vision and accomplishment and dismay at the seemingly endless creativity of Nature, whose 'thousand shapes' mock the artist's one success. Bridges says that he originally wrote many more sonnets on artistic creation, but destroyed them as being 'cold and didactic'.[13] Milton, Dante, and Shakespeare are praised in various sonnets but the tributes jar, especially those to Shakespeare which appear fulsome; in Sonnet XVI, 'Patriotism', for example, there is a characteristic portentousness that would later mar many of the poems Bridges was required to write as Poet Laureate. A tendency to generalize and use flat, rhetorical phrases is evident in Sonnet XV: 'Rejoice ye living, ye who now excel,' | 'And guard in nameless homes the sacred light.' More successful are Sonnet XXIII, a simple prayer addressed to God, 'whose name is love', and Sonnet XVII, inspired by a portrait of the poet's mother which he persuaded her to let Wooldridge paint in 1875. Bridges was grateful for the hospitality shown to his friend while he was at Rochdale, especially by Dr Molesworth.[14] The sonnet celebrates the completion of the picture:

> Tears of love, tears of joy and tears of care,
> Comforting tears that fell uncomforted,
> Tears o'er the new-born, tears beside the dead,
> Tears of hope, pride, and pity, trust and prayer;
>
> Tears of contrition, all tears whatsoe'er
> Of tenderness or kindness had she shed
> Who here is pictured, ere upon her head
> The fine gold might be turned to silver there.
>
> The smile that charmed the father hath given place
> Unto the furrow'd care wrought by the son:
> But virtue hath transformed all change to grace.
>
> So that I praise the artist, who has done
> A portrait for my worship of the face
> Won by the heart my father's heart that won.

Bridges succeeds in conveying the tenderness he felt towards his mother but the lines describing the worry he has caused her and his feeling towards the picture are awkward. Of the octave of this poem John Sparrow says, 'It is not easy to explain why these lines are so very moving. Their peculiar effectiveness is due, it seems, not only to the ideas themselves, but to their successive presentation—itself somehow suggestive of a shower of tears—and to the falling rhythm, beside which the cadence of "Drop, drop, slow tears" sounds almost crude.'[15] Some of the other poems show a psychological astuteness: Sonnet IV, 'Timidity', for example, in which the speaker avers a preference for living in doubt rather than having his fears confirmed of his beloved's displeasure with him, and Sonnet XI, 'Fame', which acknowledges that if the earth and with it all that man has accomplished were to disappear, it seems unlikely that the fact could even be noted elsewhere in the universe. Improvements being made to telescopes meant that man was becoming much more aware of the vast size of the cosmos, and Bridges catches the resultant feelings of loneliness and insignificance.

He sent the volume to Hopkins, who made detailed criticisms accompanied by warm encouragement. His judgement is summed up: 'In general I do not think that you have reached finality in point of execution, words might be chosen with more point and propriety, images might be more brilliant etc.' But he praised the beauty, 'manly tenderness', and 'flowing and never-failing music' of the work.[16] *The Growth of Love* was to go through two more editions. By 1889 the sequence had grown to seventy-nine sonnets, although ten of the original collection were dropped and numerous revisions made in which obscure lines were clarified and on occasion the meaning made more positive. However, the poems' freshness was also diminished by the greater smoothness and the change of verb endings to 'th' ('groweth' instead of 'grows', for example). In 1898, with the omission of a further ten poems, the volume took final shape as part of the collected poetical works; it contained sonnets from all Bridges' previous books. For the later volumes (1889, 1898, incorporated into *Poetical Works*) Bridges deleted the subtitle that had suggested that all the sonnets formed a single poem. As Donald Stanford has remarked, many parts of the series could be reordered without changing the overall effect very much.[17] The final collection (1898) includes examples of most of the topics that Bridges tackled during his life. There are descriptions of the countryside in all seasons, love poems and elegies, philosophical explorations, imaginative depictions of classical figures, descriptions of modern inventions, poems of religious doubt and faith, and evocations of moods, and in this final form *The Growth of Love* deserves its title in much the way that *The Testament of Beauty* does; both are explorations of diverse subjects held together by the fundamental importance that love, especially of beauty, had for Bridges. In one of the sonnets he went so far as to place beauty in the role normally thought of as God's, seeing in its existence not only the explanation of joy but also a rationale for man's sorrow:

For beauty being the best of all we know
Sums up the unsearchable and secret aims
Of nature, and on joys whose earthly names
Were never told can form and sense bestow;
And man hath sped his instinct to outgo
The step of science; and against her shames
Imagination stakes out heavenly claims,
Building a tower above the head of woe.

Nor is there fairer work for beauty found
Than that she win in nature her release
From all the woes that in the world abound:
Nay with his sorrow may his love increase,
If from man's greater need beauty redound,
And claim his tears for homage of his peace.

Among the friends from his Oxford days that Bridges saw at this time was Richard James Thursfield, a tutor at Jesus College who left in 1881 to marry, moving to London, where he became a journalist for *The Times* and subsequently the editor of the *Times Literary Supplement*. While a student in Oxford he had been secretary of a fresco committee at the Oxford Union and had been responsible for trying to coax Rossetti to complete his part of the Union frescos. Another of Bridges' Oxford friends who had some connection with the Pre-Raphaelites was Robert Bateman, who was a couple of years his senior. He was a figure-painter influenced by Burne-Jones and early Italian Renaissance artists, who exhibited occasionally at the Royal Academy and more often at the Grosvenor Gallery. In December 1875 Bridges told Muirhead that he was 'going to eat chops off Japanese plates with Chutnee made by Bateman at 6. this evening at Mad[d]ox St.—The gourmand pleasures of the rich are foolish compared to such an entertainment.'[18] A letter he sent Muirhead in 1878 shows something of his life in the midst of his friends' artistic activity:

Wooldridge tells me that he has heard from you. I write because I think you may care to hear an unprejudiced opinion concerning the picture. It was not done in time for the academy, indeed tho' the Grosvenor is 14 days later there is some doubt whether it will be in time for that [it was not]. but—it is a success. decidedly—very decidedly. One unfortunate circumstance, viz, that Aeneas we discover, shd be in armour, and though it wd very much improve the picture to put him into armour, yet there is not time. W. got an old frame for the picture, which is beautiful, and suits it admirably.—It is a remarkable production, & its excellence cannot escape the notice of the veriest fool: for it has a sort of mysterious simplicity about it that makes one look at it. as I found out when it was put in its frame. for to tell the truth I was sick of it=and thought I shd never want to see it again.

So much for the picture. Bateman has 3 for the Academy. One he has sold and one is a commission . . . The Reredos is finished [by Wooldridge for St Martin's Church, Brighton] & has gone in. it is a most gaudy 'pulticacious' dish.[19]

Bridges mentioned to Muirhead in 1875 that he had 'found rather a nice person', but no trace of her identity remains.[20] In December he acted as best man to Samuel Gee, five years his senior and a full physician at the Children's Hospital, Great Ormond Street. Gee's wife, he noted, thinking of their chances of having children, 'is I am sorry to say older than himself. this is a great pity'.[21] Gee became a specialist in children's diseases and was appointed physician to George, Prince of Wales in 1901. He had taught Bridges the technique of auscultation, and been sufficiently impressed with his pupil later to dedicate his textbook on auscultation to him by printing one of his poems on the title page. In his poem *Carmen Elegiacum* Bridges wrote, in Latin,

I see you standing over your seated flock and I recall the days when I was one of your lambs and am overwhelmed with vain longing; yet no one believes that I wish the place that fellow yonder is taking were mine. You will teach them how to tend new-born babies in the right way, how to suit delicate food to their tender digestions; they see you sounding, palpatating and percussing chests and so deducing symptoms of disease. Had you not been my guide, philosopher and friend, the learned school of medicine would be jeering at my headlong retreat.[22]

The friendship between the two men lasted until Gee's death in 1911, although Bridges' letters to him dwindled to annual accounts sent at Christmas. They shared interests in literature as well as medicine; Gee published articles on, among others, Abraham Cowley and Andrew Marvell. His productivity seems to have caused a slight uneasiness in Bridges, whose letters to him in the 1880s describing his literary work sometimes suggest that he felt a need to justify having abandoned medicine for literature.

Bridges spent two months in Paris, from mid-January 1876. It was a busy visit. Rising at 7.30 he would have a breakfast of tea, bread, and butter while dressing, then catch a taxi to the Pitié Hospital where, from 8.30 to 10.15, he would work in the wards. At 10.15 there would be a lecture by one of the eminent physiologists or doctors at the hospital. Occasionally he would be free for lunch by noon, returning to the hospital for another lecture of an hour-and-a-half and more time in the wards. After dinner at 6.30 he would go and see a play, returning at midnight. He intended to hear all the principal doctors during his two months, and attended lectures seven days a week; 'the best of all the physicians, whom I most wanted to meet', he told his mother, 'holds his chief clinical lecture on Sunday—I wonder whether you think it wrong—I wish he did—but it is most likely a great effort of self denial to him, & he is very likely lecturing out of his spare time.'[23] He also wanted to see as much French theatre as he could and expected that he would not have time to do much else.

In 1876 Bridges passed the examination for membership of the Royal College of Physicians. An anecdote concerning this was related by Sir Henry Head to Harvey Cushing:

> Nowadays, in the examination, there remains a vestigial appendix, the German or French piece for translation. This serves rather to remind those connected with the examination that they are still acquainted with culture and learning, than to intrude as an obstacle to the candidates' success. In Bridges' day there was both a Greek and a Latin passage for translation. Since there were no instructions as to the language into which they were to be translated, he put the Latin one into Greek and vice versa.[24]

Bridges resigned as house physician to Dr Black on 8 June and in December sent him a farewell poem called *Carmen Elegiacum*. It was in Latin, humorous, and written mostly, he said, while he was having breakfast.[25] He had the poem privately printed and sent a copy to Hopkins, who found it in parts '——d obscure'; 'I don't know when I remember to have read so much good Latin verse together, still I look upon such a performance as a waste of time and money (a pretty penny it must have cost you printing)'.[26] Composing a farewell in Latin was a custom at Eton, a school that Black too had attended. In the poem Bridges sketches the history of the hospital and then tells characteristic anecdotes or describes briefly his contemporaries among the staff. The final section is more serious, mentioning Black's achievements and gracefully expressing Bridges' appreciation for the many things Black had taught him and the many times he had encouraged his assistant's flagging spirits. Bridges had found life as an assistant physician almost too hard at times; he was to find being a casualty physician still more demanding.

7

The Casualty Department (1876–1881)

Bridges then began work in St Bartholomew's Hospital Casualty Ward. The department was relatively new, the first out-patients having been admitted in the 1840s and the first casualty physician appointed only in 1870. A report Bridges wrote on the department after spending a year there is informative about its state and his attitudes at the time. The paper begins with a description of the ward: a

> large hall, 90 feet by 30 feet, with rooms opening off it at the four corners, and two enclosed spaces about the centre of it, shut in with screens; the rest of the area is set out with forms. [In the middle of the long side opposite the entrance] are the counters of the dispensary of common drugs, served by nurses. One half of the hall, with the rooms off it, is devoted to the women, the other half to men. A casualty physician and a house-surgeon attend at each end; the centre enclosures contain, besides, the junior assistant surgeon, and on busy mornings, the junior assistant-physician.[1]

Four mornings a week, people would queue outside the casualty entrance. At 9 o'clock they would be allowed in one by one, directed either to the physician or surgeon according to their complaint. An hour later the doors would be closed.

> If anyone should go into the hall at about twenty minutes past nine, he would see some hundred persons standing in an orderly manner, trying to look as if they were not pushing towards the various exits and entrances, and some four hundred others ranged on the forms; the women engaged in conversation, the men waiting in silence. If he goes out again and comes in again at eleven, he will frequently find the room nearly or quite empty.

The necessity for attending to as many of the patients as possible before 11 o'clock came from the fact that out-patients were not admitted for treatment after that time, and the allocation of vacant beds in the hospital was made then for all patients who had been well enough to walk.

The casualty physicians' task was to treat patients whose ills were minor and select those who needed either further treatment as out-patients or required a stay in hospital. The difficulty of the job arose principally from the sheer number of patients who had to be treated. The dispensary, which made and supplied all the medicine used in the hospital, could not be overstrained, so the physicians had to compromise and treat as many ailments as possible with the small selection of medicines available at the dispensary counter in the casualty hall. The physicians gave tickets for these emetics, drastics, tonics, astringents, and emollients to the patients, who presented the ticket and their own container for the medicine at the counter. Quassia and iron was, Bridges stated, the tonic most frequently presented, because 'atonic dyspepsia was quite as frequent as one would imagine it would be from a knowledge of the long hours that machinists and buttonhole-makers have to work, the stale air they breathe, and the cheap miscellaneous food they are obliged to live on, and often have no appetite to eat'. But poverty and harsh conditions of work were not the only cause of ill health. Knowledge of guide-lines for health and hygiene was appallingly scant, and examples of resultant ills ranged from the 'oversuckled rickety baby whose mother prided herself on its fatness' to illness produced by drunkenness and insufficient cleanliness. Bridges was not as strident in his report of public ignorance as one of his fellow physicians who, in his account in the *St. Bartholomew's Hospital Reports*, criticized contemporary fashion for such follies as the tight lacing of girls' and womens' corsets, which led to the misshaping of internal organs; he suggested as well that all schoolchildren should be given tuition in hygiene.[2]

The problem of numbers affected not only the dispensary but the difficulty of arriving at accurate diagnosis. In his report Bridges said,

> At present it is not unusual for a casualty physician to see 150 patients in less than two hours; and I shall not be using extravagant language if I call

this quick work, and say that very great accuracy cannot be arrived at in such hasty proceedings. Indeed, it is not easy to see what he can be supposed to do except work miracles, considering that if he has only to take down the patients' names and addresses he would be over-occupied.

To the hospital authorities' demand that he act as a filter, sorting the patients into groups, Bridges protested,

It is in vain to point out that filtering is of necessity a process slow in proportion to its efficacy, while the quick filtering of patients is almost unintelligible. Making bricks without straw cannot be compared to it; that is done every day, but filtering quickly is a contradiction in terms. And yet filter he must, and filter quickly too; and be prepared to hear his quick filtrate shamefully ill-spoken of in the wards and in the out-patient rooms.

The contempt with which casualty physicians' efforts were greeted by colleagues clearly aggravated Bridges' frustration. He himself was not prepared to work as hastily as was considered necessary and, spending an average of 1.28 minutes per patient, was usually still seeing them after midday. In one year he saw nearly 31,000 patients in the casualty ward. In 1878, when he worked at St Bartholomew's three days a week and acted in addition as out-patients' physician at the Children's Hospital and at the Great Northern Hospital, he gave a total of over 50,000 interviews in the year, although not all of these were to new patients.[3]

Recalling his experience at Bart's he said,

from the first day when I, with much fear and reluctance, which I am glad I overcame, undertook the duties of filtrator, I was unpleasantly aware of the responsibility and difficulty of the task; and being afraid lest, through seeing this great number so hastily day after day, I should, from ignorance of what happened to them, slide into indifference, I made a system of hieroglyphics, by means of which I checked off each patient as I dismissed him, the sign showing me what medicine he had had, whether I considered him seriously ill or no, whether he had attended before, and if so, with what result.[4]

At first he tried to follow up patients whom he had sent for admission to the hospital, but

the ill success of the few efforts which I made to follow up my cases in the wards so discouraged me that I relinquished the idea. It is needless to say that by the time one has got to one's 150th patient, earlier impressions have faded and that one has difficulty in recognizing in a washed, placid, or even smiling countenance, pillowing its chin upon clean linen, the breathless, anxious, flurried, and neglected-looking face that one had regarded for a few seconds merely as a means of diagnosis. The change from perpendicular to horizontal is in itself perplexing, and, as far as memory went, the clue was lost. Then the only time I had for visiting the wards was the patients' dinner-time, when nobody was very glad to see me; and if they had been, they had no means of knowing which were mine, or which were anybody else's cases.

He advocated entering the name of the admitting doctor on the patients' board of particulars. The distance from which some of the patients came was astonishing:

Among the queue of patients enter a man of 40 whom you see at first glance to be seriously ill. He says he has a cough. Simply *strip to the waist.* While he does this you see and dismiss another patient. Then 10 or 15 seconds auscultation. Signs are irregular disseminated patches of aulum and silence. Hydatid suspected—where do you come from—Australia. Sheep-farming? Yes. Hydatid confirmed. Then the history of many months illness, gradually increasing and no benefit from treatment. So he had come to England for advice, had landed that morning at the docks and made his way straight to sit in the Hospital queue, faithfully believing that he wd thus get the best expert advice in London.—Immediate admission into wards. That poor fellow died. I saw him from time to time. The doctors cd do nothing for him.[5]

Bridges' report pointed out that the situation in the Casualty Department was close to unworkable and not far from crisis brought on by the growing number of patients with which it was being asked to cope. The tone at times is dryly ironic. The casualty physicians were, in Bridges' view, overworked and underestimated, their patients were not the carefully bathed, deloused, and prepared ones that the ward physicians saw, although these facts are mentioned in passing without complaint. What Bridges does object to are the things that prevent him from doing a good job: the long plaintive tales and even lies of the women—a common complaint among the doctors—patients ignoring good country doctors and making pilgrimages instead to St Bartholomew's, the noise through which he had to try accurate auscultation, one of the principal methods of diagnosis,

the rattle of carts in the street, the hum of voices inside, the slamming of doors, the noise of people walking about, the coughings of all kinds, the crying of babies, the scraping of impatient feet, the stamping of cold ones, the clinking of the bottles and zinc tickets, and, after eleven o'clock, the hammering, sawing, and tinkering of the carpenters and blacksmiths who came not unfrequently at that hour to set things generally to rights.

His impatience with those who did not need help or should have sought it elsewhere came from worry that those who were dependent on St Bartholomew's and were seriously ill would not receive the right diagnosis in time.

A later doctor at St Bartholomew's said of the report's reception,

> Although some notice must have been taken of this elegant tirade, new casualty buildings were not erected until 1906, and then only temporary ones. Sir Walter Langdon-Browne says that it also resulted in Bridges never getting another appointment at Bart's, and he warns with solicitude a student audience, 'the powers that be do not appreciate irony, and youthful reformers still find it advisable to curb their tongues and pens'.[6]

It is not possible now to tell whether this is true, although Bridges clearly did advocate reform. He himself apparently told a fellow physician that he did not want to remain at St Bartholomew's since promotion there necessitated a lengthy spell of work in the rat-infested Dead House.

Instead, he transferred his efforts to the other hospitals for which he had worked, becoming an assistant physician at the Hospital for Sick Children, Great Ormond St, and full physician at the Great (now Royal) Northern Hospital. At the latter he is credited with preventing a serious epidemic of smallpox, one of a number of outbreaks during the decade that caused numerous deaths in London. The illness was severe in the neighbourhood and two cases were reported in a ward while Bridges was Out-Patient Physician and temporarily In-Patient Physician in the absence of the doctor in charge. He acted decisively, moving all patients who had to be hospitalized to Homerton Hospital, having all who could be sent home vaccinated, bathed, and provided with clean clothing. The staff were all vaccinated, all bedding was disinfected and washed, the wards fumigated with sulphur and then every surface washed down with carbolic acid. The results were encouraging: none of the hospital's staff developed the disease and the In-Patient department was fully operational again within two weeks. The House Visitors and the Executive Committee 'expressed their great satisfaction at the excellent manner in which the emergency had been dealt with under Bridges' direction', and in 1879 he was made a full physician in the department.[7]

He was then responsible for training medical students himself. Many of them objected to his use of 'facies', wanting instead to have routine sessions in which all symptoms were discussed in detail and a diagnosis slowly deduced.[8] From Bridges' account of his time in the hospitals it would seem that there was an aggressively competitive spirit among the students and doctors that would have made for a somewhat unpleasant atmosphere, although he nowhere says this. Diagnostic techniques were still too few for some diagnoses to be confirmed rapidly, and Bridges mentions several cases when it took at least a week before more obvious symptoms appeared to confirm a diagnosis that had been openly doubted. This was wearing, and at times he evidently became weary of it. He tells the story of an occasion when he was full physician at the Great Northern Hospital:

> on my visit to the wards [I] found in one of the beds a girl of 15 whom the House physician had admitted because she seemed to be really ill but on examination had been unable to discover anything special the matter with her. He read his report and when I examined [her] I found no physical signs of disease. Then I said, 'the girl is, as you thought, really ill . . . and I suspect it is a case of incipient chorea.' Oh, he said, 'there is a history of chorea. She had a slight attack years ago. I noted it down but omitted it on reading as being of no import.'—That decides it (I said) That is what is wrong with her now—'Shall I write chorea on the board?' Yes (I said) and watch for movements.
>
> For a week she was watched without any slightest movement being detected and for so long she lay labelled 'chorea' without spasm!! Then a typical attack came on suddenly.—The respect of the House-Physician and nurses for my judgment, which had been severely tried, was now greatly advanced. But if the diet and rest had been sufficient to stay the attack (and it well might have done) then my true diagnosis wd have been scanted.[9]

In 1876 Bridges lost his sister, Julia. She had joined a house of the Sisters of Mercy at Cowley. Her life there was one of privation, and she developed tuberculosis. According to her eldest brother, John, the Bridges were prevented by the prior from having any contact with her. She was persuaded to sign over to the House the money she had inherited and the family were not allowed any say in her burial. John was evidently very bitter about her sufferings.[10] Robert must have written about this to his family at the time but the letters are not extant. The only hint left about his feelings is in the letter to Carry of 1879, in which he described himself as being full of family melancholies and praised the single-mindedness that Edward and Julia had both possessed.[11] Julia had been Robert's playmate as a child and he would have felt keenly the prohibition on using his medical knowledge to help her.

On 21 April 1877, while Bridges was working in the Casualty Department at St Bartholomew's, his stepfather died. Robert invited his mother to make her home with him in London, which she did. Although passing allusions in Bridges' letters to friends show no obvious affection for Dr Molesworth, in his letters to his mother he always showed 'the good doctor' respect and goodwill, and when he was at home he sang in the choir at Rochdale. Hopkins, who had been so solicitous and gentle over the death of Bridges' sister Harriett in 1869, merely inquired in 1877 how Dr Molesworth's will had divided his wealth.[12]

In the same month Bridges sent Hopkins his *Growth of Love* and *Carmen Elegiacum*. Hopkins, with the generous criticism he gave to work sent him by his friends, responded with a long letter which marked the beginning of a new and closer phase in their friendship. The relationship had also been helped in February when Hopkins, taking seriously Bridges' objections to the censorship of his letters, explained that the superior receiving the Jesuits' mail usually simply tore the envelope as a gesture, leaving it clear that the letter had not been removed from it.

In August 1877 Hopkins sent Bridges 'The Wreck of the Deutschland'. Bridges responded with a parody of the metre, which 'reassured' Hopkins that he had understood it though he had objected to it, calling the new metrical scheme 'presumptious jugglery' and declaring that he would not for any money read the poem again. Hopkins replied: 'nevertheless I beg you will. Besides money, you know, there is love. If it is obscure do not bother yourself with the meaning but pay attention to the best and most intelligible stanzas, as the two last of each part and the narrative of the wreck.'[13] Bridges kept the poem and the correspondence flagged until February 1878, by which time Hopkins had been moved to Mount St Mary's, Chesterfield, to which he urged Bridges to send 'The Deutschland', 'or she will in course of time be lost'. It is a comment that in retrospect appears both ironic and sad; ironic because Hopkins lost his copy of the 'Deutschland', and if Bridges had not secured two transcriptions of it the poem itself would now be totally unknown; sad, because if Hopkins' work had met with a warmer reception during his lifetime, he may have felt it worth preserving.

'Write me an interesting letter', he wrote to Bridges. 'I cannot do so. Life here is as dank as ditch-water and has some of the other qualities of ditch-water: at least I know that I am reduced to great weakness by diarrhoea, which lasts too, as if I were poisoned.'[14] Bridges must have been moved by the appeal, for Hopkins next wrote, 'your last letter was very kind indeed, but I should have lost all shame if under the circumstances I had allowed such a thing to be as for you to come hundreds of miles to cure me'. Hopkins was also pleased because Bridges and his mother had visited his family several times. In May (1878) he sent him 'The Loss of the Eurydice', which was rather less obscure or obviously new, and instructed him to 'write no bilgewater about it'. Bridges liked the poem, and was attracted by its rhythm. He did, however, find some of the lines puzzling and made a religious comment that provoked from Hopkins the admonition, 'never mingle with your criticisms monstrous and indecent spiritual compliments like something you have said there'.[15]

Hopkins' rhythmic techniques were evidently beginning to interest Bridges. He wrote to Hopkins asking for permission to experiment with them, but Hopkins does not appear to have thought it an important matter for he forgot to reply and only remembered the request a week later, when he wrote encouragingly, 'do by all means and you will honour them and me'.[16] In July Hopkins was moved to Farm Street, London. On 16 July, having called on the off-chance of finding Bridges in, he sent him three of his sonnets written at St Beuno's during his *annus mirabilis*, 1877. They were 'Hurrahing in Harvest', a second version of 'The Windhover', and 'Pied Beauty'. Three weeks later Bridges attended mass at Farm Street to hear Hopkins preach. Hopkins said of it, 'I was very little nervous at the beginning and not at all after. It was pure forgetting and flurry. The delivery was not good, but I hope to get a good one in time. I shall welcome any criticisms which are not controversy. I am glad you did not like the music and sorry that you did not like the mass.'[17] To Muirhead Bridges wrote: 'Gerard Hopkins is in town preaching & confessing at Farm St. I went to hear him. he is good. He calls here; and we have sweet laughter, and pleasant chats. He is not at all the worse for being a Jesuit: as far as one can judge without knowing what he wd have been otherwise . . . His poetry is magnificent but "caviare to the general".'[18]

In November Hopkins wrote sadly, 'I am here [Old Windsor] for my yearly retreat of eight days and shall be back in town on Tuesday week. But I am to leave London. I meant today to have brought you back your *Academys*. I will do so on my return. I daresay we may not meet again for years.' Hopkins was, however, only moved as far as Oxford, where he still had such friends as the Paravicinis and Walter Pater, who had been one of his tutors while he was an undergraduate.

By the end of December Bridges had, he told Muirhead,

> about 20 pieces *ready for the press* . .. . one or two lines still remain in a state which does not quite satisfy me. an hour or two—when I can get it—shd set all to rights. They will be better than anything I have done, and 2 of them are I hope *successful in a new metrical system* of which I hope great things. I don't know if I ever spoke to you of it. This brings me to *Gerard Hopkins*. It is useless my telling you where he is, as by this time he is not there. he never can be according to present arrangements. but when last I heard of him he was *converting Pater at Oxford*. Whether he is actually sent to undermine undergraduates steadily or not I cannot say.[19]

Clearly the penultimate remark is flippant, but the last comment is uncomfortably close to the common mistrust of Jesuits.

In January 1879 Hopkins, fearing that Bridges was now a complete atheist, made what he saw as an attempt to save his soul by urging him to give alms—to give enough of either money or time to inconvenience himself. Hopkins said later that he was afraid that Bridges would be too offended to reply. He was vexed and probably surprised; as a doctor he was, after all, devoting far more of his energy to helping those in need than most of his artistic friends. It may be a mark of how much the relationship between the two men had improved since the early 1870s that, instead of dropping the correspondence, he sent Hopkins three replies, and Hopkins smoothed the issue by explaining that it had been an attempt to secure Bridges' salvation that had led to his admonition.[20] It would not have been uncharacteristic for Bridges to have expressed opinions that were more extreme than those he actually held. If he did at this time come close to complete disbelief, it was not a state that he remained in for very much of his life, although his faith was not completely orthodox.

Bridges' next letter concerned a new project that he had in mind. He had become acquainted with Edmund Gosse, perhaps through being elected to the committee of the Savile Club on which Gosse also served. Gosse was just making his own reputation and writing reviews for such journals as the *Athenaeum*. He had written to William Scott in 1874 that 'the best thing in verse this year has been Robert Bridges in a little modest volume . . . of which no one seems to have taken the least notice'.[21] Such admiration was a promising beginning for the friendship, but rather than just advance himself Bridges was eager to help Hopkins. He wanted to arouse Gosse's interest in the hope of his mentioning Hopkins' poems in a forthcoming review, and asked Hopkins if he might suggest this. But Hopkins replied,

> No, do not ask Gosse anything of the sort. (1) If I were going to publish, and that soon, such a mention would be 'the puff preliminary', which it would be dishonourable of me to allow of. (2) If I did, a mention in one article of one review would do very little indeed, especially as publishing now is out of the question. (3) When I say that I do not mean to publish I speak the truth. I have taken and mean to take no step to do so beyond the attempt I made to print my two wrecks in the *Month*. If some one in authority knew of my having some poems printable and suggested my doing it I should not refuse, I should be partly, though not altogether, glad. But that is very unlikely. All therefore that I think of doing is to keep my verses together in one place—at present I have not even correct copies—,that, if anyone should like, they might be published after my death. And that again is unlikely, as well as remote.[22]

Early in March Bridges and his mother invited Mr and Mrs Gosse to one of their regular dinners for eight, and Bridges then tried to promote his brother John's volume of poems, *Wet Days*. Gosse, however, did not think very highly of them.[23] Meanwhile, Canon Dixon, who had taught briefly at Highgate School while

Hopkins had been a pupil there, remembered that he had won a prize for a poem, and asked if he had written more poems since. He was delighted with what Hopkins sent him and, like Bridges, wanting to win recognition for Hopkins, offered to mention his poetry in an acknowledgement for information he had provided for his *Church History*.[24] Bridges next showed Hopkins' poems to Andrew Lang, hoping that he could be persuaded to have them published but Lang found them too odd; so Bridges then, ignoring Hopkins' objections, let Gosse see the poems.[25] In triumph he told Hopkins that Gosse had liked them. However, after the turn of the century Bridges said that Gosse had not taken to them, a contradiction that may have arisen from his confusing in retrospect Gosse's reaction to Hopkins' poetry with that to *Wet Days*.[26]

Hopkins introduced Bridges to Canon Dixon and encouraged each to obtain the other's published volumes of poetry. Neither, however, could obtain the other's books from booksellers, and both had to send copies from their own stocks. Dixon and Bridges exchanged several letters, and in 1880 Bridges proposed to visit Dixon at his rectory at Hayton near Carlisle. He stayed with Mandell Creighton, who was vicar at Embleton, and then began to ramble along the Roman Wall from Newcastle towards Carlisle. The weather was so wet that he was forced to make a later start on his walk than he had intended, and had to forego the final section and travel by train. Dixon met him:

> a tallish, elderly figure, its litheness lost in a slight, scholarly stoop which gave to the shoulders an appearance of heaviness, wearing unimpeachable black cloth negligently, and a low-crowned clerical hat banded with twisted silk . . . His face . . . was dark and solemn, and as he drew near I could see that the full lips gave it a tender expression, for the beard did not hide the mouth . . . His hearty welcome was in a voice that startled me with its sonority and depth.[27]

Bridges greatly enjoyed his visit and referred back to it many times. Dixon

> was then a widower, living with his two grown-up stepdaughters a simple life full of professional engagements. The domestic round closed early, and he and I would then repair to his study upstairs, and chat by the unseasonable but comforting fire until the small hours . . . Of the many

nights spent thus, I can recall little but the inexhaustible pleasure of our conversation, and the reluctance with which we dutifully separated for our beds . . . Those nights I remember better than the days, of which, however, some distinct pictures remain: one is of Dixon's favourite walk in a deep combe, where the trees grew thickly and a little stream flowed by the foundations of old Roman masonry; another is of a game of lawn-tennis . . . The scene after thirty years is undimmed; I am standing with Dixon and two ladies in the bright sunlight on a small plot of grass . . . am more spectator than player, lazily from time to time endeavouring to place a ball where Dixon might be likely to reach it, or mischievously screwing it in order to perplex him. He like a terrier after a rat, as if there were nothing else in the world, in such rapturous earnestness that I wonder we did not play oftener.

In his Memoir, from which this description comes, the picture of Dixon at a disadvantage in sport is followed and balanced by praise of his ability as an historian. Dixon gave Bridges as a parting gift the first volume of his *History of the English Church*, which Bridges found so readable that he had almost finished it before his train-journey to Worcestershire was over. His admiration encouraged Dixon to send him requests for information from the Public Record Office and British Museum, which Bridges duly obtained.[28]

In 1879 Bridges published another volume of poems. It opened with a 'Hymn to Nature' which was never reprinted, but which shows that Bridges' love of the natural world, so evident in his lyrics, had begun to extend to the more problematical questions of the interrelationship of man and nature that would dominate his later verse. The poem's theme, that man's intimate bond with Nature arises from his being part of it, is typical of a predilection for discussing man in the context of the whole of the natural world which was fostered by nineteenth-century science, evident in the books Bridges would have used during his medical training and in Lyell's *Elements of Geology*, a copy of which he possessed and read in 1871. Admiration of Tennyson and various Romantic poets is clear in the poem, but the unusual sections in which Bridges' interest in palaeontology and his fascination with human physiology are evident sit uneasily in such traditional surroundings, emphasized as they are by his use of 'poetic' diction:

[Nature] Who makest touch a thrill, whereat the soul
Trembles ineffably; and taste and smell
Stumble on ecstasies, and are entranced.
Who causest to vibrate the tender chords
This way and that way in their subtile sheaths,
That every pulse of beauty may awake
New-born desire, and every form of love
Faithfully mirrored may record a joy,
With chosen pleasure garnered from decay.

Among other poems omitted from later collections is a verse epistle, 'Ode written to H—— ', explaining that Bridges has fled from London to recuperate at the seaside, where he finds that floods have destroyed many of the buildings he knew and disrupted the lives of the townspeople:

So here alone I pace again
The gently-shadowed downs, and climb
The bleak cliff, drenched with mist and rain,
That last I praised sweet in the prime
Of briar roses and wild thyme.

But since that day the shifting beach,
Just where it banks the cliffs with brown,
Has given way, and through the breach
The sea rolled in upon the town,
And tumbled half the houses down.

Some of the later stanzas are less good, but it is a pity that the first of these verses, in which the control of rhyme and rhythm is so satisfying, had to be cut.

The volume did not attract much notice in the press. Bridges commented to Hopkins, apparently somewhat unfavourably, on one review in the *Academy*.[29] This begins,

Poems, by the Author of the 'Growth of Love' is a mere pamphlet of some fifty pages, but contains some very remarkable work. We do not think that the author has as yet fully digested his own powers, and his work is apt to contain blemishes by the side of its beauties. But the beauties are undeniable, and what is perhaps of more importance, they are not in the least copied or reflected from the beauties of anybody else.

After criticizing the 'Hymn to Nature' for 'wilful Latinising of its language . . . a corrupt following of Milton and other and earlier seventeenth-century authors', the reviewer remarks that 'with the faults it has also a double portion of the grandeur of its models. Nothing, on the other hand, can be simpler and more charming than the piece which follows, "Will Love again Awake?"' He chooses to quote 'I have loved flowers that fade', which was one of Hopkins' favourites and was to be frequently quoted in the 1890s when it was part of *Shorter Poems*. Of it the reviewer says, 'it is not the best, because all or almost all are equally good, but it is one of the clearest and least blemished . . . We do not remember to have met for a long time any poetry so fresh, and at the same time so complete as this, which is one of the least ambitious things in the book.' The review concludes with an admonition that 'all who are interested in English poetry should certainly read [the book]', and a statement that was to be repeated time and again over the years: 'The seventeenth-century hue which we have noted prevails throughout. But it is not in the least a *pastiche*. It has rather the manner in which a poet of the seventeenth century would have written if he had lived in the nineteenth.'

The following year saw the publication of yet another volume. Three-quarters of *Poems* (1880) was devoted to sonnets written for *The Growth of Love*. These fifteen poems had been excluded from the 1876 volume, but all except one were included in the 1889 edition. They vary in quality considerably, from vivid sonnets such as 'I heard great Hector sounding war's alarms' and 'Nothing is joy without thee' to the confusing 'I will not marry thee, sweet Hope'. Bridges sent these to Hopkins before publication, and he hurriedly made some criticisms of them which seem to have provoked a crisis of confidence in Bridges for, in October 1879, Hopkins wrote, 'One thing you say in your last is enough to make me quite sad and I see that I shall have to write at some length in order to deal with it. You ask whether I really think there is any good in your going on writing poetry.'[30] Along with further explanation of his criticisms, Hopkins expressed his opinion of Bridges' poetry in the context of his assessment of Tennyson, Burns, Swinburne, and Morris:

If I were not your friend I shd. wish to be the friend of the man that wrote your poems. They shew the eye for pure beauty and they shew, my dearest, besides, the character which is much more rare and precious. Did time allow I shd. find a pleasure in dwelling on the instances, but I cannot now. Since I must not flatter or exaggerate I do not claim that you have such a volume of imagery as Tennyson, Swinburne, or Morris, though the feeling for beauty you have seems to me pure and exquisite; but in point of character, of sincerity or earnestness, of manliness, of tenderness, of humour, melancholy, human feeling, you have what they have not and seem scarcely to think worth having (about Morris I am not sure: his early poems had a deep feeling).

Then, characteristically, Hopkins turned from consideration of Bridges' poetic merits to comments based on a far more strict, religiously moral standard, the one to which he subjected many of his own actions and motives. His conviction that Bridges was an atheist because he had not thought through the arguments honestly and thoroughly enough seems to me to be included in this statement that Bridges was not sincere nor enough in earnest: 'I may then well say, like St Paul, *aemulor te Dei aemulatione* [I am jealous of you with the jealousy of God]. To have a turn for sincerity has not made you sincere nor a turn for earnest / in earnest; Sterne had a turn for compassion, but he was not compassionate; a man may have natural courage, a turn for courage, and yet play the coward.' He thus sent Bridges the encouragement of a friend and the strictures of a priest, and Bridges would have appreciated the concern that lay behind the combination.

The remaining quarter of the volume contains some of Bridges' best lyrics. The book opens with 'Indolence', which, using the method Tennyson had made popular of evoking a state of mind through describing a landscape, suggests the growing lethargy of indolence through the description of a sculling trip.

But past the bridge what change we found below!
The stream, that all day long had laughed and played
Betwixt the happy shires, ran dark and slow,
And with its easy flood no murmur made:
And weeds spread on its surface, and about
The stagnant margin reared their stout heads out . . .

Beyond, deserted wharfs and vacant sheds,
With empty boats and barges moored along,
And rafts half-sunken, fringed with weedy shreds,
And sodden beams, once soaked to season strong.

No sight of man, nor sight of life, no stroke,
No voice the somnolence and silence broke.

Then I who rowed leant on my oar, whose drip
Fell without sparkle, and I rowed no more;
And he that steered moved neither hand nor lip,
But turned his wondering eye from shore to shore;
And our trim boat let her swift motion die,
Between the dim reflections floating by.

A shorter poem, 'The evening darkens over', extends the technique:

The evening darkens over
After a day so bright
The windcapt waves discover
That wild will be the night.
There's sound of distant thunder.

The latest sea-birds hover
Along the cliff's sheer height;
As in the memory wander
Last flutterings of delight,
White wings lost on the white.

There's not a ship in sight;
And as the sun goes under
Thick clouds conspire to cover
The moon that should rise yonder.
Thou art alone, fond lover.

As in 'Indolence', a literal description of a scene is given, but there is another possible level of meaning, most evident in the simile in stanza 2 in which the fading of happy memories is made vivid by comparing it to the eye losing track of birds wheeling up into the sky. In other lines common associations turn individual elements of the scene into metaphors of aspects of the lover's situation: the dark night replacing the bright day suggests the change in his happiness, and less directly, the fact that there is no ship in sight intimates that he has nothing to look forward to. There is duality too in the choice of individual words: 'conspire' for the gathering clouds, for example, is enriched by its etymology; 'fond' adds notions of folly and innocence to the lover's affection; and 'latest seagulls' rather than 'last' frees the darkness of suggestions of death. Over the years Bridges developed this indirect expression of emotion and used it for some of his most effective and powerful poems.

The final three poems are all in Bridges' version of sprung rhythm, the justly popular 'London Snow', 'The Voice of Nature', and 'On a Dead Child'. In a note at the beginning of the volume Bridges explained:

> The poems in the smaller type, like those similarly distinguished in the author's last series, are written by the rules of a new prosody, which may very well exist by the side of the old. It is left to the judgment of the reader: but the author hopes that these verses will be read with attention to the natural quantity and accent of the syllables,—for these are the interpretation of the rhythm,—and not with the notion that all accents in poetry are alternate with unaccented syllables, nor with the almost universal prejudice that when two or more unaccented syllables intervene between two accented syllables the former must suffer and be slurred over: a prejudice which probably arises from the common misuse of unaccented for short syllables.
>
> The use of feet which correspond to paeons, and the frequent inversions of feet in these new rhythms, render it possible for four or five unaccented syllables to follow on each other.
>
> The author disavows any claim to originality for the novelty: this is almost entirely due to a friend, whose poems remain, he regrets to say, in manuscript.

This note should be contrasted with Hopkins' own explanations of the benefits he saw from sprung rhythm. He explained to Bridges:

> Why do I employ sprung rhythm at all? Because it is the nearest to the rhythm of prose, that is the native and natural rhythm of speech, the least forced, the most rhetorical and emphatic of all possible rhythms, combining, as it seems to me, opposite and, one wd. have thought, incompatible excellences, markedness of rhythm—that is rhythm's self—and naturalness of expression—for why, if it is forcible in prose to say 'lashed: rod', am I obliged to weaken this in verse, which ought to be stronger, not weaker, into 'láshed birch-ród' or something?[31]

Hopkins' use of sprung rhythm increased the proportion of stressed syllables. In many of his sonnets he did this in part because he considered that, in comparison with the Italian sonnet, the English was 'short, light, tripping and trifling'.[32] Bridges, on the other hand, generally used the metre to allow into his verse more unstressed syllables in a manner closer to speech. The shared use of the rhythm was of the best possible sort, each poet seeing a different potential and exploring it in ways that enabled each to retain his identity.

'On a Dead Child' is the only example of a poem written completely out of Bridges' medical experience. Hopkins disliked it[33] but the poem is sincere and free from the sentimental religiosity that sometimes mars Bridges' attempts at serious human subjects:

Perfect little body, without fault or stain on thee,
With promise of strength and manhood full and fair!
Though cold and stark and bare,
The bloom and the charm of life doth awhile remain on thee . . .

So quiet! doth the change content thee?—Death, whither hath
he taken thee?
To a world, do I think, that rights the disaster of this?
The vision of which I miss,
Who weep for the body, and wish but to warm thee and awaken thee?

Ah! little at best can all our hopes avail us
To lift this sorrow, or cheer us, when in the dark,
Unwilling, alone we embark,
And the things we have seen and have known and have heard of,
fail us.

Although Hopkins considered that Bridges was 'less at his ease' in sprung rhythm, 'On a Dead Child' shows that he understood it well. He uses monosyllables to take most of the stresses in the first stanza, weighting the bleak words. The ebb and flow of the rhythm, accentuated by the short third line, emphasizes the flux of emotion, and its rubato is balanced and contained by a variety of patterning devices—alliteration, related consonants, repeated or parallel syntax, and end-rhyme, of which he would later grow tired. The word order is unusually straightforward for Bridges' early poems, and strengthens the impression of dignity and strong emotion. Bridges valued sprung rhythm because it enabled him to achieve a more meditative tone, slowing down the pace of lines, allowing long, polysyllabic words to escape from unidiomatic accent, and permitting the placing consecutively of two or three unaccented syllables without tempting a reader to slur them.

In 'London Snow' he used the flexibility of the rhythm to aid the description of the snowflakes drifting downwards softly but implacably, gradually covering all surfaces until a new world emerges. As so often his descriptions are enhanced by his ability to communicate recognizable, characteristic sounds; here, for example, he remarks on the 'busy morning cries' that sound 'thin and spare' when reflective surfaces are muffled with snow:

When men were all asleep the snow came flying,
In large white flakes falling on the city brown,
Stealthily and perpetually settling and loosely lying,
   Hushing the latest traffic of the drowsy town;
Deadening, muffling, stifling its murmurs failing;
Lazily and incessantly floating down and down:
   Silently sifting and veiling road, roof and railing;
Hiding difference, making unevenness even,
Into angles and crevices softly drifting and sailing.
   All night it fell, and when full inches seven
It lay in the depth of its uncompacted lightness,
The clouds blew off from a high and frosty heaven;
   And all woke earlier for the unaccustomed brightness
Of the winter dawning, the strange unheavenly glare:
The eye marvelled—marvelled at the dazzling whiteness;
   The ear hearkened to the stillness of the solemn air;
No sound of wheel rumbling nor of foot falling,
And the busy morning cries came thin and spare.

Hopkins wanted Bridges to make the rhythm more dramatic and abrupt, but that would have been inappropriate to the subject. It seems a pity that Bridges used sprung rhythm so little. He had an acute ear for the music in verse—when he wanted to pay attention to it, although that was not always his aim—and the flexibility of sprung rhythm offered him opportunities that he could surely have explored further. Instead, he experimented with more ambitious projects and metres more suitable for discursive subjects.

8

The Change of Course (1881–1884)

In June 1880 the *Agammemnon* of Aeschylus was performed in Greek by Balliol College, Oxford, the first modern production in England of a Greek play in the original language, and it started a fashion. Bridges saw the performance (as did Browning, Tennyson, and Andrew Lang) and wrote enthusiastically of it to Hopkins. It may in part have been this resurgence of dramatic interest in Greek tragedy outside the demands of the educational system that prompted Bridges to begin a 'mask' on the story of Prometheus. He must have alluded obscurely to the new project in a letter to Hopkins, who inquired in April 1880 what the '1,000-line poem' was about.[1] But then, at the end of June 1881 Bridges contracted pneumonia. It was a severe attack. Hopkins received a note telling him of it on 2 July and visited him the following week, but Bridges was too ill to talk long and Hopkins went away 'gloomy and sad at heart'. His condition then deteriorated, and Hopkins found that 'when I called I was not allowed to go up'.[2] It was not till 29 July that the daily doses of morphia were stopped. Still in a fever, Bridges was allowed to sit on a sofa during the evening of the following day, and the day after that was able to write, in an unrecognizable, shaky hand, a short note of thanks to Muirhead for sending flowers accompanied by a doggerel poem of good wishes. By 10 August Hopkins was working in Glasgow, initially intended as supply-work for two weeks but extended to nearly two months. In September he wrote to Bridges, 'I am very glad you do improve. Still your recovery is very slow and I cannot understand it. You did run well, like the Galatians: how has your good constitution been so unhappily bewitched? I hope nevertheless that all your strength will return.'[3] He commented to Dixon on Bridges' 'wearily slow' convalescence, adding: 'He is at Hampstead now, where my family live, but they happen to be staying near Winchester.'[4]

Bridges wrote several times to Hopkins in August, believing that he was still in Liverpool, but partly through 'leisurely' forwarding received no reply till the middle of September. From Hopkins' letter of 16 September, it is clear that Bridges, whose slow recovery was causing concern, had begun himself to fear that his health would be permanently impaired. Hopkins' response was probably made more tardy than it otherwise would have been by Bridges' frank admission that he had found 'what is unusual in expression' in Hopkins' verse 'less pleasant' while he was in a weak state. Hopkins responded stoutly, but no doubt with a sigh,

> I find myself that when I am tired things of mine sound strange, forced, and without idiom which had pleased me well enough in the fresh heat of composition. But then the weaker state is the less competent and really critical. I always think however that your mind towards my verse is like mine towards Browning's: I greatly admire the touches and the details, but the general effect, the whole, offends me, I think it repulsive.[5]

This is an overstatement. Bridges certainly did not like all of Hopkins' poetry; with the 'Wreck of the Deutschland' for example, he was still wishing in 1918 that 'those nuns had stayed at home', but the attitude in that poem to human beings' physical suffering is one with which Bridges could not agree—Edward Thompson was later to notice Bridges' extreme sensitivity to human beings' physical pain.[6] However, his reaction to much that Hopkins wrote was more positive. Like Hopkins, he took his friends' poetry seriously, and responded to it with forthright criticism sometimes sweetened with praise and encouragement. He had tried hard to get public notice for Hopkins, and in April 1881 had shown himself willing to defend his work even at the expense of his own reputation. Hall Caine was at that time compiling an anthology of English sonnets expressly designed to 'demonstrate the impossibility of improving upon the acknowledged structure whether as to rhyme-scheme or measure'.[7] Dixon and Bridges were asked to contribute, and Dixon in turn urged Hopkins to send in some of his poems. Hall Caine, faced with Hopkins' obvious dissatisfaction with the standard English sonnet and his numerous modifications to form, rhythm, and syntax, reacted, according to Hopkins, like a 'she bear robbed of her cubs' and refused to print his poems. Hopkins played down the incident when writing of it to Bridges but his disappointment was detectable and Bridges, furious with Hall Caine, withdrew his own work in support of his friend.[8]

In the first week of October Bridges went to Torquay, where he remained for most of the month. The pneumonia had been further complicated by emphysema, and he was still so weak and cramped with rheumatism that he was unable to stand straight. He was advised to spend the winter months in a warmer climate, and on 2 November left London under Lionel Muirhead's care. They travelled via Amiens, Torino, Genoa and Nervi, and reached Rapallo on 19 November. There, on 10 December, Muirhead drew Bridges as he sat well wrapped up, reading a book, perhaps a copy of Shakespeare's plays since that and Aeschylus' *Prometheus* were the only books he had with him until his mother posted him more in late March. On 12 December they settled in La Spezia where they spent the next two weeks. Bridges was now able to wander about for four hours a day, and he started boating daily in the bay. He found scarves in the local shops to send to Hopkins and Dixon for Christmas, and spent time walking with friends of his mother who were also travelling for reasons of poor health.[9] On 29 December Bridges and Muirhead left for Pisa, where they spent two days before settling in Florence, where a friend of Dr Barlow, whom Bridges had known at Barts, kept an eye on him. Bridges was still much bothered by rheumatism but could now stand straight and was looking well. By the middle of January he had begun to play lawn tennis for short periods, and his poem 'Prometheus', he reported, was growing. He still had to be careful not to overdo things. Waking early, he would spend most of the day reading or writing, exploring the city for a few hours in the middle of the day until it was time for his daily Italian lesson at 4.15. Taking lessons in Italian while recuperating was characteristic of Bridges, who, even when he had an excuse for being idle, made use of some of his time to learn. After dinner it was 'whist or laziness till bed time' at 10.30. He found several good whist players among the other guests at 12 Fecca Vecchia, Lungarno, including a retired naval officer who had known his brother George, and two elderly Scottish ladies who were pleasant company. In the pension there was a colonel who had served in the Middle East and with whom Muirhead spent hours chatting about Baghdad, three English ladies who would not talk to the other guests because they had not been properly introduced, and an American and his son for whom it was all new and whom the others unkindly shamed into silence.[10]

Hopkins corresponded with Bridges while he was in Florence. Having visited the Victoria and Albert collection in South Kensington, he remarked, 'amidst the bewildering wealth of beautiful things my attention was fixed by the casts from Michael Angelo, the David, two figures of slaves for Julius II's tomb, a Madonna, and others. I thought of the advantage, for which nothing can completely make up, you have of seeing these things on the spot.'[11] Typically, Hopkins was not content with this praise and speculated more generally,

> In the arts of painting and sculpture I am, even when most I admire, always convinced of a great shortcoming: nothing has been done yet at all equal to what one can easily conceive being done. For instance for work to be perfect there ought to be the sense of beauty in the highest degree both in the artist and in the age, the style and keepings of which the artist employs. Now the keepings of the age in which for instance Raphael and Angelo lived were rich, but unsatisfactory in the extreme. And they were both far from having a pure sense of beauty. Besides which they have several other great shortcomings. But in poetry and perhaps in music *unbetterable* works have been produced.

Bridges and Hopkins were united in theoretical discussion on the necessity for beauty in good poetry, but what they meant by that notoriously difficult term would seem from their poems to have been rather different. Neither strove consistently to make all his poetry beautiful; the sense of humour they both possessed and to which, to the disapproval of each other, they gave vent in their poems, would alone have seen to that. But they were also keenly interested in wider truth that cannot be expressed with conventionally beautiful poetry, so that while Hopkins marred the musical beauty for the sake of expressing psychological truth, Bridges explored scientific ideas whose terminology was disruptive of rhythmical ease.

In March Bridges and Muirhead moved on to Sorrento, where Bridges spent the mornings riding in the hills on a donkey and in the afternoons rowed and occasionally bathed in the sea.[12] In April

Muirhead went to Rome while Bridges settled in Naples, contented with reading and the good company of an English officer and a pleasant American couple. By the middle of the month he had been joined by Owen Wethered and his friend John Faussett, and on 12 April the trio went to Pompeii, two-and-a-half hours away by carriage. Bridges was pleased to find that he was well enough to make the final four-hour ascent and descent of Vesuvius and still have the energy to sit talking till ten o'clock at night. He decided to join Wethered and Faussett, who were planning to explore Sicily for three weeks. Palermo delighted him, and he was able to enjoy travelling round the island and visiting Mount Etna. Then, in mid-May, he returned to England by boat.[13]

It is not possible to estimate how much of *Prometheus the Firegiver* Bridges had written when work on it was interrupted by his illness. He offered to send Hopkins a partial draft in February 1882 but Hopkins, who was reluctant to spend time on literature during his tertianship, replied, 'I should hardly wish you to send me your poem here [Roehampton]. Either send it to me at Preston or keep it awhile. I am sorry to put off the pleasure, but the time does not suit.'[14] In fact it was not until the following June that Bridges, having reached his goal of 1,000 lines, gave Hopkins the manuscript. The occasion was one of the rare meetings of the two friends. Dixon saw a less complete copy at about the same time. Dixon, whose poems Hopkins and Bridges had criticized for insufficient finish, complained to Bridges that he found *Prometheus* 'too finished'. Bridges hastened to assure him, 'I am within 100 lines of the end of my poem. I wrote 100 yesterday, which was a good 2 hours work. It ought not to be too finished, that?'[15] The speed with which Bridges wrote many of his poems was commented upon by Coventry Patmore after he visited him in 1884.[16] But the fear aroused in Bridges by Dixon's criticism was that his real opinion was that there was not 'much in it'. He wrote, 'A poem cannot be too finished?', questioning the idea for the first time. Hopkins, with his meticulous craftsmanship, would not have raised the question, yet when Bridges later came to edit Hopkins' poems for publication in 1918 he sometimes chose early versions in preference to later ones because he found them fresher.[17]

Prometheus was complete by 4 August 1882, and Dixon expressed his opinion of it to Hopkins in December: 'Prometheus seems to me a very good poem: particularly the choruses: extremely Greek in feeling. The difficulty seems to me the impossible state of things, without fire, what the story supposes.'[18] but Hopkins defended the likelihood of a civilization not discovering fire. What annoyed him was Bridges' manner of publication: 'this private printing of *Prometheus* may turn out unfortunate. I have myself no taste for what is called dainty in the get up of books and am altogether wanting in the spirit of a bookhunter. 10s seems like what is called a prohibitive price. I could not recommend our library to get such a book and till the second edition I shall not see the poem in print.'[19] He told Bridges the same thing, just as brusquely, but added in a postscript: 'I am rueful and remorseful about P.F. But what else could come of handmade Dutch paper? I regret that Daniel [Bridges' printer] made his offer. And I hope the 2nd edition will be this one's Jacob.'[20]

Bridges, who had been introduced to Henry Daniel by James Thursfield early in 1880, shared with him an interest in beautifully produced books. However, as he later explained, there were also financial considerations that had led to his using Daniel as a publisher:

> critics copied each other in asserting that I withheld my poems from the public. Here are some facts—Daniel wished for something to print: so I gave him my Prometheus. He printed 100 copies & sold them at ten shillings, giving me an immediate return of £15, altho' some of the 'subscribers' never paid up. That was in 1883.—Humphry Ward meeting me at Yattendon complained that Daniel's bk was unprocurable, & that he wd be constrained to have the poem copied by hand if I did not 'publish' it. I told him that no publisher wd take it. He laughed at me: so I handed him the poem to do as he liked with it. He found out that I was right: but eventually persuaded Ewd Bell, who was a friend of his, to publish a small edition. That was in 1884 and the editn was not sold out until 1893 when the total profit was £4. 17. 6.[21]

One of the early projects Bridges had suggested that Daniel undertake at his press was a collection of work by five poets: Dixon, Dolben, Hopkins, John Affleck Bridges, and Robert himself. But Daniel had not been sure enough of his ability to carry out the job and Bridges, afraid of causing him regrets, had let the matter drop.[22]

Bridges subtitled *Prometheus the Firegiver*, 'A mask in the Greek manner', but it is Milton's *Comus*, an atypical example of the masque-genre, that *Prometheus* most resembles. This is especially true in the opening lines, where many of the images are close to those in *Comus*. Albert Guérard has commented that, in the prologue, Bridges accomplished 'the first perfect imitation of Miltonic blank verse in two hundred years of experiment', with an effect that is closer to elevated prose than poetry.[23] However, Bridges' use of his mythical source is closer to Shelley than to Milton, in its depiction of a change from the old dispensation to the new. Bridges writes a 'history' of religion, amalgamating the stories of Genesis with the Greek tale. Thus he explains the flood as a deliberate attempt by Zeus to kill man, not because of his evil deeds but because of a rumour that he is to be deposed by a human. Man is, according to Bridges' masque, foolish in his worship of Zeus (actually God) and in his rationalizing of its futility. Prometheus mocks Inachus' inability to explain why Zeus should have withheld the gift of fire:

> Pr. Is this thy wisdom, king, to sow thy seed
> Year after year in this unsprouting soil?
> Hast thou not proved and found the will of Zeus
> A barren rock for man with prayer to plough?
> In. His anger be averted! we judge not god
> Evil, because our wishes please him not.
> Oft our shortsighted prayers to heaven ascending
> Ask there our ruin, and are then denied
> In kindness above granting: were't not so,
> Scarce could we pray for fear to pluck our doom
> Out of the merciful withholding hands.
> Pr. Why then provokest thou such great goodwill
> In long denial and kind silence shown?
> In. Fie, fie! Thou lackest piety.
>
> (ll. 394–407)

At times Inachus is too close to a straw man for Prometheus' wit. However, the overall result of the approach is not simply the depiction of the growth of Christian belief in place of Old Testament attitudes, but a basic questioning of religious faith. This concludes with an assertion that man's inherently spiritual nature is an adequate guide to conduct, an attitude which Guérard calls dangerously close to 'Rousseauistic primitivism', and which Bridges was to explore in greater detail in later works.[24]

Masques were traditionally not intended to have marked dramatic qualities, but rather to be decorative not only in spectacle but also in their poetry. Hopkins, who postponed comment until 4 November 1882, wrote:

> Although . . . the action is so good and its unity so well kept and . . . the style so beautiful I have doubts about the play's acting. Experience only can decide; but I do not think it has in a high degree a nameless quality which is of the first importance both in oratory and drama: I sometimes call it *bidding*. I mean the art or virtue of saying everything right *to* or *at* the hearer, interesting him, holding him in the attitude of correspondent or addressed or at least concerned, making it everywhere an act of intercourse—and of discarding everything that does not bid, does not tell . . . It is most difficult to combine this bidding, such a fugitive thing, with a monumental style. Your style is monumental. But it can be done: witness Greek plays—and Shakespeare's, but those are more monumental and less in bidding, his more bidding and less monumental . . . This will be of more importance in your Nero.[25]

It was shrewd advice. The masque was performed by a boys' grammar school at Newbury, a performance that Bridges saw, but his comments on it are not extant. The well-known classicist J. W. Mackail gave the published version a favourable review in the *Academy* (22 Nov. 1884):

> Mr Bridges does not attempt to restore the lost play of Aeschylus, if there ever was one. He adopts the ancient legend, and treats it as a Greek artist might have treated it, according to its own beauty; not rationalising it, or using it to give an illusory freshness to overridden modern ideas; nor, on the other hand disfiguring it by futile and clumsy archaism. He is a scholar who dares to be natural.

Bridges was later to be criticized for not adapting the play to more personal themes, but the religious attitude that he saw in the story and brought out in the masque was an expression of the religious position which he had reached. Seeing the play as fulfilling the promise evident in *Poems* (1873), Mackail commented, 'there is now sustained power, and a mastery of rhythm and language almost of the first rank'. He pointed out the range of metres that Bridges has used, from the alternating anapaestic and iambic measures of the entrance-chorus to the pure dactylic of the ode on wonder, and the 'Samson' lines 1200–1211:

Or if some patient heart,
In toilsome steps of duty tread apart,
Thinking to win her peace within herself,
And thus awhile succeed:
She must see others bleed,
At others' misery moan,
And learn the common suffering is her own,
From which it is no freedom to be freed:
Nay, Nature, her best nurse,
Is tender but to breed a finer sense,
Which she may easier wound, with smart the worse
And torture more intense.

A more exacting review appeared anonymously in the *Athenaeum* (24 Jan. 1885). It begins, 'If this were a translation it would be a good one'. It criticizes the rhythm in a few lines and, more seriously, the handling of the story of Io for a lack of dramatic intensity: Io's parents' do not show convincing concern when they learn of her fate, and the 'geography lesson' of her journey is not interesting in itself. These are criticisms akin to those Hopkins made. However, remarking that, like Shelley, Bridges' Prometheus is the 'spirit of man', to be worshipped instead of Zeus, the reviewer concludes,

Mr Bridges's use of the Promethean myth is subtle and suggestive. His parable is inexact—for Prometheus is an individual being, as distinctly personal as Inachus or any other of the worshippers, thus as conceivable an object of worship as the Zeus he supersedes, which cannot be said of the spirit of mankind without embodiment—but it is well put, and is worth the thinking out.

Bridges had reason to feel encouraged by these mostly favourable reviews.

Hopkins remained in London until August 1882. During his tertianship (October 1881 to August 1882) he met Bridges a number of times. Early in June Robert brought his sister Maria's son, Bertie Molesworth, with him when he visited Hopkins at Roehampton, but Hopkins felt the undergraduate's presence was a 'restraint upon confidential talk'.[26] The two men do not seem to have been at ease, and it was an unhappy visit; Bridges attempted to accept or buy peaches from the gardener as a gift to Hopkins (and presumably also for Bertie) but Hopkins protested. He later wrote 'you could not make me wretched now by either stealing or buying fruit',[27] suggesting that the incident remained a sore point. Alluding to the occasion in *The Testament of Beauty*, Bridges said that Hopkins had refused the fruit because of its sensual attractiveness and, when teased, accepted but only to avoid giving offence:

> . . . And so,
> when the young poet my companion in study
> and friend of my heart refused a peach at my hands,
> he being then a housecarl in Loyola's menie,
> 'twas that he fear'd the savor of it, and when he waived
> his scruple to my banter, 'twas to avoid offence.
> But I, upon thatt day which after fifty years
> is near as yesterday, was no stranger to fear
> of pleasure, but had grown fearful of thatt fear; yet since
> the sublimation of life whereto the Saints aspire
> is a self-holocaust, their sheer asceticism
> is justified in them; the more because the bent
> and nativ color of mind that leadeth them aloof,
> or driveth, is thatt very delicacy of sense,
> whereby a pinprick or a momentary whiff
> or hairbreadth motion freeth the detent of force
> that can distract them wholly from their high pursuit:
> wherefor they fly God's garden, whose forbidden fruit
> (seemeth to them) was sweeten'd by a fiend's desire
> to make them fond and foolish [. . . yet]
> the doctrin esoteric in their rapt divines
> and their diviner poets—this the novice knew—
> is the reincarnation of their renounced desire.
>
> (Book IV, 433–52, 456–8)

The two ideals are clear here as they probably were to Hopkins and Bridges on that day: a repression of sensuality channelled into religious fervour or a reconciling of it with higher aims. Hopkins' happiest poems are those in which he reconciles his sensitivity to sensual pleasures, especially of sight, by thinking of them as means of communication with God immanent in nature. Bridges was to express his very similar belief in *The Testament of Beauty*.

The following week Bridges attended a Corpus Christi procession in which Hopkins participated, but he was not impressed and Hopkins reacted:

it is long since such things had any significance for you. But what is strange and unpleasant is that you sometimes speak as if they had in reality none for me and you were only waiting with a certain disgust till I too should be disgusted with myself enough to throw off the mask. You said something of the sort walking on the Cowley Road when we were last at Oxford together—in '79 it must have been. Yet I can hardly think you do not think I am in earnest. And let me say, to take no higher ground, that without earnestness there is nothing sound or beautiful in character and that a cynical vein much indulged coarsens everything in us. Not that you do overindulge this vein in other matters: why then does it bulk out in that diseased and varicose way in this?[28]

However, he enclosed a copy of the ceremony's hymns, which Bridges had not had, and Bridges evidently responded with questions about the significance of the procession. Hopkins' rebuke made an impression on him; five months later he was still concerned about having hurt his friend.[29]

Bridges intended to visit Hopkins early in July and certainly did on Sunday 29 July. He remarked to Dixon, 'those Jesuits do bully their men dreadfully. He [Hopkins] shuns even his Jesuit fellow creatures—perhaps though these more than others.'[30] In August the visits came to an end when Bridges and his mother moved to Yattendon, near Newbury, and at the end of the month Hopkins was appointed lecturer to the undergraduate Jesuits at Stonyhurst College in Lancashire.

The Yattendon estate had been bought in 1876 by the architect Alfred Waterhouse, who built a home for his family on the hill overlooking the village. They moved into this in April 1881, vacating the estate's eighteenth-century manor-house, which was then let. The house was very close to the church and Bridges, thinking that this would suit his mother, took it, moving there with her on 8 August 1882. A fellow practitioner at St Bartholomew's Hospital noted in his pocket-book, 'on Tuesday, 8 August 1882, I walked with Dr Robert Bridges, and he left London at 4 p.m. to commence poet at Yattendon, and turned his back on the critics'.[31] Bridges was later to remark that the move from London not only broke his ties with medicine, it all but ended a number of his friendships too.

It has been said and repeated that Bridges became a doctor with the intention 'to practise medicine until he was forty, when he would retire; the experience would give him knowledge of men for his work as a poet'.[32] The statement, however, requires considerable modification. At the time, men in a wide variety of professions maintained serious interest in the arts without trying to relate their creative work to their jobs. Robert was not specially endowed by his father's will, which gave an equal income to all the sons, and it is noticeable that all his brothers chose and followed careers. Tom and George entered the army and navy respectively; John, who considered himself the main literary figure in the family and published some novels, volumes of poetry, and memoirs, was also a farmer. Why did Robert choose medicine? The training and practice were extremely arduous and deeply shocking to his sensibility. The dedication required to carry out the work and the exceptional conscientiousness with which Bridges acted make it most unlikely that he was simply gaining 'knowledge of men for his work as a poet'. With rare exceptions, the influence on Bridges' poetry of his scientific study and medical practice was not the deeper psychological perception of the artistic observer, but a tendency to place man in the natural world and analyse him as part of that. His best 'poetic' writing simply does not reflect the experience.

Bridges' reasons for becoming a doctor were, I suspect, more positive and less selfish than has been suggested. He had lost his father and two brothers to disease, and in at least one of these instances thought that medical incompetence, not just the state of the art, had shortened their lives. Medicine in the 1870s was benefiting from advances in scientific knowledge as never before and entering an exciting phase. It clearly seemed to him an exacting and worthwhile profession. The lecture on his experience as a doctor given by Bridges to medical students at Ann Arbor does not suggest that he entered medicine as a temporary measure. In it he says that he gave up practice as a doctor because he realized that he 'had not the necessary . . . disposition':

First of all the uncertainty of medical science and the possible complications in any difficult case gave me an intolerable anxiety—Then again since medicine was not nor could ever be my sole or chief interest in life, I could not face the perpetual industry which was needful in order to keep up with continuing and rapidly expanding knowledge—and this was also in my case the more difficult from the fact that I have no mechanical memory.—For instance it was impossible for me to remember the various strengths of the various preparations of the drugs which one had to prescribe—and I was always finding this a considerable inconvenience—I suppose that nobody ever found a medical student's work more uncongenial and disagreeable than I did.[33]

These were difficulties that he had not foreseen in 1869. He drew a telling comparison between himself and one of his fellow doctors:

Among my colleagues there was one man in whom I saw in their perfection the gifts which I lacked—Thomas Barlow with whom I worked at the Children's Hospital and who has ever since been a dear and good friend.—Son of a Lancashire cotton farmer, he renounced the full fortune which he might have inherited, because he felt a higher call in life—and as you know he came to the top—I do not wish to speak of his professional work here—you will know of that. But I wish to tell you this—that of all the Doctors I ever knew he was the one who had most intimate personal sympathy with his patients.

It is of course not only somewhat dangerous for a physician to allow such feelings full play—they may disturb his scientific judgment—But to bestow a genuine fellow feeling on all your patients daily is a burden which it needs almost superhuman effort to assume—to say nothing of the difficulty of sustaining it. But Barlow's fellow feeling was inexhaustable and unwearied. So far was it from injuring his judgment that it led him often to a sounder and clearer insight into his cases—and while it strengthened his own hopefulness and determination it also helped his patients toward recovery by evoking the emotional side of their confidence.

Spoken nearly forty years after Bridges gave up medicine, this plays down both his own talent and the dedication with which he had practised. Bridges' situation in 1882 was modified by various things. His serious illness gave him time to assess the life he had been leading and to think about what he most wanted to do. His financial situation was doubtless eased when his mother joined him to form a household. He also had by then several volumes in print which had been encouragingly received in some quarters.

Hopkins' reaction to Bridges' new intentions was to say, 'I should be sorry to think you did nothing down there but literary work: could you not be a magistrate? This would be honourable and valuable public duty. Consider it'.[34] In time Bridges did take several public posts, as a member of the local Board of Guardians (Bradfield) and as choirmaster at Yattendon Church, the nineteenth-century church of St Peter and St Paul.

The tiny village lies in a characteristically English landscape of rolling hills, with copses of deciduous trees that divide the area into small, isolated pockets; even today it gives one a feeling of being isolated in time as well as geographically. Once settled there, Bridges began seriously to lead a 'literary life'. One of the first topics he tackled was revision of Dixon's long narrative poem, 'Mano . . . a poetical history . . . concerning the adventures of a Norman knight'. Perhaps knowing the discouraging circumstances and isolation in which the poem had been written, Bridges undertook the task with gusto. According to his memoir of Dixon, the prelate had established a schedule for himself by giving a finished section of the poem to a colleague at their monthly clerical meetings. Only when he had finished the six volumes did he discover that his 'treasurer' had 'never had the curiosity to read a line of it; so he [Dixon] took his sheaves home with him, and garnered them in his cupboard with other poems and epics that slept on the shelf gathering grime'.[35]

Bridges had written enthusiastically to Hopkins about 'Mano' from Florence early in 1882, but during his tertianship Hopkins expressly asked Dixon to defer sending the manuscript to him. Bridges sent Dixon a long letter in September proposing various types of alteration, such as the pruning of some of Dixon's more obscure vocabulary (which Hopkins had punningly suggested required a 'Dixonary'), a smoothing of the rhythm, and a tightening-up of the early cantos. 'It is absolutely necessary that we should meet over this work', he declared, suggesting that Dixon spend a fortnight at Yattendon; 'if not and you would wish it I will try and manage to pay you a visit—Unless indeed my interference is not mere conceited impertinence'.[36] By December Dixon wrote wearily to Hopkins, 'You speak of "Mano". I am revising him from Bridges's suggestions: and find it rather a toil: I only give off days to it. I have not quite reached the end of Book I. Bridges likes it, and has taken vast pains about it. Nearly everything he says is right.'[37]

When Bridges had settled in, he encouraged Muirhead, and Dixon and his second wife (whom he had married in 1882) to visit him. He also began to transcribe those of Hopkins' poems of which he had copies into a second album, a practical way of showing him that he valued them. Hopkins disliked making fair copies of his poems, and with his many moves and his ambiguous attitude to his poetry, did not always preserve them, but Bridges wanted copies that he could send to friends. He was afraid that if his first album went astray in the post, some of Hopkins' best work would be totally lost. As he made his transcriptions, he sent his friend questions about interpretation. Encouraged, Hopkins sent him copies of new poems. 'The Leaden Echo and the Golden Echo' prompted Bridges to suggest that he had been influenced in it by Walt Whitman; he himself had a copy of the first edition of *The Leaves of Grass*, but Hopkins declared that he had seen little more than Saintsbury's review of the revised edition (1874).[38] The review included the whole of Whitman's poem 'Death Carol', and Bridges may be excused for suspecting some influence. Hopkins was very much more anxious than Bridges to avoid echoes of other writers: they are, he declared when he thought that Bridges was echoing in his *Nero* lines from an earlier play, 'a disease of education, literature is full of them; but they remain a disease, an evil'.[39]

The first person to whom Bridges wanted to send the album was Coventry Patmore. Patmore, who was a Catholic convert and a poet with an established reputation, had visited Stonyhurst in August 1883 and the rector, probably because he knew of Hopkins' interest in poetry, asked him to look after the guest. When Hopkins mentioned Bridges, Patmore expressed admiration for those examples of his poetry that he had seen in reviews but said that he had been unable to purchase copies at booksellers. Informed of this, Bridges sent Patmore copies of his books and all three poets began a correspondence about prosody. Patmore had published an essay on 'Metrical Law' as a preface to his poem *Amelia* in 1878. Hopkins examined it carefully and sent Patmore notes on where he disagreed with his analysis. Bridges, seeing a slightly different opportunity, wrote:

> The interest which you take in the grammar of English verse has led me to hope that you would not be disinclined to give an account in print of

what Hopkins and I call the new prosody. We both regard it—without prejudice to the conventional prosody, which you will have seen I use independently of it—as the true solution of English verse. Perhaps we write it rather differently; I should say Hopkins more correctly, I more popular or practically—but I think that we both want an outsider to say something. Your learned essay gives you a standpoint, and . . . your judgment would be at once unprejudiced and weighty . . . I shall never write on prosody myself. I think it likely that Hopkins might so do, but I am very anxious that there should be something dogmatic written soon, as people are already beginning to copy the style without understanding it. The rules are very simple but difficult to observe.[40]

This seems to have been the first indication Patmore had that Hopkins wrote poetry, and it awakened his interest. Bridges wrote to ask if he could send Patmore the album, but Hopkins was not particularly pleased:

I had not meant Mr. Patmore to know I wrote poetry, but since it has come naturally and unavoidably about there is no more to be said and you may therefore send me your book and I will point it and make a few corrections. You were right to leave out the [metrical] marks: they were not consistent for one thing and are always offensive. Still there must be some. Either I must invent a notation applied throughout as in music or else I must only mark where the reader is likely to mistake, and for the present this is what I shall do.[41]

After he had made his changes, Hopkins sent the album to Patmore. Bridges had already tried to interest him in Dixon's 'Mano' but Patmore had been disappointed by it, so he forewarned him about Hopkins' poetry:

I have some misgivings lest I may have spoken too warmly of these poems, and prepared your mind for a disappointment like that which I so regretted in the case of *Mano* . . . lest you should be ill-prepared for these poems I should tell you that Gerard Hopkins is affected in style. His affectation is somewhat natural to him, however, and subservient to general effect. I should say it was artistically used, tho' not always pleasant. I think of him, as of Dixon, that he must always be treasured by poetic minds on account of his original beauties. I hope you will think so.

By 'affected in style' Bridges would seem to have had in mind Hopkins' use of nouns as verbs, the omission of relative pronouns, and other techniques that violate the ordinary rules of English idiom in order to achieve particular effects. His concern in showing the poems to Patmore, as later in the question of publishing them, was not just that they should be liked, but that they should not adversely affect acceptance of sprung rhythm. He continued:

As to the prosody which should be the subject of this letter, H. pushes it to its extreme limits. If there is an *ad absurdum* of it he exhibits it. He has (for instance) in my opinion, an absolutely wrong notion of rhyme. He does not consider that it makes necessarily any pause in the rhythm. This would affect his rhythm to my ears unfavourably in whatsoever prosody he wrote, and you will exclude the effect produced by it from the proper effect of the prosody . . . Tho' there is much in his poems which I should not defend as useful prosody, yet you will find plenty of passages where the full force of the system, his originality, which I advocate, is well shown.[42]

But Patmore did not take to Hopkins' poems, and although praising the least unconventional of them as exquisite, he told Hopkins that he viewed his poetic innovations as 'self-imposed shackles':

It seems to me that the thought and feeling of these poems, if expressed without any obscuring novelty of mode, are such as often to require the whole attention to apprehend and digest them; and are therefore of a kind to appeal only to the few. But to the already sufficiently arduous character of such poetry you seem to me to have added the difficulty of following *several* entirely novel and simultaneous experiments in versification and construction, together with an altogether unprecedented system of alliteration and compound words;—any one of which novelties would be startling and productive of distraction from the poetic matter to be expressed.

System and learned theory are manifest in all these experiments; but they seem to me to be *too* manifest. To me they often darken the thought and feeling which all arts and artifices of language should only illustrate.[43]

To Bridges he remarked that he would be 'more sorry' than he could say if his criticisms hurt Hopkins, but the poems seemed to him like 'veins of pure gold imbedded in masses of impracticable quartz'. When Bridges did get the album back he found that Hopkins had made many changes, sometimes cancelling the neatly written pages with untidy lines. He does not, however, seem to have made any comment about this.

★

It is clear from Hopkins' letters that by November 1882 Bridges had started work on a play about Nero.[44] He later wrote to Samuel Butler,

> I always wished to write drama—I began at school. When I seriously set to the work I approached the difficulties thro' a masque 'Prometheus the Firegiver'.
>
> Next I took a historical subject which gave me characters & plot, and used the Shakespearean form as that best known to me: and I wrote 'Nero Pt I'. I never meant it for more than an exercise, else I shd not have taken the cumbrous Shakespearean form, with its innumerable drampers [dramatis personae] and frequent changes of scene.[45]

In a letter of 3 March 1900, Butler said that he admired this and Bridges' other plays, but admitted that had they been written by anyone else he would not have read them. V. S. S. Coles, who similarly did not especially respond to verse, liked both *Nero* and later *The Return of Ulysses*, while being less keen on Bridges' lyric poems. *Nero*, unlike the rest of Bridges' plays, was not intended for the stage, as is clear from its published notes. It reflects the Victorian admiration for closet drama, a genre that views a play as another form of the long poem. For *Nero, Part I*, Bridges used Tacitus as his main source, exploring aspects of character and motivation that are only hinted at in the Latin.[46] He also seems to have been influenced by Thomas Gray's sketch for a proposed play to be called 'Agrippina'. The only important drama on the subject of Nero before Bridges tackled it was Racine's *Britannicus*, which he mentioned to Hopkins, remarking that 'it was wonderful that the story had not been made . . . more use of before'.[47]

There is 'plenty of story and action' for the reading play that Bridges intended, but Hopkins astutely remarked that on the stage it could be criticized because too much of the action was reported rather than shown and the plot contained incidents not made essential enough to the main action.[48] The most interesting of the characters are Nero and Seneca whose degenerating, and complex, vacillating characters are well caught. They fulfil Guérard's definition of the 'dramatic' as establishing 'significant relationships between character and event which emphasize or illustrate important psychological or philosophical truths'.[49] Although Guérard thought the play as important as *The Testament of Beauty* and Ivor

Winters considered it comparable to Shelley's *The Cenci*,[50] none of Bridges' plays have had many ardent admirers, partly because his attempts to amalgamate classical and Renaissance forms were contemporary with the establishing of the taste for prose plays dealing with modern life and its difficulties. Guérard suggests that they would be more widely admired if they were thought to have been written in the sixteenth century; certainly the dialogue in many of them has an Elizabethan character.[51] But there are other problems too, as is clear from *Palicio*, his next play. This 'Romantic drama in five acts in the Elizabethan manner' was based on Stendhal's story 'Vanina Vanina', about political rebellion in Sicily. However, Bridges' plot is too intricate and, although the basic story could have been turned into an exploration of social injustice, he shows an unexciting preference for the *status quo*. Diminishing the political element leaves the romance to carry the play's interest, but this is not written in a particularly convincing way. Bridges himself may not have been very pleased with the drama at first; he never sent a copy of it to Hopkins and spoke to Muirhead in January 1885 of having *Nero* and *Ulysses* printed by Daniel, omitting any mention of the work written between them. But he took the manuscript away with him on holiday in September 1886 and reported that he thought that he had 'nearly cured him',[52] and when going through the proofs in 1902 for volume 4 of *Poetical Works* he found himself more contented with it.

While waiting with a certain impatience for his wedding in the summer of 1884, Bridges wrote *The Return of Ulysses*. It was, he noted, 'a dramatising of the chief scenes in Homer's *Odyssey*' and 'not a recast of the story in dramatic form'. Bridges evidently took some pains with the characterization and creation of suspense, but some of the speeches are simply weak, and Hopkins, commenting in May 1885, criticized the use of Elizabethan diction and the inclusion of Athena because both led to unreality. While in *Prometheus the Firegiver* Hopkins had accepted the presence of Prometheus among men, because he had interpreted the story as an allegory in which every character had symbolic value, he objected to Athena:

being an unreality she must talk unreal . . . What did Athene do after leaving Ulysses? Lounged back to Olympus to afternoon nectar. Nothing can be made of it . . . The background of distance and darkness and doom which a tragedy should always have is shut out by an Olympian drop-scene; the characters from men become puppets, their bloodshed becomes a leakage of bran.[53]

The objection is, however, too sweeping as the power the Greek tragedies still have today proves.

Yeats, who wrote about the play in 1896, had precisely the opposite reaction, applauding *Ulysses* for being

perfect after its kind, the kind of our new drama of wisdom, for it moulds into dramatic shape, and with as much as possible of literal translation, those closing books of the *Odyssey* which are perhaps the most perfect poetry of the world, and compels that great tide of sound to flow through delicate dramatic verse, with little abatement of its own leaping and clamorous speed. As I read, the gathering passion overwhelms me, as it did when Homer himself was the singer, and when I read at last the lines in which the maid describes to Penelope the battle with the suitors, at which she looks through the open door, I tremble with excitement . . .[54]

He was later to suggest staging it.

By the end of 1884 Bridges was contemplating a new play, a comedy eventually called *The Feast of Bacchus* which, like Hopkins' 'St Winefred's Well', was to be written in twelve-syllable lines. Bridges wanted to write six-foot lines that would not be alexandrines, but Hopkins doubted that he could avoid the medial caesura so common in the metre. He had himself struggled to overcome this and found that 'the metre is smooth, natural, and easy to work in broken dialogue, so much so that it produces nearly the effect of 5 foot blank verse; but in continuous passages it is a very different thing. In passionate passages I employ sprung rhythm in it with good effect.'[55] By the middle of April Bridges reported to Muirhead that he had nearly completed two acts of his 'Menander-like play on the lines of the self tormentor'. 'I do not like the work', he added, 'but it will be amusing I hope.'[56] He may have sent a sample to Hopkins, who returned it on 1 April, sending some of his own 'St Winefred's Well' for comment. Bridges responded encouragingly. At this point he was proposing to start writing the second part of *Nero* in July, something he did not in fact do for nearly nine years.

In 1887 Hopkins visited Yattendon and Bridges gave him a copy of *The Feast of Bacchus*. Hopkins wrote of it,

The Menandrian period appears to me the dullest and narrowest world that one could choose to lay an action in, a jaded and faded civilisation; moreover I have a craving for more brilliancy, more picturesque, more local colour: however you austerely set these things aside and I am to take the play for what it is. In its kind then, which has for me no attraction, and in its metre, which has to me no beauty, I think it a masterpiece. The language is a strong and chaste English; it is, I suppose, for us much what the French admire in Télémaque and in Racine's plays. The dialogue is everywhere nature, than which more cannot be said . . . I daresay the metre will serve its purpose, which is, I suppose, to give a slight form and pressure to the language and a corresponding degree of idealisation, and it may work well on the stage: in itself I do not admire it. The only particular fault I find is that there are many lines in which the pause in the middle, without which, as it seems to me, it is merely prose rhythm and not verse at all, is wanting. I may add that the continual determination to be smooth and lucid in style gives upon the whole a sort of childish effect. I have only read it once through and therefore add no more now. I do not however think that I shall have much more to say. I could not recommend you to write more Menandrian plays.[57]

However, by Christmas he said,

My judgment is in substance the same as at the first reading, but my feeling is changed: I *enjoy* it more. It is 'an excellent piece of work: would 'twere done'—on the stage. In its own kind I believe it could not be bettered . . . The rhythm wd. I believe have an excellent effect in performance. I will not now say it has no beauty of itself: as verse it has to my ear none; but as a form, as a simple rhythm given to diction, and making such diction intermediate between verse and prose it is elegant. The value of the play is, like Terence's, as a study of human nature and in that it is firstrate; in *vis comica*, in fun, like Terence too, it is not strong: still there is enough to make me laugh aloud sometimes. This is, I believe, all I have to say and shall say on this subject and I will send the book from Dublin.[58]

In July 1884 Hopkins wrote to Bridges, 'I find that 2557 is divisible by nothing till you reach 20, beyond which I have not tried: what then can the length of the stanza be? And what is the subject of the poem?' The poem was 'Eros and Psyche'. Bridges said that in it he 'pretended neither to originality nor loftiness. The beautiful story is well known, and the version of Apuleius has been simply followed.' He expands Apuleius' story from the *Metamorphoses* by adding a number of descriptions—of Juno's dress, of the landscape, and a particularly imaginative one of Psyche, sitting in a dimly lit room surrounded by unsorted seeds, suddenly becoming aware of the first of the helpful ants (December, st. 1–3). In a note to the 1885 printing Bridges said that he had used a gentler handling of motive than Apuleius and had substituted Hellenism for 'latin vulgarity'. Most of Bridges' changes are improvements—the main characters become more attractive, and Eros, whom Apuleius says is primarily responsible for adulterous love, is made the source of annoyance in all love and a gentler, kinder husband to Psyche. Bridges' revisions for the 1894 edition increased the emphasis on conjugal tenderness, and in an envoi to that edition he drew attention to his own happy marriage, which had evidently influenced the alterations.

The story of Eros and Psyche had considerable popularity in the nineteenth century, though Bridges said that he had read no English version of it; among others, Pater was to make use of it in *Marius the Epicurian* (1885), and as a young man Edward Burne-Jones had made a series of drawings of it to illustrate Morris's version in the *The Earthly Paradise*. That particular edition had been abandoned and the drawings left unused. Bridges came to know of them and Dixon arranged for him to visit Burne-Jones in July 1897 to discuss the possibility of their being used in an edition of his poem, but Burne-Jones was by that time elderly and ill and the drawings, which had been done on tracing paper, were faded and discoloured, so the project was abandoned. It was only in 1935 that the Gregynog Press had woodcuts made of twenty-four of the most suitable drawings, which were included in a limited edition in which the poem was printed in a hand-set type, 'designed to harmonize with the engraving'.[59]

A reviewer of the second edition of *Eros and Psyche* pointed out in *The Saturday Review* (1895) that,

> it is a tale which should be dealt with lightly by the imagination and also by the understanding; some of its situations suggest a passionate treatment, but being essentially a fairy tale, to insist strongly upon the element of passion is to do injury to its true character. And none the less it is wronged by the grave interpreter who, not satisfied with its elusive suggestions, would read a system of moral doctrine into the myth.

Judged by these criteria Bridges succeeds admirably. Hopkins praised the work for its 'equable beauty . . . and freshness' but an anonymous reviewer in the *Spectator* commented,

The poem was written after Morris's 'Earthly Paradise,' and though there may not be direct imitation, the point of view is the same. The story is told with a technical finish which Morris never attempted, but told, like his, simply for the sake of the story,—a strange thing in this particular legend, which tempts almost irresistibly to symbolism. But Mr. Bridges has rather concealed than drawn out the inner meaning of the myth, overlaying it with images of beauty. Each action is literally pictured. Here, for instance, is a Burne-Jones canvas put into words: the scene where Venus is met suddenly by the apparition of Psyche, who returns to her cruel taskmistress, having accomplished the impossible:—

'And now it chanced that she had called her son
 Into her presence chamber, to unfold
Psyche's destruction, that her fate might stun
 What love remained by duty uncontrol'd;
And he to hide his tears' rebellious storm
Was fled; when in his place another form
 Rose neath the golden lintel; and behold

Psyche herself, in slow and balanced strain
 Poising the crystal bowl with fearful heed,
Her eyes at watch upon the steadied plane
 And whole soul gather'd in the single deed.
Onward she came, and stooping to the floor,
Set down the cup unspill'd and brimming o'er
 At Aphrodite's feet and rose up freed.'

Yet, excellent as the whole poem is, it is the sort of thing that one may read with extreme pleasure and never desire to re-read. Nothing new is added to the tale; only the old beauty is burnished up and set again before us; and the reason for telling an old story in verse should be that it has for the poet some new and personal significance . . . You may read 'Eros and Psyche' ten times, but you will get no nearer to Mr. Bridges.[60]

For Bridges, the underlying idea in *Eros and Psyche* was of the necessity, not only for each human being (represented by Psyche) to be guided by love, but the desirable change wrought in love itself (personified by Eros), by tempering sexuality with compassion. The theme is neither new nor outdated but the critic's final comments suggest he felt that Bridges was not vitally engaged with the subject throughout. This seems true, Bridges' interest does appear to flag, and despite the beauty, must limit estimation of the work.

9

Marriage

(1884–1895)

In April 1884, at the age of 40, Robert became engaged to Monica Waterhouse, the elder daughter of the architect Alfred Waterhouse. Monica had had a happy and privileged childhood. Born in Manchester in August 1863, the year Robert became an undergraduate, she had spent most of her life at Fox Hill near Reading, one of four estates into which Whiteknights Park had been divided after it passed out of the hands of the Duke of Marlborough. The original house was owned by Alfred's parents, and Fox Hill had been built on the neighbouring plot. Florence, Monica's younger sister, later described aspects of their childhood there for her nephew:

> The chief beauty of the garden at Fox Hill was the large lake bounding it on the south side, which we shared with the neighbours whose fields enclosed it on two other sides; a public road ran along it to the east. As ours was the only garden that came down to its shores, it seemed to belong more to us than to our neighbours, and it was a great fact in our lives. The Grandparents' home stood away from the Lake, but it had a very beautiful garden full of rare trees (planted by the old Duke of Marlborough . . .) and with great stretches of lovely lawns and glades, winding between huge bushes of flowering azalias and rhododendrons. Among other attractions for us children was Jacko, the Peacock, who was nearly always prophecying rain at the top of his shrill voice, and who strutted about the garden strewing tail feathers for our benefit. There was much coming and going between Whiteknights and Fox Hill—and we often went to the Grandparents to tea on Sunday afternoon, and stayed for a long hymn-singing afterwards. The Uncles and Aunts and Father also, were all enthusiastic singers; but Mother [whose Quaker upbringing had discouraged any interest in music] . . . often felt left out. These occasions were not all pure joy to us children either for the Moody and

Sankey hymns, with their long choruses, seemed endless sometimes; and there is a limit to one's powers of standing on one leg and wondering when the performance will come to an end.[1]

Their father's architectural practice kept him away from home most of the week. Sometimes he managed to return by tea-time, 'and on those occasions', said Florence, 'we nearly always spent the evenings with him, often having a wildly exciting game of hide-and-seek all over the house. Father was the catcher, and ran up and down stairs in stockinged feet, only to be heard approaching, in the dark, by the jingling of the little things on his watch-chain . . . We adored this game.' On most days, however, from tea until bed-time, the children had what they called 'everins',

the happiest times in the day; they were spent in Mother's boudoir (as her sitting-room was called), and we all settled to whatever occupation we fancied: drawing, stencilling, pasting scrap-books, painting, fancy-work—while Mother read to us. When we were little, she read things like Hans Anderson's Fairy Tales, which she translated from the German as she went along . . . As we grew older she . . . tried to make us as keen about poetry as she was herself. She read us much narrative poetry, such as Scott, Southey, and William Morris; also Longfellow and Mrs Browning.

Pictures of Elizabeth Waterhouse show a face with delicate features and great sweetness. She was an intelligent and exceptionally well-educated woman of strict Quaker stock who joined the Church of England a few years after her marriage, though her religious views were strikingly undenominational. Each morning in the middle of their lessons she would read a religious book to the children, and each Sunday evening she would have a 'private talk' with each child before saying for them a prayer of her own. She wrote a number of devotional books and compiled collections of homilies and poetry.[2] Hopkins sent poems through Bridges for her to see or use on several occasions. Although she had been brought up to shun music, appreciation of art had been encouraged and she was adept at painting and handicrafts—gifts which Monica inherited. Mr and Mrs Waterhouse frequently went away together to the Continent, taking their sketching-and-painting 'tackle' with them, sending the children illustrated letters. As a Quaker, Mrs Waterhouse had been taught to address people as 'thee' and 'thou', and continued the practice within her family; Monica always addressed her sister as 'thee' in her letters. This sort of usage was common in nineteenth-century poetry, but for Bridges the daily use from his wife and her family would have given the words a greater naturalness and significance which is of relevance in assessing his love poems.

Between 1876, when Alfred Waterhouse bought the Yattendon estate near Newbury and started building a home for his family, and April 1881, when they moved in, the family spent their holidays in the old Yattendon Manor House. They collectively took on the role of village squire, providing the community with its first proper well, a reading-room, and a lending library. They ran evening classes and handicraft groups, and played host to the village at Christmas. Their social circle was not restricted to Yattendon. Each February and March the family spent several weeks in London, and they also entertained guests at home. Bridges would have known Alfred Waterhouse from the Savile Club, but his acquaintance with the family may have been increased through such mutual friends as Edmund and Nellie Gosse, who were guests on a number of occasions at the Manor House—Edmund wrote for the children's Christmas play a 'drama for private acting' called *The Unknown Lover*, dedicated to Elizabeth and published in 1878. The Gosses were also guests of Bridges and his mother and reciprocated their hospitality on at least one occasion in 1878, when the Waterhouses were present.[3]

Bridges' search for a place to which to move in 1882 coincided with Alfred Waterhouse's need for a tenant for the Manor House. Florence said that

> One day Father told her [mother] that the author of the first Triolet in the English language had offered himself as tenant for the Manor House. This of course was Robert Bridges, who, after settling in Yattendon and becoming a delightful and friendly neighbour, eventually became a member of the family. The coming of Robert and his mother to the Manor House brought more into the life at Yattendon than I can attempt to go into now; but one of the chief results was a great intellectual kindling and quickening in the place. A year or two after Robert came, Mr Beeching (Dean Beeching as he was to be) was given the Living at Yattendon, which also added to the literary and poetical element. Moreover, all the interesting friends of our neighbours would sooner or later find their way up the hill.

The 'poetical element' was relevant on Sunday afternoons at Yattendon Court. Bridges and Mr Beeching were welcomed to the Sunday afternoon teas, when it was the custom after tea for each person to read out a poem they had chosen. Florence remembered that, 'though it was amusing listening to the other readers, it was a terrifying ordeal for some, when our turns came. The only thing that guided my choice of a verse was its shortness.' But 'the corner of the [family's] Library devoted to the poets was Mother's delight, and she was constantly adding new volumes of modern poetry'.

In the late 1870s, when Monica first met Bridges, she was no more than 15 or 16. She must have found him a somewhat overawing figure—over six feet tall, bearded, and strikingly handsome, a doctor who wrote poetry and composed music. By the time he proposed she was 20. One of the sonnets from *The Growth of Love* may belong to the period of their engagement, a poem suggesting a stage in their relationship before trust was as deep as commitment. Its interest lies in the suggestion that Monica was psychologically more fully Robert's equal than might be expected from the discrepancy in their ages, able within the relationship to demand what she needed as well as fulfil his wishes.

> *O my goddess divine* sometimes I say:—
> Now let this word for ever and all suffice;
> Thou art insatiable, and yet not twice
> Can even thy lover give his soul away:
> And for my acts, that at thy feet I lay;
> For never any other, by device
> Of wisdom, love or beauty, could entice
> My homage to the measure of this day.
>
> I have no more to give thee: lo, I have sold
> My life, have emptied out my heart, and spent
> Whate'er I had; till like a beggar, bold
> With nought to lose, I laugh and am content.
> A beggar kisses thee; nay, love, behold,
> I fear not: thou too art in beggarment.

They were to develop an extraordinarily close partnership; Monica took an active part in many of his literary projects and he placed considerable value on her literary judgements. Among the letters of congratulation Monica received on her engagement in 1884 was one from Edmund Gosse, who confessed that he felt that he could never please Bridges; but he was, he said, confident that her future husband would have a place in English literature in the long run, outlasting 'many a noisy reputation that occupies the world now'.[4] It is a letter that shows the kindliness and sensitivity of which Gosse was capable.

Perhaps because Lionel Muirhead expected to be away in July 1884, Bridges wrote to Hopkins asking him to be his best man, which suggests the warmth of the friendship at the time. Hopkins, who had been transferred against his will to Dublin, was unwell, and while congratulating Bridges he did not take the invitation seriously. It was only when, with the initial date of July for the wedding approaching, Bridges wrote more urgently to Hopkins that the latter realized that his friend was indeed serious. He declined, 'pleasant and honourable as the position would be', explaining that the examination schedule would not allow him to be out of Ireland at the time.[5] He may also not have liked to ask for permission to attend an Anglican service, since it would almost certainly have been refused. Bridges then asked Muirhead, who was able to oblige since the Waterhouses wanted the wedding to be postponed until September, a few days after Monica's twenty-first birthday.

In August Bridges visited Dixon at Warkworth in Northumberland, for what he called a 'Nero clearing expedition' to finish his play, which removed him from the bustle of preparation surrounding the bride's trousseau. The canon returned with Bridges to Yattendon and officiated at his wedding. Robert and Monica spent their honeymoon in southern England, visiting Salisbury then spending two weeks at the Saxon town of Swanage on the south coast, and a few days at Dorchester and Wimborne on the way home. They were lucky with their weather and Monica, who was delicate, returned happy and in exceptionally good health. They sent a joint letter to thank Muirhead for his wedding present. It purports to be 'dictated' by Robert to Monica, but shows the styles of each and suggests the couple's enjoyment in each other's company. One passage reads:

> also I am told to say that we hope you are not really thinking of giving us another easel, as this one amply supplies all our wants in the easel line and

is indeed most useful. You have been much too generous already, and we hope that now you will begin to easel off a little—(Please remember that all this letter is in quotation marks and that I am only writing what I have been told to say.)[6]

Hopkins was delighted at Bridges' marriage. He considered, he said, that a single life was difficult and not altogether natural; it was better for those not living in communities such as the Society of Jesus to marry. He had, besides, a 'spooniness and delight over married people', and expressed his pleasure at the account of married life that Bridges sent him in November.[7]

Some of the love lyrics Bridges wrote in the 1880s and 1890s have the air of ecstatic new-found love, such as this from Book IV of his *Shorter Poems*:

My spirit kisseth thine
My spirit embraceth thee:
I feel thy being twine
Her graces over me.

In the life-kindling fold
Of God's breath; where on high,
In furthest space untold
Like a lost world I lie.

And o'er my dreaming plains
Lightens, most pale and fair,
A moon that never wanes,
Or more, if I compare,

Like what the shepherd sees
On late mid-winter dawns,
When thro' the branchèd trees,
O'er the white-frosted lawns,

The huge unclouded sun,
Surprising the world whist,
Is all uprisen thereon,
Golden with melting mist.

Guérard notes how 'the last two stanzas give a breathless rush which subsides only with the slow last line. The image immediately personalizes the poem . . . diction and rhythm combine to achieve the feeling rhetorically announced in the first stanza.'[8] 'New Poems' (1899) contained the poem:

My delight and thy delight
Walking, like two angels white,
In the gardens of the night:

My desire and thy desire
Twining to a tongue of fire,
Leaping live, and laughing higher;
Thro' the everlasting strife
In the mystery of life . . .

Hand in hand as we stood
Neath the shadows of the wood.
Heart to heart as we lay
In the dawning of the day.

In his pamphlet on Bridges John Sparrow wrote that 'for all the art that went to the shaping of them, these poems impress one as absolutely spontaneous'. Bridges wrote to Muirhead in 1899, 'the question arises whether the public will take for granted that they are to my wife, and whether in that case it is well to print them'.[9] It is difficult to see how else to take a poem like:

Since we loved . . .
All my joys my hope excel,
All my work hath prosper'd well,
All my songs have happy been,
O my love, my life, my queen.

He also strengthened several of his earlier love sonnets in this period by changing them from the third person to direct address, as in 'When first I saw my love' of 1876, which became 'When first I saw thee, dearest'.

Monica became pregnant in the summer of 1885, but was miserably unwell and miscarried in August. Hopkins, who suffered from depression for much of 1885, was in England that month, but did not try to see Bridges. He wrote afterwards, 'I did not know that visitors would at that time be very welcome and it would have been difficult to me in any case to come. I am sorry to hear of Mrs Bridges' disappointment: somehow I had feared that would happen',[10] an apprehension perhaps arising from Monica's frequent bouts of ill health. In fact Hopkins was not to meet her until May 1886 when he visited Yattendon, after which he wrote that she 'was not as fancy painted her (indeed fancy painted her very faintly, in watered sepia), but by no means the worse for that'.[11] After a second visit, in August 1887, he was to say: 'I may write now that when I was last in Yattendon I had the impression I had never in my life met a sweeter lady than Mrs Bridges. You may wear a diamond on your finger and yet never have seen it in a side light, so I tell you.'[12]

In the autumn of 1886 Bridges and his wife took a holiday at Fishguard in South Wales, Bridges reporting to Muirhead, 'we are enjoying ourselves immensely, the weather being perfect. I think the deep sea bathing is what I enjoy most.'[13] Muirhead was suffering from eye-trouble, and instead of being able to carry out designs for a stage-set for Bridges' *Ulysses*, which was being printed by Daniel, could not even read the play himself. By November, however, he was on the mend.

From Fishguard they went to stay with Monica's relatives, the Frys, at Bristol. Her 19-year-old cousin, Roger Fry, was reading science at Cambridge but was already keenly interested in questions of art and aesthetics. After a few days of the Bridges' visit Roger wrote to Charles Ashbee,

> there is a standard of beauty somewhere, and if there is not, the sooner we chuck the whole business the better. Just as to a morally-minded person it is inconceivable that there is not a right and a wrong absolutely, to which we constantly approximate, so to the artistically-minded man it is inconceivable that we have not got something at which we constantly aim. This is the result of some discussions with a certain poet Robert Bridges who has been staying here, a most delightful man. It was great fun hearing him uphold the standard of Beauty against my sceptical parents, and it has cleared my views much. He is very great on the severity of art and the necessity of enormous study on the technical parts without the least subordinating the higher aims to the technique. I have learnt much from him . . .[14]

Fry's respect for Bridges was reciprocated. They were both men of strong and independent mind, and the family bond was strengthened by a real friendship that sometimes erupted in explosive disagreement.

While staying with the Frys Bridges made an excursion to

Tyntesfield House to visit friends and see the stained-glass windows that Wooldridge had designed. He thought them

> extremely good. though the people there hate them, & the old archdeacon whom they keep as a private chaplain cd not imagine why I shd think them worth looking at. they are in every respect but one successful. but the workman who did the faces was evidently incompetent & has spoiled the effect by making rather silly & ugly saints. The colour is excellent & the whole decorative effect the best I have ever seen in stained glass.[15]

Bridges' friend Dr Gee, whose own writing was done in the time he could spare from the hospital, seemed to have some apprehension that Bridges was affecting the role of professional writer. Bridges replied, 'I have 3 unprinted plays . . . when I do print it will be privately. Without pretending to superhuman virtue I can say that I despise the whole thing as much as I loathe the vulgar treatment which any one who is at all noticeable above the crowd receives from journalists. nothing on earth wd persuade me to pose as a poet or even a member of the literary profession.'[16] He was always exceptionally unassuming as a poet, but at Yattendon he came in time to think that he had settled rather too fully into the life of the village to develop his literary abilities. By the end of 1885 he was, for example, busy training the Yattendon church choir, an occupation that gave him considerable satisfaction. In August 1886 he wrote to Dixon that 'we always sing now on Wednesday evenings without the organ. I give the key note from a pitchpipe & they sing by the book & give no trouble. Last Wednesday the chants were very difficult & went without a hitch. It is very nice to have one's work so well repaid.'[17] The responsibility of choosing music for the choir prompted Bridges to compile his own hymn-book, a task which he was to continue and expand in the 1890s. He was also participating in politics, campaigning in December 1885 for the local Conservative candidate and, in the second of the two elections of 1886, helping with the local registration of voters. The most controversial issue was Home Rule for Ireland. Parnell's filibustering was making it impossible for the British Government to govern England, let alone Ireland, and Gladstone went twice to the electorate that year, winning the first time and losing the second.

The question of Ireland provoked an irritable exchange between

Bridges and Hopkins, who was depressed by the growing unrest he saw daily. Gladstone's decision to support Parnell's call for Home Rule seems to have occasioned a scornful remark from Bridges about the government losing the will to govern Ireland, prompting a hot but well-argued reply from Hopkins about English ignorance and mishandling of the situation. The other main political issue of the day was the extension of the franchise, and this time Hopkins and Bridges do not seem to have crossed swords. Bridges shared the widespread wariness of democracy of his class. Although he was later to agree with suggestions that unearned, inherited wealth should go to the state, he wrote to Samuel Gee in 1886: 'the impending democracy is not likely to be a final step, nor in my opinion will it last very long if it shd actually establish itself at all', feelings with which Gee agreed.[18]

Hopkins' letters suggest that he was feeling increasingly frustrated and lonely. There is at times an irritability that reinforces his statements that he felt himself under too much pressure. Meanwhile Bridges was moving closer to Muirhead, whose circumstances were closer to his own and whose visits were becoming more frequent. Several times in 1886 Hopkins distributed copies of Bridges' works to people in Dublin whose interest he had aroused in them, but a series of petty disagreements mar the correspondence. They argued about the excellence of William Barnes' poetry and the novels of Robert Louis Stevenson and Mrs Gaskell, to aspects of all of which Bridges objected. His interlineated defence of his actual objections show that his views were not the complete condemnations that one might unwarily deduce from Hopkins' response.

Released from the constraints of his medical duties and encouraged by his wife, Bridges was able to give rather more time to his friends in the 1880s than had been possible during the previous decade. In April, 1886, for example, he visited Mandell Creighton at Worcester, where he was now canon. Creighton had also been made a fellow of Emmanuel College, Cambridge, in 1884 and Professor of Ecclesiastical History. Dixon had just begun to get to know him in June 1884 when Creighton's new appointments moved him away from his vicinity. Bridges had written to Dixon,

> I am sorry that you are losing Creighton, especially as you had just got to know him a little. It is difficult to get near a man who talks so wildly. But

he is really very sensible and warmhearted. and has been such a good friend of mine that I shd have liked you to know him. His main deficiency is a sensuous artistic one. which he is mainly unconscious of. & this leads him very wrong in the subjects which we care most for.[19]

Creighton was a few years Bridges' senior. At Oxford he had been an enthusiastic reader of Browning and Carlyle, writers that Hopkins and Bridges agreed in criticizing.

The winter and spring provided a number of social occasions. Wooldridge spent Christmas 1886 with the Bridges, a visit long postponed. He had agreed to sing in a concert at Yattendon on 23 December but Bridges, evidently aware of a certain absent-mindedness in his friend, said, 'we hardly expect him, though his name is printed on the programme—he will probably miss his train'.[20] But Wooldridge did come and Bridges found him 'most amusing and entertaining and as usual instructive. He seems too in fairly good preservation'; like Hopkins, Wooldridge frequently suffered from ill health and depression. This was more evident during a second visit three months later, when Wooldridge was unwell and easily became fatigued. He found initially, to his surprise, that in the Bridges' company he was rather less depressed. They spent evening after evening making music together and Wooldridge sang regularly in the choir. At Bridges' request, he even started a portrait from a photograph of Hopkins, who sent a description of his colouring. However, Wooldridge's despondency returned, making Bridges in turn depressed and fretful, so that he was relieved at his departure.

There were social occasions too when, in January 1887, Muirhead became engaged to Grace Ashhurst, and Robert's brother John made one of his rare visits to Yattendon. John's memoirs suggest that he was much more conservative in his attitudes than Robert, much more the gentleman farmer, more cynical and somewhat self-pitying. He had tried farming in North America, and after settling in England took part in local politics. Perhaps influenced by Robert's example, he was to retire from farming in 1889 and, devoting himself to writing, publish several volumes of verse and memoirs, but in 1887 his literary work amounted to little more than journalism for newspapers and magazines. At the end of February the Bridges spent three weeks at Seaford, where there was 'snow on the beach and the salt pools' were 'frozen thickly', then visited the Patmores in Surrey and spent a couple of days seeing relatives in London. In July Bridges visited Dixon in Northumberland.

Yattendon itself was not entirely to Bridges' satisfaction. He had begun to think of moving from the Manor House, which was too expensive to allow the couple to travel as much during winter as he would have liked. He also found his involvement in local institutions distracting. In 1886 he had not written a single complete work and, at 42 beginning to notice his age, he wondered if his vein had 'run out'. But, by the end of January 1887 he was working on the fifth act of a play he had started in 1886—*The Christian Captives.* For the play he read a lot of comedies, mainly by Lope de Vega, which he read in Spanish, and came to the conclusion that 'they are not up to their reputation but there are some good things . . . They are dreadfully alike—without characterisation. I return to Aeschylus.'[21] He did not complete his own play, which is one of his stronger ones, until late in 1888. In 1887 he finished another play, *Achilles in Scyros*, and, with Monica's help, planned a comedy in three acts, *The Humours of the Court.*

In mid-August, during a short visit that Hopkins paid to Yattendon, Bridges evidently discussed with him a paper that he had been asked to write on Milton's blank verse. The request had come from the local vicar, Henry Beeching, who wanted the essay to publish with the first book of *Paradise Lost* in an edition intended for sixth-form pupils. He wanted to counter the general tendency to distort the natural accent of the words so that the lines could be forced into an inflexible iambic pentameter. Bridges' solution was to suggest that Milton's metre was syllabic, a 'learned systemization of Chaucer's practice'. By making a distinction between a strict metric base (ten syllables per line) and a flexible, superimposed speech-rhythm (variable iambic pentameter), he opened up the possibility of far more sensitive interpretations of Milton's cadences. Examining metrically anomalous lines, he found no examples in *Paradise Lost* of lines having fewer than ten syllables. Those which had more than ten could be explained in one of two ways: either they had a final additional syllable creating a 'feminine ending', or they were explicable through a set of rules of elision, which he tried to deduce by expanding classical conventions.

Bridges' essay was subsequently published separately and met with a mixed response. He was criticized for insufficient consideration of phonetics, an impression which he tried to correct in 1904 through three 'letters' to the *Athenaeum*.[22] However, partly on account of the general advances in the study of phonetics, and partly because Bridges' knowledge was the self-teaching of a talented amateur, the criticism remains valid. Nevertheless, he was able to answer those, like George Saintsbury, who believed that Milton was working in a tradition of extra-metrical liberties, by pointing out to them that the verse must be syllabic since Milton's extra syllables are always elidable into disyllabic units; anyone writing accentual trisyllabic feet, he said, would use unelidable monosyllables as well. Although analysis of Milton's verse is still a decidedly controversial subject, most modern critics concur with Bridges' contention that it is basically syllabic, and he has been called the forefather of modern studies of Miltonic prosody.

Edward Thompson points out that Bridges also changed attitudes to *Samson Agonistes*:

> Before Bridges effected what was nothing less than a revolution in our attitude towards *Samson Agonistes*, the common judgement was that of Macaulay: 'We are by no means insensible to the merits of this celebrated piece, to the severe dignity of the style, the graceful and pathetic solemnity of the opening speech, or the wild and barbaric melody which gives so striking an effect to the choral passages. But we think it, we confess, the least successful effort of the genius of Milton.'

Bridges showed that the 'rhythm was "always ready to follow [Milton's] thought, a habit with him so essential to his style and so carefully trained" that when unusual action is depicted or a striking new motive emerges these are not passed over "without some exceptional treatment"'.[23] The 'barbaric melody' is not barbaric, but carefully calculated. The essay went through two further editions, each time with additional material.

In April 1887 Bridges was invited to prepare a translation of Terence for publication by Macmillan but declined:

> I cannot imagine a more thankless task. Terence's Language is more faultless than Virgil's, and does not offer the escape into elevation which Virgil allows. Then, when all is done, the best modern equivalent brings

one into very rough contact with Latin manners. It was for these reasons that I recommended the reprinting of Cooke's version: because the colloquialisms of his date being now out of vogue one is removed from everyday life without effort or affectation.

'Englishmen who do not know Latin', he suggested, 'shd read Plautus & Terence in the French.'[24] It would be difficult to find modern critics who would agree with this rather Victorian verdict. On the other hand, his views five years later, when he was asked by A. H. Bullen to translate three poems of Anacreon, would still receive assent: 'I do not like translations unless the original is good enough to suggest an English form, and not perfect in itself. When the original is perfect there is nothing to do: because the translation of the perfection is impossible, the poet always making the poetic best of his own language, which is *different* in another. Therefore the best translation must be alteration.'[25]

Bridges' views on several contemporary writers emerge from his letters of this period. The winter of 1887 was cold with heavy snowfalls, giving him plenty of time to read. He tried but did not get far with, Browning's drama, *A Blot in the 'Scutcheon*. He tried Darwin's *Life and Letters*, but thought that in his autobiography Darwin failed to do himself justice.[26] He found that Edward Dowden's biography of Shelley, who had been one of his favourite poets, left him sickened with its subject:

That is his biographer's fault. Dowden will not allow the reader to think that Shelley was mad . . If you may not sometimes laugh at Shelley you soon loose your patience with him. | Did ever any other man take to himself a woman in the lifetime of his wife, & ask his wife to accompany him on his travels with his new love. | A family tree of the Godwins & Shelleys should be published showing the suicides etc.[27]

When Dixon had sent some of his own work to Bridges for comment, among Robert's reactions was an opinion of Dickens:

I object to your writing any ode or anything else on the death of Dickens. I have a contempt for his pathos. & regard him merely as a very amusing writer in a vulgar style. In that inimitable and unsurpassed. Your reflection is that he said how near sorrow & joy were. the smile and the tear . . I don't think he knew what joy was. perhaps I wrong him, but Query, if he did know, is he the man who told us this first. or better than anyone else? Thus R.B.[28]

Then, during the rainy summer that followed, he found Charles Doughty's *Arabia Deserta*, which he liked enough to make him write to its author, who was still in Palestine. Doughty had created a prose style based on sixteenth-century English to describe his journey among the Arabs, and this seems to have struck a chord with Bridges, who had used Elizabethan English in his plays and some lyrics. It is striking, however that he never did this in his own prose. He recommended the book to Hopkins, who replied,

> since you speak so highly of his book I must try to see it: to read 1200 pages I do not promise. But I have read several reviews of it, with extracts. You say it is free from the taint of Victorian English. H'm. Is it free from the taint of Elizabethan English? Does it not stink of that? for the sweetest flesh turns to corruption. Is not Elizabethan English a corpse these centuries? No one admires, regrets, despairs over the death of the style, the living masculine native rhetoric of that age, more than I do; but ''tis gone, 'tis gone, 'tis gone'. He writes in it, I understand, because it is manly. At any rate affectation is not manly, and to write in an obsolete style is affectation. As for the extracts I saw they were not good even as that—wrong as English, for instance calling a *man* a jade; and crammed with Latin words, a fault, let do it who will.
>
> But it is true this Victorian English is a bad business. They say 'It goes without saying' (and I wish it did) and instead of 'There is no such thing' they say a thing 'is non-existent' and *in* for *at* and *altruistic* and a lot more.[29]

Certainly Doughty's style now seems a rather ponderous eccentricity, bearing out the truth of Hopkins' observations. Bridges defended his own use of Elizabethan English in verse in a letter to Lowes Dickinson:

> About Elizabethanisms, I think these are chiefly in 2nd person sing[ular] of pronoun & verb.—It must be remembered that Shakespeare is permanent and will never age. The diction of our time will in 100 years or 200 years be antiquated but not Shakespeare's diction.
>
> Secondly blank verse always requires elevation, & a remoteness from *common talk*. In proportion as you let the characters be perfectly natural in their utterances you require some artificial raising of their speech. This is easily helped by using the 2nd person sing[ular] for the colloquial plural.
>
> Thirdly—the translation of the Bible gives it a familiarity and solemnity.
>
> Fourthly—the difference of attitude between speakers is shown by the use of sing[ular] or plural address. and if the singular be given up a tremendous power is lost (read carefully the prison scene in 'Measure for

Measure,' III i after Isabella enters—& see how the 2 numbers are used by Claudio and Isabella. every change meaning a change of attitude of mind.) Whereas if it is used at all it must be used pretty frequently. Also the plural is used in such a play as Nero for Royalty, & this distinction wd also be lost.

You mention also *doth*, and probably wd include the *th* ending of 3rd pers[on] sing[ular] of verb for the modern *s* as *writeth* for *writes*. I use this whenever I can as a means of getting rid of a sibilant. English is so full of them, that with all one can do one has too may ss.

Consider these things & tell me if they weigh with you. I am abused by Lang for being 'Elizabethan' but really my use of these Elizabethanisms is most reserved and intentional.[30]

But familiarity with the Authorized version of the Bible and the subtleties of Shakespeare's use of language is not so common now, and appraisal from critics that accommodates Bridges' aesthetic sensitivity to the sound of English will be necessary before his usage will be seen as anything but a handicap.

The summer of 1887 was exceptionally hot in Britain, and since Monica was again pregnant and this time forbidden to travel, Bridges spent most of the summer writing, directing the choir, and playing cricket. In December they moved to London so that Monica could be looked after and on December 5 their first child was born. They named her Elizabeth. She was left in the care of her grandparents when, from 28 December 1888 to the end of January the Bridges and Mary Plow, Robert's niece, visited the south of France and Italy. Bridges described the trip to Muirhead: 'we came via Calais stopping at Arles. where we were detained by tremendous storms, part of the line giving way. all the country between Toulouse and Nice under water. We drove from Nice to Sanremo. train to Genoa. one day there. had intended to drive to Spezia: hadn't time—one night at Pisa. saw all things again well. found nothing improved', an allusion to Muirhead's complaint during a trip to Italy the previous spring that the beauty of Rome was being ruined by the installation of modern inventions. The weather, Bridges said, had been lovely; 'We think of spending a fortnight here [in Rome]—are in pension au 4[eme] at this hotel [Hotel Molaro]. with very sunny rooms. a wood fire & Roman tobacco . . . Rome seems a good deal altered. But it was lovely as ever on Pincian this afternoon.'[31] He was, however, less happy with Rome's inhabitants, complaining of the Swiss touters and the Italians—'they lie and cheat and play the fool and mismanage your luggage worse than ever'; he had had most of his belongings stolen from his hotel room on a previous visit in 1874. On his return home, Bridges developed a liver complaint and rheumatism, which stopped him from walking; he sent Hopkins a grumpy letter, full of petty complaints about the Italians, complaining of their slovenly appearance and inability to sing in tune. Hopkins pointed out that exactly the same faults and worse were to be found among the English.

By March 1889 Hopkins was ill. Bridges was told in May, and wrote:

> Dearest Gerard.
>
> I am so sorry to get a letter from one of your people telling me that you are ill with fever. And yesterday I sent you off a budget of notes on Milton's prosody. and when I last wrote I never mentioned your ailing tho' you told me in your letter that you interrupted it to lie down.
>
> What is this fever? F. Wheeler says that you are mending. I hope you are recovering properly. let me have a line—I wish I cd look in on you and see for myself. You must send me a card now and then, and one as soon as possible to let me know about you.
>
> Meanwhile I must be patient.
>
> I think that if you are really mending Miltonic prosody will be just the sort of light amusement for your mind—I hope you are well enough already—and will make a quick recovery and complete for which I pray . . . Yrs affc. R.B.[32]

He sent a copy of the new edition of *The Growth of Love* as well as *Milton's Prosody*. Messages sent to Bridges in May suggested that Hopkins was recovering, but then on 12 June came news of his death. The last six months of Hopkins' life had seen a widening of the rift between the two men. Hopkins had teased Bridges about not attempting to become better known, but Bridges' works were too little in demand for him to see a joke on the subject. Hopkins, leading the isolated existence that he did, was nevertheless far more in touch with the progressive artistic trends of his time than Bridges. 'So far as I see', Hopkins wrote to him, 'where we differ in judgment, my judgments are less singular than yours; I agree more than you do with the mob and with the *communis criticorum*.

Presumably I should agree with these still more if I read more and so differ still more from you than now. Who for instance is singular about Dryden, you or I?'[33] Hopkins did not send Bridges his sonnets of desolation, and those poems he did send towards the end of his life—'Harry Ploughman', 'Tom's Garland', 'That Nature is a Heraclitean Fire', 'St Alphonsus Rodriguez'—Bridges found more incomprehensible than his earlier work. Bridges wrote to Dixon of Hopkins' death:

> How can I tell you—the terribly mournful tidings of Gerard's death reached me two days ago. It is possible that you may not have heard. I hope you have. I shd have written to you at once, but heard that you were from home. This morning I got your letter from Warkworth.
>
> I had had only favourable reports from Dublin. In fact the people who wrote to me described his illness as a slight & not dangerous attack.
>
> Still he was of course too ill to write himself..I do not know whether he died suddenly. or as is more likely in a relapse, & when the worst was feared chose deliberately not to see any one in his prostrate condition. One can only guess. Still I had no message of any sort from him after the last favourable one.
>
> His last letters to me & the two last poems are if not a foreboding of it, yet full of a strange fitness for the end.
>
> The last poem but one was an address to God, most powerful and plaintive. the last was a sonnet to me, explaining some misunderstanding which he thought existed. You will be anxious to see them & I will, when I am more in the mood for writing, copy them out & send them..
>
> In answer to your letter. I am sorry that you are so overworked & have not been well. I hope you will get through all right . . .[34]

He added a controversial footnote: 'that dear Gerard was overworked, unhappy & would never have done anything great seems to give no solace. But how much worse it wd have been had his promise or performance been more splendid. He seems to have been entirely lost & destroyed by those Jesuits.' Bridges' opinion of Hopkins' achievement rose considerably when he saw the sonnets of desolation, which he considered some of his best poems, a judgement with which most subsequent critics have agreed. But in his letter there may also be an attempt to escape from his realization that he could have done more to make Hopkins' last years happy. Bridges had only discovered after Dolben's death that his last eight months had been lonely. This deeply affected him, and he wrote that he had never been able to shake off the remorse he felt at having allowed himself to lose sight of his cousin.[35] The guilt he felt over failing Dolben may have been repeated in a more complex form over Hopkins.

At Daniel's suggestion, Bridges proposed shortly after Hopkins' death to edit a volume of his poems to be privately printed. Knowing that he would be busy for some months, Bridges organized the volume so that Daniel could proceed with the book without being held up until the preface was complete. The plan was to include two portraits of Hopkins, samples of his handwriting and drawings, a memoir of 48 pages, Hopkins' preface to his poems, and a selection of his poetry (61 pages). Bridges wrote to Mrs Hopkins that he was not finding Hopkins' Catholic friends very communicative but was hoping to see one or two of them in London in September; by November he considered the memoir a 'disagreeable difficulty', although he was still convinced that the poems should be printed. In August 1890 he wrote to Mrs Hopkins:

> Mr Daniel says that he will print a selection at any time, free of charge—up to 150 copies. yourselves and friends to take a certain number, & the rest for private sale among interested outsiders. Perhaps you will like this plan..The Memoir must I think be given up for the present, but perhaps a short 'preface' might be written which shd put the poems out of the reach of criticism. I shd not like the poems to be printed without some word of that sort, and it is a difficulty which a memoir wd have got over. I shd myself prefer the postponement of the poems till the memoir is written, or till I have got my own method of prosody recognised separately from Gerard's. They are the same, and he has the greater claim than I to the origination of it, but he has used it so as to discredit it: and it wd be a bad start in favour for the practice we both advocated. & wished to be used. Readers wd not see that the peculiarities of his versification were not part of his metrical system, but a freakishness corresponding to his odd choice of words etc. in which also his theories were as sound as his practice was strange.
>
> In this I am not considering myself: but the prospect of introducing this new way of writing, in which if there is any reputation to come to him, it will be from the recognition of the principles which I think his own verse wd damage.
>
> I have no doubt of the adoption of the system. and when once it is recognised his verses will establish his claim to foreseeing (not to say outgoing) the limits of it.

> A year or 18 months is all the delay which I expect will be necessary for this—and I shd like it for the reasons I give I hope not unintelligibly.[36]

That Bridges was sincere in this argument is suggested by the similarity between it and the letter he sent to Patmore about Hopkins' poetry in 1884. Patmore's negative reaction then may have swayed Bridges towards the delay in publication.

The first selection of Hopkins' poems that Bridges shepherded before the public was included in A. H. Miles's collection, *The Poets and the Poetry of the Century*, in 1893. Bridges chose for it some eleven poems, seven of these complete, and he quoted most of three others in the introduction. He warned Hopkins' family that Miles might reject the poems when he saw them, 'as everyone else has done', 'everyone' being those in a position to publish them, but Miles was enthusiastic and the tone of Bridges' letter to Mrs Hopkins after he received this response was markedly more relaxed and hopeful than his earlier note had been.[37] His account of Hopkins' life in the introduction is not well written—his later memoirs of friends are far superior in style—and the tone is peculiarly tense: powerful and unresolved feelings lie just below the surface, visible in the lack of critical distance in his discussion of Hopkins' poetic style and the vehemence that develops in his account of the life. It begins conventionally with a sketch of Hopkins' early promise and accomplishment as a poet at school and at Oxford, and his first-class degree, but then Bridges mentions his love of subtlety and uncommonness:

> and this quality of mind hampered their author throughout life; for though to a fine intellect and varied accomplishments (he was both a draughtsman and musician) he united humour, great personal charm, and the most attractive virtues of a tender and sympathetic nature,—which won him love wherever he went, and gave him zeal for his work—yet he was not considered publicly successful in his profession.

This was true. But Bridges' disapproval of Hopkins' becoming a priest and his dislike of the Irish Catholics among whom he had worked is too obvious. Hopkins' letters show that Bridges has some foundation, although he exaggerates, in saying that the 'vice and horrors' of the Irish community in Liverpool 'nearly killed him', and that the 'drudgery [of being classical examiner in Dublin] . . . and the political dishonesty which he was there forced to witness, so tortured his sensitive spirit that he fell into a melancholy state . . . he was attacked shortly after by the material contagions of the city, and making no effort for life . . . died of the fever in his prime'. There is anger here and a sense of loss, but the importance Bridges places on Hopkins' state of mind at his death and the guilt Bridges had felt in Dolben's case over failing to support a lonely friend suggest that he was also experiencing as he wrote a combination of guilt and self-justification. How much responsibility should a man take for his friends' happiness?

Of Hopkins' poetry Bridges wrote:

> The octetts above quoted ['Thou art indeed just . . .' and 'To seem the stranger . . .'] are in his best style, the dated specimens below are from all periods of his writing. The first two of these he would not have wished to be printed ['A Vision of the Mermaids' and 'The Habit of Perfection'] but it is necessary to give them in proof that the unusual and difficult rhythm of his later work were consciously sought after, and elaborated from the common types which he had set aside. Poems so far removed as his came to be from the ordinary simplicity of grammar . . . had they no other drawback, could never be popular but they will interest poets; and they may perhaps prove welcome to the critic, for they have the plain fault, that, aiming at an unattainable perfection of language (as if words—each with its . . . value in sense and in sound—could be arranged like so many separate gems to compose a whole expression of thought, in which the force of grammar and the beauty of rhythm absolutely correspond) they not only sacrifice simplicity, but very often among verses of the rarest beauty, show a neglect of those canons of taste which seem common to all poetry.

Bridges' analysis of Hopkins' poetry is harsh and reminiscent of Patmore's objections, but it cannot simply be dismissed as jealousy. Bridges clearly had no wish to write as Hopkins did. He thought of him as having achieved some beautiful and moving effects, but he also considered him potentially a pernicious influence in his abuse of English. He sent the introduction to Dixon, who felt it was too severe, and to Hopkins' family for comment before submitting it for publication, saying that if they liked they were welcome to rewrite it, but they raised no objection. The reaction among reviewers to Hopkins' poems was limited and mixed. Bridges did not alter his introduction when the second edition of Miles' anthology was published in 1906.[38]

★

1. Harriett Louisa, Edward, and Frances C. Bridges (Carry), *c.*1854

2. Julia Bridges, *c.*1854

3. Lieut. George L. Bridges, *c.*1860

4. Robert Bridges at Eton, *c.*1863

5. The Reverend J. E. N. Molesworth

6. The Eights Crew, 1864: (*back row, l. to r.*) C. J. Pearson (3), J. B. Reid (6), C. F. J. Bowka (2), Robert S. Bridges (stroke); (*middle row*) F. F. Lambert (4), C. J. Manning (5), J. C. Ingram (cox); (*front row*) E. Ridley (7), H. G. Woods (bow)

7. Gerard Manley Hopkins, *c.*1867

8. Robert Bridges (copy of a photograph once owned by Willoughby Furner), 1869

9. Harry Ellis Wooldridge drawn by Lionel Muirhead, *c.*1874

10. Monica Bridges, *c.*1885

11. Mrs Molesworth (Robert Bridges' mother) painted by Harry Wooldridge, 1875

12. Yattendon: the Manor House, home of Robert Bridges and his family *c.*1882–1906

13. Chilswell, the Bridges' home near Oxford before the fire in 1917

14. Edward Bridges, the poet's son, 1914

15. Margaret Bridges, the poet's younger daughter, *c.*1918

16. (*below*) Elizabeth Daryush, the poet's elder daughter, 1933

17. Robert Bridges wearing Lionel Muirhead's cape, 1929

In 1889 the second edition of *The Growth of Love* was published, expanded to seventy-nine sonnets and printed almost illegibly in black letter. The following year four of Bridges' plays were issued, and the *Shorter Poems*, divided into four 'books'. The first three of these consisted of his selection from the pamphlets of 1873, 1879, and 1880 respectively. 'Book IV', composed of some thirty poems, was new. Bridges told Gee that he had more manuscripts ready for printing but could not afford to have anything more published until he got some money from those already in print. *The Humours of the Court* he held back until 1893. It was later performed by the Oxford Dramatic Society at the Arts Theatre in London in January 1930, with Edith Evans as Diana. Eddie Marsh, who saw the performance, sent Bridges an account of how the audience had enjoyed the play's humour.

In a survey of contemporary writers published anonymously in the *Edinburgh Review* in 1893, Bridges' plays and *The Growth of Love* were commented upon. Of the plays it was said that they were 'modern-antiques which do not interest us very much', although *Achilles in Scyros* was singled out for its 'vivacity and picturesqueness' and the metre of *The Feast of Bacchus* was called an experiment worth attention for comic drama. The reviewer objected to the care that had been lavished on the appearance of *The Growth of Love*, considering it irrelevant and distracting, but praised the sonnets as 'finely written, manly in tone, and very varied in their range of subject and sympathy', and considered them Bridges' best work.[39] It is a pity that he does not seem to have known *Poems* (1880).

A reviewer in the *Saturday Review*, after rebuking Bridges for not making his poems more readily available, remarked of the *Shorter Poems*:

> Mr Bridges's poetical characteristics require no very large expense of critical praelection. Though an extremely scholarly, he is at his best (as most men are at their best) a very simple, writer. He once indulged himself in experiments in a 'New Prosody,' which we do not think a success, and of which we are not sorry to find that he has not reprinted many examples here . . . Sometimes, though rarely, he further indulges in unnecessarily exotic words. We do not ourselves like 'nenuphars' and 'myosote' in English verse, and we think 'spathe' might be left to the scientific man; but blemishes of this kind are exceedingly rare and of little

importance. Beyond legitimate poetic transposition of words, there is absolutely no element of obscurity in Mr Bridges's style, as shown here. Further, he is quite free from the curse which weighs on so much contemporary verse, the curse of trying to be fashionably 'thoughtful'. His verse is, indeed, as full of thought as it is accomplished in form and melodious in sound; but it abides by the principal things, and does not busy itself with the things that are not principal.[40]

A review of the same volume in the *Athenaeum* criticized his poems in freer metres, although liking the volume overall. Of the short lyrics, the reviewer said,

It is remarkable . . . considering how much other writings of Mr Bridges [such as *Eros and Psyche* and *Prometheus the Firegiver*] show him to have imbued himself with the spirit of ancient Greek literature—that these lyrics are quite without traces of that spirit. Their thought is as essentially English as their treatment . . . in a kind agreeably akin to the strong, subtle, and quiet lyrical method of the sixteenth and seventeenth centuries. Something there is, too, which, without actually resembling Heine's verse, is at times suggestive of it.[41]

Bridges' cautious approach to the publication of Hopkins' poetry needs to be seen in the context of the dislike shown in reviews for his own much more conservative experiments.

He received a complimentary letter about *Shorter Poems* from George Saintsbury in October 1890 and sent back an appreciative response, but commented to Muirhead on the academic's 'inability' to distinguish the good poems from the bad.[42] He was to disagree with Saintsbury over metrical analysis later, but corresponded with him for the rest of his life. Letters of admiration were responsible for the start of a number of Bridges' friendships. Sometimes, as with Saintsbury, Bridges was the recipient, but more often he sent the initial letter, especially to younger writers whom he wanted to encourage. This was the case in November 1890 with Goldsworthy Lowes Dickinson. Bridges had seen Roger Fry's copy of Dickinson's volume of poems, *Jacob's Ladder*, and liked it so much that he asked Fry to get him a copy. Praising Dickinson for 'a promise of poetry of original and rare character', he cautioned him against marring his work by following elements of Browning's manner, which he personally found 'detestable'.[43] He sent him some of his own axioms: that 'it is the function of art to beautify' and, 'to quote another who has expressed my meaning well: "Rien n'est plus vite banal que les hardiesses de mauvais gout."' He hoped, he said, that Dickinson would write more, and invited him to visit Yattendon.

By February 1890 Bridges was enthusiastically reading about Peter the Great, Henry I, and Henry II and planning to write plays about all of them. However, although he was to begin a drama on Peter the Great in August 1892, it was never completed and he wrote nothing about the English kings. He had more success the following January when he started investigating the stories about Nero and the burning of Rome. He concluded that the emperor could not have been responsible for the conflagration, and early in 1892 incorporated his ideas in the second part of *Nero*. This, the last play he wrote, was not published until 1894 and has been criticized for being too loosely structured.[44] Bridges recognized this himself; he wrote to Dickinson, who had sought his advice about writing a history play:

> the chief mistake I made was that I thought I could get more in than is possible. The plot cannot be too simple, and the general lines too clear. else the drama degenerates into mere intrigue & incident. & becomes only amusing. I am quite sure of this. that in a tragic or quite serious play the main lines cannot be too simple—and this is the chief difficulty of an historical drama—because history supplies you with such authoritative details that you cannot miss them out without being untrue—& admitted they ruin your drama. Now from the point of view of the dramatist it is better to be false to history than to spoil one's drama. and as I suppose that your interest will be chiefly historical I do not know what line you will take.[45]

In July 1892 Bridges read Carlyle's *Cromwell* and wondered whether he could write a play on the subject. 'He puzzles me very much', he told Dixon. 'I don't understand his face. What do you think of his face. do you see the man or is it a mask? and if it is a mask is it only the mask of his religious delusions and enthusiasms. or did he consciously make it?'[46] There is no evidence that Bridges overcame his puzzlement sufficiently to begin the play.

In December 1892 Bridges saw one of the volumes William Morris had printed at his Kelmscott Press, and thought that he would like to have something of his own printed there. By

February of the following year, however, he had changed his mind. He wrote to Muirhead,

I have seen the Kelmscott press books. I think they disappointed you: they did me. The paper is good, and the printing well done, and it is very easy to read. Otherwise I do not see that Mr William Morris has cut much above Ye Leadenhalle Presse. It is wonderful why he so admires old work, when it is plain that he does not see why it is good. His printing is like his poetry: that he considers in the manner of Chaucer: but it lacks all that makes Chaucer admirable.[47]

At least part of Bridges' own admiration for Chaucer was technical: on several occasions he praised him for using terminal vowels and inflexions that gave to his heroic verse a buoyancy that made it an attractive form for narrative.

In January 1893 Bridges wrote to Muirhead, 'there are now and then signs that my work is getting better known and more read: but the common critic is afraid of drama, and the pretentious critic only writes nonsense about it, so that I do not get much mention except for my lyrics, and they sell very slowly now'.[48] Among the critical opinions published at this time was one by J. C. Bailey in *Temple Bar* for autumn 1893, concentrating on *Achilles in Scyros* and *The Shorter Poems*. He thought that the best of the lyric poems owed their strength to Bridges' close observation and love of nature. Given no biographical facts, he wondered if

Mr Bridges, as befits a poet, has been earlier than the rest of the world in his 'return to Nature'. Perhaps he never left the country; but, however that may be, every line of his poems tells of his present life there, and of the observant eye, the habit of quiet, leisurely contemplation, and, above all, of the gift of imagination, which make that life so delightful and so rich. A life of this sort is in itself a rebuke to the majority of us; and Mr Bridges' way of writing and publishing a still stronger rebuke, if he would but feel it, to the average man who writes and publishes. Here is a poet who issues three or four volumes of poetry, at intervals, quite quietly, for private circulation only, and then modestly selects a small number of them to offer to the public! But modesty has its disadvantages when one stands alone in practising it, and Mr Bridges has paid for his by remaining little known.

Of *Achilles* he said that

the dramatic faculty is not among the special gifts of Mr Bridges. It is just the gift which a quiet life in a country village cannot possibly produce. For the life and movement and passion a man must be willing to sacrifice repose and plunge into Johnson's 'full tide of human existence'. He must not refuse to surrender the living of his own life in order to observe how other men live theirs. This has not been Mr Bridges' way, and the consequence is that his play has many merits as a poem, but not many as a play.

These were the sort of remarks that were to be made time and again of Bridges: his public image was one of a man who had led a comfortable, sheltered, and happy life in the country, which he described with delicate, carefully crafted verse.

By October of that year Bridges was able to say that an American edition of *The Humours of the Court* and some twenty new lyrics would soon be published simultaneously with their English editions. He was also 'beginning to print the hymns which we have collected or set for the choir here'.[49] Most of Bridges' books published at this time were also issued in editions printed on handmade paper. When *Milton's Prosody* was published in this way in 1893, the Clarendon Press decided not to print the regular edition until all the special issue had been sold, with the result that Bridges had to exert himself to get it noticed. He wrote to Norman MacColl, the editor of the *Athenaeum*, appealing for help, in response to which a favourable review appeared in March 1894.

In December 1891 Monica's brother Maurice died suddenly. Maurice had been so delicate that he had not been able to go away to school but had been tutored at home. He was just 22 and it was a bad blow for the family. Bridges wrote to Muirhead, 'We have been in trouble. Maurice Waterhouse is dead, he got a chill skating in London, and died in 5 days. I do not know if you know how much beloved he was. The funeral is to be here on Monday.'[50] To Mrs Humphry Ward he said, 'Maurice's death was a terrible misfortune. I never met a nicer fellow. great natural gifts of all kinds and a most gentle nature. He was intending to take orders, & wd have been one of the sort in whose existence, you (not without reason) disbelieve.'[51] Bridges wrote a commemorative poem for the Waterhouses, choosing for it a tight rhyme-scheme:

I never shall love the snow again
    Since Maurice died:
With corniced drift it blocked the lane
And sheeted in a desolate plain
    The country side . . .

We fed the birds that flew around
    In flocks to be fed:
No shelter in holly or brake they found.
The speckled thrush on the frozen ground
    Lay frozen and dead.

We skated on stream and pond; we cut
    The crinching snow
To Doric temple or Arctic hut;
We laughed and sang at nightfall, shut
    By the fireside glow.

Yet grudged we our keen delights before
    Maurice should come.
We said, In-door or out-of-door
We shall love life for a month or more,
    When he is home.

They brought him home; 'twas two days late
    For Christmas day:
Wrapped in white, in solemn state,
A flower in his hand, all still and straight
    Our Maurice lay.

And two days ere the year outgave
    We laid him low.
The best of us truly were not brave,
When we laid Maurice down in his grave
    Under the snow.

The shock of this unexpected loss seems to have precipitated a stroke in Robert's mother that left her with delusions and depression. His eldest sister, Maria Lady Molesworth, came to help in looking after her and an attendant was hired, but Bridges was considerably upset and found it difficult to settle to any work. He and Monica had planned to go to Venice in the summer but abandoned the idea. They did, however, spend time going to concerts and exhibitions in London. Bridges and Roger Fry seem to have disagreed about the value of landscape painting. Robert tried to smooth their differences while sending him an account of the exhibition they had seen in London:

You need not defend landscape painting to me. I must have said more than I intended against it.—I do hate 'sketching' and have suffered from it.—This year there was an exhibition in London—you saw it before you left [for Italy] I expect—in which English landscape carried all before it. The old Italians were poorly represented, and Walker in a square 6 inches licked a wall side of Florentines. Also another victory of England over Italy to my mind is the contrast of certain portraits. Gainsboroughs and Romneys, with 2nd rate Venetian grandees. our 18th century admiral with his background of sea sky and cannon was godlike beside those snuffy stolid musty councillors. It was plain that he could not only beat them at fighting or dancing but wd strip much better, & there was an island breeziness about him, much more poetic than the velvet business.[52]

Bridges gave a similar 'breezy' account of another such trip to London in the first week of February 1893, when he and Monica stayed with the Barlows while their children were looked after by their grandparents. They

had not a bad visit altogether, crowding in many distractions, seeing pictures & hearing music, none of the best. the modern music gets to my taste worse and worse. The new concerted vocal music, part-songs by Brahms & Henschel, is extraordinary stuff. in my humble and stiffening opinion just intellectual rot. The pictures too were a melancholy spectacle. At least a gallery full of Burne Jones is depressing. at first sight of his best one is struck with admiration, but it is sad how the more one looks the less one admires. I never saw such badly drawn feet any where, his angels in the Creation have both gout and rickets, which is discouraging to the hopeful mortal who dreams of some day getting rid of deformities in heaven. and strange too it is that with his born artistic instinct and faculty he shd cut off parts of his chief figures with the frame. Insanity is not as great an enemy to art as affectation and ill conceived mannerism. London itself gets more and more intolerable every year. and the aesthetic development of the average man is very lamentable. every thing is self-conscious. Even the poor coalscuttle, which used only to don the ornaments of trade, and had no ambition above the 51 exhibition, is taking hints from Ruskin. One thing is an improvement: the electric light indoors. The house where we stayed had it, and the convenience was immeasurable.[53]

This is one of Bridges' grumpy but witty letters, more indicative of his mood than his considered opinion. He wrote elsewhere, for example, of Henschel as 'worth hearing' and of Brahms as the family's favourite composer, and in 1897 tried to persuade Burne-Jones to let him use his illustrations for an edition of *Eros and Psyche*.

In June 1893 Bridges and Fry had the first of several disagreements about portraits Fry had painted of Bridges' family. The first of these was of Elizabeth, and Robert objected that Fry had given her too large a head and too little childlike bloom of complexion. Later disagreements on such subjects were to be stronger. Bridges was rather more pleased with a portrait of himself by Charles Furse later in the same year. He also had contact with another artist, Robert Bateman, an old friend from London, asking him to do some woodcuts to illustrate the second edition of *Eros and Psyche*. Although Bateman sent Bridges sketches which he described as 'rather good', finished pieces were probably not completed in time for publication. June and July 1893 were spent on the Sussex coast at Bognor. Bridges told Fry, in a letter written to ease the tension between them, that 'our visit here has not been quite a success. None of us are I hope the worse for it. but we have not got as much benefit from the sea air as we thought we had a right to look for. It is a dreary and relaxing place, only the sands, the attraction, have not disappointed the children.'[54] Since Elizabeth, the Bridges had had two more children, Margaret in 1889 and Edward Ettingdene in 1892. Bridges was a devoted father, and after 1887 most of his letters to his friends contain anecdotes about the children. They visited Bosham, then spent three days at the Patmore's home, Feldmore, before returning home on 4 July.

In 1893 A. H. Miles decided to call the final volume of his series of the 'Poets and the Poetry of the Nineteenth Century' *Robert Bridges and Contemporary Poets*, and to use a photograph of Bridges as the frontispiece. This was probably the first public sign Bridges had of his growing reputation. Saintsbury made the encouraging comment that he deserved the prominent position.[55] In October Robert and Monica visited Herbert Warren, president of Magdalen College, Oxford, who was to write the introductory essay on Bridges for Miles' collection. In it he describes the poet as having a close affinity with early Milton, the Milton of the lines on Shakespeare, and the lines 'At a Solemn Music', of 'Comus' and 'Arcades'. . . He is content to be within the direct legitimate classic line. But he has advanced his art. He has rediscovered the forgotten metrical perfection of Milton, and has carried it still further . . . As a metrist, he is among the most subtle of our time, learned even to difficulty. Of blank verse especially, now that we have lost Lord Tennyson, there is no more nice, absolute, or various master living.

Warren spends considerable time on the plays, saying of them that, though 'they do not suggest the modern stage; yet I believe some of them would act exceedingly well'. However, he finds *The Growth of Love* Bridges' most impressive work, with the greatest range of thought and feeling. The 1895 introduction ended,

Selections are seldom satisfactory, least of all . . . in dealing with a poet whose beauty is not concentrated in purple patches or brilliant epigrams, but diffused through all this writing . . . Mr Bridges is a poet of this sort. His charm is subtle and wins gradually on the ear and on the mind . . . He has little or no rhetoric . . . Healthy, harmonious, happy . . . no living English poet more English or more true.

Bridges was to receive more concrete evidence of his status in November of 1894 when he was elected, with John Ruskin, an honorary fellow of his old Oxford college, Corpus Christi, and the following year nominated for the Chair of Poetry at Oxford, 'urged by an impressive list of supporters'.[56] He withdrew in favour of Courthope, saying that he wanted to spend his time in writing, not lecturing, but a letter to Muirhead shows that he was very pleased at the nomination.[57]

In April 1894 Wooldridge visited Bridges, who plunged into discussion of literature as well as music with him. At the time Bridges was reading a lot of Dante Gabriel Rossetti's poems in the complete edition that had just been published, and wrote to Dixon, who had been a friend of Rossetti's,

there is some shockingly poor verse got in especially a journal to and in Belgium—Also I am quite sure that his sonnets bore me profoundly. You used to admire them. I doubt whether you cd read them now without being of my opinion that they are sensuality affected to dullness—I think The White Ship is the best of his poems—it is magnificent. The Staff and Scrip, which you liked best is nearly as good. it wd be better if it did not betray a lot of affectations—it has splendid things in it. better than the ship—but the few blots put it in the second place.[58]

It seems quite likely that the tone of these comments characterized many of Bridges' letters to Hopkins about his poetry: enthusiasm, some warm praise, blunt but uncalculating criticism that disregards any sensitivity that might sway critical judgement.

In the same month A. H. Bullen asked him to prepare a critical introduction to an edition of Keats's poems. Bridges was unsure of being able to carry out the task successfully:

of course I think J. K. one of the highest gifted poets that was ever born into the world—and to give a worthy portrait of his mind, & at the same time a clear philosophical acc[oun]t of his ways towards nature and art etc—may prove beyond my powers.

I shd wish to get at more interesting and precise generalizations than the literary critics do. Otherwise Colvin's Keats is good. In any case I shall ask you to promise me that you will reject my essay if you do not like it.[59]

To Dr Gee Bridges wrote:

It used to be the fashion to say that he [Keats] was killed by a review in the Quarterly.

This nonsense has now given place to the tale that he was a feverish hectic lad with the 'seeds of consumption' in him, & that he died of an inherent malady aggravated by falling in love with Miss Brawne.

The true story has always seemed to me to be this.

(1) That his mother who after her second marriage led a very unhappy life, contracted 'consumption' in a not unusual manner. & then (2) infected her youngest child Tom. as is very common. (3) after her death John Keats nursed Tom till he died & in doing this caught the disease (4) so far from his being *especially* liable to it—tho' that he caught it shows him not to have been immune—he showed I shd say a peculiarly long resistance to it. He had what I shd conclude to have been a phthisical laryngeal affliction for nearly two years before he first spat up blood.

I shd like to say this if it is the right impression, and have wondered whether in the next month you wd have time to read *his letters*, & see whether you agree.

I recommend them on their own merits as one of the most interesting books I know they are perfectly straightforward & transparent . . .[60]

The essay also prompted correspondence and discussion with Margaret Woods, the wife of the President of Trinity College,

Oxford, who was establishing a reputation as a poet and novelist. After wrestling with the revised 'Hyperion', Bridges wrote to her:

the more I read it the more there seems to be in it. 2 or 3 things seem certain. (1) that Keats was influenced by Dante when he wrote it (2) that all the new visionary part is intended to be allegorical. Much of it is of course quite directly and unmistakably so.

I confess however that I cannot yet make out what it all means. What is the fire of the rainfall—or rather what is it that is being consumed, and on the consumption of which his life depends? And what is that life? And what is the feast? And what the drink which when he has drunk he swoons away—and awakes in a temple? (3) This also is clear, that on the interpretation of the new part the signification of the old Hyperion depends. It was not like Keats to try to work up an old poem into an allegory when he had not originally intended it for one . . . The extremely direct and severe style forbids one to suppose that there was any muddling about it, or a meaning only suggested and not carried through?[61]

Dixon, Wooldridge, and Maurice Hewlett, another poet and novelist, were also asked for advice. The essay was delayed in August by a couple of visits that Bridges made to Oxford in connection with the printing of his book of hymns, and in September he was distracted from it when Monica became ill with a lingering attack of bronchitis. He finally submitted it on 9 October. An anonymous reviewer in the *Times Literary Supplement* wrote (14 April 1905),

The most important thing in the muses' Library Edition is the introduction by Mr Bridges. Mr Bridges is not only a poet, but a profound student of the poetic art, and this thoughtful and suggestive essay is probably the best thing that has been written on the art of Keats . . . Mr Bridges always gives us the impression of . . . viewing the problem from the poet's point of view as well as the critic's.

But he disagreed with Bridges' explanation for the abandoning of 'Hyperion', saying that he had misunderstood the plot. Andrew Lang, in 'From a Scottish Workshop', wrote about Bridges' handling of 'Endymion': 'Mr Bridges . . . has, by his explanations, made the poem "readable as a whole, suggestive of meaning, and full of shadowy outlines of mysterious truth." This, of course, is the true and legitimate function of criticism . . . The necessary function Mr Bridges fulfils throughout his introduction to Keats with extraordinary tact and sympathy and poetic knowledge.'[62] In 1914 Bridges revised the essay, writing comments in the margin where he now disagreed with his original remarks. Of the abandoning of 'Hyperion' he wrote:

> Continuation in this vein was impossible at least to an artist like Keats. What ever mental qualities go to make a born artist, none is more essential than an unconscious enthralment to his creative conception. When any true and sane artist has strayed into a fault that falsifies his conception then his inspiration comes to a stand. Cd he go on, as if all were well, it wd be because he was lacking in the essential faculty wh makes artistic work good—Keats never rightly discerned the cause of his dissatisfaction.[63]

Like much good criticism, the essay is stimulating rather than completely convincing. Unfortunately, what has been filtered out and passed down in Keats criticism has been Bridges' objection to describing the nightingale as 'immortal bird', rather than his far more interesting remarks on rhythm and poetic form. Thompson points out that

> what admirers of Keats have most cause to thank Bridges for is the overwhelming proof he brought that the poet was determined to weed out inadequacies in his way of thinking and an unworthy attitude towards men and the world. This resolution to strengthen his work's intellectual content is clear in Keats's letters. But it was Bridges who first revealed it as actively at work in what had hitherto been taken to be a flaccid tentative redrafting [of '*Hyperion*'].[64]

10

Musical Collaborations (1891–1897)

In August 1891 Bridges' friend, the musician W. S. Rockstro, stayed with the family. He was not well off and appreciated having summer holidays at his wealthier friends' homes. The whole family liked him very much. 'He was,' said Bridges, 'the only thoroughly bad whist player that I ever enjoyed playing with: his wrong cards were offered with such genuine modesty and abundantly courteous apology that they were more than welcome.'[1] He contributed greatly to the music-making, and as an enthusiastic admirer of Homer who had compiled a dictionary of place-names connected with the *Iliad*, provided Bridges with literary discussion too.

Around the turn of the century there was in England a renaissance in both the writing and performance of music. The number of concerts and recitals in Britain increased and provincial music festivals grew in size and prestige. As interest in music as an academic subject spread, with more people applying for musical qualifications, the general standards of performance and ensemble work improved. Among the British composers active at the time three were prominent: Hubert Parry, Charles Stanford, and Edward Elgar. Bridges had been a friend of Parry since their days together at Eton, and, during the 1890s he devoted much of his energy to music and the relationship of words to music, collaborating with Parry and Stanford and discussing collaboration with Elgar.

The first of Bridges' musical collaborations was *Eden*, an oratorio composed by Stanford and now considered one of his more successful works. Hoping to obtain advance publicity, Bridges sent copies of the text to Saintsbury and to Gosse, who suggested that it should have been written in stanzas throughout, an idea that

Bridges rejected. According to Stanford's later account of the collaboration, he had noticed in the Wren Library in Cambridge the manuscript of Milton's initial ideas for *Paradise Lost* as a tragedy. It occurred to him that Milton's sketched plot would be suitable for an oratorio. 'There was happily,' Stanford said, 'one poet, as interested and knowledgeable in music as in his own craft, who was steeped to the lips in Milton, and whose style was more indebted to that master than any of his contemporaries, Mr Robert Bridges.'[2] Stanford was Professor of Music at Cambridge and could only compose in the vacations. This made for a schedule in which a lot was done in a short time, and Bridges was forced to write the three-act work more rapidly than he would have liked. The first act was set in Heaven and Bridges suggested using for it 'early modal methods, so as to contrast with the modern colouring of the second and third (Hell and Earth)'.[3] Stanford agreed to taking a series of lessons in modal writing from Rockstro, who was then living in Torquay.[4] Stanford decided to use the modes in the second act too for their associations with angels and devils; 'Mi contra Fa est Diabolus in musica' was incorporated in a witty musical parody. Bridges' description of the fall of Adam and Eve is far less condemnatory than Milton's: Adam is not seen as concupiscent and it is Eve who, recovering hope first, persuades the despairing Adam to turn to God in repentance. The third act contains three masques, visions of war, plague and famine, and the vision of the angels of Music and Poetry as comforters of Sorrow. Much of the gruesome detail that Bridges used in the first two of these can be found in Milton's sketched tragedy and in Book XI of *Paradise Lost*. The oratorio ends with Christ's words, 'Come unto me Ye weary and heavy-laden' and a chorus describing Adam and Eve falling asleep comforted by the promise of Christianity.

The Bridges attended the Birmingham Festival in October 1891, where *Eden* was performed. It received and has since been given a mixed reception by critics: George Bernard Shaw said of it, 'I caught not a single definite purpose or idea at all commensurate with the huge pretensions of the musical design. That pretension is the ruin of *Eden*.'[5] John Porte noted that 'from the purely constructive point of view' *Eden* is 'one of the most remarkable of Stanford's large works', but there are passages where, finding the music uninteresting, listeners should 'dip deeply into the libretto',[6] though he added, 'the conflict for first position in the eyes or ears of the audience hardly produces the finest possible effect'. J. A. Fuller-Maitland, reviewing Stanford's career in 1934, was more positive. After blaming the work's initial lack of success on the fact that 'the beauty of the ancient modes had not yet dawned even on the more intelligent part of the public', he described part of the music:

> The quotation from the hymn 'Sanctorum meritis' serves as a motto-theme for the whole of the first part, and the six-part chorus 'God of Might!' is a grand conception grandly carried out. The absence of the bass voice in this number is compensated in the baritone solo for the Angel of the Sun, with its most picturesque accompaniment. The climax of the scene is the 'Madrigale spirituale' in five parts *a capella*, a thing of radiant beauty. The final chorus 'of all angels' still without basses, makes a most effective ending to the 'act'. In the second 'act', after an introduction which recalls that to the second act of *Parsifal*, a chorus of 'all devils' parodies the first scene, and the triple apostrophe to Satan is a counterpart to the angels' triple address to God; at the very end of the act the angelic hymn is heard immediately after its parody, carrying out Satan's reference to
>
> the song, whose echo
> Sometimes makes vibrate here our iron vault.
>
> The part of Satan needs a singer of the calibre of Henschel, who sang it with perfect conviction both at Birmingham and in London, and the opportunities it gives to a great artist are as many in the third 'act' as in the second, if not more, because of the craft the tempter must indicate. The lovely pastoral introduction and duet, the clever *scherzando* movement where the serpent is seen, and the fruitless interjections of the angelic choir warning Eve of her danger, lead to a declamatory solo describing Adam's remorse; there is a prayer, and Michael and two angels join their voices with his (what becomes of Eve, by the way?). What remains can hardly fail to come as an anticlimax; Adam is shown a pageant . . . followed by words of Christ sung by six baritones of the chorus, a kind of lullaby in which the influence of Berlioz is to be detected, and a fine broad final chorus of all angels, this time complete with bass voices.[7]

Bridges' detailed awareness of the interrelationship between the words and music is clear in a letter he wrote to Stanford while they were preparing the text for publication:

I congratulate you. The words I wrote for the bad place are (I mark the bars and suggested rests)

Behind them 𝄾 [O happy| sight!] 𝄾 my sons I see 𝄽 | crowned and bright as the | Seraphim 𝄾 | 𝄾 that in God's | presence 𝄽 sing the | threefold hymn.

I should like *God's* a semibreve. If you must move on it I myself prefer ♩. ♪ to ♩ ♩.[8]

He also commented to Stanford that he had in fact changed his wording at one point, turning 'to soil the glory of God' into 'to soil the might of God'. *Eden* was dedicated to Hubert Parry because he had generously abandoned plans for a similar project when he heard of Stanford's work.

Wooldridge spent January 1891 at Yattendon, visited again in May and June, and again spent Christmas with the Bridges, clinging to the fireside and refusing to take exercise in the cold weather. He wrote several good double chants for Bridges' hymn-book, but Robert was not sorry when he left. The Hymnal grew out of Bridges' nine years as precentor of the Yattendon choir, a post he resigned in 1894 through growing dislike of the local vicar's sermons. After this, instead of going to two services each Sunday he seldom attended the church, and replaced direct work with the choir with work on providing a hymnal for them and for more general use. He explained: 'when I gave up my office, I printed the first twenty-five hymns for the convenience of the choir, and also for the sake of the tunes by Jeremy Clark [the seventeenth-century composer whom he considered the originator of English hymnody], which I had been at some pains to restore, and for the preservation of the tunes composed on our behalf by Professor Wooldridge.' In his essay, 'A Practical Discourse on some Principles of Hymn-singing' Bridges explained his choice of composers. He started from the premiss that,

Music being the universal expression of the mysterious and supernatural, the best that man has ever attain'd to, is capable of uniting in common devotion minds that are only separated by creeds, and it comforts our hope with a brighter promis of unity than any logic offers. And if we consider and ask ourselves what sort of music we should wish to hear on entering a church, we should surely, in describing our ideal, say first of all that it must be something different from what is heard elsewhere; that it should be a sacred music, devoted to its purpos, a music whose peace should still passion, whose dignity should strengthen our faith, whose unquestion'd beauty should find a home in our hearts, to cheer us in life and death . . .[9]

'Good melody', he said, 'is never out of fashion', and the plainsong melodies whose unbarred rhythms 'dance at liberty with the voice and sense' instead of 'plumping down . . . on the first note of every bar whether it wil or no' have clear advantages.[10] Finding that many of the tunes he liked had no suitable texts, he provided over forty out of the final collection of one hundred hymns with new words, generally translations.

The bulk of the melodies were by nine composers: 4 tunes from Heinrich Isaac; 13 from Louis Bourgeois; 4 from Christopher Tye; 8 from Thomas Tallis; 8 from Orlando Gibbons; 13 from Johann Crueger; 9 from Jeremiah Clark; 8 from William Croft, and 8 from J. S. Bach. Wooldridge wrote seven tunes and Lionel one. Most of these required harmonizing, which was done by Monica and Wooldridge, who used for the plainsong melodies a Palestrinal harmonization intended for unaccompanied singing in four parts. Bridges continued with his family the custom of his childhood of spending Sunday evenings gathered round the piano singing hymns. Convinced that too frequently those who could not afford expensive things were forced to accept the 'cheap and nasty', he arranged for a cheap but aesthetically pleasing edition of the hymnal in addition to the luxury edition produced by Oxford University Press. Bridges hoped that the latter would be 'one of the handsomest music books ever printed'. He told Samuel Gee that, 'the type is being cast for me at the Clarendon Press from some old matrices that were brought to England from Holland by Dr Fell in 1670 or thereabouts. They have never been used. They are also recasting a contemporary word fount to match.—It will be very beautiful. I shall bring out some 32 pages at a time. If I do as I intend it will be the beginning of a lot of music printing.'[11] Over the next five years (1894–9) four parts containing twenty-five hymns each were published, as the *Yattendon Hymnal*, along with the *Small Hymn-book* giving the words but not the music, the *Yattendon Hymns* containing hymns not in *Hymns Ancient and Modern*, a composite edition, and several limited issues. The Hymnal was noticed by members of the committee formed to revise *Hymns Ancient and Modern* who considered it 'too short for congregational use' but 'within its limits', of 'incomparable value'. They expressed the wish that 'we may some day see it enlarged and made more easily accessible'.[12] Thirteen of the hymns were included in the English Hymnal. Bridges was asked to join the committee, but finding that it was likely to spend much of its time on hymns that he thought insipid and sentimental, he declined the invitation.

Musical friends came to stay at Yattendon in the summer of 1892 and Bridges reported to Dixon that there were 'no end of trios and string quartets in the air'.[13] A new friend, G. E. P. Arkwright, who edited a great deal of old English music, generously sent the Bridges several volumes of madrigals by Byrd and Kirby. Wooldridge was also at work on old music at this time, re-editing Chappell's *Popular Music of the Olden Time*.

In October 1894 Bridges wrote to Parry,

> Squire has written to me to say that you might be writing a Cantata or short choral piece for the Leeds Festival next year and that you would do an 'Ode to Music' which might also serve for the Purcell Festival, and that you [would] like to hear my ideas on the subject . . . I write at once to you to say how glad I should be to do it with you, lest you might think I was indifferent. Also to prevent there being any misunderstanding. I should wish you to understand that whatever passes between us I shall never consider you in the least bound but free to give up the notion at any time.
>
> On my side I can't promise to have the requisite inspiration to order, but I see a splendid opportunity for something new, and popular. My idea is to show music in its various relations to the passions and desires of man: as something supernatural mysterious and consolatory: which it always is to me. Also it seems to me that something quite new might be done in the music by the blending of the different attitudes of mind or spirit instead of their merely isolated contrast as in Handel's *Alexander's Feast*.[14]

Bridges would have liked closer consultation than was allowed by Parry's busy new schedule as Director of the Royal College of Music, and tried to compensate for the lack of discussion by providing Parry with a variety of musical opportunities from which to choose.

The ode marks a fresh departure in Parry's musical development—a turning away from the style of oratorio towards forms that have been compared with Bach's cantatas. He was to set three works of this sort to words by Bridges—the *Invocation to Music*, *A Song of Darkness and Light* (published 1898), and *The Chivalry of the Sea* (published 1916, and performed by the Bach Choir in the Albert Hall on 12 December 1916), and the two also collaborated on an *Eton Memorial Ode* (1908). Bridges' letters reveal that, although he tried to give Parry as free a hand as he could with the *Invocation to Music*, he often felt that the composer was fussing unnecessarily. But Parry's delay may suggest not pernicketiness but the importance he accorded the work. Dedicated to Purcell, the ode was given a first performance at the Leeds Festival in 1895, then put on later that year at the commemoration for Purcell in London. Bridges was away and missed Parry's letter listing the dates of the performances. He told Parry,

I am very sorry to have missed the opportunity, but I doubt whether if I had been home I could have managed to make all the prearrangements necessary to secure reasonable comfort . . . I had to content myself with buying all the penny papers as I came up in the train yesterday, and reading what the critics said. I gathered two things. 1st that the Ode had really been a success, and 2ndly that the critics are a poor lot. It is extraordinary that they cannot give one a better notion of what has taken place.[15]

Bridges sent the ode to Dixon and, when it was returned, commented,

I was rather disappointed at your having nothing to say about the Dirge—which I fancy is as good a thing as I have written. I guess that its Ecclesiastes vein was unsympathetic to you. But the point of it was to express that view of the matter—and the moral of it is that the poetical expression of it is *the* (or at least *a*) cure for the melancholy. This it seems to me is what art has to do. To satisfy by expression. In the ode Sorrow complains that art having left the country she has no expression for her soul—and she asks for comfort. Music gives her the comfort of this most melancholy dirge—the next movement is more cheerful, and passes off into a sort of triumph.[16]

The 'dirge' is prepared for by the movement (no. 6) that Bridges described to Dixon in which Sorrow asks Music to give her a means of expressing her grief. Yet in the dirge itself the refrain of loss appears at the end of the second verse, where it comes almost abruptly to end the description of man's joy in the beauties of nature. In literature and choral work the pervasiveness and unexpected arrival of death is often presented in a more overtly threatening way. Here it is introduced gently, almost with euphemism. It opens a refrain that is lovely and characteristic of Bridges in its ahistorical mixture of diction:

> Then he hideth his face;—
> Whence he came to pass away
> Where all is forgot,
> Unmade—lost for aye
> With the things that are not.

Fuller-Maitland considered that, although 'it happens very rarely with Parry that his music fails to enhance the beauty of the words he sets . . . his treatment of Bridges's fine *Invocation to Music* . . . must be admitted to fall below the poem in emotional value. The pastoral pictures at the end of the tenor solo, and the "dirge" for bass, are its most remarkable points, and there is an impressive seven-part close.'[17]

In 1931 the dirge caught the attention of Gustav Holst, who wrote a second setting of it. Called *Choral Fantasia*, it was first performed at the Three Choirs Festival. Holst's daughter, Imogen, in a detailed description of the work, believed that it contained movements in which Holst managed 'to find the warmth [of tonality] he had been searching for' ever since listening to a performance of the Schubert Quintet that had provoked a crisis of confidence in 1929. 'He was to lose [the warmth] again, in moments of weariness, during the few remaining years. But having once found it, he could shake off the horror of numbness and isolation. There was to be no more despair.'[18] She concluded that as well as marking a turning-point in Holst's career, showing him 'able to move forward' into the final phase of his writing 'with all the strength of his mature experience', it was a composition of immense personal importance to him.

When the *Invocation* was published in 1896, Bridges wrote a preface for it in which he stated his objection to the popular trend of giving poems declamatory choral settings. His objections were not, he said, to the setting that Parry had given his ode, which 'far beyond its deserts, honour'd and beautify'd' it, but to Parry's apparent advocacy of the declamatory method in his book, *The*

Art of Music (1893). Bridges pointed out that since the declamatory method is close to *recitativo secco*, it is not the most effective way of marrying words and music. The formal structures of music and verse are different, so that rhythms, cadences of phrases, and distribution of climax all achieve different effects. Bridges claimed that the two forms can be more effectively united if the differences of the two arts are respected: 'the best musical treatment of passages of great poetic beauty is not to declaim them, but, as it were, to woo them and court them and caress them, and deck them with fresh musical beauties; approaching them tenderly now on one side, now on another, and to keep a delicat reserve which shall leave their proper unity unmolested.'[19] Parry was able to accept that Bridges was not making a personal attack on him but challenging a contemporary practice that he considered seriously flawed. They collaborated on two further occasions and after Parry's death it was Bridges who in 1921 wrote the memorial inscription to him that was placed in Gloucester Cathedral.[20]

In addition to Bridges' musical collaborations, poems by him were set to music by a number of composers. Stanford's *Six Songs of Robert Bridges* (1891–2) are considered 'among the best of the composer's smaller vocal works'.[21] His setting of 'Since thou, O fondest and truest' was described as 'exquisite' by Fuller-Maitland.[22] Parry also set a number of Bridges' poems, among them the sonnet paraphrasing the Lord's Prayer from *The Growth of Love*, which he set as a motet in six parts; two poems in *Six Modern Lyrics* (1897–8); 'Ye thrilled me once' in *Eight four-part Songs* (1898); and 'My delight and thy delight' which he found a 'thoroughly congenial' subject in 1910.[23] In 1916 Frank Bridge, who had studied under Stanford and was to teach Benjamin Britten, set Bridges' early triolet, 'All women born are so perverse', for voice and piano. Gerald Finzi, who became Professor of Composition at the Royal Academy of Music, wrote part-songs to Bridges' poems between 1934 and 1937. And between 1925 and 1927 Holst set seven of Bridges' poems as 'Seven Part-Songs for Female Voices and Strings'. Although Bridges may not always have been completely happy with the results, he was excited about these new experiments and, through his collaboration with contemporary British composers, became part of this renaissance.

★

In 1895 the Bridges spent their summer holiday in Cornwall, where they stayed at St Ives, taking up Sir Arthur Quiller-Couch's long-standing invitation to visit his home at Fowey. From there they went to Oxford where they stayed with the Daniels, and Bridges began a campaign to have Wooldridge elected as Slade Professor of Art at Oxford, a position for which he was chosen in July. In September the Bridges returned to the south-west, 'assisting' at a stag hunt near Porlock Weir in Exmoor. It was a well-earned rest from the combined efforts of the critical essay on Keats, the *Invocation*, and seeing the first part of the *Yattendon Hymnal* through the Press.

The opening months of 1896 were spent on the second volume of the Hymnal. This section, which Bridges considered of higher quality than Part I, included a number of translations of Latin hymns. Like Hopkins, Bridges made a translation of part of the long, twelfth-century hymn, 'Jesu dulcis memoria', although his version is less successful, largely because he tries to rhyme all four lines whereas Hopkins had used couplets within the quatrains. The work on the hymn-book kept him busy and that, combined with worry about Monica, who fell ill at Christmas and took some months to recover, probably led to his responding a little brusquely to Mrs Hopkins' enquiry as to whether he would like to look through some of Gerard's musical compositions.

> I shd of course very much like to see them and I shall hope to do so some day when I am at Haslemere again, which I shall hope to be ere long, but unless you have any particular reason for sending them I am sure that I have not time just now to enter into their subtleties. Gerard had a notion of starting music, as everything else, on new lines, and I cannot without great difficulty follow his intentions so as to do them justice. Honestly I think that his ingenious inventions do not lead to anything. and I have not myself the delicacy of ear to fully understand them.[24]

Wooldridge too did not think very highly of Hopkins' compositions, believing that he used too many inverted chords and that he needed to practise strict harmony; recent work, though, has suggested that, with encouragement, his ideas might have been productive.[25]

Hoping to hasten Monica's recovery, Bridges took his family to Seaford for a week at the end of March and beginning of April.

From there he wrote to Muirhead praising Wooldridge's lectures as Slade Professor of Art: 'I suppose there has never been anything of the kind so good.'[26] His audience grew during the series until every seat was filled and people sat on the floor at the front and leant against the walls at the back. He was twice re-elected to the post. Wooldridge was still collaborating with Bridges on the Hymnal and was to contribute to the third part, but then devoted himself, to Bridges' regret, to the writing of a textbook on counterpoint. He was also editing music for the Purcell Society.

In July 1897 the whole family made what was to become an annual visit to stay with Edward Moore, one of Bridges' mother's relatives. Bridges had come to know him in London when they acted together as executors for his mother's favourite brother, George Danby. Moore was an Irish Orangeman who, said Bridges, 'as many Irishmen, was able to be humorous without affronting intelligence'.[27] He had inherited his aunt's property in 1892 and had bought a somewhat ugly Victorian stone-built house a mile from Wells on the lower slopes of the Mendips. During morning prayers Bridges would position himself in the bay window and gaze down on the cathedral and the small hills stretching away to Glastonbury Tor. The house faced south and had a wide lawn ending in a ha-ha held up by a wall covered with ferns and toadflax on which Bridges used to stretch out, reading and dozing. Monica practised riding a bicycle. If no special excursion was planned for the day the Bridges would set off to the cathedral, where Percy Buck was organist. The choir was good and the acoustics excellent, and Bridges admired the choir's traditional chanting which preserved the speech-rhythms of the psalms.

By August Monica was well again and was becoming more adventurous in her bicycle riding. Bridges ordered a machine for himself. Although the roads for several miles around Yattendon were in bad condition, he thought that it would be possible to ride over to the Muirhead's home near Reading, but they do not seem to have done this very often.

11

A New Generation of Writers (1894–1899)

Throughout his life Bridges dipped into books that were popular and newly published. His reading in 1894 included Benjamin Kidd's *Social Evolution*, with which Bridges found himself in general agreement, and Alice Meynell's *Rhythm of Life and Other Essays*, which Patmore sent him—he thought that one or two of the essays were 'really as good as possible'. Of John Davidson's *Ballads and Songs* he wrote that he was disappointed. Davidson had, he declared, 'more imaginative poetic power than any man of my time, & yet he can't put a thing together decently, and now has gone off on common claptrap fads, & mere flash. I am afraid he will never do well'[1], an opinion shared by W. B. Yeats. When Daniel visited the Bridges with his family in April 1895 he brought with him the proofs of a volume of poetry by Laurence Binyon. Bridges had begun to correspond with Binyon in May 1890 when the latter, at that point still an undergraduate, had sent him a letter on his *Milton's Prosody*. Having seen some of Binyon's poems in July 1891 he had suggested that he needed to make a conscious effort to escape from Byron's influence and use more 'elevated expression'. The new volume of verse that Daniel showed Bridges in 1895 impressed him; the poems reminded him of Dixon's, but used a new prosody and, although not 'quite masterly', he thought them full of 'poetical beauty'. Other critics thought he was influenced by Bridges. Binyon, Robert predicted, would do well: 'he has good feeling, a true mind and a wonderful visual memory.'[2] He had taken a job at the British Museum cataloguing books where he made his career, becoming an expert on Oriental art and eventually the Keeper of the large Department of Prints and Drawings. The friendship between the two men lasted for the rest of Bridges' life, fostered by mutual concern. As an old man Binyon remembered having had an attack of influenza in the 1890s for which Robert has sent him three bottles of his best wine with an offer of more.

Among the other poets of the younger generation whom Bridges met at this time was Henry Newbolt, whose background was much like his own and who, like him, had been a student at Corpus Christi. There his interest in poetry had brought him into contact with Bridges' friend, Margaret Woods. On leaving Oxford Newbolt had gone to London and been called to the bar, but had continued to write. His interest was sustained by a small literary society, 'the Settee', founded by his wife Margaret. He wrote poems, not only for the magazine of his old school, Clifton, but also for such journals as the *Spectator*, *St James Gazette*, and, at the instigation of Andrew Lang, *Longman's Magazine*. The Newbolts were friends of the Waterhouses and it was while staying with them in 1896 that Henry first met Bridges.

At dinner that evening almost the only guests besides ourselves were Robert and Monica Bridges, who walked up from the Manor House below . . . The general talk after dinner turned for a time upon a charge of idolatry recently made against those who were for placing carved figures upon a church screen. After several opinions had been heard, Bridges came suddenly out of his silence and argued decisively that no human beings, not even the heathen, could in any true sense of the word worship wood or stone. I asked him if that implied approval of all ornaments or ritual. 'It would', he said, 'if they were in good taste, but they are generally hideous'.[3]

It was agreed that the Newbolts would visit the Bridges in April 1897, staying at Pargiters, a house in the village adjacent to the Manor House. Robert asked to see Newbolt's verse, much of which was of a patriotic nature in vogue at the time. Partly, no doubt, in preparation for the encounter, Newbolt read Bridges' poetry and found that he liked it. In April, once he and his wife had established themselves at Pargiters, Newbolt collected some of his poems and set out for the Manor House. He later recalled,

I found Robert Bridges lying in the sun on his own doormat, with his spaniel Ben beside him. There were some six or seven steps up to the entrance and dog and master were both stretched comfortably against the front door, where there was just room for me to join them. Bridges was dressed with the most elegant shabbiness, in an old grey felt hat, an old but well-cut lounge coat, and narrow lavender-grey trousers of nankeen, a material then so obsolete that I never saw it worn by any other man, except, I think, Mr Wyndham of Clouds.

Like so many other people, Newbolt has left a record of his admiration for Bridges' appearance and manner: 'his fine stature, his masculine beauty, the rich character that sounded in his voice . . . every tone and every trick of him had the rarity that we call distinction.'

'"Now", said Bridges when I had settled down opposite to him, "You've got some verses for me—is that fat book full of them?" "No", I said, "there are only a few, and I think they're quite legible".' The first poem Newbolt showed to Bridges was 'Drake's Drum', which he praised warmly. Typically, during the rest of Newbolt's visit, Bridges tried tactfully to interest the younger man in learning more about prosodic theory. According to Newbolt, Bridges advised him to give up the bar and concentrate on his writing, advice which he was to follow with great success.

Bridges' style was nothing like Newbolt's but Victorian imperialist patriotism had been growing since the 1860s and, like Hopkins, Bridges was susceptible to the appeal of such subjects; he liked much that Kipling wrote while taking exception to the swearing and some of his colloquial language. But Bridges was a poet who wrote best out of his own observation, and patriotic subjects were sufficiently far from his personal experience that he wrote practically nothing successful along these lines, although he tried on a number of occasions. He planned, for example, in 1896 to write an heroic poem on the Siege of Gibraltar, for which Newbolt lent him two books, but these merely left him with 'a strong impression of the general follies of man. especially of the paradoxical desertions from side to side, which appear to follow some law, like that of the unaddressed letters in the Post Office—& of the waste of ammunition'.[4] There is no trace of such a heroic poem among Bridges' papers. Two years later he attempted to write some verses on the Boer War, in which two of his nephews were fighting, but did not like the poems sufficiently to include them later in his *Poetical Works*. In 1900 he commented on the war to Samuel Gee,

> You say you have been reading the newspapers. as for me. when I found out that our military authorities had taken none of the necessary precautions & made none of the common sense preparations, which I or any intelligent layman cd have told them of years ago; & that our generals were behaving in a foolhardy way: after about 3 sleepness nights I gave up looking at the papers, and never in my life I think have kept myself so studiously uninformed as to what was going on. It was no use worrying as one could not help. Now they tell me things look better, and I read the paper yesterday. But I do not believe in their advantage at this Spion's Kopje: It seems to me that it was practically undefended, and that we lost any number of men as soon as we got there. It seems as if it might be another trap. | The behaviour of the country & and the Colonies and the private soldier has been splendid: no better sign of national life cd be wished. 15 years ago no one wd have thought it was possible.[5]

He did not reveal his misgivings so clearly to Newbolt. Later he was to comment to him on the Russo-Japanese War: 'It seems to me that this war is a very favourable opportunity for persons who have the ear of the public to make a general protest in favour of a European concert for arbitration & mutual reduction of armaments—Do you think anything could be done?'[6] It is little wonder that he later approved so heartily of a League of Nations.

In 1898 Newbolt dedicated his volume of poems, *The Island Race* to Bridges, a compliment that he failed to notice in his first reading of the book but which, finding it a week later, he appreciated. The Newbolts also organized a dinner in London expressly in the hope 'of seeing Bridges as the Londoner he had once been'. This, Newbolt records,

> 'was a complete success—he was a new man, a resplendent figure and a gay and confident talker. He discoverd by some instinct, during dinner, what I did not myself know, that Basil Levett, who sat near him, was an expert in English Hymns, and they became so thick together over their wine and their church music that we were very late in reaching the drawing-room. There, to my astonishment I saw Bridges take possession of a stool and seat himself at Lady Margaret Levett's feet for the rest of the evening, flashing wit and humour from every facet . . .[7]

Bridges' admiration for Newbolt's poetry seems to have faded. In May 1905 he only reluctantly prepared a selection of his poems for inclusion in an expanded edition of A. H. Miles' *Robert Bridges and Contemporary Poets*. He consulted Newbolt about the choice of poems to be included and appealed to him for information for the preface. His criteria are interesting:

> The thing is to write something which interests a general reader—criticism is best avoided in the case of a living writer and a friend—I fancy the subjects of your muse might give occasion for reference to pedigree, (which does interest people). with that and the main biographical facts: and some material statistics of bibliographical success there shd be no difficulty in making a distinguished & interesting memoir.[8]

Bridges' introduction is only two pages long and the pedigree is worked into the first paragraph:

> Mr. Newbolt's fame is associated with the flush of patriotism which so suddenly overspread England in the last decade of Victoria's reign, and for his subject-matter and simple appeal he has been reckoned a follower of Mr. Kipling; he is, however, artistically independent of that writer, and drew even his Indian interest directly through his own family, while his general sentiments were probably uninspired by fashion. Of such an author the interest of a line of forefathers settled in one place, from the 15th to the 20th century, is worth recording, and that one of his ancestors was Mayor of Winchester in the year of the Armada, and stood arrayed to fight, if need were . . . and that his grandfather, as a midshipman of eighteen, steered the Menelaus in the cutting-out expedition of San Stefano.
>
> (p. 561)

The penultimate paragraph contains Bridges' technical assessment:

> Mr. Newbolt holds not only the literary and the common reading public, but his songs have been sung by camp fires, and his pages thumbed in military hospitals. Praise and description are unnecessary, and I have only one critical remark to append: The old ballads and songs, with which his own range so worthily, owe much of their masculine vigour to a roughness of composition that lies outside metrical art. Mr. Newbolt by a learned use of a free accentual rhythm has come to retain this effect without violating metrical structure. As his enthusiasm never degenerates into nonsense, so his rhythmical liberty does not offend the musical ear or the metric rule . . . Few poets, for the real satisfaction and pleasure which all the pieces will give to all readers, could match the following selection.
>
> (p. 562)

The praise is not mean but measured. It does, however, suggest that although Newbolt's verse may have been widely popular, by 1905 Bridges himself admired rather than liked it.

Another of the younger generation of writers, and another member of 'the Settee', whom Bridges met in 1895 or 1896 was Mary Coleridge, great-grand-niece of Samuel Taylor Coleridge. One of Monica's relations, Violet Hodgkin, made a copy of Mary's poems, 'all in printing capitals, in a little book which she carried about with her. She was anxious that the poems should be published, and got permission from Mary C. to show them to [Bridges] anonymously, on the understanding that if [he] approved of them she would have them printed.' She left the volume with Bridges, who thought so well of the poems that he persuaded Henry Daniel to print them in 1896.[9] Mary became a good friend of the family, visiting Yattendon several times. In March 1897 she wrote to Newbolt, 'here they live artistically, not demanding of life what it cannot yield, but drawing out all that it can. Nothing is wasted, and they are not self-conscious nor restless . . .' She described working on a translation with Bridges: 'the words come swarming, buzzing round, like bees—the smoke curls up from his pipe—the eternal possibilities of every tiny paragraph bewilder and stimulate me so that an hour goes like a moment. Monica joins the dance when she has time; she is astonishingly good.' It was, she concluded, 'a magnificent lesson in style'.[10]

In 1896 Bridges also read W. B. Yeats's *Poems* (1895), which their mutual friend, J. W. Mackail, had drawn to his attention. *Poems* contained work printed in *The Wanderings of Oisin*, *Crossways*, and *The Rose*. Some of the lines in 'Oisin' were, Bridges said, 'as good as Homer', but he noted in the margins the frequent recurrence of such words as 'pale', 'old', 'dim', 'glimmer', and 'dreary'. To Yeats he wrote in June 1896 one of his charming, self-effacing letters:

Dear Sir,

I have been reading your poems which my friend Mr Mackail introduced me to. I write to tell you how much I admire a great deal of them, and what pleasure they gave me.

I know that I run the risk of being considered impertinent, but I had rather you should think that than perhaps misinterpret my silence.

Hoping that you will excuse the liberty that I take in writing, and that you will write more and meet soon with the success which your work must ultimately reach.[11]

Yeats finally responded to Bridges' note with an absent-mindedly unsigned letter in December. He remarked, 'your praise of my work gave me great pleasure as your work is to me the most convincing poetry done by any man among us just now . . . Your work alone has the quietude of wisdom and I do most firmly believe that all art is dedicated to wisdom . . .'[12] Yeats had seen the copy of *Prometheus the Firegiver* that Hopkins had given to Professor Dowden. He was now working on *The Shadowy Waters*, and discovered in Bridges qualities that he was aiming at in the play: 'a more remote wisdom . . . a visionary harvest', qualities that critics were to find unappealing.

By January 1897 Yeats was planning to establish a small theatre for the performance of romantic drama, and one of the plays that he wanted to produce was Bridges' *Return of Ulysses*. Bridges invited Yeats to visit Yattendon in the spring for a discussion on rhythm since he had detected in *Poems* rhythms that were 'entirely new'. Yeats accepted, adding, 'I . . . would much like to discuss with you questions of rhythm, for though I work very hard at my rhythm I have but little science on the matter and as a result probably offend often. Without a consistent science it is difficult to distinguish between license and freedom.'[13]

Newbolt was present during Yeats's visit and later described it. Yeats had worn a 'long frock-coat with gracefully flowing skirts, and round his neck an enormous tie of purple silk, tied in a bow end floating down to his waist uncontrolled by waistcoat or pin'. This costume made it very difficult for Yeats to join in the Sunday afternoon's entertainment of 'small cricket', but he had been more in his element talking about the Tarot. Bridges was interested and, although not prepared to experiment himself, was intrigued and disturbed by Monica's experience when, pressing one of the cards to her forehead, she immediately had the vision that Yeats had predicted. Afterwards, Bridges walked up and down the garden with Newbolt trying to explain the vision in scientific terms. He spent the evening with Yeats and, thinking that a short discussion of the Tarot might put the younger man at his ease for a talk about rhythm, found himself instead smoking pipe after pipe as Yeats talked on and on about the occult. When the Irishman left the following day Bridges urged him to come again and stay longer, but to bring some work to do and avoid talk of visions. Despite his fears of the effect of Rosicrucianism and the occult on Yeats, he told Newbolt 'he's a great poet: a better poet than I am'.[14]

Yeats had meanwhile been reading Bridges' work in preparation for an article which was published in the *Bookman* in June. Retitled and greatly shortened, it was later included in *Ideas of Good and Evil*. In it Yeats extended the comments he had made to Bridges about *The Return of Ulysses* and added notes on his other plays and *Prometheus*, which he found 'vigorous and simple, though a little slow in its motion'. The others, he said, 'appear to me rather loose in their hold on character and incident, and . . . do not move me greatly'. The criticisms are astute and much like those he was later to apply to his own *Shadowy Waters*. Yeats faulted Bridges for insufficient negative capability, for arranging characters and events according to his knowledge of history rather than relying on his instinct. In part this was intentional and a difference in taste between the two poets, since Bridges felt that Yeats's fault was too heavy a reliance on his instinct. Yeats concluded his review with comments on the poems. 'I know', he said, 'of no poet of our time, and few of our Century, who can so perfectly knead thought and rhythm into the one mystical body of faint flame.' He said much the same thing to Tagore in 1915, adding, 'I feel that he is the head of my craft in England and have felt so since the death of Swinburne, or from before it for Swinburne's abundant genius repelled me.'[15] When contributing to the purchase of the clavichord given to Bridges in 1924, Yeats told Sassoon, 'I am very glad indeed to do so as I have always so greatly admired his work. It has an emotional purity and rhythmical delicacy no living man can equal.'

Sending Bridges his collection of short stories, *The Secret Rose*, Yeats asked for criticism of it and *The Celtic Twilight*. Bridges annotated about three-quarters of *The Secret Rose* and told Yeats that he admired the style in which the tales had been written, but suggested that their effect was marred by an 'apparent insistence on the part of the writer to have them taken otherwise (i.e. more seriously) than he suspects the reader would naturally take them'.[16] He noted that 'some of the stories of course are more telling and interesting than others—I do not however fall in comfortably with the humour of crucifying the beggar'. He added, 'I expect that while we agree absolutely about the necessity for mysticism, we do not take quite the same view of the value of the phenomena in themselves, but I can't write about this'. Bridges' view of the world, as it is seen in some of his essays, and most clearly in *The Testament of Beauty*, does indeed have a mystical basis but it is of a broadly Christian kind.

Bridges continued to urge Yeats to use Yattendon as a place to which to retire while he worked. Like Lady Gregory, whose home was soon to provide just this sort of haven for Yeats, Bridges, with his doctor's eye, probably saw that Yeats was rapidly undermining his health with overwork and a scanty diet, and was badly in need of a refuge. In his offer Bridges was not moved just by the wish to aid a greatly gifted man, but hoped too for the excitement of literary discussion with him. When in June 1899 Yeats sent Bridges an inscribed copy of *The Wind Among the Reeds*, he found that Bridges had already purchased it. In the back of the volume are order forms placed there later for *Poems* (1906), on which Bridges transcribed the second stanza of 'The Withering of the Boughs' and the fifth stanza of 'Adam's Curse'. He also owned *Autobiographies*, in which he marked sections about people he had known, *Reveries*, *The Trembling of the Veil*, which was given to him by S. B. Jackson, and *Responsibilities*. Yeats sent him two more volumes in 1915. Though the friendship was not close, Bridges and Yeats did correspond over the years and met on a number of occasions. Bridges wrote in 1907:

> My dear Poet,
>
> I have not heard that you have got married since I saw you last, therefore you must rely on your dramatic imagination to tell you what you wd do if your mother-in-law were an anthologist and she were to ask you to make use of the slight friendship between us (which you have so selfishly neglected) to persuade me to allow her to print some of my poems in her anthology. It is as you may have guessed Mrs Waterhouse of Yattendon who insists on approaching you in this roundabout way, and I enclose her request . . . I do not wish that out of kindness to me you shd do anything unusual. I have a great abhorrence of these anthologists, tho' I now and then get something out of them. But I believe that the multiplication of their poetry books does really hinder the sale of poems.[17]

He ended the letter with an invitation to Yeats to visit the family.

A number of portraits of Bridges were done in 1897–8. Yeats's friend, William Rothenstein, who drew many of the figures of the day—Hardy, Yeats, Verlaine, E. M. Forster, Pater, Einstein, Sir

Henry Acland—did a number of drawings of Bridges and a lithograph, which was exhibited among his *English Portraits*, as was one he did of Dixon, which initially Bridges liked enough to frame. However, he later wrote to Dixon, 'I have had your portrait hanging up now for some time and I think I know what I think about it. It is a wretched piece of work.'[18] Despite this recognition that Rothenstein was capable of somewhat careless work, and the fact that Bridges found him hard to get to know, he liked and respected him and sat for two more drawings in 1916. Monica reported to her sister that during his 1897 visit Rothenstein had been very 'entertainable', playing whist well, drawing beautiful pictures for the children, and accompanying the family on a bicycle tour to Newbury. Others who painted Bridges at this time included Muirhead, who completed a portrait, and William Strang, who did an etching. Bridges concluded that Strang thought him 'a cross between Moses and an old lion', with the result that 'the etching had the disadvantage of not being very like' him.[19]

Bridges' mother died suddenly on 14 December 1897. Bridges felt that they had parted long ago when her memory and capacity for coping with everyday life had declined. 'I feel', he told Samuel Gee, 'that I shall have to face the sorrow which her loss will be to us, when the old memories return as they will do after the sad routine of these last years has faded away'.[20] But the new generation absorbed his attention too. His children were sufficiently old now that he engaged a governess for them. She was, he said, tongue-in-cheek, 'a success—so far. She can play whist.' Bridges, however, found himself missing the stimulus of the circle of artistic and literary friends that he had had in London. Now 54, he was beginning to feel his age and was not as fit as he might have been. Partly in search of variety, he visited Dixon at Warkworth in September 1898, the final visit he would pay him, although Dixon visited Yattendon for the last time the following year. In December the family went to Ramsgate for a fortnight thinking that the sea air might improve Bridges' health, and had a 'continuous blustering time instead of the perpetual rain that fell to the lot of everyone inland'.[21]

In spite of his ill health, however, during 1898 Bridges managed to write a 'Hymn of Nature' which Hubert Parry set to music for the Gloucester Festival, when it was performed as 'A Song of

Darkness and Light'. Bridges told Muirhead that it was to be published in the September number of the *Cornhill*. He remarked that 'it contains some queer words to sing in a Cathedral, but I hope it won't be the last time that such things are allowed. I should have told you that they sing "Blessed pair of Sirens" for an anthem at Wells.'[22] There is great variety in mood from section to section, giving opportunities for very different musical settings within a relatively small compass. Section IV is an example of the way in which Bridges absorbed into his verse imagery of contemporary society:

Or else, in crowded cities gathering close,
He traffics morn and eve
In thronging market-halls;
Or within echoing walls
Of busy arsenals
Weldeth the stubborn iron to engines vast;
Or tends the thousand looms
Where, with black smoke o'ercast,
The land mourns in deep glooms.

This contrasts with the more rural imagery of some of the other sections. Bridges felt that it, like most of his other poetry of the time, expressed his faith clearly. 'I am not sure that it may not be a pretty widely received expression of the thought of our time', he said.[23] But it did not make much of a stir, and although it is clearly very well suited for singing, it is not one of his best works.

At Christmas both Robert and Monica had books published, Part III of the *Hymnal* and Monica's *A New Handwriting for Teachers*, in which she advocated the use of italic script. Although Bridges was interested in handwriting and did some work with Monica on it, the questions of phonetic spelling and type for printing were of more importance to him. It was phonetic spelling which first brought together Bridges and Henry Bradley, a year his junior. Bradley came from a poor family and had grown up in the Midlands. Illness and a capacity to learn very rapidly, outpacing his teachers, made his formal schooling brief. After a couple of jobs as a tutor, he became the foreign correspondent to a cutlery firm and taught himself many languages. He then tried his hand as a free-lance writer in London, but overwork caused a breakdown and in 1896 Bradley and his growing family moved to Oxford, where he eventually became Senior Editor of the *New English Dictionary*. It was in this capacity that Bridges first wrote to him about orthographic reform. Bradley's response was not very enthusiastic, but the two men discussed the topic many times and both eventually wrote pamphlets on the subject. With their shared interest in language, they were to become very good friends.

Work on the *Hymnal* had made Bridges more aware than ever of the quality of paper, print, and good layout. In June 1899 he wrote to Muirhead,

> when I was last in Oxford I made the discovery of some really good old black letter—must be early 16th century. They had not enough to work with, but told me that they could get more in Germany. I intend buying enough to print with, and having a good book at last, I know how to get good paper. It will be delightful if after a lifetime of failures one gets a good book done at the end.—Still I am not altogether discontented with the hymnal, when it is not compared with a book of the best period.[24]

Bridges is credited with having encouraged Daniel to use the Fell type in his *Garland of Rachel* (1881), a collection of poems by eighteen writers including Bridges, which is considered the first 'adequate specimen' of a Fell type. Bridges had *The Growth of Love* printed in Fell black letter, a type which many people dislike, finding it difficult to read. *The Yattendon Hymnal*, however, used the Fell small pica, a typeface which many people considered so good typographically that Horace Hart decided that the type should be among the established founts of Oxford University Press. They printed over fifty books in it between 1902 and 1927, including Bridges' masque, *Demeter*.[25] Stanley Morison, with whom Bridges was later to become friendly and who redesigned the type for *The Times*, considered that 'but for the Yattendon enterprise it is almost certain that the use of the Fell types in our time would have been restricted to private use'.[26] Bridges' interest in type was evident in all his published volumes, including the editions he made of his friends' poetry and his wartime anthology, *The Spirit of Man*.

Just before Christmas 1899 Bridges bought Samuel Butler's book, *The Authoress of the Odyssey*. Bridges considered the *Odyssey* 'the best book in the world'. He was dubious although not dismissive of Butler's theory that it had been written by a woman and praised many of Butler's incidental observations. Butler then sent him a more recent book on Shakespeare's sonnets, suggesting that Shakespeare had not intended the poems to be published and that they were the record of a homosexual affair in his youth. Bridges agreed that the sonnets seemed to belong to Shakespeare's early writings, but objected to

> 1°—The mean personality of W. H. which disagrees with the hints that other poets wrote of and to him, & that books were dedicated to him. 2°—The worthlessness of his character & conduct, which disagrees with the very frequent assertion of his reciprocal affection, which is so beautifully and passionately told. 3°—The idea that Shakespeare wd have disliked the publication of the sonnets, in face of his plain statement that they wd immortalise the recipient; which implies that they were intended to be read. 4°—and what follows from this, That whereas you make the explanation of certain expressions to be shameful, it is impossible that they can have been so. 5°—your assumption that the sonnets not addressed to W. H. shd be put with those addressed to him. Surely by the nature of the case they cannot have been . . .[27]

Bridges' own 'key' to the sonnets was that they were about ideal love and, feeling some of this ideal love for W. H., Bridges said, Shakespeare sought to give it poetic expression. It was the very absence of sexual feeling that freed him to use sexual imagery. 'This sexual imagery', he asserted, 'is of universal application in metaphor, and could only be excluded from a treatment of ideal love by secondary considerations of propriety and the fear of a misunderstanding which S[hakespeare] did not fear. His boldness here is quite logical, tho' it is unparalleled.' Bridges' reasoning would not find wide acceptance today in regard to the sonnets, although similar arguments are used in discussions of *In Memoriam*. He continued to investigate the subject and found it increasingly difficult to refute Butler's case, although he remained unconvinced, suggesting that Butler had not paid sufficient attention to the artistic shaping of the sequence, interpreting as 'successive [biographical] experiences or states or reflections' sonnets that had been 'composed with definite [artistic] relation to each other'.[28]

The year 1899 was highly productive for the Bridges. Monica prepared a larger and cheaper edition of her book on handwriting,

Part IV of the *Hymnal* was published in October, and a selection of the hymns was printed separately by Daniel in black letter and by Oxford University Press in a collection they called the *Small Hymn Book*. The same year also saw the appearance of the second volume of Bridges' *Shorter Poems* printed by Smith and Elder. The 'Shorter Poems' comprised two-thirds of the book, while some of the remaining eighty pages were drawn from past work and some were the product of two months of 'poetical spurt'. 'I hope', Bridges wrote to Muirhead, 'that you will like the new work. It is in some respects better, I think, than what I have done before, clear and simple. Wooldridge is coming partly to read these things for me, because I have no time to let them soak.'[29] Bridges always encouraged his friends to criticize his work while it was in progress, but in fact over the years he does not seem to have made many alterations in response to their remarks. The criticisms may have affected what he wrote subsequently, but it seems likely that it was enjoyment of the discussion, the exchange of ideas about writing, that prompted both the requests for criticism of his own work and his readiness to offer suggestions about that of other people.

The volume contained some of the love lyrics Bridges wrote in the 1880s and 1890s, and although Bridges was concerned in case they revealed too much of his relationship with Monica he has since been criticized for not writing personally enough. But when biographical details are provided, many of Bridges' love poems have a striking intimacy.

The volume also contained several eclogues based on discussions with friends and, amongst the miscellaneous remainder of the collection, a picture of 'November' which is one of the more successful poems in the book:

> The lonely season in lonely lands, when fled
> Are half the birds, and mists lie low, and the sun
> Is rarely seen [. . .]
>   Out by the ricks the mantled engine stands
> Crestfallen, deserted,—for now all hands
> Are told to the plough,—and ere it is dawn appear
> The teams following and crossing far and near,
> As hour by hour they broaden the brown bands
> Of the striped fields; and behind them firk and prance

The heavy rooks, and daws grey-pated dance: . . .
And here and there, near chilly setting of sun,
In an isolated tree a congregation
Of starlings chatter and chide,
Thickset as summer leaves, in garrulous quarrel:
Suddenly they hush as one,—
The tree top springs,—
And off, with a whirr of wings,
They fly by the score
To the holly-thicket, and there with myriads more
Dispute for the roosts; and from the unseen nation
A babel of tongues, like running water unceasing,
Makes live the wood, the flocking cries increasing,
Wrangling discordantly, incessantly,
While falls the night on them self-occupied;
The long dark night, that lengthens slow,
Deepening with Winter to starve grass and tree,
And soon to bury in snow
The Earth, that, sleeping 'neath her frozen stole,
Shall dream a dream crept from the sunless pole
Of how her end shall be.

Again, it is Bridges' appreciation not only of the appearance but also of the sounds of the landscape that gives his descriptive poem its strength. The final lines absorb into the description the scientific belief, necessary before the discovery of nuclear reaction, that the sun's radiation would dwindle, leaving the earth's atmosphere to condense and form deep layers of ice, a 'frozen stole' over the planet. Tennyson had referred to the same idea in 'Locksley Hall Sixty Years After'.

The *Shorter Poems* were also published in a shilling edition by Bell, of which seven hundred copies sold in a month. Although Bridges was by no means the first poet to utilize speech-rhythm he was the most successful of his period, and 'freedom of speech-rhythm was, at the time of their first appearance, the distinguishing stylistic feature of the *Shorter Poems*.[30] By comparison, Guérard considers that Swinburne's modified anapaestic metres are less subtle, Arnold has less variety, and Browning is seldom as natural. The stylistic models for such success are Keats and seventeenth-century writers such as Herbert, and Bridges' affinity with them was commented upon by many critics. Guérard points out that in only three of the *Shorter Poems* did Bridges 'resort to the easy device of allowing the phrase to dictate the length of the line'. A review in the *Academy* (22 April 1899) noted,

This little book is the discreet and exquisite expression of a rapturous love of nature and the best things of life. None the less, we fancy that Mr Bridges will remain always a poet's poet. His ear is too delicate, his experiments in metre are too nice. The ordinary reader is so often baulked in the pleasant occupation of keeping time to the syllables with finger or foot. It is the poets who go *tip-tippety* that find their way to the large circulations; Mr Bridges, we can believe, is peculiarly disappointing at times, for he chooses the *tip-tippetists*' subjects, and brings to them an austerity usually associated with the poetry rather of the soul than of nature.

The reviewer quoted six poems, 'Who has not walked upon the shore', 'The clouds have left the sky', 'Spring goeth all in white', 'Nightingales', 'September', and 'The idle life I lead', and ended: 'By these extracts we have done Mr Bridges less than justice . . . They may, however . . . send many persons to the book.'

By the turn of the century Bridges was receiving serious and complimentary attention in such journals as the *Academy* and the *Athenaeum*. The *Academy* (5 February 1898), reviewing his achievement, noted,

of metre Mr Bridges is a master, as befits one who has written learnedly and with insight on the rhythms both of Milton and of Keats. He delights in metrical experiment, and, by skilful resolution of syllables and shifting of accent, manages to secure an almost inexhaustible variety of effect. He has left the English lyric a far more flexible thing than he found it, and one seems already to trace his influence in the versification of such younger writers as Mr Stephen Phillips and Mr Laurence Binyon. Another point to which Mr Bridges has paid considerable attention is the relation of verse to musical setting. We do not know whether many of his lyrics have actually been set, but there are not a few which sing themselves as you read them . . . Such are the fine lines beginning, 'Awake, my soul, to be loved . . .' After, perhaps before, his nature-poetry, it is as a love-poet that Mr Bridges excels. . . The lines just quoted ['I made another song, In likeness of my love'] have the simplicity, the exaltation of the best Caroline work. And there are many other poems in which the passion of love finds high and romantic expression . . . If we were asked to define Mr Bridges's crowning literary characteristic, we should say that it was style, in the ultimate sense of style—that is, distinction.

On 11 January 1902 an article in the *Athenaeum* primarily devoted to *Poetical Works*, volume III, which contained the first part of *Nero* and *Achilles in Scyros*, ended with criticisms of too mechanical a reflection of emotion in the rhythms of *Achilles* and a more general comment:

Mr Bridges is always a theorist; he has made many experiments in metre, with not less taste and learning than boldness. But he is occasionally so interested in the theory that he forgets to look at the result. In spite of a few defects of his own choosing, Mr Bridges is one of the few contemporary writers of verse who are poets both born and made. Many of his 'Shorter Poems' have the sudden, irresistible charm of the lyrics in the Elizabethan song-books, and they are like nothing which has appeared in English poetry from the time of Elizabeth to the present day. He stands aloof in a place of his own, not without worshippers, but without the general applause, almost unknown to the crowd. He will live by his lyrics, not by his plays; but nothing that he has written is without some touches of an excellence in which he is unique.

Arthur Symons, in a long article on Bridges' work, also chose to comment on his handling of rhythm. He quoted a passage from *Milton's Prosody* in which Bridges had said, 'I will only add that when English poets will write verse governed honestly by natural speech-stress, they will discover the laws for themselves, and will find open to them an infinite field of rhythm as yet untouched. There is nothing which may not be done in it, and it is perhaps not the least of its advantages that it is most difficult to do well.' Symons remarked,

All Mr Bridges' work in verse is an illustration of this theory, and it is because this theory is, as he says, 'too simple to be understood,' that he has been accused of writing verse which is difficult to scan. Read verse for the sense (that is what he really says to us), and if the verse is correctly written the natural speech-emphasis will show you the rhythm. Take, for instance, the last of the 'Shorter Poems.' The last stanza reads:

Fight, to be found fighting: nor far away
Deem, nor strange thy doom,
Like this sorrow 'twill come,
And the day will be to-day.

The first line of the poem reads:

Weep not to-day: why should this sadness be?

a line which appears quite normal, from the conventional standpoint of syllables and according to a conventional accent. Yet what a surprising and altogether admirable variety is introduced into this metre by the first line which I have quoted from the last stanza! Read it according to the rules by which, we are commonly taught, English verse is governed, and it is incorrect, scarcely a verse at all. Read for the sense, say it as you would say it if it were prose, and you were speaking it without thinking about accents or syllables, and its correct ease, its legitimate beauty, its unforced expressiveness, reveal themselves to you at once . . . It is only in one point that Mr Bridges seems to me inconsistent with his own theory, in which natural speech is so rightly accepted as the test and standard of verse. He admits . . . inversions which would be impossible in natural speech . . . It is a 'poetic licence,' and for poetic licences poetry, at all events modern poetry, has no room.

Speaking more generally, Symons said: 'Mr Bridges' art is made for simple thoughts, and indirect, though delicate, emotions; these it renders with a kind of luminous transparency', and he concluded that the qualities of his poetry, 'apart from its many qualities as an art', would be summed up by the words 'wisdom' and 'temperance'.[31]

12

In Search of Health

(1900–1906)

Early in January 1900 the family contracted influenza, which did not affect Robert or the three children very much but Monica, who was expecting another child, was seriously ill. The baby seems to have been born late in May, two months premature, and did not survive long. Bridges described it as 'one of those arrangements that make it almost impossible for a mother to live'.[1] It was some months before Monica regained her strength.

Bridges was saddened too when, on 23 January, Dixon died. R. Wilkins Rees, who was thinking of writing an article on Dixon's work, asked Bridges for his memories and views. Bridges replied that he considered Dixon's most important work to have been his five [actually six] volumes of Church history, 'written throughout in a fine and imaginative style. It is already recognized as a text book and authority—and will in my opinion take its place among the best "Histories" in our language.'[2] Bridges had edited a collection, priced at a shilling, of Dixon's poems published by Elkin Matthews in 1896, but this had not received the appreciation he had hoped. The Church of England too, he considered, had been insufficiently aware of Dixon's talents: 'his fate [was] to work all his life devotedly for the Church (being one of the most gifted and brilliant of the clergy) without any recognition save that of an honorary Canonry', but his feelings about the parallel disregard of Hopkins' talent by the Jesuits had been very much stronger and more complex.

At the end of January 1901 the Bridges moved to Oxford for the Hilary term, staying until the end of March. Elizabeth was sent to the Ruskin school for drawing lessons, Margaret had violin lessons, and Edward was at school. The house they took, 17 Bradmore

Road, was in a quiet street just north of the University Parks and ten minutes' walk from the town centre. Initially Robert thrived: 'so far', he told Muirhead, 'I am enjoying myself more than I deserve. I have a great many friends here: and the society of people at once so friendly and accomplished, all active and interested in life is a great pleasure. Also there is plenty of music.'[3] By the end of March, however, the whole family were glad to get back to their own home. Bridges considered the trip successful, but 'it did not make us wish to live in Oxford. I shd never have believed how entangled one gets. I did absolutely nothing and was always too much occupied to fulfil my engagements.—I made some very pleasant acquaintances, but saw almost nothing of old friends.'[4] His visit had been complicated by bad weather and having twice to see relatives in Somerset who needed help.

Among the friends with whom Bridges had been able to spend time in Oxford was V. S. S. Coles, now Principal of Pusey House; he also began to get to know Henry Bradley. When he had moved back to Yattendon one of the early topics of discussion in their letters was a book by George Santayana, to whose work Bridges had been introduced by Laurence Binyon, who thought that he would find *Interpretations of Poetry and Religion* (1900) attractive. Bridges disagreed with some of Santayana's ideas, such as his explanation of the Platonic ideal and his inability to find what corresponds to religion in Shakespeare, but concluded,

> I do not think that I have ever met with anything so much like my own notions as his general position. I always seem to see man as the centre of concentric spheres, the nearest to him being the 'circle' of common sense and matter-of-fact, beyond this the circle of science and intellect, and beyond that, stretching out to infinity, the realm of imagination, which imagination, if it be present radiates from the centre, and is related to everything, at least if it be present at all.[5]

The diagram is as much a hierarchy of values as the mapping of the relationship of aspects of mind. After the publication of *The Testament of Beauty* in 1929, Santayana came to see more clearly than Bridges that there were significant differences between their views of how the mind functions.

Bridges' interest in philosophy and the amount of time he devoted to reading it gradually increased in the new century. He wrote to Samuel Gee in July 1901, 'I read a lot of Locke yesterday & the day before. together with Fowler's life of him. He wd be very pleasant to read (Locke) if there was not something to pull one up in every other section. My philosophy has somewhat matured—I shall yield to the temptation someday of writing metaphysics.'[6] By December he was reporting, 'I read a lot of Nietzsche the other day . . . He is excellent amusement—a sort of Ruskin in philosophy . . . opinions extreme and paradoxical, but a lot of truth mixed up.'[7] The philosophical reading found vent first in what Bridges described as 'an Epistle to Burns on moral philosophy in the Scotch stanza which he uses so well'. He thought that the poem contained 'some original philosophy . . . which I believe to be quite sound. Perhaps it is not original. I have however always missed it in books, i.e. since I came to think it.'[8] Called 'An Epistle on Instinct', the argument is the basis of that in *The Testament of Beauty*. Bridges starts with an evolutionary pattern, tracing the possible development of the instincts into man's reason and moral conscience. His ambivalent attitude to reason is already clear; it differentiates conscience from the instinct for survival but can also paralyse the will with doubts and over-fine analysis. Hamlet would commonly be cited as the literary exemplum of this, but Bridges accused himself of the same failing:

For Nature did not idly spend
Pleasure: she ruled it should attend
On every act that doth amend
    Our life's condition:
'Tis therefore not well-being's end,
    But its fruition.

Beasts that inherited delight
In what promoted health or might,
Survived their cousins in the fight:
    If some—like Adam—
Prefer'd the wrong tree to the right,
    The devil had 'em.

The stanzas provide a very clear example of the way in which, in the new century, late Victorian thought, which integrated religion, evolution, and anthropology into one pattern of progress from antiquity to the present day and beyond, was extended.

Bridges may well have considered innovative the thought about the transition from instinct to moral conscience and the relation of reason to instinct. This was an area that was receiving recognition as a central problem in the rapidly developing science of psychoanalysis and by biologists and philosophers dissatisfied with the motivating force in Darwinian evolution.

The Scotch stanza was an attempt to find a metre in which discursive poetry could be written. Earlier in the year Bridges had started to compose an epistle to Muirhead in heroics, but found that 'as soon as they [the heroics] lack absolute beauty they are dull in my opinion'.[9] His next experiments, in December, were along entirely new lines. In May 1899 Robert had met William Stone, the son of E. D. Stone who had been a master at Eton when Bridges had been a pupil there. William Stone, a master at Radley College, showed Robert an article that he had written in which he maintained that it was possible to write quantitative verse in English 'governed by rules equally strict and perfect [as those in Greek and Latin], and producing on the ear the same pure delight'.[10] There had been numerous attempts in the nineteenth century to write in stress hexameters, from Longfellow's *Evangeline* (1874) to Clough's *Bothie of Tober-na-Vuolich* (1848) and Kingsley's *Andromeda* (1858). But, as Stone pointed out, these poems did not show the possibilities of quantitative verse since their metres were based on stress and not on vowel length. Bridges was interested by Stone's theories. He had long considered that Greek and Latin were taught illogically because teachers confused stress and the length of vowels, both features necessarily being present. The length of the vowels in classical languages, determined as it is by a set of rules, is far more easily established than in English, and he was dubious about how successfully quantitative metres could be transferred to a language in which stress was so dominant. However, he promised Stone that he would make some experiments and he had the essay bound with his own extended edition of *Milton's Prosody* (1901). Tragically, Stone caught pneumonia in March of that year and died after only a few days illness. Robert, who had liked him from their first meeting, spoke of him as 'most delightful' and 'exceedingly clever'.

When in November Monica became seriously ill, Bridges used the time spent sitting near her while she slept to start the promised experiments with Stone's 'patent classical English phonetic quantitative versification'. It was initially a frustrating business. By Christmas he was writing to Newbolt,

> I have during the last fortnight made use of my broken times to accustom myself (as far as I can) to make verses in Stone's quantitative method. It always seemed to me impossible, for one had never regarded words in this way and again had no rhythms in one's mind to build on. One has to write a good deal before one finds what rhythms English gives one in this manner. This is such tedious work that I shd never have done it but for the imposed heelkicking of last month.[11]

Then a visitor, Alfred Crawley, a master at Bradfield, astounded Robert by the facility with which he could compose English verse in quantitative metre. Crawley was to publish a version of *Omar Khayyam in Greek Elegiacs* in 1902. No doubt helped by seeing another's skill, Bridges persevered and found that it surprised him 'very much to find how the difficulties which seemed insuperable gave way'.[12] He felt that it was necessary to try a variety of quantitative metres and to write sufficient to explore the new possibilities. He sent Muirhead hendecasyllables and scazons in February. He experimented in the poem 'The Flute-Player' with hexameters, the metre which next to the iambic he considered the most difficult and least amenable to English. His experiments continued until 1909, and included the two long epistles, 'Wintry Delights' (1902) and 'To a Socialist' (1903) and verse translations of part of Book VI of *The Aeneid* (1904–5) and Book XXIV of the *Iliad* (1909). He noted in 1905 that his own 'valuation of syllables' had come to differ considerably from Stone's. What Bridges was trying to achieve was something that was parallel to and not imitative of classical verse. W. H. Auden said that he thought Bridges had been the first poet to write quantitative verse in English ignoring stress altogether:

> thus the following extract is written in hexameters, but no ear that listens for stress will hear them as such
>
> What was Alexander's subduing of Asia, or that
> Sheep-worry of Europe, when pigmy Napoleon enter'd
> Her sovereign chambers, and her kings with terror eclips'd?
> His footsore soldiers inciting across the ravag'd plains,
> Thro' bloody fields of death tramping to an ugly disaster?

Shows any crown, set above the promise (so rudely accomplisht)
Of their fair godlike young faces, a glory to compare
With the immortal olive that circles bold Galileo's
Brows, the laurel'd halo of Newton's unwithering fame?
Or what a child's surmise, how trifling a journey Columbus
Adventur'd, to a land like that which he sail'd from arriving,
If compar'd to Bessel's magic divination, awarding
Magnificent Sirius his dark and invisible bride.

'Wintry Delights', ll. 121–133[13]

Albert Guérard suggests that the effort to write quantitative verse, the most exacting of Bridges' many experiments, led him to use a much wider vocabulary with far more polysyllabic, archaic, technical, and Latinate words in order to satisfy the demands of the quantitative feet.[14] The more philosophical and scientific topics Bridges wanted to write about also broadened the diction towards the technical and Latinate. The epistles in quantitative verse accustomed him to writing long, discursive poems and, with the introduction of Miltonic elisions into his later experiments in such metres, taught him to detect potential elisions, a necessity for his subsequent exploration of syllabic verse.

Finally, quantitative prosody incorporates a theory of equivalence which accepts as a convention two short syllables in place of a long one. Critics now generally agree that this was a convention in both Greek and Latin verse and not true to the actual proportionate length of the vowels. Bridges realized that the much greater variety of syllabic length in English makes such a theory of equivalence suggest a condition even further from the real state of that language. And any poetic convention that departs from the true nature of a language opens the door for significant differences between the theoretical prosodic organization and the actual rhythm. He explained how he thought that quantitative verse had evolved into accentual-syllabic verse by comparing a fourth-century Latin hymn written correctly in classical iambic metre with a later one written in imitation of the earlier style.[15] Unfortunately, because the latter poet's knowledge of vowel-quantity was faulty, he incorporated only the more easily apprehended characteristics of stress and syllable-count. The deduced rules were transferred to verse in the Romance languages and then, by Chaucer, into English. In the process, the classical division into feet was retained but the length of the vowels was ignored so that terms such as iambic and trochaic ceased to refer to long and short vowel-quantity, and came to indicate the pattern of light and heavy stress. From observations of Shakespeare's and Milton's verse, Bridges suggested that in the sixteenth and seventeenth centuries the process of development away from classical verse had been carried still further, more polysyllabic metrical feet being introduced and the extra syllables prosodically accounted for by many more rules of elision than in the classical languages. This meant that stress, which remained unchanged, became a much more important organizing principle.

Many of the opponents of quantitative verse condemn it on the grounds that English is so heavily a stress language that any other attempt at prosodic organization is quickly overpowered. What Bridges was looking for was more subtle. He understood the importance of stress and wondered 'whether, if the speech-rhythm be the beauty of the verse, it may not be a sufficient rule for it; whether indeed, the rhythms of *Par. Lost*, *Samson*, or even of Dante's *Commedia* are any the better for their strict syllabic scheme and prosodic fictions'.

> Theoretically the problem is this, whether in poetry the speech as determined by its accent and rhythm can be made so persistently beautiful in form as to dispense with all the subtle assistance which it derives from interplay with a fundamental metrical form, which never relaxing its conscious guidance gives special significance to every deviation from it, and overriding all irregularities blends them into a consistent whole; or whether, in renouncing this it must not, if it should do well, create a prosody of its own?[16]

That 'prosody' would of course be free verse. The experiments that Bridges made for the rest of his life were attempts to gain the best of both worlds; to have some of the flexibility of free verse but also the unity and counterpoise of regular, unobtrusive metres.

In November Monica became dangerously ill again, and for nearly two months Robert did not venture out and they had no visitors. He read to her Jane Austen's novels, *Middlemarch*, and half of *Tom Jones*. He had read all George Eliot's novels when he was an undergraduate. Returning to her over thirty years later he found that she still made him want to read on even when he was not particularly enjoying the story. He did not see this as entirely admirable, and she was, he thought, 'overserious in her exposure of the faults of foolish & young thoughtless persons. [She] . . . does not see that they are only good to make fun of. Her very humour is generally stilted. and there are whole chapters of conversations in the public houses. supposed to be very witty I believe. but as tedious to me as the smell of stale beer.'[17] But what he disliked most was 'her careful analysis and dissection of monsters of her own creation. That Bulstrode. a beast. I don't believe there was ever anyone like him. and if an artist is going to invent, why invent beastliness. and beastliness without fun.' Nevertheless, the family's library contained *Scenes from Clerical Life*, *Romola*, *Felix Holt*, and *Silas Marner*. Fielding's *Tom Jones* he found surprisingly successful when read aloud to Monica, but before they had got half way through it they were 'sick of it chiefly I fancy from the persistence of the unnecessary coarseness. But to the last we found plums—but threw it, plums and all, aside.' Both books, however, were a greater success than the more sedate Trollope, whom they found provided no 'temptation to make one take up the book a second time'.

Once Monica was well again most of 1902 drifted by, with Bridges contentedly experimenting with various quantitative metres. In June he wrote to Samuel Gee that he now so disliked coming to London that he neglected things he ought to attend to there. The tranquility of Yattendon and his growing family clearly absorbed him. 'We are supposed to be all pretty well', he said.

> My wife has got to look quite strong again. in fact she seems to me to be above her usual standard. The children are also very flourishing. My second girl, who is about 12½ has quite outgrown her elder sister, and weighs nearly nine stone. Despite this rainy season they manage to get on merrily, and the Peace has certainly lightened all hearts. The Coronation [of Edward VII] is a monstrous nuisance, but we shall not I hope have very much of it here. I am busy in various ways. We have now perfected our calligraphic phonetic writing and I hope that I may get my book on it done before Xmas. I have also a new style in poetry which will amuse you. Today we have Miss Coleridge staying with us. She and my wife are gone up to tea with the Waterhouses, and I am using the interval.[18]

The account he sent to Muirhead in August is rather more relaxed in tone:

We had a good day on the river last week—and are going to try and get another tomorrow. Spokes [Edward] has rather a good schooner, which sails well—a toy one of course.— Ben [Bridges' spaniel] has a bad ear, and he doesn't like my cauterising it. We have a few visitors engaged to come here next month, some of them musical . . . Elizabeth is doing water colour. Margaret nearly through Mozart's violin Sonatas. My wife has with my assistance about perfected the phonetic writing.[19]

Later, while the family were living at Yattendon they had more pets whom Bridges evidently observed with some amusement:

Our parrot was on good terms with the cat, and in winter the cook wd complain that she could not get to the fire for the animals, the cat the parrot and the two terriers (Chremes & Menedemus, whom she called Many=demons) who all arranged themselves in a semicircle about it, nor ever quarrelled with each other except for the best place, which the parrot generally secured for itself by walking round and biting the tail of the quadruped that occupied it.[20]

During the year Bridges completed the longest of his original poems in classical prosody. 'Wintry Delights', whose subject-matter provided more problems than the metre, surveys some of man's achievements in the sciences and the effect of these on his view of the world. Bridges starts with geology and palaeontology, noting that the fossil record forms 'the only commandments | By God's finger of old inscribed on tablet of earth-stone' (ll. 103–4). He then turns to astronomy, describing some of the discoveries that have been made:

. . . when Adams by Cam, (more nearly Leverrier in France,)
From the minutely measur'd vacillation of Uranus, augur'd
Where his mighty brother Neptune went wandering unnamed,
And thro' those thousand-million league-darknesses of space
Drew him slowly whene'er he pass'd, and slowly released him!
(ll. 134–8)

The control of the pace in that last line is masterly. In the poem he touches on physics, chemistry, anthropology, medicine, and, harking back to the nineteenth-century quarrel between evolutionists and those who took the Bible as history, refutes:

That trouble of Pascal, those vain paradoxes of Austin,
Those Semitic parables of Paul, those tomes of Aquinas,

All are thrown to the limbo of antediluvian idols,
Only because we learn mankind's true history, and know
That not at all from a high perfection sinfully man fell,
But from baseness arose: We have with sympathy enter'd
Those dark caves, his joyless abodes, where with ravening brutes,
Bear or filthy hyena, he once disputed a shelter;—
(ll. 348–55)

By the middle of 1903 he had finished a second Epistle, nearly as long as 'Wintry Delights', and this time addressed 'To a Socialist'. In it Bridges musters various arguments against socialist doctrine, from Malthus's projections of the effects of the exponential increase in the earth's population to man's 'predilection . . . for Magnificence, Force, Freedom, Bounty; his inborn | Love for Beauty, his aim to possess, his pride to devise it' (ll. 221–3). The arguments are logical but suggest that rampant individualism is not only characteristic of man but unchangeable. Roger Fry objected to Bridges' apparent 'doctrines' in the Epistle, and to him Bridges wrote, 'I guess from your last letter but one that you did not approve of the doctrines in my Socialistic epistle. I don't either, but they must be met by Socialists before they can win the confidence of the world.'[21] Bridges' dislike of socialism did not mean that he thought the plight of the poor could simply be ignored. He was charitable to the local poor, but he did not see the fight for a more equitable distribution of wealth as a cause to which he wanted to dedicate himself.

Robert's widowed sister, Carry, approved of the poem except for its criticism of the clergy; she had married the Revd William Glover in 1858. Bridges replied,

I quite understand your thinking that I was hard on the priest, but I don't think I am. I believe that the priests are . . . making the Christian religion impossible, and the way in which I speak of them is the way in which most people speak of them behind their backs . . . Yesterday we went to hear the French Benedictines . . . sing plain chant. It was very odd to see all their old fashioned elaborate ritual in a corrugated iron building . . . It might have looked fine in a beautiful ancient abbey. The prior was a charming old man. While he was chatting to us before the service all seemed attractive—the thing itself as exhibited in the chapel ridiculous beyond conception.—One sees how necessary it is to detach them from these old buildings, at least if they will not move forwards.[22]

Carry's letters suggest that she was a highly conventional Anglican of Victorian propriety, and Bridges' views may have scandalized rather than unsettled her. A letter from Bridges to Muirhead about Elizabeth's confirmation shows quite clearly his feeling that the Church was in many ways decadent:

I took Elizabeth in to Exeter the other day to be confirmed . . . The organ there is lovely. I did not admire the ceremony. The service was ruined by the introduction of some of the most maudlin and washy hymns with their tunes out of HAM. I was earnestly praying the Preserver of Souls that my dear little girl might be safe-guarded thro' life from the unholy spirit that all the parsons seemed to be invoking, and that she might have the Spirit of Wisdom, and understanding, and the Spirit of Might, instead of that Spirit of bosh and ignorance, and weakness—which sounded in the air and was apparent in nearly all the faces of the clergy.[23]

'To a Socialist' also attracted the attention of Logan Pearsall Smith, but his interest was not in the content but the use of a Greek metre for English verse. In November 1902 Smith had sent Bridges verse that he had written in iambics. Bridges had not been overly encouraging—'I don't fancy that much is to be made of that metre in English'[24]—but this was no more than his honest opinion of what he considered to be the classical metre least suited to the English language. Smith was undaunted and a friendship was slowly established.

Five years later, when Pearsall Smith was compiling an anthology that included a number of Shakespeare's sonnets, he asked Bridges' opinion about which ones to use. Bridges replied,

. . . Considered as perfect poems I am not nearly as enthusiastic about S's sonnets as I once was . . . The sonnets are excellent poetic reading, but they very seldom satisfy one throughout, and it is perhaps for that reason that I have put among those which I select some which in their general strength argument and intention are complete, altho' these are deficient in the poetic beauty for which some more imperfect sonnets are conspicuous.[25]

He included 'The expense of spirit' and 'Then hate me when thou wilt' for the strength of their expression. 'Thy bosom is endeared' because he considered it 'the most beautiful in meaning of all the sonnets', and among others such popular ones as 'When to the sessions', 'How like a winter', and 'Let me not to the marriage'.

Such a selection he thought would provide poets with what they were likely to want, but he suggested that if Smith had some other audience in mind then further thought and discussion would be desirable; but nothing came of the project.

The family holidayed on the Isle of Wight in August 1903. The weather, wrote Bridges,

> seems rather broken up—and we do not suffer from extreme heat. Indeed it is a difficulty some times to get completely warm again after bathing. Walking & cycling fill up the rest of the day, and I am often more fatigued than I like. I have got Mantell's geological guide with me. It is rather old fashioned now, but it is a good book, and helps the children to pick up geological ideas, and also encourages them to pick up stones which they do not always carry home for themselves.[26]

In September Margaret became ill and feverish with what was at the time diagnosed as influenza. By Christmas she was still unwell and the following February developed pneumonia. Monica meanwhile contracted what at first was thought of as a throat complaint and lost her voice. After some four months tuberculosis was diagnosed in both of them, and by the end of July they were in a sanatorium in the Cotswolds. For six months Monica was to be forbidden to speak except on rare occasions. On 30 July Bridges wrote, 'I saw my wife in London 3 days ago. She had an interview with the specialist coming up from her Sanatorium . . . and returning the same day. He gave a good account of her, and she was allowed the use of her larynx for 30 minutes which she was glad to use in a conversation with me. She is probably to return home in September. she is expected to get practically all right.'[27]

During the first few months of Margaret's illness, when her fever lasted for week after week and its diagnosis for someone with Bridges' medical training was unconvincing, he was writing a masque for the opening of a new library at Somerville College, Oxford. It was a task that had been requested by Roger Fry's sister, Margery, and he had 'got settled into the thing' when Margaret fell ill. Her illness left him depressed and worried, emotions that he thought 'may have strayed into the play'.[28] It was performed on 11 June, again by request on 22 June, and published in May 1905. In many ways *Demeter* is more satisfactory than *Prometheus the Firegiver*. The syntax is generally far more straightforward, so that the lines flow more easily and naturally. Some of the speeches, such as the Prologue and Demeter's praise of flowers, convey a factual accuracy with imagination and delicacy and the masque is notable for successes of this sort. The characters and their emotions, however, are not particularly convincing. Bridges also initiates in the masque an exploration of the underlying metaphysical scheme of the world, and has Demeter and Persephone assert respectively that the origin of all things is entirely good and entirely evil. But these ideas are neither developed nor resolved but swept aside by Demeter in an ending that was probably distorted when Margery Fry insisted that Bridges turn his pessimistic conclusion into a more positive one. For the performance dances were arranged for the choruses which Bridges had written in quantitative metres. *The Times* of 13 June 1904 carried a report of the opening, and remarked that 'the performance was one of which Somerville has every right to be proud. Perfectly simple and unpretentious, the memory which it leaves of quiet colour, graceful movement, and harmonious words will not easily be lost.' Henry Bradley, who saw the performance, praised the masque to Bridges for its beauty. It was subsequently acted at Liverpool three times in 1908, with Shelley's version of Euripides' *Cyclops*.

Bridges rented a stone cottage at Birdlip, Gloucestershire, 'just at the top of the steepest highway in England, looking North over Gloucester', and there he, Monica, and Elizabeth lived until Margaret was well enough to leave the sanatorium, when they intended to go to Switzerland. Bridges explained to Muirhead, 'it is a very queer house. tho' very small it has 5 external doors. and as we live on "the open door" system the rooms are full of dead leaves and stray cats. of an evening the lamps blow out and it is impossible to go about the house with a lighted candle after dark.'[29] It was here that Bridges wrote what he called his 'impeachment' of John Bunyan, whose *Pilgrim's Progress* had been the most copiously printed book of the nineteenth century. While gathering material for it, he asked Margaret Woods whether she had reread *Pilgrim's Progress* since childhood, liked it, and thought it had done her any 'moral or spiritual good???'[30] He sent similar questions to some forty other people and tabulated the responses in his essay. They reinforced his impression that children loved *Pilgrim's Progress* mainly because it was 'the consecrated means of their indulgence in adventures and fights with giants and fearsome monsters on a Sunday, when their favourite pastimes are forbidden'. Bridges attempted to counter what he saw as excessive and undiscriminating praise of the book, concluding that 'Bunyan himself would have been horrified to find that the secret of his fame was literary excellence, yet without that he would have perished long ago. In this regard his book is like Milton's Epic, which was at first esteemed for its plot and theological aspect, and is now read in spite of them.'[31] Bridges' approach, as so often, was a practical one, an investigation here of the attraction and effect of a book that he was reading to his children.

In February the family moved to St Columb's, Foxcombe Hill, to the south of Oxford and very near Boar's Hill where they were eventually to settle. From St Columb's Bridges could cycle into Oxford in about twenty minutes, but it took, he said, forty-five minutes to get back home. Throughout the spring of 1905 he cycled long distances round the area trying to find a new home for the family, something of an achievement for a man over 60. The Bridges had mixed feelings about giving up their house at Yattendon into which they had put much effort and money but, according to family legend, Dr Barlow advised that Monica and Margaret would be healthier living on a hilltop at least four hundred feet high with falling ground to the south and east and protected from the north and west.

In May 1905 they moved into a furnished house called 'Boar's Hill Heath', and began preparing to go to Switzerland at the end of June. Besides house-hunting, Bridges had the task of clearing the Manor House at Yattendon so that it could be let while they were away. He was also trying to finalize arrangements for Edward to enter Eton, but on a visit to introduce Edward to his tutor decided that the room offered to his son was unacceptable, since its window was directly above the dining-room ventilator and the kitchen refuse. The current headmaster refused to make any changes. However, when he retired the following term the problem was quietly solved and Edward entered the school in May 1906. He left his preparatory school near Newbury at the beginning of August 1905 and, with the help of Bridges' friends, travelled out to Basle where Bridges met him and took him to join the rest of the family at Stoos in the mountains above Urner See. Bridges sent the

Newbolts a letter of thanks for equipping Edward for his journey and an account of the latter part of it:

we . . . had ½ an hour at Lucerne before we took shipping . . . I had reckoned on dining in the boat. This was made impossible by the crowd, on whom the 2 waiters cd make no impression; but now came the great success of the whole 'voyage': I wish you cd have seen it and my delight at the discovery of the precious remains of your generous provisions for Edward. How much he had already eaten of it I don't know, but his sack when explored still revealed a good part of a roast fowl, bread and butter both brown and white buttered buns with cress, biscuits, cake, gingernuts, bananas and cheese: all done up in separate papers: also ½ a bottle of excellent lemonade . . . I arranged [these treasures] all in a row on one of the deck-tables, to the great scandal of the correct tourists, english and german-apeing english, who were sipping deleterious iced squashes and waters: I on the other hand ordered a bottle of Veltliner Sassella, and in the face of all the gaping staring fellows and families who never thought how I was playing on them, I took the paper parcels in order. I think my breaking up the cheese ostentatiously with my fingers disgusted them most: but you shd know that I had on a hat old enough to take anyone's character away. Imagine how I enjoyed myself! Ed of course assisted, and, when he had finished the lemonade, joined on to the wine, which was good. I watched the horror and contempt of my spectators pass gradually thro' wonder into natural envy and honest admiration, while the curious miscellany of viands was successively and impartially assimilated & the papers one by one emptied and folded up flat, till nothing was left but the bare bottles and glasses. I seldom enjoyed a meal better: and I narrate it in confidence that *Mrs Newbolt will like to know that not a crumb of her excellent provender was wasted.* Thus we came happily to Brunnen pier, where on landing we saw a strange sight. There were some American passengers named Pyne, the disbarking of whose baggage employed all the able bodied men of the district. The innumerable boxes & cases as they were piled up on shore made a heap that soon rivalled the neighbouring mountains: and the last thing we saw, as we drove off, was a party of half-tipsy tourists who having come upon this obstacle unexpectedly from the southeast just when they thought they had finished their day were angrily making its ascent with their alpen stocks and knapsacks, and jodelling loudly as they clambered up its precipitous heights.[32]

Bridges' relief at Edwards's safe arrival and his initial holiday exuberance make this one of his most light-hearted letters. The area near Brunnen is a very beautiful part of Switzerland but Bridges could not be at ease in such rugged country for long, and by October when the family had moved to St Moritz he wrote to Muirhead,

> I hate Switzerland as man has made it, and don't really much care for it as created—though I must praise as I enjoy the bright clean air and the beauty of the valleys, where I have spent delightful hours wandering among the rocks and pines and streams & eating the wild raspberries. The mountains to my thinking are merely damnable; though of course such monstrous masses must under the changing atmospheric conditions sometimes make strange and great effects.[33]

This opinion may have been made bleaker by his loss of heart over a relapse in Margaret's condition. Having seen in his youth one after another of the members of his family die, Bridges must have felt as if he were entering a nightmare in which he might lose his younger daughter and perhaps his wife in the same way. Although their house in St Moritz, Villa Gentiana, was comfortable and fitted with central heating, he feared that its wooden structure was vulnerable to fire. He also found life away from his friends and the culture of England dreary until, prompted by Muirhead's writing of epigrams, he returned to the writing of poetry. In April 1905 Muirhead had given Bridges a pocket-sized edition of the *Aeneid*, which he had since carried around with him, reading in it frequently. He now decided to experiment further with Stone's prosody, translating part of the sixth book of the *Aeneid* into hexameters and systematizing his modifications to Stone's rules. Some of the initial thinking was done while skating. He wrote, 'it is very curious work. Virgil being untranslatable. and the paraphrase consequently a matter of extreme ingenuity. It is astonishing how long a time one can spend over one line . . . as you no doubt discover with your epigrams. It is a wonderful time killer.'[34] A comment Bridges made in December serves to show the sort of problem he was thinking of:

> his [Virgil's] passage on the gates of sleep seems plainly to assert not only that the whole was a vision in the cave—but he very well excuses the awful pessimism of his Hell by sending Aeneas out at the ivory gate. IBANT is therefore almost impossible to translate. it means 'They found themselves walking.' 'They seemed to be walking'—This is a difficulty that I can't get over without spoiling the passage.[35]

The translation was later published under the title, 'Ibant Obscuri', the opening words of Book VI. Muirhead's objection to Bridges' translation was to the number of sibilants it contained. Although true, this was an old-fashioned comment; following Hopkins' advice on a closer relation to contemporary idiom would have served him far better.

In the first few months of 1906, at the request of A. H. Bullen, Bridges wrote an essay on Shakespeare's drama, later called 'The Influence of the Audience'. He had decided to make an 'emotional'—i.e. not intellectual, analysis of Shakespeare's work, and separate off all that *offended* . . . The process is simple and . . . entirely free from the usual blemish of testing a great *intellect* by a smaller one.' He found that he 'never tired' of Shakespeare but added,

> there is something very strange about him . . . My lucubrations have not at all changed my opinion . . . nor do I think that I shd be able to solve the problem which his extraordinary mixture of 'brutality' with extreme, even celestial, gentleness offers, but the examination supposing it to be successful would define the brutality (the word is not mine) and that wd be unpleasant to most readers. It has always puzzled me very much.[36]

He expected that the essay would not be an acceptable contribution to the selection of critical essays on Shakespeare that Bullen was preparing as the last of ten volumes devoted to the writer.

In March the family returned to England. Edward, who had been working with a private tutor during the winter, passed his entrance examinations for Eton and Bridges reflected, 'I do not think that we have wasted the time'.[37] Elizabeth and Margaret had started to learn German and Italian, Margaret and Monica were both pronounced 'fit' again, and Bridges, slowly recovering from a bout of influenza that left him with sciatica in the legs for months, was feeling relatively pleased with his essay on Shakespeare. His main argument, that Shakespeare only included obscene jokes and brutality in his plays because his audience demanded it, is unconvincing. However, when he shifts his focus to that of consistency of characterization and looks at *Measure for Measure*, *Macbeth*, and *The Winter's Tale*, he has some thought-provoking observations about the disjunction between character and action and the increased dramatic effect of leaving extreme emotions, such as

Leontes' jealousy, without motivation. Although it is more seriously flawed than most of his essays, some of its statements could usefully be reconsidered today. Edward Thompson called it a 'penetrating if somewhat capricious essay', and was enthusiastic enough to want to republish it, only to find that Bridges had forgotten that he had sold the rights to it to Frank Sidgwick.

One morning in 1926, however, Bridges (as was his manner) strode unannounced into our drawing-room and happened to meet me on my way to my study outside. 'You said you rather liked my Shakespeare essay. They've just printed a hundred copies of it in America in a rather special way and have sent me three for myself. I'm sending one to the King. I'm keeping one for myself. You can have the other if you care.' He tossed it down on a table. I asked him to put our names in it. 'Not with *your* pen!' He went off. This was not so brusque as it sounds. He wrote always with a quill—I have often come upon him whittling a point to a goose feather—and knew that I did not possess one. He inscribed the book later, with the proper implement—in red ink, since red ink happened to be handy.[38]

13

Moving into Prominence (1906–1912)

Bridges decided to build a house on Boar's Hill. It seemed the only way of meeting all Dr Barlow's recommendations. Alfred Waterhouse, who had been ill since 1901 when a stroke forced him to retire, died in August 1905 and bequeathed the family a legacy which left them 'very much better off. Indeed', Bridges wrote, 'I shall be richer than I ever expected or wished to be, neither desiring nor deserving.'[1] The money was, however, extremely helpful in setting up the new home, which Paul Waterhouse designed for them.[2]

Bridges lost no time once the family were resettled on Boar's Hill in enjoying the concerts available in Oxford, but he also encountered the people gathering for Eights-Week rowing races and declared, 'I never saw such crowds of useless-looking people anywhere'.[3] However, his temper when writing the letter was somewhat soured by the family's temporary lodging, a 'houselet', 'intolerable in any weather but the most propitious'. In September they moved into Whitebarn, a more comfortable house. Work on their own home went ahead steadily and Bridges' manuscript notebook contains six lines of verse used as a dedication for the foundations. He noted that they were 'MMB's birthday verses 1906 she and all children laid first bricks Aug. 31—9 a.m.'

Come hither all earth-graces, and all heaven's company, that make
In the dwellings of men your hallowing residence,
Bless these foundations which we long homeless assembled
By the running wellspring lay in the sandy summit:
Viewing a house where love may abide with door ever open
And keep life's holidays holy with ample honour.[4]

By November the family were at work on those parts of the garden that were clear of construction, and Bridges appealed to Muirhead for 'any odds and ends which your gardener would have "no use of" as they say in Berkshire'. Their own gardener, 'a very exceptionally practical and intelligent fellow' was 'doing very well' for them.[5] By Christmas the roof-timbers were nearly all on the house, the gables built and faced with stone, and the planting of the garden had gone well but Bridges was restless. He contemplated editing Campion's poems for Clarendon's series of Tudor reprints but on reading his Latin poems found, 'I never was so bored in my life'.[6]

In July 1907 the Bridges moved into the new house, which they named 'Chilswell', which Thompson explained (p. 78) 'was at the very heart of the enchanted country dedicated to the Gipsy Scholar; the name is that which Arnold (I believe, in error) spelled as Childsworth: "Runs it not here, the track by Childsworth Farm?" At the poet's gates was the wood which (no longer) "hides the daffodil"; a few yards' walk gave an uninterrupted view to "the fir-topped Hurst".' Robert wrote contentedly to Muirhead in mid-November

> our final building-accounts have come in, and are more favourable than we had dared to hope: so Monica (who does all these things) says that we ought to be able to finish up the library at once. This will be delightful for me, as it is my room, and at present it cannot be said to be comfortable, though it is a great luxury when we wish for music. We have got the designs completed for the bookcases: and we find that we must have the corridor which connects the house with the library glazed in from the wind for when there is any wind it collects at high pressure in the corridor, and makes great efforts to get into the house.[7]

Both the plot of land and the shape of the house were slightly unusual. The land was narrower in the corner where the drive met the road. From the road the house was hidden by trees through which the drive gently curved, dividing near the house so that a short spur led to a turning circle in front of the entrance while the rest swept past the kitchens to the stables and gardener's house. The turning circle was formed by curved banks of stacked light-grey slate harmonizing with the gravel and topped with plants. The flat roofs and unornamented balcony and patio would have made the main view of the house ugly without creepers, bushes, and trees. Most unusually, the front door was at the side, opening to a central passage that bisected the building into public rooms on the right and a large kitchen on the left. The living-room, the first entrance on the right, was an oblong room, well lit by a large window opposite the door and overlooking the garden and a smaller window along the side (entrance) wall. Next was the dining-room, rather darker and with a door leading to a patio that was almost enclosed. This opened on to a grassed terrace. Above the dining-room was a square balcony to which the bedrooms had access. From the terrace, steps led down to the main level of the garden, with its flower beds and a rose garden. Beside the library, which was a separate building attached to the house by a covered walkway, was the well, and extending back from there a large vegetable plot edged with apple trees trained along wires. From the upper storey and garden it was possible to glimpse through the trees the distant towers of Oxford, three miles away across the fields in the valley below. The family also bought a boat, which they kept on the Thames above Oxford.

One of the people with whom Bridges resumed acquaintance at this time was A. C. Benson, poet, novelist, and later Master of Magdalen College, Cambridge. Benson had been a master at Eton and had sent Bridges a volume of his poetry in 1892, with an accompanying letter, mentioning that Bridges' poems were read there. He now sent him two pamphlets on education which provoked the response:

> It seems to me absolutely inhuman to set boys of 10 to 14 to learn the grammar of two dead languages, which their teachers cannot themselves speak or even pronounce. Boys of 10 can learn any language rapidly and almost without effort by ear. This faculty is *entirely neglected*: they are 'taught' languages by those who do not speak them, in a method which is both unnatural and difficult. I believe that nothing more foolish could well be invented.[8]

The 'wretched *scholarship examinations*' for which all the public schools crammed their pupils should, he thought, be redesigned to baffle cramming. Instead he advocated that 'no boy shd begin Greek before he was about 16 years old', that modern languages should be examined viva voce by native speakers, and that all grammatical papers for boys under 14 'should be confined to translation into the foreign language (Latin or French or German), and to the analysis or explanation of the sentences actually occurring in the "seen" and "unseen" passages set for translation into English'. In addition, he suggested some 'good miscellaneous papers, involving original application of elementary mathematical and scientific methods, in order to bring out ingenuity and practical intelligence: and also, (if this were not enough) optional papers which might exhibit any special aptitude whether—e.g. for music or drawing or mechanics'. Bridges' innovative comments were based in part on his observation of the education his son was receiving; Edward's reports had shown that he was no more than competent at Greek and not particularly interested in it, but 'accurate, quick and diligent' with arithmetic. Bridges also thought that much of his own time at school had been wasted and advocated the inclusion of scientific subjects on the basis of their immediate usefulness to boys. He waged a long campaign over contemporary teaching of Latin and Greek, and improvements were made gradually as the views of various like-minded reformers became influential.

Bridges was now in a position where the institutions in which he had been educated turned to him as a celebrity. An indication of his status can be seen in the additions that Herbert Warren made to his introduction to Bridges' poems in the 1906 edition of A. H. Miles' *Poets and the Poetry of the Nineteenth Century*, where he pointed out that *Shorter Poems* had been reprinted four times in the previous five years and that Bridges had formed something of a 'school', his influence clearly seen in the work of younger men. Early in 1907 Bridges was asked to write the scenes on Charles I for the University of Oxford's historical pageant, but on reading about Charles he came to the conclusion that he 'didn't at all understand' him, and he therefore declined the request only to be asked to provide an ode and the pageant's opening scene on the early history of the university. William Sanday and V. S. S. Coles, Bridges' two High Church friends in Oxford, told him that they could not comprehend his ode, a remark he interpreted as disapproval. He considered the subject, an 'Invitation to the Pageant', a magnificent one but bewailed the fact that he would have to use rhymes, which he described as 'useless appendages . . . terrible obstacles in the way of one's saying exactly just what one wants to say'.[9] The pageant was performed in fields beside the Cherwell that are now school playing-fields. Sir Hugh Allen conducted the orchestra, which included the wind section from the London Symphony. Each of the historical scenes was acted to music that was, where possible, appropriate to the period, and musical interludes, written by Sir Hubert Parry and Donald Tovey, 'foreshadowed each scene in the terms of modern musical art'.[10]

In 1908 Bridges wrote an ode requested for the opening at Eton of a new Memorial Hall dedicated to Etonians who had died in South Africa. A considerable sum of money had been donated, and the fund-raisers decided to build a museum, library, and a hall capable of holding all the boys and their masters. These memorial buildings were formally opened by King Edward accompanied by the Queen and other members of the Royal Family on 18 November 1908.[11] Bridges' ode was sung to music by his fellow Etonian, Hubert Parry. Parry apparently disliked the words, and Bridges, whose verse had been altered to suit Parry's music in their two previous collaborations, was adamant that this time he would change nothing. Edward reported that his schoolfellows had not liked the piece, but Bridges, while declaring that 'my Ode . . . as a performance was a mere failure' also noted that 'some of the great ladies however, who had suffered in the War thanked me in an unmistakably heartfelt manner: and they were the people whom I wished to please'.[12]

Bridges wrote a number of critical essays at this time. Although most of these were on writers whose reputations he wanted to help, he did write one on the nineteenth-century Irish poet George Darley and contemplated writing on Robert Louis Stevenson and Tennyson. The article on Darley had been requested for the *Times Literary Supplement*. In January 1908 he told the editor, Bruce Richmond, that he had finished reading Darley—'which was no joke—about a week ago', and had written over two-thirds of the paper. 'I hope', he added, 'that I have not made an error in judgment in thinking that, as his work is quite unknown to the public, it would be best to write very explicitly and somewhat separately about the different plays and poems'.[13] He used a similar strategy for his next essay, on Lascelles Abercrombie, a young writer whose work he liked. Wanting to help Abercrombie establish himself in the literary world, Bridges recommended him as a potential reviewer to Richmond. He also gave him careful advice and encouragement about his poetry, but Abercrombie's bent was not that of Bridges and he went his own way. At the end of 1911 Bridges was asked to review his new volume for *TLS* and, deciding that he did not like the book, tried to decline the job, but he harboured no resentment over the younger man's independence, and in 1929 suggested that Abercrombie, who by then had a chair of English at Bedford College, London, be asked to become a member of the committee of the Society for Pure English.

When, in August 1907, Mary Coleridge died, Newbolt, who was her literary executor, set about compiling a memorial volume of her poetry. He asked Bridges to write a preface for the edition, but Bridges had also been asked to write a memoir of Mary for the *Cornhill* and preferred the latter task. This was the first of a series of memorial essays that he wrote over the following four years on creative writers who had been his friends. He sent Newbolt his opinion that from Mary's two published volumes it would be possible to make an 'incredibly beautiful' selection of nearly one hundred poems. Bridges finished his article towards the end of September, but delayed submitting it until it had been criticized by Newbolt and Monica, who was away with Elizabeth at Harrogate for a month. In the essay he described Mary's poems as 'an absolutely truthful picture of a wondrously beautiful and gifted spirit, whom thought could not make melancholy, nor sorrow sad; not in conventional attitude, nor with fixed features, not lightly to be interpreted, nor even always to be understood, but mystical rather and enigmatical'.[14] In the course of the article he suggested that poetry needs to combine 'the Greek attainment [technical excellence] with the Christian ideal' or it will fail to 'command our highest love or satisfy our best intelligence'.

Bridges' attitude arose from the role which he believed art should play in society. In a newspaper article of 1909, in which he advocated the construction of a national theatre, he wrote that while he enjoyed farce, comedy, and even some melodrama, it was also necessary to provide plays showing 'man's pathetic conflict with destiny, the strife of spiritual powers, the saintliness of heroism, the life of the soul . . . the inspiring delight which should lift us away from all the rubbish and worldliness of daily existence, from all those impediments to man's greatness which the common playwright selects for his subject matter'.[15] It was especially important, he thought, that children should find in the theatre 'some worthy portrayal of the poetic aspects of life' for

> they are indeed in that happy state when man looks to art for more than it can give him: they have to learn the disillusionment of human limitations: they do not analyse their expectations, but they expect, and have the right to expect, to find in the theatre some . . . portrayal of an ideal existence, where their virginal emotions are treated with the dignity that is due to the eternal springs of man's highest aspirations.

Bridges did not always attain these goals in his own writing, and he is susceptible to criticism at points where he is not rigorous enough in distinguishing between idealism and convention, but he became increasingly aware of this himself, and his later work is stronger in this regard.

In August 1908 Bridges made his first visit to Scotland. After staying with relatives in Northumberland, he left Monica and Margaret and, with Elizabeth, visited Edinburgh and then went north to Wooldridge's cottage just south of Inverness on the Caledonian Canal. The canal, designed by Thomas Telford and opened in 1847, linked four lochs to provide a passage between the Irish Sea and the North Sea. Bridges told Gee,

> I visited Wooldridge chiefly because I feared he must be very ill [he suffered from diabetes]—but I found him far better than I had ventured to hope. He has aged very much lately, and it is a great misfortune for him that his wife cannot live out of London. She engages herself in good works, & cannot be detached. Moreover he is somewhat dependant on intercourse with her kind.[16]

After a week with Wooldridge, Bridges and Elizabeth travelled by boat through three of the lochs to Fort William, where they took the West Highland Railway which snakes around the north of Ben Nevis and through the Grampian Mountains of Argyllshire down past Inversnaid on Loch Lomond—where Hopkins had gone on his brief trip into the Highlands—to Glasgow. Argyllshire Bridges described as a 'revelation of desolation'. 'How foolish it is', he declared, 'to think one can imagine a country without having seen it.'[17] From Glasgow they went east to Northumberland to rejoin Margaret and Monica at Bamburgh, where Edward came to join them and they 'spent a fortnight in some old cottages by the sea'.

On returning home towards the end of August Bridges settled down to the first of two critical memoirs that he intended to write in the autumn. He expected them to be difficult: 'a great opportunity of doing well, but of desperate complexity'.[18] The first of these was of R. W. Dixon, the second of Digby Mackworth Dolben, both published initially as prefaces to collections of poems. In 1932 Monica agreed to their being republished with Bridges' memoir of Henry Bradley in a book called *Three Friends*, but noted that she had reservations about separating the preface to Dolben's poetry from the selection of his poems because, unlike the selection of Dixon's and Bradley's work which had been made by other people, Bridges had planned the preface to Dolben's poems with those poems he wanted to include very much in mind.[19] The memoirs are amongst Bridges' very best prose. They use to the full his gift for vivid description through the selection of memorable and characteristic detail, which is one of his main strengths as a poet. The memoir of Dixon has been called 'the best account of Dixon, and might be claimed to be one of the best appreciations by any English poet of another'.[20] Bridges' affection for his friend is clear and winning:

> The characteristic of Dixon which was most outwardly apparent was his humility. With many it passed for shyness or gaucherie, whereas he was at his ease in any company, with sympathy and observation both actively engaged. This modesty was entirely natural, and so excessive as to reach the pitch where modest manners assume distinction and a position of veritable advantage. Thus he always took the lowest room, and involved his host in the trouble of bidding him come up higher, or in the shame of neglecting to do so. When I rallied him on this, saying that he must at heart be very proud, since true modesty would shrink from giving needless trouble . . . he would laugh at himself, but was evidently unaware that he was ever advantaged by his mode of conduct; while, on the other hand, of his being unpleasantly imposed upon he had experience enough and to spare.[21]

Nevertheless, Bridges' affection does not cloud his critical judgement in the essay. He considered that Dixon's main achievement was his *History of the English Church*: his poetry, he said, was more uneven in quality. The criticisms are interesting when assessing his statements about Hopkins' poems, of which he was more appreciative. Of Dixon's he said,

> Dixon's poetry cannot be defended against the charge of inequality, the occurrence of poor and faulty passages of various defect, which easily offend a taste that cannot relish his excellences; they work also to discredit him with those who are merely impatient and inattentive, and it is fair to add that he does not command in his poetry, as he does in the History, the art of making attention easy. His appeal, moreover, was to an audience whom Tennyson educated to be specially observant of blemishes, and who came to regard finish not only as indispensable, but as the one satisfying positive quality. The lack of it in Dixon was due to the artistic deficiences of his Oxford training, which the distractions of his professional life never allowed him to supply. It is thus that he varies his form more than he masters it, and when he encounters a technical difficulty he is content to override it with the readiest means at command, neither avoiding nor fearing detection. That he commanded unusual and learned resources may have satisfied his artistic conscience, but this often only makes matters worse, for what might have been overlooked or condoned as a mere weakness, becomes remarkable as a pedantic queerness or an awkward obscurity.[22]

Bridges noted elsewhere that Dixon 'observed the golden rule of never forcing' his writing. The result was a spontaneity that gave his poetry 'its rare truth of temper and sentiment—for this can come only of the live blending of feeling with idea—as also it may have been indirectly the cause of his poetical defects, since these are generally of the kind that it requires technical deliberation to avoid'.[23]

Bridges submitted the memoir of Dixon in mid-December and wrote to Muirhead: 'I am meditating much on the Dolben Memoir, and wonder whether you cannot help me with reminiscences. I am sure that you must remember a lot of things and persons that I have forgotten.'[24] The memoir presented two main problems: Dolben had had an adolescent crush on a fellow pupil, whose name appeared in the poems and whose widow in 1909 was unwilling to have the matter made public; and he had carried out various religious escapades, such as wandering through the streets of Birmingham barefoot and in a monk's habit. Bridges treats both enthusiasms as aspects of his youth, preserving the impression of Dolben's idealism and his own affection for him. He makes much more extensive use of expurgated letters from his subject than in the memoir of Dixon. The claims Bridges makes for Dolben are large—for example, that towards the end of his brief life he was capable of poems 'that will compare with, if they do not as I believe excel, anything that was ever written by any English poet at his age; and the work is not only of rare promise but occasionally of the rarest attainment, and its beauties are original'.[25] It was not until February 1910 that Bridges considered himself 'pretty well satisfied' with the memoir and selection of poetry. Henry James sent Logan Pearsall Smith a letter that was promptly passed on to Bridges praising the memoir, characteristically exploring in minute detail Dolben's personality and the problems of presenting it sympathetically.[26] Today, however, it is probably most frequently read for the light it throws on Bridges and Hopkins.

Preparation for the memoirs led Bridges to reread some of Hopkins' letters. Interest in his poems was now growing: Bridges received a request to reprint a couple of them in September 1908 and a similar request in March 1910, and in January 1909 Katherine Bregy's article, 'Gerard Hopkins: an Epitaph and an Appreciation', appeared in *Catholic World*. It was a perceptive and sympathetic assessment but treated him as a Catholic poet. Robert lent it to Mrs Hopkins and, thanking her for its return, remarked, 'the Catholics are very hard up for any literary interests. and are glad enough to make something of Gerard's work. I hope you will like my references to him in my Memoir of Canon Dixon . . .'[27]

Elkin Matthews, the publisher, asked Edmund Gosse to edit a volume of Hopkins' poems early in 1909, a request which he at first accepted but subsequently declined, perhaps on being told that Bridges was effectively the literary executor. Bridges asserted that Gosse was

> not only incompetent (of this particular work) but when he was visiting the Waterhouses at Yattendon in the seventies, I tried to get him to recognise the merits of Gerard's verse. He exhibited extreme antipathy . . . His belief that something might come of it now—wh is implied by his negociations—is no doubt not unfounded; but it wd be merely in the scheme of 'booming' Roman Catholic pretensions to artistic eminence: just as they pull all the strings to glorify Francis Thompson.[28]

Gosse had a reputation for inaccuracy, not a promising characteristic for the editor of an exceptionally problematic text, but Bridges would seem to have confused Gosse's reaction to Hopkins' poetry with that to his brother John's volume, *Wet Days* (see pp. 92–3 above). As an alternative to Gosse's edition he proposed to Mrs Hopkins that, 'when the time comes, "If ever that time come" I shd wish a selection of Gerard's letters to accompany his poems. In a limited edition, with R-C patronage such a book wd be sufficiently well received, and it wd I think be valuable, and take its place among "dappled things". I shd like to know your wishes.' Bridges' reluctance to consider an edition at this time probably arose from the difficulty he was having with the memoir of Dolben, and the fact that, although Hopkins would have been delighted if his poetry had been used to glorify Catholicism, Bridges wanted to avoid this. He would have helped his friend but not the religion he considered had destroyed him.

In May he received a request from Father Keating for permission to have Hopkins' poems edited by a committee of Jesuits at Farm Street. Father Keating considered that the Society of Jesus was in fact Hopkins' literary executor, but Bridges was not inclined to be helpful. The people who supported Hopkins now had not taken the offered opportunities of publishing his poetry when he was alive, and this, added to Bridges' distrust of their motives and editorial ability, made him uncooperative. Father Keating published three articles on Hopkins in the *Month* (July, August, and September 1909) in which he included Cannon Liddon's letters to Hopkins at the time of his conversion. Bridges objected on Liddon's behalf because the letters had been private and on Hopkins' because according to Father Keating, Liddon had been Hopkins' confessor: 'he might have stated their contents in general terms without offense' he added.[29] But the interest in Hopkins' verse made him feel that something should be done, and he agreed to see if the Oxford University Press would print privately 'The Wreck of the Deutschland', but nothing seems to have come of this until the edition of 1918.

Living in such proximity to Oxford, the family were increasingly drawn into the life of the university. In December 1908 Bridges undertook to write 'a lot of new things' in the part-books of New College. He dined with university friends in Oxford and was invited to special feasts such as the Christmas Gaudy at New College. The numerous concerts attracted him, and there he heard not only Palestrina and organ recitals, but orchestral concerts, in some of which Margaret played the violin. Bridges wrote to Muirhead of one such evening, 'why were you not at the concert? I went, the sole representative of our family. It was magnificent, and I had never heard the 4th Beethoven [piano] concerto before. It gave me as much pleasure almost as any music that I ever heard.'[30] Sir Hugh Allen, in whose orchestra Margaret played, put on a performance of Aristophanes' *The Frogs* in 1909, for which Parry had written the music, as well as *Fidelio* in 1910 and *Der Freischütz* in 1911. There were plenty of musical occasions at Chilswell too. In January 1909 Bridges noted, 'Monica is practising the piano part of a Mozart clarinet trio, which she expects to be called upon to play this afternoon'; a scratch performance of Schubert's Unfinished Symphony is mentioned on another occasion, and in January 1911 the violinist Joachim's nephew was at Chilswell getting a quintet together.

To Bridges' delight his son obtained a scholarship to Magdalen College, Oxford, in 1910, and in general this was for Bridges a time of contentment. In the summer of that year he wrote to Muirhead,

> Flowers music and philosophy account for me, and we have had a delightful summer so far in spite of the somewhat frequent rain, and occasionally necessary fire on the hearth. I must not forget the strawberries: but everything has been prolific and beautiful. we are extravagantly gay (florally) and all the many immigrants from Haseley flourish. I am really becoming a gardener, which I never expected, and spend many hours propagating.[31]

He did not write much poetry but concentrated on memoirs and, with his children at an expensive age, essays for which the journals would pay, including an essay on Kipling for *The Times*, one on handwriting for the *Times Literary Supplement* and three for Arkwright's musical *Antiquary*, the first of these on prosody (October 1909), the second and third on Anglican plainchant (April 1911 and January 1912). In these latter he suggested changes which would match the words of the psalms very much more closely with the music than was often the case. As with his work on prosody, he thought that he had deduced a convincing theory of how contemporary practice had evolved. Inevitably there are similarities between his historical sketch of the development of chanting and his suggestions about the shift from quantitative to accentual syllabic prosody, since in both cases he sees the change evolving out of the use of English words in Latin forms. The gist of his case is that the replacement of Latin words with English ones caused a shift from penultimate accentuation to stress on the final syllable, a shift that only became evident when the flexible plainchant melodies were harmonized, making the placing of stress far clearer. He concluded that many chants would have to be rewritten to make them more suited to the natural tendencies of the English language.

The relation of words and musical cadence was a subject in which Yeats too was interested. Yeats believed that poets wrote with distinctive verse tunes in mind. He hated the contemporary style of public reading of verse and sought a way of ensuring that his own tune could be reproduced by writing the notes and rhythm he envisaged. The effect he wanted was not that of singing, and obtaining the balance between emphasis on the music of the verse and its meaning was extremely difficult. He sent Bridges an account of his early experiments with Florence Farr, who used a psaltery:

> In our experiments in London we found your verse the most suited of all verse to this method. She [Florence Farr] recites, your 'Nightingales' your 'Muse & poet' ['Will love again awake'] and a third poem of yours whose name I forget . . . We found that the moment a poem was chanted one saw it in a quite new light—so much verse that read well spoke very ill. Miss Farr has found your verse & mine [&] a little modern lyric verse to be vocal, but that when one gets back a few generations lyric verse ceases to be vocal until it gets vocal as song not as speach is, as one approaches the Elizabethans.[32]

Bridges replied,

> I agree about the recitation, I think. It is a very difficult matter. Setting *song* aside—which has several degrees—the mere reading of poetry, if well read, is full of melodious devices, which it is the art of a good reader to conceal, so that he gets his effects without calling attention to them. The word recitation—and the presence of an instrument—makes open confession of his art, and without becoming a singer he ceases to be a reader. The hearer has his attention called to the method itself—and as I have never had any experience of good chanting or recitation I do not know how I shd like it. There was a kind of recitation fashionable some years ago in London drawing rooms—satirized by Anstie—and it even crept

into the churches. I have heard the Old Testament 'recited' in Westminster Abbey. This used to draw tears from me—tears of laughter. I shook as at a French farce. This is the only sort that I ever heard. I can't really imagine a recitation which I shd myself like as well as good reading (in which the same art wd be disguised) but I think that there must be such a thing—and I hope you and the lady will discover it.[33]

Chanting, on the other hand, did not try to hide the importance of the music. Bridges had heard the effect he wanted in Percy Buck's choir at Wells, and was also indebted to his old friend Sir Hugh Allen, who held similar views.

Music brought him too the acquaintance of Francis Brett Young, a poet and physician himself, who first wrote to Bridges in January 1910 asking if he could set some of his poems to music. Bridges replied,

musical song-form is a very cranky subject, and I doubt whether many of my little lyrics are suitable for music.—The one 'Awake my heart to be loved' was written with a musical intention, and one or two of those that you had chosen seemed all right, but generally I fancy that I use expressions which lose their meaning if they are sung. Schubert has set Heine's 'Ich stand in dunkeln Traümen' but it is plain that the last two lines

Und ach, ich kann es nicht glauben,
Dass ich dich verloren hab'!

can hardly be spoken, much less sung. They overwhelm one by their simplicity and, to liken my lesser things with these greater, I think that they are not often 'musical'.

Instead, he suggested, 'Do you know Miss Coleridge's lyrics, or Canon Dixon's? I think some of theirs wd be grateful material—and no one has tried them much yet, tho' I think that I saw that Sir Cha[rle]s Stanford was bringing out some of Miss Coleridge's.'[34] Hopkins had written musical settings for several of Bridges' poems as well as some of Dixon's, and Monica had set some of Dixon's, though none of these had been published. Bridges later invited Young to Chilswell, and the latter subsequently—in 1914—wrote the first critical book about him.

In the spring of 1911 Muirhead commissioned Sir William Richmond to paint a portrait of Bridges about which Robert wrote in April, 'I wish I could report on it but he is evidently very sensitive about being watched so that . . . none of us has ever gone behind his easel. when he has done for the day, he sets the picture with its face to the wall, and no one disturbs it.'[35] In late June it was finished and, with the exception of Elizabeth, the family liked it and Muirhead and Sir William were both pleased.

The summer of 1911 was unusually hot and much of the country suffered severe drought. In July the Bridges went to Dunwich on the coast of Suffolk. The family rented a bungalow in a wood a few hundred yards from the almost deserted sandy beach. For three weeks they sunbathed and swam. Bridges occupied himself with playing patience and doing embroidery. He had read George Tyrrell's *Christianity at the Crossroads* in June, amid the flowers and humming bees of Chilswell, and found Tyrrell's 'analysis most lucid and his thought profound and clear'. At Dunwich he read his *The Church of the Future*, and wrote to Bradley that he considered Tyrrell's 'apology for religion' in some respects 'the best' that he had seen.[36]

In 1910 Edmund Gosse formed 'An Academic Committee of English Letters'. It was to have no more than forty members and 'to represent pure literature in the same way that the Royal Academy represents the fine arts, the Royal Society science and the British Academy learning', and was under the jurisdiction of the Royal Society of Literature. Gosse intended its aims to be like those of the French Academy: 'to maintain the purity of the language' (which Bridges might have understood in a rather different way from Gosse) and to reward literary achievement. The committee included Bridges, Laurence Binyon, Joseph Conrad, Henry Dobson, J. G. Frazer, R. B. Haldane, Thomas Hardy, Henry James, Andrew Lang, John Morley, Newbolt, Arthur Wing Pinero, Yeats, Sir Walter Raleigh, and George Bernard Shaw. Bridges and Gosse inevitably clashed over its aims. Gosse wanted to hold centenary celebrations of Browning, but Bridges disagreed somewhat vehemently during a meeting in December 1911 and, writing to make peace with Gosse, explained,

I am much more sympathetic with Bernard Shaw's proposal that we shd do all we can to associate our activities with rising movements—I should be content if we could get *two* or *three* young men amongst us. If we cannot actually catch a genius we could secure ourselves by seeing that the younger men whom we selected had actual proved solid attainments, & that they would not eventually disgrace us.[37]

It may have been the Academic Committee that first brought Bridges and Walter Raleigh together. Raleigh, like Henry Bradley, was a fellow of Magdalen College and his home was at Ferry Hinksey, a short detour for Bridges on his walk from Chilswell into Oxford. In a letter Raleigh described one such visit in October 1912:

Robert Bridges has just been in on his way down the hill. He is delightfully grumpy. He mentions thing after thing which is commonly believed and says that of course it's not so. He's always right. His intellect has been so completely self-indulged that it now can't understand rubbish. He has never obeyed anyone or adapted himself to anyone, so he's as clear as crystal, and can't do with fogs.[38]

This flippant description, apart from the grumpiness, could have been applied still more justly to Raleigh himself since the two men were both outspoken in their assessments of contemporary institutions and taste. Edward Thompson notes that another reason why Bridges liked to take this route into Oxford was that it avoided the built-up areas. However, it forced him to cross the river. 'If the ferryboat happened to be the wrong side, Bridges did not always bother to shout for it. At least once, when he was over seventy-five, he merely waded, carrying his trousers, since the water comes up to your waist.'[39]

One of Bridges' projects that was a long time in coming to fruition was a phonetic type to be used by Horace Hart at the Clarendon Press. Bridges chose a series of mostly Anglo-Saxon letters from several founts at the Press. He wrote to Muirhead early in March 1909 that he expected that in a very short time he would be able to send him a '"Lord's Prayer" or some short sample which we shall have to set up before we plunge into casting the fount'. He hoped to be able to use it to print a few books by subscription. Bridges generally had to contribute to the publishing expenses of his various volumes and experiments, and a shortage of money restricted what he and Monica were able to do with the phonetic type. Bridges wrote a paper on English pronunciation for the

English Association in 1910 to advertise it. Interest in modifying English spelling was, of course, not a new idea. In the 1840s impetus for reform had come from the development of Pitman's shorthand, which emphasized its irregularities. Further calls for revision came after 1870 with the efforts to broaden the spread of education, when it was claimed that 'teaching our anomalous system of spelling to the children of the poor is in most cases impracticable . . . when the task is in exceptional instances accomplished, it entails either the loss of much other instruction . . . or the sacrifice to indigent parents of a child's possible earnings during a considerable period'. At the turn of the century the Simplified Spelling Society was formed, and Walter Skeat wrote its first pamphlet, *On the History of English Spelling*, in 1902. It was later to have the backing of professors Gilbert Murray and Daniel Jones. The system was to use no new characters or diacritics but to make each symbol as self-sufficient as possible. G. H. Vallins commented that 'it would seem that the Society in an effort to respect the old spelling has failed to secure that perfect (or almost perfect) correspondence between sound and symbol which is deemed essential to any rational and workable system of reform.'[40] It is, however, still in use. Bridges regarded 'Simplified Spelling' as having been developed 'on an unscientific and non-literary basis'. Trying to persuade Bradley to withdraw his support from it, he advocated a more fully phonetic script, explaining:

> My notion is that if you can get intelligent people to think about the matter they will see that the ordinary conversational way of speaking is slovenly, and immediately they realise what sounds they say nature, neycher—saxifrage, saxerfidge etc., they will do something. and what they do will have a conservative attitude and tend to restore things which are in danger of disappearing.
>
> I advocate such a system of spelling as would be at once literary and careful, and more or less consistent. then when that is once fixed let people pronounce it as they now pronounce for all that I care, but they would know what the better pronunciation was. I do not care what means are taken to this end. whether mute final e's might not be retained to lengthen preceding vowels, and double consonants to shorten them. But I think the main matter is to get people to realise what they say.
>
> It seems to me that some form of phonetic spelling will prevail with our democracy—& I want people to see what that will mean. It does not

concern me what will happen, only it shall not be my fault if things take a worse turn.[41]

In 1911 and 1912 Bridges revised his tract on the Present State of English Pronunciation (1910, 2nd impression 1913), adding an appendix. He attempted to persuade Bradley to write on the subject, preferably a note that could be included in the pamphlet. But Bradley replied,

A lot of words will have to perish from the language if we get phonetic spelling . . . The reformers are wrong in saying that adoption of phonetic spelling would not affect the language itself. It would do so profoundly, so far as the literary language is concerned; in some respects no doubt the result would be for the good, but the breach with the past, for all but the highly educated, would be, so far as I can see, an evil.[42]

He later put these ideas into a paper that has been reprinted many times as one of the standard documents on the subject, 'On the Relations between Spoken and Written Language, with special reference to English' (1913). In his reply Bridges failed to meet Bradley's objection and he did not finish his revisions until December 1912.

After Christmas 1911 Bridges settled down to writing an article on Wordsworth and Kipling. Published in the *Times Literary Supplement* on 29 February 1912, it was formed around a review of a concordance to Wordsworth's poems and a *Dictionary of the Characters and Scenes in the Stories and Poems of Rudyard Kipling, 1886–1911*. He was not enthusiastic about the concordance, which was four times the volume of Wordsworth's poetry, primarily because it had been compiled on alphabetical rather than philological principles. He used the review to discuss the use of dialect to regenerate decaying language, remarking on Synge's attitude as expressed in the preface to *The Playboy of the Western World*, to which Yeats may well have introduced him. Although Bridges did not quote Synge accurately, his analysis of the effect is valid. He remarked that Synge's use of dialect was 'a very welcome freshness and a gracious beauty of motion, which his genius made the best of; but the charm of it soon palls, and its strangeness becomes itself a mannerism more mannered than that which it supplanted'.[43] From diction Bridges turns to poetic form, and his impatience with rhymed accentual syllabic verse is clear. He is as assertive as

T. S. Eliot in stressing the need for modification of old forms if they are to be used for modern verse, and he criticized Wordsworth for thinking that he could 'purify the diction and revivify English poetry by putting a new content into the old verse-forms'. Bridges had already experimented with new forms; he was to become increasingly adventurous in this from now on, and writing the article may have contributed to his conviction of the necessity of further experimentation.

Towards the end of 1912 or the beginning of 1913 Bridges proposed to establish a Society for Pure English whose expenses he would guarantee. The society was not designed to be an English version of the Académie française, but to publish regular tracts in which various linguistic and stylistic issues were discussed and new books reviewed. He wanted as members of the group only people who agreed with and were prepared to practise the society's aims; their influence on English was to be entirely by example and he hoped that the newspapers (and, later, the BBC) would become interested practitioners. What is desirable, said Bridges, 'is that our language in its future development should be controlled by the forces and processes which have formed it in the past; that it should keep its English character, and that the new elements added to it should be in harmony with the old'.[44] To this end the society favoured the use of English forms of adopted foreign words; the use of English words to create new compounds; and the encouragement and preservation of dialect words in preference to technical ones drawn from classical roots. Finally, in order to preserve the rhythms of English literature of earlier periods, it recommended the increased use of the enclitics that had been branded ungrammatical in the eighteenth century. The richness of tradition was, Bridges thought, worth considering in deciding about the direction in which the language developed. His general attitude to its growth may be seen in a paper on aesthetics when, in discussing the change from 'es' to 's' endings as in 'postes' to 'posts', he said,

> the monosyllable *posts* is a longer and more difficult word to say than the older disyllable *postes*: and *god's* is longer and more ill-sounding than *Goddis* or *Goddes*. At the time that this particular change was taking place there was probably complete ignorance of what was going on, and certainly no machinery for supervision; but now when we cannot plead

ignorance, and are well supplied with machinery, the attitude of blind indifference is inexcusable. Is it not our duty to exercise ordinary foresight and do what we can to obviate the inconveniences that threaten our language?[45]

The original suggestion of forming the society was made, according to Logan Pearsall Smith, during one of his visits to Chilswell.[46] The first person Bridges sought to interest in it was Henry Bradley, whom Bridges later described as the 'mainstay' of the group. Preparations for launching the society came to a halt with the outbreak of war in 1914 and did not resume until 1919. The society then issued regular tracts until 1948. During Bridges' lifetime the most frequent authors were Thomas Fowler and Otto Jespersen. Though Bradley wrote no complete articles for the SPE—he was just writing his first when he died—he vetted all its publications; 'many pages in the Tracts have profited by his correction', said Bridges. 'Some of the papers were carefully edited by him, and here and there he added valuable notes.'[47] Bridges asserts that Bradley's reluctance to write articles stemmed from his fear that the fee might come from his friend's pocket. It was probably a qualm without foundation. Minutes for the society only exist from the 1920s, but these show that the tracts were so popular that at one point membership-charges were actually reduced while the fees paid to contributors were raised and a part-time secretary hired.

The founding members elected a small committee to prepare tracts and handle the finances. This consisted initially of Bridges, Logan Pearsall Smith, Henry Bradley, and Walter Raleigh. Monica was often an invited guest at meetings, taking an increasingly important role as Bridges entered his eighties. After his death she became a member of the committee. Initially the meetings were held in Corpus, 'in the little drawing-room overlooking the garden . . . Curried chicken, apple-tart, and a bottle of claret was the regulation fare.' There they would talk 'by the open windows till 3 o'clock . . . wishing the hours were longer.'[48] Raleigh would enliven the meetings with his witty mockery of anything smacking of bureaucracy. The facetious objection to a proposed new member on the grounds that 'he's a windbag and Socialist, a vegetarian—he's pro-Boer; he writes filthy prose', which Edward Thompson mistakenly attributes to Bridges, was one of Raleigh's jokes, as Pearsall Smith noted.[49]

Wanting to influence Daniel Jones, a member of the Simplified Spelling Society, whose phonetics seemed to him flawed, Bridges invited Jones and his wife, 'a very young Frenchwoman', to stay at Chilswell. Bridges told Bradley, 'we got on well with them. and I had great discussions about the points that I fight for—and he was not at all unsympathetic. He seems a really learned phonetician, very clearheaded and generally reasonable. His wife "quite a dear".'[50] Bridges probably learnt a lot from Jones and initially thought that he in turn had influenced him to 'be more scrupulous about the tendency of his teaching: for he saw the point of my contention, and, as I said, he was not unsympathetic'. However, by February 1913 Bridges was explaining to Abercrombie that his phonetic system was intended as an experiment to be developed by other people. Jones had evidently criticized it as clumsy and Bridges wanted to 'get the pamphlet [*A Tract on the Present State of English Pronunciation*] out separately with some answers to the enemy Jones & Co.' George Bernard Shaw, he added, 'is on my side'.[51] In 1921 the Clarendon Press told Bridges that his tract was in danger of dying: 'there are no plates or stock in trade'. Do you, they asked, 'wish to revive or revise it?' But he had become a bit bored by the subject even in the course of making his revisions in 1912 and replied, 'let it die'.[52] His views on pronunciation were motivated by his desire to increase the beauty of spoken English. Bridges, who has been called 'the author of the largest body of entirely beautiful poetry in the language',[53] had a keen ear and a readiness to adopt what sounded well to him, as is evident from an incident he described to Bradley: 'Yesterday at the Clarendon Hotel I had to ask the ostler where my wife had driven to, & he said "To Beaumont Street" pronouncing *Beaumont* fully. i.e. the first syllable as a French word the second as an Italian—& I felt how much better it was than my own pronunciation. Henceforth I shall say it as he says it.'[54]

In 1912, Bridges rashly became embroiled in a public dispute with Logan Pearsall Smith over his book, *The English Language*, which seemed to him to draw heavily on Bradley's *The Making of English*. Bridges wrote to both writers and *The Times* saying as much.[55] The charge hurt Smith, who pointed out that his work appeared so close to Bradley's because they had both drawn on a common source. This refutation and Bridges' 'diplomatic' reply accepting the explanation and withdrawing his charge then appeared in the *Times Literary Supplement* on 20 June 1912, but his final letter to Bradley on the affair suggests that he was not totally convinced by Smith. It is also clear from the correspondence that he felt far closer to Bradley, although throughout the incident and for some considerable time afterwards he tried, while making his point, not to break his friendship with the younger man.

14

Poet Laureate

(1912–1914)

In June 1912 Bridges was, with Henry James, awarded an Honorary D.Litt. at Oxford. Responding in high spirits to Muirhead's congratulations, he said,

'I am as you say very much honoured—which I attribute partly & chiefly to the whiteness of my beard . . . The reason why I am glad to have this degree is that I am more or less responsible for the gown which was chosen some four years ago for the full dress of the Litt. & Scientific Doctor's degree, and the tailors make it of a wrong shade. Now I shall try and get the right colours (though I shall not be able to do this in time for the Encaenia, when they will provide the gown for me for the day) and set the matter right.[1]

He added more seriously: 'Now in these revoluntionary times, when a million men are on strike, & the whole of Europe on the edge of a catastrophe and general shifting of all things, the smallness of this motive is so apparent that it shows a certain amount of faith in the stability of things in any one who can entertain it.' Bridges was clearly delighted at the honour and thoroughly enjoyed the ceremony (Encaenia), with its associated conviviality. Muirhead wrote to Monica that he and Grace thought that they had never seen him looking more well and happy.

The day after Encaenia the Bridges went to Cheltenham for a performance at a girls' school of *Achilles in Scyros*:

There was [he said] a deal of cheering and bestowing of bouquets at the end: but the thing was a failure. I felt at first somewhat depressed at the flatness of it until it struck me that since the girls did not (with the exception of Deidamia who looked & acted well) in any way appear like the persons whom they represented, and since one could not hear exactly what they said the effect was natural.[2]

But the play, or rather masque, is not one of Bridges' best—he had made no attempt to use the myth as allegory for more profound ideas, and this left the piece with little more than 'slender fanciful charm'.[3]

In November Oxford University Press issued their first edition of Bridges' *Poetical Works*, combining a selection from all his previous volumes of poetry with a few other poems. One of these, 'Johannes Milton, Senex', written in scazons, is probably his most successful piece in a quantitative metre. Much of its impetus derives from the poem's logical structure, which impels the reader through the first few lines in search of the consequences whose existence is implied by the opening word, 'since':

Since I believe in God the Father Almighty,
Man's Maker and Judge, Overruler of Fortune,
'Twere strange should I praise anything and refuse Him
praise,
Should love the creature forgetting the Creator,
Nor unto Him in suff'ring and sorrow turn me:
Nay how coud I withdraw me from His embracing?

The beautifully balanced phrases of the simple antithesis of lines 3, 4 and 5 are made still easier for mind and tongue by the repetition of words and sounds in them: praise–praise, creature–Creator, suff'ring–sorrow. The second and third stanzas qualify the statement of the first verse, setting out Bridges' creed:

But since that I have seen not, and cannot know Him,
Nor in my earthly temple apprehend rightly
His wisdom and the heav'nly purpose eternal;
Therefore will I be bound to no studied system
Nor argument, nor with delusion enslave me,
Nor seek to please Him in any foolish invention,
Which my spirit within me, that loveth beauty
And hateth evil, hath reprov'd as unworthy:

But I cherish my freedom in loving service,
Gratefully adoring for delight beyond asking
Or thinking, and in hours of anguish and darkness
Confiding always on His excellent greatness.

This is by far the clearest and most concise statement of his belief, showing his broad Christianity and doctrinal unorthodoxy.

Bridges was one of only two living authors whom the editor Charles Williams allowed in the Oxford Standard Poets series. Bridges told Muirhead that, while he appreciated the honour and hoped that the variety would make the volume popular, he had so long ceased to feel any satisfaction in the poems that he took 'no sort of pleasure in seeing them in the market'.[4] Indeed, he told Newbolt, 'the interest that I take in my Clarendon Press edition is the foolish position that it will put me in if it does not sell'.[5] He need not have worried; 27,000 copies were sold in the first year alone,[6] and its popularity probably had a significant influence on the choice of Bridges as Poet Laureate. A number of critics reviewed the volume in conjunction with Edward Marsh's first volume of *Georgian Poetry*, which had been 'dedicated to Robert Bridges by the writers and the editors'. Several of the reviews praised him as the greatest living master of verse in England, and suggested that the Georgians showed an 'assimilation of verse to the manner and accent of natural speech' derived from Wordsworth and Coleridge and, more recently, characteristic of Bridges.[7] However, Bridges, himself aware of fundamental differences, wrote to Marsh,

> I do not wish to criticize [and] I may say that I think I am mainly sympathetic with the psychological tendency of the 'school', which is generally, I suppose, a reaction agst intellectualism. As far as a new moral position is deduced from this, I feel that the necessity of its being subordinated to aesthetic beauty is in danger of being lost sight of. I feel sometimes as if I were being reminded of postimpressionists' pictures. You know however that I am not opposed to novelties and that I welcome any assault against dead conventional bondage.[8]

Marsh's criteria for inclusion were 'intelligibility, music and raciness' but, since Bridges' ideas of raciness would have been constrained by the Victorian decorum in which he had grown up, he could not have been comfortable with all that Marsh published. However, he continued to take an interest in *Georgian Poetry*, praising the work of D. H. Lawrence, Wilfred Gibson, and Rupert Brooke, three of whose poems he included in *The Spirit of Man*. He also tried to get Marsh to accept Herbert Palmer among his

Georgians for 'the genuine imaginative quality' of his sonnet 'Ishmael', but Marsh refused and Bridges wrote protesting, 'Graves and I wd say that you do not recognise the sort of excellence that this man has'.[9]

Logan Pearsall Smith sent Bridges Charles Vildrac's *Livre d'Amour*, to which he responded, 'I do not know when I have been so much interested by new work. I have ordered the book . . . and also his announced volume about French rhythm, which ought to be very interesting.'[10] He considered that the poems were not 'above detailed criticism', but he appreciated Vildrac's novelty in attitude and prosody, and his excellence: 'I have enjoyed reading it very much and put the author in a very high rank.' There have not been very many Englishmen of nearly 70 who have been so willing to read new work in foreign languages. Although Bridges objected to aspects of most of the things he read in his life, he also had a capacity, even as an old man, to appreciate literary qualities that were different from his own. Vildrac was a friend of Roger Fry, who had been introduced to him by Ezra Pound. He belonged to a group of French writers and artists who had tried to live as a community, supporting themselves with their garden produce and the sale of books that they printed. The experiment had run out of money but prompted Jules Romains to write *La Vie unanime*, which Bridges was later to praise for its psychological insights into group emotion. It may also have influenced Fry in his setting up of the Omega Workshop.

In 1913 the *Journal of Education* 'offered a prize for a list of the "three greatest poets in order of excellence." The winning list was determined by plebiscite . . . The vote gave first place to Kipling, second place to Watson, and third place to Bridges.'[11] That year Alfred Austin died and the question of who was to succeed him as Poet Laureate arose. When in 1892 there had been discussions as to who was to follow Tennyson as Laureate the principal names mentioned had been Swinburne, Kipling, and Bridges. Sir Edward Grey had backed Bridges bringing him to Asquith's notice for the first time,[12] while at Arthur Balfour's insistence Kipling had been asked whether he would take the post, but he had refused because 'he thought he could be of more use to the country and do better work if he were free to write as he chose'.[13] In 1913 the two names were Kipling and Bridges. According to Lady Violet Bonham-

Carter, 'the obvious choice was Kipling. Bridges was the alternative in my Father's mind. What weighed with him was . . . that Kipling was inspired and could not write to order. Bridges with his chiselled gift would be more likely to be able to do so.' This was a misunderstanding of Bridges, but in mid-July he was invited to become Poet Laureate. He replied to Asquith:

> I judge from your letter that you really desire me to accept: and if that is so, I do not think that I have a right to refuse. I therefore very humbly and gratefully accept the honour which you are so good as to offer me.
>
> This is all that you will care to hear, but I wish to add that my hesitation, which caused the delay in my reply, was due only to a sense of my unfitness, and to a dislike of the personal inconveniences that have, I am afraid, gathered round this rather peculiar office.[14]

Indeed, had it been known what would be required of the Poet Laureate in the next five years Bridges would not have been chosen. If Newbolt had not been serving in the navy, he would almost certainly have been able to fulfil the role during World War I more easily and convincingly. Bridges was not a Poet Laureate who ever wrote well to order. Complaints made in Parliament that he was not writing enough during World War I underestimate how hard he tried, but while the honour gave him a confidence and made him better known than he would otherwise have been, both the official subjects and the traditional poetic forms he felt obliged to tackle were inimical to the direction in which he wanted to develop. What the experience of the war did contribute to his poetry was a deeper thoughtfulness about the darker sides of man's nature.

Bridges' first publication as Poet Laureate was in Harold Monro's influential *Poetry and Drama*. 'Flycatchers' was a very slight poem, an experiment in free verse that had been written in February. He had, he noted, shown the poem to Sir Edward Grey before publication and received his approval, but there is in it an element of cocking a snook at the establishment; a suggestion before his appointment that he would not naturally like to be restricted to the versifying of official views.

> Sweet pretty fledgelings, perched on the rail arow,
> Expectantly happy, where ye can watch below

Your parents a-hunting i' the meadow grasses
All the gay morning to feed you with flies;

Ye recall me a time sixty summers ago,
When, a young chubby chap, I sat just so
With others on a school-form rank'd in a row,
Not less eager and hungry than you, I trow,
With intelligences agape and eyes aglow,
While an authoritative old wise-acre
Stood over us and from a desk fed us with flies.

Dead flies—such as litter the library south-window,
That buzzed at the panes until they fell stiff-baked on the sill,
Or are roll'd up asleep i' the blinds at sunrise,
Or wafer'd flat in a shrunken folio.

A dry biped he was, nurtured likewise
On skins and skeletons, stale from top to toe
With all manner of rubbish and all manner of lies.

Bridges suggested that he withdraw from the Society for Pure English because of 'possible misunderstandings'; perhaps he had in mind that his new position might suggest that the SPE was an official government institution, closer in its role to the Académie française than he wanted. He seems to have been rapidly reassured and the work of gathering new members proceeded smoothly.

For a time he participated in some of the social events that were part of the national poetry 'scene', taking part, for example, in one of Monro's evenings of poetry reading at his Poetry Bookshop. His metrical experiments at the time included translating some two hundred lines of the final book of the *Iliad* into quantitative hexameters. But by November he was attempting 'to work out an altogether new sort of thing', and warned that this 'third manner' of his would be very different from his earlier styles. It was to prove to be more personal and discursive, with wry humour and a more colloquial tone and in general the loosest of regular prosodical schemes. He explained to J. W. Mackail that he was trying to 'make an English prosody . . . *independent of rhythm*'. There were, he thought, 'two lines to take—(1) the system which Milton arrived at, i.e., a fixed syllabic basis with a free rhythm superimposed. (2) The free rhythm, governed by stress, independent of syllabic numeration'.[15] He had, he said, tried both systems and found that both worked. Bridges' notes in *New Verse* (1926) and *October and Other Poems* (1920) expand the explanation. In *New Verse*, for example, he records how for many years he had had the complete subject of a poem in mind but had been unable to give it a form: 'one cannot originate a poem in an unknown metre, for it is familiarity with its framework which invites the words into their places.' He found that writing it in twelves with a mid-caesural break solved the problem, and the poem 'ran off quite spontaneously to its old title "The Flowering Tree", which is dated in my book November 7, 1913':

> The sunlight was enmesh'd
>   in the shifting splendour
> And I saw through on high
>   to soft lakes of blue sky . . .

Three other pieces in this metre were published in *October and Other Poems*: 'Noel', dated 28 November, 'In der Fremde' (12 December), and 'The West Front' from 1917. Bridges noted that they were:

> strictly syllabic verse on the model left by Milton in 'Samson Agonistes'; except that his system, which depended on exclusion of extra-metrical syllables (that is, syllables which did not admit of resolution by 'elision' into a disyllabic scheme) from all places but the last, still admitted them in that place, thereby forbidding inversion of the last foot. It is natural to conclude that, had he pursued his inventions, his next step would have been to get rid of this anomaly; and if this is done, the result is the new rhythms that these poems exhibit . . . It is probably agreed that there are possibilities in that long six-foot line which English poetry has not fully explored.[16]

All four poems can still be scanned as fairly regular accentual metres, although with extra freedoms as in the opening lines of 'In der Fremde'—'Ah! wild-hearted wand'rer | far in the world away.' The technical weakness in these poems, as elsewhere in Bridges' work, is the choice of words or ordering of syntax to satisfy the rhyme, such as the use of 'forby' at the end of the stanza: 'hearing the wind to sigh: | 'Twas thy lover calling | whom thou didst leave forby.' Moving away from verse that used end-rhyme was thus to be of exceptional benefit to Bridges, allowing emphasis to fall on his strengths, such as the interplay of grammatical and verse units or the more subtle patterning of sound.

Characteristically, he also began to use his enhanced position to try to further the cause of writers whose work attracted him. His first endeavour was to try to help R. Piccoli to obtain an Italian scholarship to Cambridge. A few months later he was attempting to persuade Monro to include a review of Willoughby Weaving's first volume of *Poems*, 'by a critic who will take him seriously, and not merely make fun of his mistakes. He is a very shy nature and needs encouragement: at least if his work justifies it',[17] as Bridges clearly thought it did. In 1916 he wrote the introduction to Weaving's volume called *The Star Fields and Other Poems*, which Weaving then dedicated to Bridges. However, Bridges was also aware that his post was a political one. Yeats invited him to a restaurant dinner in honour of Wilfred Scawen Blunt in December 1913. Bridges declined, replying that he admired Blunt's work, but that, besides disliking restaurant dinners, he was apprehensive of being involved in 'ostensibly' honouring someone who had 'unfortunately a very political or impolitical side' (Blunt was an ardent champion of Irish and Indian nationalism).[18]

Bridges' first official publication as Poet Laureate was 'Noel', a Christmas poem which he sent as a greeting to the King and which, since it was impersonal, the King had published in *The Times*. 'Noel' is in syllabics, with elisions that have the effect of occasional trisyllabic feet. Since the poem was intended to be popular, its elisions, with one exception, were made immediately apparent and easily assimilable into the speech rhythm:

> . . . from many a village
>   in the water'd valley
> Distant music reach'd me
>   peals of bells aringing:
> The constellated sounds
>   ran sprinkling on earth's floor
> As the dark vault above
>   with stars was spangled o'er

Critics, somewhat to Bridges' amusement, suggested that he was trying to imitate Langland with 'perhaps unjustifiable liberties'.

During 1914 Bridges revised his Dolben memoir and his essay

on Keats. His translations of Virgil and Homer were published and he finished a tract on Daniel Jones' dictionary, the preparation for which he had found tedious. He also read Clive Bell's book, *Art*. In it Bell suggests that most people only 'recognise' things in the world or see them in terms of their utility. The artist, on the other hand, sees the essence of a thing or even the universal or divine in it—its 'significant form'. He calls this the emotional way of perceiving the world. The viewer's perception of the artist's ecstasy in his work is 'aesthetic emotion', an appreciation of art that he distinguishes from appreciation of beautiful things in the world. Art lifts the viewer above the mundane and frees him from human interests; it is a state which he compares to that of the pure mathematician when rapt in his studies. The perception of the emotional significance of the universe is also found, he asserts, in religion although art is not the expression of religion. Bridges told Roger Fry that he liked Bell's book and generally agreed with him, but thought that he should have considered music as the artistic medium most susceptible to analysis. He found Bell's description of the artist's devotion exaggerated, and said that his insistence on 'what he calls primitive qualities' leads him to 'exclude and underrate quite necessary complications'.[19] Bridges may well have been thinking of the relationship he saw between the response to beauty and spirituality, the potential for which he believed all men possessed. The next few years were to test his faith in the theory.

15

War

(1914–1918)

Some of the atmosphere of the Bridges' home at this time may be caught in a note Monica wrote to Muirhead, thanking him for a portrait he had given the family. The picture had arrived the previous evening, 'and had to be unpacked immediately . . . I have just got a chance to write to you today, as the organist from the Cowley Fathers has come to tea, and while he and Margaret play a Handel concerto, I write this for him to post—All the same it is impossible to write while music goes on—but please read my pleasure and gratitude, in spite of poor expression.'[1] In May Monica's throat again began to give trouble, leaving Bridges worried and unsettled, but she was better in June and early in July they went down to Littlehampton on the Sussex coast where he reported that they were 'splashing like Nereids in the brine—and the brine at 70° F.' during a heatwave.[2]

The international picture, meanwhile, was steadily worsening. Conflict had been growing between Pan-Slav and Pan-Germanic movements in Eastern Europe and the Balkans. The final chain of events is now well known: the assassination of the Austrian Archduke Franz Ferdinand and his wife on a visit to Serbia, an event seized on by Austria to move to open confrontation with an ultimatum to Serbia and declaration of war on 28 July; Russia's general mobilization on 30 July, Germany's the following day; the declarations of war by Germany against Russia on 1 August and against France on 3 August, on which day *The Times* reported, 'Europe is in arms, the greatest war of modern times is upon us'. On 4 August England declared war on Germany. It was Edward Bridges' twenty-second birthday. The following day he graduated with a First and started looking for war work, but because he was short-sighted, was not among those first chosen as combatants. He had been a member of the Oxford University Officers' Training Corps and drilled recruits in England until August 1915, when he was accepted for service in France. Five days after the declaration Bridges wrote to Muirhead, who was anxious about his son Antony:

the war is dreadful in its possibilities. on account of the unknown capacities of these airships. It is bewildering to think of, and I have great difficulty in not giving way to senseless excitement. The resistance of the Belgians was quite unforeseen. Neither William [the Kaiser] nor our Foreign Office gave them credit for anything: and their glorious bravery has not only disconcerted the German plans. but established an immense moral discouragement to them—I am wild with delight at their prowess.[3]

Bridges, like most people, was convinced that confrontation with Germany had been inevitable but had no conception of how long or dreadful a struggle it would be. He wrote 'our case hangs on the imminent Battle of the North Sea—I wish I could not think of it.'[4] He was soon in a state of continual anxiety. Each day for the first week of war *The Times* carried a patriotic poem. Bridges' contribution, 'Wake up, England!', was published on 8 August. He told his sister Carry that he had tried to say 'what was quite simple and would be universally approved':[5]

Thou careless, awake!
  Thou peacemaker fight!
Stand, England, for honour,
  And God guard the Right!

Thy mirth lay aside,
  Thy cavil and play:
Thy foe is upon thee,
  And grave is the day.

The monarch Ambition
  Hath harnessed his slaves;
But the folk of the Ocean
  Are free as the waves.

For Peace thou art armed
  Thy Freedom to hold:
Thy Courage as iron,
  Thy Good-faith as gold.

Through Fire, Air, and Water
  Thy trial must be:
But they that love life best
  Die gladly for thee.

The Love of their mothers
  Is strong to command;
The fame of their fathers
  Is might to their hand.

Much suffering shall cleanse thee;
  But thou through the flood
Shalt win to Salvation,
  To Beauty through blood.

Up, careless, awake!
  Ye peacemakers, Fight!
ENGLAND STANDS FOR HONOUR,
  GOD DEFEND THE RIGHT!

Bridges' expectation that the poem would win widespread approval was based on the fact that he had incorporated a number of sayings and attitudes commonly voiced at the time. The title, 'Wake up, England', had been 'the King's well-known call to the country in 1901 at the Guildhall', the ideals of selfless service to a country watched over by God had given Kipling and Newbolt enormous popularity. The unsavoury idea that the country would be purged by the war was Bridges' reaction to the reorganizing of the social fabric from an undemocratic order to one recognizably modern which had resulted in civil violence over Irish Home Rule, women's suffrage, and bad working conditions, and the crisis over the House of Lords' rejection of Lloyd George's 1911 budget.

At the end of August Bridges wrote to his sister,

the war is awful. I can scarcely hold together. The crisis is so tremendous, but we ought to be very grateful to that deceitful William for putting us so absolutely in the right. Also, it being evident what his schemes are, it is certain that if we had not joined in the issue now, we shd have been both morally and materially in a far worse position after it. Humanly speaking the conditions could scarcely have been better for us—and there is also this on the good side, that is, that we were sick with domestic boils & broils which it needed some vast fever to drive off. I trust & pray that all may go well. Have you read what is called 'The White Paper'? you can get it for 9d. It is the Parliamentary copy of all the negociation preceding the war . . . It is sickening to think of those millions of men in Germany fighting bravely for the wrong. And this will probably continue for about two years.—Just at present I am far too disturbed to write, the communication with my subconscious mind is broken off . . .[6]

He remarked, 'I have never in my life known so beautiful an autumn, nor so prolific a general harvest. It is strange that it should concur with an eclipse of the Sun, and the death of the Pope.' By and large, however, Bridges' sense of humour, like his poetic ability, was muted by the war. His letters frequently suggest that he was 'off balance', and many of his opinions on subjects unrelated to the war were less perceptive than was normal with him.

In December Bridges was asked by Charles Longman, whose son had been killed in the war, to compile an anthology of poems and prose extracts that the grief-stricken would find consoling. He also intended it to entertain those serving at the Front. Bridges, suggesting that people get consolation from beauty rather than philosophy, set about making 'a book of beauty, excluding sexual passion and mirth'.[7] Although he has been criticized for excluding sexual passion, there would seem to be practical reasons for doing so given that the book was intended for those in the trenches and those left alone at home. He asked a number of his friends to help, among them Logan Pearsall Smith, William Sanday, J. W. Mackail, Gilbert Murray, and Walter Raleigh. 'The unity of the book', he warned 'will be that it only has *things that I like* in it.' The resulting volume, *The Spirit of Man*, shows Shelley, Shakespeare, Milton, Keats, and Amiel with over twenty extracts each, Blake, Wordsworth, and Dixon with over fifteen. He chose eleven passages from Coleridge, ten from Plato, eight each from Yeats and Pascal, seven from Marcus Aurelius, and six each from Hopkins and Dolben. There were a number of passages from French authors in French but all else was translated, and Bridges worked on many of the passages from the Greek and Latin himself. He also included Indian and Persian extracts, acknowledging: 'In all my Oriental quotations, I owe everything to my friend Hasan Shahid Suhrawardy for putting his taste and wide learning at my disposal.' Bridges said to A. H. Bullen, 'English pietists should be surprised to see their George Herbert ranging with Jellaludin and Kabir, with no difference between them but their prosody!!'[8] The anthology contained many beautiful and unfamiliar pieces, and great care was clearly expended in their juxtaposition.

Bridges' war effort took other forms besides the preparation of the anthology. At the age of nearly 70 he was a member of 'Godley's army' (a regiment of Oxford citizens past military age), drilling three miles between 7.00 and 8.00 a.m., crawling through hedges, with afternoon drills and route marches.[9] In December 1914 he apparently overdid it and was ordered by his doctor not to take so much exercise. He then bought a car, which Elizabeth soon learnt to drive. She was to work in several convalescent hospitals in England during the war. In 1915 Margaret went to France where she worked in the kitchens and played in concerts in a convalescent hospital. John Masefield had hoped to set up a hospital in the Argonne and invited Margaret, who was a family friend, to join him, but the plans fell through and she spent most of the war in Boulogne.

H. J. Grierson sent Bridges his edition of Donne's poems, perhaps because in his introduction he had quoted Bridges' 'Awake, my heart, to be loved . . .' with the comment, 'Donne has written nothing at once so subtle and so pure and lovely as this'. Bridges was grateful for the compliment, but remarked to Grierson that Donne's 'psychology (espec[iall]y of sensual love) seems to me bad as well as ugly', and 'his "learning" . . . seems to me pestilential. I shelve him with Burton's Anatomy of Melancholy, and Sir Tho[ma]s Browne's lucubrations—whereas I adore Montaigne'.[10]

In October Francis Brett Young had sent Monica a copy of his book, *Robert Bridges: A Critical Study*. In an essay written in 1920 Bridges alluded to it when referring to a 'writer—whom I as highly esteem for his talent as I pity him for the misfortune he fell into when he contracted to write my "life" without even any acquaintance with its meagre materials—who described me, I believe, as a child of the English Prayer Book'.[11] He told Brett Young that he wished he 'had been able to say' more about Hopkins' influence on his writing. Although he and Hopkins had initially experimented with stress prosody independently—Bridges had used it for one of the poems in his first published volume (1873)—after a meeting in July 1877 Bridges said, Hopkins 'was no doubt responsible for my developments. He was a very accurate hairsplitting analyst and grammarian, and his patience supplied me with just what I needed, often showing me the justice of my own contention when we disagreed'.[12] He also acknowledged that Hopkins' advice had improved his pamphlet on *Milton's Prosody*.[13]

As far as the publication of Hopkins' own verse was concerned, Bridges admitted that although a number of people were now urging him to prepare an edition, he believed that the time was still not right. Hopkins' poetry was, he said, of a 'very difficult & unpopular nature', and he feared that publication would only lead to 'adverse criticism & ridicule'. On the other hand, refusing to publish the poems, he realized, also led to problems: 'I am really (by my doing nothing) laying myself open to the charge of suppressing the work of a man to whose originality I owe so much.' This charge has been levelled at Bridges repeatedly ever since the appearance of his first edition of Hopkins' *Poems* in 1918, and the question of what he owed to Hopkins is therefore worth considering. Hopkins' detailed criticisms certainly helped Bridges to become a more careful craftsman and his experiments encouraged him to be more adventurous rhythmically. However, as Donald Stanford has remarked, Bridges used Hopkins' most important metre—sprung rhythm—for a comparatively short time and the effects he wanted it for were generally different from those Hopkins produced.[14] It is noteworthy too that Bridges referred to Shelley's 'Away the moor is dark beneath the moon' as another of the sources for his interest in sprung rhythm and was clearly influenced by it in 'On a Dead Child'.[15] Similarly, Hopkins used hexameters for his incomplete tragedy, 'St Winefred's Well' where Bridges chose the metre for the comic *Feast of Bacchus*. This indirect stimulus and productive disagreement—echoes of Hopkins are rare in Bridges' work—make Bridges one of the poets most successfully, although too briefly, influenced by Hopkins.

In February 1915 Bridges, returning to his earlier interest in Italy and Italian, accepted an honourary membership of the Oxford Dante Society at which papers were given on such subjects as 'Quotations in Dante' and 'Virgil and Dante's Italy'. Bridges' friends Herbert Warren and J. W. Mackail were already members, and over the next six years he attended some half-dozen meetings. Bridges' copy of the *Divine Comedy* shows by his annotations that he continued to read it closely over many years.[16]

In June W. B. Yeats made his second and last weekend visit to Chilswell. He discovered that Elizabeth had published anonymously a volume of poems entitled *Charitessi* about which he was initially very enthusiastic, calling it 'the best poetry done by any woman in our time'.[17] He sent Bridges a selection of his poems printed in Germany and *The Green Helmet and Other Poems*, and Lady Gregory's two volumes of Irish mythology. Bridges told Yeats that, reading the preface of her *Gods and Fighting Men*, 'I thought wonderfully well of Lady Gregory until I got to the last page of it and saw your name at the bottom'.[18] On 23 June Yeats sent him Ezra Pound's *Cathay*, 'his book of Chinese translations'. Bridges' library also contains copies of *Canzoni and Ripostes* and *Personae and Exultations of Ezra Pound*, both annotated. Bridges met Pound on 27 February that year at a lunch at 10 Church Walk in Hampstead with Eva Fowler,[19] the daughter of the Attorney-General of Hawaii. Pound sent his impressions of the Poet Laureate to Dorothy Shakespear: 'Bridges is quite disarming—called his job "This Professorship", was very quaint about [Henry] James, invited me down to Oxford, showed a flattering familiarity with my works, went on to dine with the King . . . Bridges was really charming.'[20] Bridges, who had spent a lot of time with the publisher Elkin Mathews over the previous few days, told him that he considered *Personae and Exultations* unquestionably Pound's best work.[21] Bridges evidently repeated his invitation to Pound, because on 8 March Pound told Dorothy: 'Professions of admiration from the Laureate this A.M. I shall go up to Oxford for half day sometime probably next week—it appeals to my spirit of mischief. I wonder can I get him to issue a manifesto abolishing Gosse.' She wrote back on the 17th: 'You are now with The Laureate—I am really very amused to hear that he seems a decent kind of person: so unexpected.'

In 1922 Pound started an anecdote that he later incorporated into the *Cantos*: 'Years ago when I was just trying to find and use modern speech, old Bridges carefully went through *Personae and Exultations* and commended every archaism (to my horror), exclaiming "We'll get 'em all back; we'll get 'em *all* back." Eheu fugaces!',[22] thereby probably contributing to the misapprehension that Bridges' attitude to diction was dominated by a taste for the antiquated. But, as Pound himself once acknowledged, Bridges was a serious craftsman who regarded English as a craftsman's tool to be made as subtle and powerful as possible for the job of expression. He certainly struck out 's' sounds where he could in the books and it may have been his efforts to persuade Pound that he had been right in his earlier use of the softer 'th' endings that gave rise to the anecdote. But he also marked a number of other things in the volumes, querying for example, Pound's use of the passive where an active would be expected, as in 'Famam Librosque Cano', lines 3–4: 'when the night | Shrinketh the kiss of dawn.' There are a number of places where Pound omits hyphens or uses them for no clear reason, and these Bridges altered or questioned. He seems to have liked rather more of *Canzoni and Ripostes*, marking as excellent four of the sonnets: 'Chi e Questa' (changing line 4, 'the day's end end' to 'day's ending end'); 'Sonnet in Tenzone'; 'Ballatetta'; and 'If on the tally-board'. He considered six others good, praising in 'The Flame' not the archaic words but the phrase 'glad hair gone gray'.[23] Most of his criticisms are of obscurity, use of the opposite voice from what the sense seems to require, occasional 'awkward rhythm', and some superfluous words. In 'The Seafarer' he commented that Pound had used 'hold' and 'list' without seeming to be aware that the context would bring to mind their unwanted nautical meanings. In 1922 Pound put at the top of a list he sent Felix Schelling of things that he had learnt from critics: 'One caution against homophones, recd. from Robt. Bridges.'[24] In August 1915 Pound, who was editing the magazine *Poetry*, wrote to Harriet Monroe:

> Bridges' new booklet is privately printed, but he has given me permission to quote the poems. It amounts practically to making a free contribution, I suppose. I think the two poems quoted in full are quite good, especially the short one. And the cadence of the other is exquisite. I suppose I shall have to wait till he dies before I can do an appreciative character sketch.—[25]

He quoted 'The Flowering Tree', remarking on how Bridges' free verse had been strengthened by his work with quantitative rhythms, and the epigram, 'Who goes there?':

> Who goes there? God knows. I'm nobody. How should
>   I answer?
> Can't jump over a gate nor run across the meadow.

> I'm but an old whitebeard of inane identity. Pass on!
> What's left of me to-day will very soon be nothing.

It was, said Pound,

> worthy of a place in the Greek anthology, not only because it is hard and concise as their epigrams, but because it is novel. It is the only poem I can think of which shows quite this sense of the attrition of personality through living. It is not age which speaks, but a mood that is permanent and recurrent in life, and therefore so fine a matter of art.[26]

Writing in 1934 to Laurence Binyon, whom he greatly admired, Pound remarked, 'as Bridges and Leaf are no longer on the scene, the number of readers possessed of any criteria (however heretical) for the writing of English verse and at the same time knowing the difference between Dante and Dunhill is limited'.[27] But two years later, in replying to T. S. Eliot's request for an article on Bridges, Pound was less flattering:

> I spose I can cite what I once said of Britches? I managed to dig about 10 lines of Worse Libre out of one of his leetle bookies. Onct. And then there iz the side line of Hopkins. Couldn't you send and/or loan? In fact the pooplishers ought to donate a Hopkins and the Hopkins letters so az to treat Britches properly. Background for an article that wdn't be as *dull*, oh bloodily, as merely trying to yatter about wot he *wrote*

comments that contrast markedly with his earlier public statement made when he was himself still interested in quantitative verse: 'Beyond dispute, his [Bridges'] command of the sheer mechanics of quantitative verse can be looked on with nothing but envy. I have a grave respect for any man who is restless and persistent in the study and honor of his craft'.[28]

Someone who was surprised to find the facilities at Chilswell less luxurious than he had expected was George Santayana. A naturalized American of Spanish ancestry, he spent the war in England and met Bridges late in 1916. Bridges told Muirhead that he 'often if not quite always lunches at the George Cafe. If you go at 12.50 you catch him in the small room. We often meet there.'[29] However, Bridges evidently invited Santayana to stay at Chilswell and Santayana was somewhat horrified to find that hot water was not readily available; Bridges' daily bath was a cold one. When on

Sunday morning Santayana rang for hot water with which to shave, it was not a servant but Monica who appeared in answer to it.[30] In his autobiography, Santayana takes the opportunity of making several snide comments about Monica, whom he found less sophisticated and intellectual than Lady Ottoline Morrell. However, of Bridges, he said he was 'the only real friend I ever had much older than myself'; 'his manners . . . and his conversation were of the most unpretending, easy and charming kind, those of the simple, affable English gentleman who remains always young'. Bridges' 'acquired habits of mind' were 'for mocking English prejudices, while adoring England'. It was for this 'that he valued my writings; and though we seldom or never discussed our respective works, I knew that it was this liberating outlook, partly in the Catholic and partly in the naturalistic direction, that he cared for in me'.[31] Bridges and Santayana corresponded over a number of years. Most of Bridges' letters have been destroyed, but Daniel Cory's edition of Santayana's letters shows that he wrote to Bridges more seriously about philosophical topics than to any other English person.

In August 1915 Bridges submitted his anthology, *The Spirit of Man*, to the press; it was to prove very popular, requiring reprinting three times in 1916 alone. With the book safely lodged with Longmans, Green and Co. he went on holiday to the Lake District, which he had not seen before, and to Sheffield, which he thought beautiful. Then Edward was posted to the Western Front and the majority of Bridges' letters mention the fact, not only because it was the most important thing to him at the time but because, although he was proud of this family contribution to the war effort, he sought the support of fellow-feeling by signalling his own anxiety and understanding of others in a similar position. During Christmas 1917 Bridges was to write a poem called 'The West Front' subtitled 'An English Mother, on looking into Masefield's "Old Front Line".' For it Bridges recalled his own feelings during the previous eighteen months:

No country know I so well
 as this landscape of hell.
Why bring you to my pain
 these shadow'd effigys

Of barb'd wire, riven trees,
  the corpse-strewn blasted plain?

And the names—Herbuterne
  Bethune and La Bassée—
I have nothing to learn—
  Contalmaison, Boisselle,
And one where night and day
  my heart would pray and dwell;

A desert sanctuary,
  where in holy vigil
Year-long I have held my faith
  against th' imaginings
Of horror and agony
  in an ordeal above

The tears of suffering
  and took aid of angels:
This was the temple of God:
  no mortuary of kings
Ever gathered the spoils
  of such chivalry and love:

No pilgrim shrine soe'er
  hath assembled such prayer—
With rich incense-wafted
  ritual and requiem
Not beauteous batter'd Rheims
  nor lorn Jerusalem.

He used for it lines of twelve syllables with a medial caesura, the form with which he had started experimenting in 1913.

Anti-German feeling reached a high-point in Britain in the latter part of 1915: each day *The Times* published the names of some two or three thousand men killed, gassed, or wounded; there was a zeppelin raid on London in October which killed women and children, and the shooting of Edith Cavell provoked public outrage. The mood was reflected in the preface Bridges wrote for *The Spirit of Man*:

> The progress of mankind on the path of liberty and humanity has been suddenly arrested and its promise discredited by the apostasy of a great people, who, casting off as a disguise their professions of Honour, now openly avow that the ultimate faith of their hearts is in material force.

In the darkness and stress of the storm the signs of the time cannot all be distinctly seen, nor can we read them dispassionately; but two things stand out clearly, and they are above question or debate. The first is that Prussia's scheme for the destruction of her neighbours was long-laid, and scientifically elaborated to the smallest detail: the second is that she will shrink from no crime that may further its execution . . . From the consequent miseries, the insensate and interminable slaughter, the hate and filth, we can turn to seek comfort only in the quiet confidence of our souls; . . . our habits and thoughts are searched by the glare of the conviction that man's life is not the ease that a peace-loving generation has found it or thought to make it, but the awful conflict with evil which philosophers and saints have depicted; and it is in their abundant testimony to the good and beautiful that we find support for our faith, and distraction from a grief that is intolerable constantly to face, nay impossible to face without that trust in God which makes all things possible.

We may see that our national follies and sins have deserved punishment; and if in this revelation of rottenness we cannot ourselves appear wholly sound, we are still free and true at heart, and can take hope in contrition, and in the brave endurance of sufferings that should chasten our intention and conduct; we can even be grateful for the discipline: but beyond this it is offered us to take joy in the thought that our country is called of God to stand for the truth of man's hope, and that it has not shrunk from the call.

A number of people including Elizabeth thought that he had expressed himself too strongly, but there were many who agreed with particular parts of the statement.

A combination of wishing to help with the war and an obligation to speak out as Poet Laureate led Bridges to make a number of speeches in 1916 and 1917. Edward said that Bridges disliked making speeches but, with so many people fulfilling unpleasant tasks, he did what he could. In April 1916 he spoke at the initial meeting of the short-lived 'Fight for Right' Society. The justification for such a society was, he felt, twofold. It was necessary not only that national frontiers be protected but that the spirit of the people be preserved. The dangers that the nation be 'blinded by passion, led astray by self-interest, drowsed by false security, bewildered for want of wisdom and reflection' needed to be guarded against. Thus, the society was not to try to *create* a 'national spirit'; that, Bridges believed, Britain already had, not that such a thing could in any case be created by a society. The second aim was to organize among the non-combatants principles of order, right, and patriotic duty, so that when the armed forces returned home they would 'find something to join hands with'. Bridges called that day of peace a 'day of supreme trial', not only, one suspects, because of the psychological problems in reuniting people who had had very different and traumatic experiences, but because he was concerned that the sudden lifting of fear would lead to behaviour he considered undisciplined and self-indulgent.[32]

Bridges took part in a conference on the Reform of Education in 1916. This gave him the opportunity of stating ideas about education that he had long held and on occasion expressed privately. The first resolution before the delegates was 'that . . . it is a matter of urgency, in order to promote national efficiency in the near future, that the natural sciences should be made an integral part of the educational course in all the great schools of this country, and should form part of the entrance examination of the Universities of Oxford and Cambridge as well as of the newer Universities'.[33] The resolution was seconded by Bridges, who gave it his 'full and hearty support'. He took the opportunity of suggesting once more that not only was the introduction of science into the curriculum desirable, but that a more scientific method of language-instruction was needed. The current system of classical education he criticized for confusing the 'sensitively clear' minds of boys and fatiguing them with effort that was 'misdirected or unduly sustained'. The normal growth of a boy's mind was, he believed, slow, but the current educational system branded far more boys as 'stupid' than his own observations led him to believe likely: 'I should say that a stupid boy is a rare being, and that an average boy can learn almost anything in which he is interested, if only he is in contact with a competent teacher.' He commented on 'the low standard of intelligence that obtains among our clergy, and from which the nation suffers great drawbacks', a criticism that was greeted with laughter but which he meant, blaming the fault on an unbalanced classical education. The objections to the introduction of science in the curriculum were, Bridges said, that it was too materialistic a subject, not working 'in the sphere of ideas, which are the essential basis of character and culture'. He asserted that science need not be this, pointing out that it teaches man 'of the things among which he must pass his life; . . . it is the living grammar of the universe, without which no man can ever hope to read in its full significance the epic of his spiritual experience'. As for art, by giving the artist an earlier and deeper acquaintance with the laws of nature, science might well, he thought, improve the present 'contemptible' standard 'of the average school art of our Royal Academy'.

In October 1916 he addressed the Swindon Branch of the Workers' Educational Association, and again worked round to the subject of education.[34] The talk is very much a product of its time. Bridges expresses the doubts that he had felt about democracy and his sense of relief as the country unified in the face of war. Democracy would work, he was sure, in a small state where the electors knew their political representatives well, but in large countries Bridges feared that the politically ambitious would seek to bribe voters with short-term promises. An educated electorate, he suggested, would be less easily swayed by false promises. Bridges initially defined education as the 'drawing out of the mind', and sketched his conception of it. It has, he said, three layers, the most basic of which is the instinctive level which we share with animals and which is a much more complicated and sophisticated mechanism than we understand. He quoted as an example of its baffling excellence the case of American horses transported some distance from their farms escaping and returning home, not by following the route along which they had been taken but in a bee-line. The middle section of the mind is also below our conscious awareness, a storehouse of thousands of impressions in which man's ideals, common sense, and in rare cases genius, form. Genius he defined as the exceptional organization and creative combining of ideas. Finally there is man's reason, his conscious analytical power. Bridges then redefined education as the drawing out of a love of beauty inborn in all people; he equates beauty with good. To nurture this drive three things are necessary: opportunity or environment; the 'right choosing and using of goods', which he calls values or wisdom; and knowledge. Writing at a time when there was still considerable movement from the country to the cities and towns, he commented on the fact that, although the towns often provided a livelier community and more diverse amusements, the living conditions were frequently poor owing to uncontrolled capitalism, and many of the offered amusements, such as imported cinema films, simply trivialized human emotions.

He supported the workers' demand for more leisure-time as a necessity for further education, suggesting that they ask too for better housing, and proposed the building of 'colleges' for unmarried workers with good, inexpensive food and central heating, a common-room for meals and lectures, and three or four smaller rooms for classes that would be available to married men too. He imagined the men playing in orchestras, visiting museums and art-galleries, or reading alone; in fact doing much as he had done while he was at St Bartholomew's Hospital. The latter part of the talk is remarkable for the sincerity with which Bridges set out his beliefs and values: his hatred of what he saw as the pretensions of the middle classes, his adherence to a simple way of life, his religious faith. Returning to the distinction he had earlier made between reason and instinct, he asserted, 'the existence of God is not demonstrable by logic. It lies beyond. But Reason wil approve of a truth that she could not discover . . . our best Faith is just this reasonable trust of our deeper natur and better desires; to doubt which wer destructiv of any human ideal, and of Reason itself' (p. 188). This is the essence of his belief.

In November Bridges completed *Ibant Obscuri*, his translation into English, using Stone's prosody, of the sixth book of the *Aeneid*. He included an appendix showing his differences from Stone's evaluation of the length of some syllables. He also spent some time revising his book on Milton's prosody and expanding notes at the back of earlier editions into a chapter on accentual verse. He evidently put it aside, returning to it in 1921 when it was published in its final form.

The winter was cold. Edward was home at Christmas, to Bridges' delight, and on 5 February 1917 he sent an amusing letter to W. B. Yeats to comply with his request that he write something to identify Ezra Pound as an American citizen who was in the country as Yeats' secretary. But the following day disaster struck as the whole of the upper floor of Chilswell was gutted by fire. The cold temperatures had left the well-water frozen, and it was with some difficulty that the blaze was controlled. Monica was away with Margaret, who was on holiday before returning to France. Although the family's clothing was lost, the fire was not allowed to spread along the roof of the covered passage which led to the library (housed in a separate building) so that the books and music were saved, as were things from the ground floor. In March when the family were occupied by further troubles, Bridges wrote to Kate Hopkins, Gerard's sister: 'We did not suffer any bodily nor even mental pangs and pains from the conflagration, but it was an extreme inconvenience, among other things *all* our clothing being destroyed. I have been attempting to answer letters of condolence by the enclosed card.'[35] It read: 'I thank you very much for your friendly letter of condolence. As we find it impossible to write replies to the many kind letters we have received, I beg you will accept this formal acknowledgement. We are thankful that everything was saved from the lower rooms; the detached library was not touched by the fire.'

Monica and Robert moved into Postmasters [scholars] Hall, 14 Merton Street, in Oxford, which he described as an 'Elizabethan house and prettily furnished' and which gave them access to Merton College gardens. Elizabeth stayed with friends. It was to be over two years before they were re-established in Chilswell.

On 17 February Wooldridge died, and Bridges lost the critic and artistic adviser he most valued for his 'rare intuition, wide reading and full memory'.[36] Four years later, he told Newbolt that he had 'never since Wooldridge's death been able to supply his loss in any degree! which of course must seem ridiculous to everyone but myself and one or two people who knew him well.'[37]

Late in February, while he was involved in the fighting on the Somme, Edward was wounded in the arm. By coincidence the Red Cross hospital to which he was sent near Boulogne was the one in which Margaret was working in the canteen, and she was able to send their parents messages about his condition. The wound was serious; both bones of the right forearm were smashed and the surgeons were unable to remove all the shrapnel, some of which remained there for the rest of his life. He was lucky not to lose the limb. It was several weeks before his temperature was stable enough for him to be sent back to England, and not until May that he was allowed to spend time away from the hospital.[38] To visit him Bridges and Monica stayed in a succession of lodgings near London.

While Edward was in hospital he read some of General Jan Christian Smuts's speeches and essays about international affairs and was impressed by them. Smuts was in London as a member of the British War Cabinet and Minister without Portfolio. He was a leading advocate for the formation of the League of Nations, a broader plan of a type that Bridges had hoped to see implemented in 1904 during the Russo-Japanese War. Edward drew his father's attention to Smuts's writing and the latter, deciding that he wanted to meet him, wrote to him. Smuts responded by asking father and son to lunch.[39] Bridges subsequently invited the General to Chilswell, and the two men exchanged books and letters during the second half of the 1920s, at which time Bridges was interested by Smuts's theory of evolutionary 'Holism'. The problem that Smuts attempted to address was expressed by J. Arthur Thomson: despite retrogressions, evolution tends 'towards the growth of intelligence and fine feeling, towards increased control, towards lives that are increasingly satisfactions in themselves, as we see when we compare birds with worms'.[40] The question is, why. Smuts suggested that the answer was 'holism', an innate tendency in the universe to form wholes, which he defined as more thorough syntheses than the juxtaposition of parts would produce. There is an increase in the amount of central control and initiation of action as one moves through the evolutionary series from mere physical mixtures through chemical compounds, organisms, and minds, to personality. This last is the 'most evolved whole among the structures of the universe, and becomes a new orientative, originative centre of reality'. The theory invents an internal force to satisfy objections to Darwinian evolution that the response of structures cannot always be fully explained by the external influences on them. The most complete and whole personality is seen by Smuts as being that which has greatest self-regulation and self-direction and is as free as possible from outside stresses. What he pictures is not

> the ascetic suppression of primitive healthy human instincts, but their refinement and sublimation, their subordination and co-ordination in the growing whole of the Personality under the hegemony of the later and higher ethical factors [though] Personality, at the present stage of its history, is not yet fully developed . . . it is imperfect as a whole even in the highest individuals.[41]

The belief in the value of individualism and the use of evolutionary theory for sociological explanation have a nineteenth-century flavour, but the problems with Darwinian theory that Smuts faced are still actively being investigated. Bridges remarked to Smuts how closely his general conception of the ideal and evolution of personality coincided with his own beliefs, although in *The Testament of Beauty* he was to extend that evolution far beyond Smuts's scheme.

Paul Lambrotte asked Bridges if he would speak at memorial celebrations for A. Émile Verhaeren, the Belgian poet, in March 1917. These were under the aegis of the Royal Society of Literature, whose president was Edmund Gosse, 'l'inlassable ami des lettres françaises', and they packed the society's meeting hall in Bloomsbury Square. Any funds raised were to be given to the families of those Belgians deported to Germany. In November of the previous year Bridges, tired of the Belgians in Oxford, had written that he was glad that he had 'never gone in for them'. However, appreciation of Verhaeren was different. Bridges' contribution was printed in *Mercure de France* on 1 April. English ignorance of Verhaeren was, he said, testimony to the indifference of the English to French verse in general, although Chaucer's importing of French metres meant that English verse was in fact founded on a broad European base. The criticism was undoubtedly true of the general reading public, but it ignores the interest aroused by Arthur Symons at the turn of the century in the Symbolists and the almost contemporary advocacy of poets such as Pound and T. S. Eliot, through whom the influence of French verse on English was again growing. Bridges' own admiration was of long standing and independent of Eliot's views. He compared Verhaeren with Walt Whitman for his attachment to his country. However, perhaps with poems like 'Starting from Paumansk' in mind, he contrasted Verhaeren's 'intense vision de la vie ardente et implacable' with Whitman's 'bénédictions complaisantes et indolentes' for modern civilization.[42]

In April Margaret, who was still in Boulogne, became ill with measles; accompanying pleurisy eventually meant a convalescence of several months and she was sent back to England on 20 April. By July Edward and Margaret were both living with the Farrer family, whose house at Abinger in Surrey was being used as a home for convalescents. While staying at Crossways Farm in the same parish, Bridges wrote a lecture that was later published as 'The Necessity of Poetry', which he delivered on 22 November to the Tredegar and District Co-operative Society. It is one of his most interesting essays. 'I am here to talk about poetry, and you little think how surprised you ought to be', he begins.

> Let me explain why an artist is unwilling to discourse on his own art. The fact is that in every art it is only the formal side which can be formulated; and that is not what people congregate to hear about, when they call for Art-lectures. The grammar of any art is dry and unintelligible to the layman: it seems unrelated to the magic of its delight. In Poetry it is even deemed beneath the dignity of a poet to betray any consciousness of such detail. But, if you bid the artist leave this dull and solid ground to expatiate on Beauty, you invite him on to a field where speculations appear to him fanciful and unsound: and the venture cannot rashly be indulged in.

Nevertheless, Bridges then embarked on an examination of his topic that was exceptionally wide-ranging for the time; beginning with the relationship of words to ideas. In scientific or philosophical prose, a premium is placed on overcoming the discrepancy in meaning that words have for different people by disregarding all but central, definable meanings. However, 'it is difficult to quiet a suspicion that the natural indefinite quality of our ideas may be a healthy condition; and that the key to the mysteries of life, which is withheld from philosophical exactitudes, may lie in that very condition of our thought which Reason rejects as unseizable and delusive'.[43] He illustrates how emotion colours a word's meaning with the example of the different meaning the word 'father' has for a child, a bachelor, and a man who is himself a father, differences which lie in the word's associations. This brings him to an examination of the organization of concepts. Bridges stresses the spontaneous activity of their interrelationship. He defines poetry as representing these 'spontaneous conjunctions as they affect the imagination . . . producing vivid emotional pictures of scientific or rational ideas, and its magic then lies in the imagery which satisfies even without interpretation. It goes home, as we say; and is accepted as easily and naturally as it was created.'[44] As far as the sound of words is concerned, Bridges deduces that rhythm satisfies man's innate love of pattern and that syntax should be governed by the order in which the writer wants the reader to receive the ideas, although he sometimes used inverted syntax to make lines of verse less prosaic.

He then explores the relation of poetry to morals and religion. His assumptions that man is intrinsically good and that art should express the Ideal are so deeply ingrained that he seems unable to answer arguments for naturalism. His objections to unidealistic literature are similar to his views on aspects of contemporary religion, and doubtless gave his audience a shock. The poetry of the Bible and religious services seemed to him to have done man a disservice, and he blamed its beauty for mentally enslaving the English people to

> a conception of God altogether unworthy and incompatible with our better notions . . . The Christian churches wil not leave the old ruts. The Pope stil hankers after temporal power, and to get it would crown Tiglath-Pileser in St. Peter's while our Protestant church still begins its morning devotions by singing of 'God swearing in his wrath that his people should not enter into his rest.'
>
> Now in the religion of Christ, which, whether we wil it or not, whether we know it or not, is deeply ingrain'd in our heart's reverence and the life of our souls, and is ever rebuking and overruling our conduct—in this world-conquering Christianity the essentials are love and unity and brotherhood. But look at the Protestant sects, all quarrelling about crude absurdities and ridiculous unessentials. And ask yourselves how the Church shall be purify'd and edify'd when those who should compose it remain outside of it.[45]

He ended the lecture with an exhortation to further work on poetic technique, the advice he gave all poets who came to him.

Robert and Monica moved into the cottage they had originally had built for their gardener and Bridges spent the days working in the library. Margaret decided that she wanted to work for the Forestry Commission and began a training course in the summer; by August she was working in Wales. And Elizabeth, who had become interested in Oriental languages, went to Cambridge to study them. The wound in Edward's arm necessitated his return to hospital in September. In 1917, as a contribution to the local war effort, Bridges sometimes participated in Mrs Daniel's group in the Provost's Lodgings at Worcester College, preparing splints and bandages. At the end of the war a volume of Blake's poetry was presented to Mrs Daniel by the group in gratitude for the hospitality she had provided for them. Bridges wrote a doggerel poem of some 250 lines to accompany the gift. In it he reflected lightheartedly on such things as the sculptured heads around the Sheldonian, the benefit of being a sportsman rather than a 'swot', and such innovations since he had been a student as afternoon tea-parties:

> . . . if one calls on
> A nephew, ten to one the blade is
> Giving a teaparty to ladies,
> His room with cigarette-smoke stuffy;
> Wherat he spends, on tea and coffee
> And butter'd buns, so sober-minded,
> As much as we on beer and wine did.
> No don survives now whom it vexes
> To see this ease between the sexes,
> And we'd some dons dead as those dummies
> Carven on tombs to look like mummies
> Waiting until the resurrection
> To put their trowsers and their neck-tie on.

In October Logan Pearsall Smith asked Bridges if he would review his collection of extracts from the philosopher, George Santayana's books. Bridges replied that he was willing to undertake the task provided he did not have to tackle Santayana's metaphysic, explaing that 'he did not understand' metaphysics. Yet the review does not avoid tackling philosophical ideas, and succeeds in displaying the range of Santayana's thought and the dexterity of his aphorisms. At several points Santayana would seem to have confirmed Bridges' ideas on, for example, the relation of reason to morality. In his 'Epistle on Instinct' Bridges had sketched the relation that he felt pertained and he was to expand on the theme in *The Testament of Beauty*. His summary of Santayana's views is very close to this: 'Reason, which follows consciousness upon the scene, harmonizes the various instincts and impulses, and establishes an ideal of good—that is, corrects instinct by experience 'with a view to attaining the greatest satisfaction of which our nature is capable.'[46] In this, trust is placed not in convention and man's institutions but in the natural world and man's place within it. It is a more sophisticated version of the basic idea Bridges had expressed in 'The Hymn to Nature' (1879) and not entirely true to

Santayana's views, something that was only to become clear to both men late in the 1920s.

On 7 September 1917 Bridges wrote to Mrs Hopkins suggesting that the time was now right to publish an edition of Hopkins' poems, since those included in *The Spirit of Man* had been praised and he had been urged by a number of people, including Raleigh, whose opinion he greatly respected, to prepare an edition. He thought that the Oxford University Press would be willing to publish the book. Bridges wanted the English edition 'to be *limited and very well printed*',[47] and proposed a separate American edition. A letter to Kate Hopkins of 13 September makes it clear that he started the project with the idea that 'every scrap' that Hopkins had written was to be included, although he later modified that. In the new year he devoted himself to the task. He said afterwards that he had worked seven or eight hours a day at it, completing the job in only four weeks. This seems to have been something of an underestimate of the time it took.[48] He adopted a general principle of using Hopkins' final version, but in some cases where he had a strong preference for an earlier version he used that or combined several versions. Some of the editing, for example the untangling of the scrambled, copiously altered draft of 'Epithalamion'—part of which Hopkins had evidently written while invigilating—required considerable patience. For 'Epithalamion' Hopkins had used sheets from an examination booklet and Bridges underlined some of the instructions to candidates that seemed appropriate: 'Fill up the following blanks', and 'The rough work and calculations as well as the final results, should be shewn in this book'.[49] He found the work as interesting as it was troublesome, and told Kate Hopkins of Monica's growing admiration for the poems. As often in Bridges' old age, she worked with him. The couple also took considerable care over making the book attractive, cutting and pasting the initial sheets to get the balance between text and ornament right and the layout pleasing. The annotation Bridges provided treated Hopkins as a 'classic' by giving careful notes of poems' dates and manuscripts and citing principal variants, as well as explanations of poems or phrases that Hopkins had sent in his letters. He also wrote a dedicatory sonnet for the edition and sent it to the Hopkins family for their comments. He feared that its allusions to Hopkins' melancholy made it too sad, although he did not think that Hopkins' depression could be hidden, since his late sonnets would make that impossible. And, besides, he thought that it would be a 'good thing to tell the truth about, and show that medievalizing does not always produce complete ease of mind'.[50] 'Medievalizing', a term he had also used for Dolben's interest in Catholicism, emphasizes his conviction that it was an anachronistic faith.

Bridges' preface to the notes to Hopkins' poetry deals solely with critical appreciation rather than placing the poems within a biographical setting, a marked difference from his editions of Dixon and Dolben. The criticisms fall into two categories: taste and technique. In the latter he pointed out the unenriching ambiguities caused by the omission of the relative pronoun and the use of homophones in grammatically ambiguous syntax. He was severe in dealing with Hopkins' rhymes: 'the rhymes where they are peculiar are often repellent, and so far from adding charm to the verse that they appear as obstacles. This must not blind one from recognizing that Gerard Hopkins, where he is simple and straightforward in his rhyme is a master of it—there are many instances—but when he indulges in freaks, his childishness is incredible'. He cited as examples, 'eternal' 'burn all' from 'The Loss of the Eurydice' and 'boon he on', 'Communion' from 'The Bugler'. Bridges had expressed his strong disapproval of some of Hopkins' rhymes to him and to Patmore, and had been equally criticized by Hopkins for his own rhymes. The passage on 'errors of taste' shows a degree of repugnance which today's readers would not feel for the examples he quotes, and this must raise questions about the reasons for it. It could not have been simply that he wished that he had been the writer of Hopkins' poems; those qualities he praised in other poets, and everything he wrote himself, confirm his expressed disapproval of much of Hopkins' style. He may have been alarmed that the flaws he considered so important should be dismissed as negligible by Hopkins' admirers, and he would certainly have wanted to stop others copying what he saw as these abuses of the English language. His antipathy to Catholicism explains his reaction to the Marianism, and his Protestantism, his dislike of the combination of 'sensualism and asceticism'. In the final paragraph, which is more positive than the ending to the preface to A. H. Miles' selection had been, although the tone is still severe, Bridges put forward his genuine opinion—that Hopkins' 'terrible . . . sonnets' were his best work. He was, as well, throwing down the gauntlet to the Catholics, who he was afraid would 'puff' Hopkins as a Catholic rather than considering him as a poet. The closing sentences read:

It is lamentable that Gerard Hopkins died when, to judge by his latest work, he was beginning to concentrate the force of all his luxuriant experiments in rhythm and diction, and castigate his art into a more reserved style. Few will read the terrible posthumous sonnets without such high admiration and respect for his poetical power as must lead them to search out the rare masterly beauties that distinguish his work.

It was near the end of August 1918 before Bridges passed the final proofs of the volume. The Press had difficulty setting the book, with resultant difficulties for him. The notes, however, had been well set and the book appeared in October with a dedication to Mrs Hopkins turned into Latin by A. E. Housman. Sending a copy of it to Logan Pearsall Smith, Bridges commented,

As for the poems. I am afraid that you will not make friend of them. You will however no doubt read my editors remarks, and I have nothing to add to them, except that I can tell you my experience, which is that after many years acquaintance with them I admire them more than I ever did, and editing them (which implied detailed verbal attention) increased my admiration. They are full of happy phrases which one can never forget. These you will either find or not find for yourself.[51]

In January 1920 Bridges wrote to Kate Hopkins saying that he expected that at some point Hopkins' letters would be printed, and suggesting that the family note details that could be used for an accompanying short biography. The letters, which he greatly admired, would, he thought, make a very remarkable book.

On 29 January 1918, New College choir performed four psalms pointed by Bridges. Through his friend Sir Hugh Allen, Bridges had been invited to join the committee for the reformation of English chanting in 1916. The new version of the psalms put into practice the theories that he had devised with Sir Hugh's help and which he had expressed in his essays of 1911 and 1912. The aim was 'to bring freedom and flexibility into the old Anglican chanting' through introducing additional time-values that made the music match more closely the natural prose rhythms of the chants. The performance went well and Bridges was cock-a-hoop; it was, he said, 'an unqualified success, and everyone was convinced and delighted.—It came out just as lovely as I said it would.'[52] From 1918 he began setting the Psalms, eventually writing settings for fifty-nine of them. His system was more complex than that normally used in that he employed two units of time, which could be represented as regular time values and as the reduced value of notes written in triplets or even four notes in the time of three and five notes in the time of four. As with his later experiments in the writing of poetry, he was aiming at greater flexibility of rhythm.

A friend remembers finding [Bridges and Allen] together once in the Museum Road [Oxford]. Bridges was declaiming against the use of Gregorian chants for the English Psalter on the grounds that it was using tunes made for a language with the accent usually on the penultimate syllable for a language with quite different accentuation. When Bridges left, Allen said: 'I always like him best when he's violent, but then he generally is'.[53]

Bridges was made a member of the Senior Common Room at New College to which Sir Hugh belonged, and took to going there rather than to Corpus. He wrote to Newbolt,

I still go down to Oxford a good deal—walking always—as we have no kind of conveyance: and there are a few men still left there. but the place is wholly given up to the 'military'—I have been made a member of the Senior common room at New Coll[ege] and usually go there in preference to our old C.C.C wh is not very lively. The President [Thomas Case] has published *music*! a volume of songs, two of which have his own words!! The music I shd describe as very elegant. He is very well, and I sometimes make use of his hospitality which is on the antique magnificent scale. But now that the clocks have been put on an hour I suppose I shall take no meals with him before next winter, for he refuses to change his timepieces, & so his usually late hours become impracticable. Lunch for instance is at 2.30. If you are ever coming to Oxford let me know.[54]

At the time New College was enjoying a period of success. Its undergraduates included six future cabinet ministers, its choir was thought by many to be the best in Oxford, and its first Eight was always within the first four places on the river. Among the dons were J. B. S. Haldane and Julian Huxley, although they left soon afterwards for other universities. The Warden of New College, W. A. Spooner, had been Bridges' exact contemporary as an undergraduate. Spooner was a little man, 'short-sighted, very pink-faced, and with the white hair of albinism'.[55] They shared a disquiet over the Allies' attitude to the Germans at the end of the First World War, Spooner insisting that the college record the names of Germans who had been members of the college and had subsequently fought for Germany. Another bond was formed when Margaret married H. W. B. Joseph, senior tutor in philosophy at New College, and joined the group.

Early in April 1918 Mrs Waterhouse became terminally ill and Monica was called to Yattendon. Robert wrote that the old lady was 'dying of old age in the peaceful way in which a fire goes out, or a piece of ice melts'.[56] She died towards the end of the month and after the funeral Bridges moved into rooms in New College while Monica was away sorting out her mother's things. Edward, who had gone to work in the Treasury while his arm mended, sometimes came home for weekends; he was expecting to be sent to rejoin his battalion in Italy at the end of September. At the beginning of that month Muirhead sent Edward a duplicate he had done of an earlier allegorical picture of various symbolic figures associated with Eton. Three of the saints pictured were given the faces of Bridges, Dolben, and Coles. The original, to Edward's dismay, had been lost in the fire at Chilswell.

Bridges tried to sell some of his pictures, including Charles Furse's portrait of him, in order to raise more money for the repairs to the house. He told friends that the effect of the fire he minded most was the inability to have visitors to stay: to Roger Fry he remarked that he had not known 'how much that counted for until the luxury was entirely cut off'.[57] He was steadily putting his papers and manuscripts 'in order', reading through old letters and discarding many, and having some of the literary manuscripts bound so that the family would not have a lot of trouble when he died. Sometimes he was prompted to write to old friends such as Muirhead or William Sanday letters full of memories and appreciation of their friendship. When his eldest sister, Maria Molesworth, died in February 1919 at the age of 89 he wrote to Mrs Hopkins (herself 98): 'Her widower is over 90. They had been married 65 years. It is pleasant to be made to feel so young as I must feel in comparison at 75.'[58]

Maria had spent part of her life in Ceylon and India, where her husband, Guilford Molesworth, had directed many important engineering projects. Bridges' ideas about India would have been influenced by the attitudes of his family, and of his friends from Corpus Christi who had also been connected with the British administration there. Molesworth once called it 'the most able and pure . . . in the world; it contrasts favourably with our British Parliamentary system, which too often subordinates the welfare of the country to a vote-catching policy, sacrificing sound principles to party contingencies.'[59] But there were other, more contemporary influences too. Indians studying at Oxford were frequently guests at Chilswell, among them Hassan Shahid Suhrawardy, who later became Professor of Fine Arts at Calcutta University. Bridges' interest was also shared by his friends, Raleigh, R. C. Trevelyan, and William Rothenstein, who had founded the India Society in London in 1910 and, worried about the teaching of art in India, had gone there in the winter of 1910–11 to meet Indian artists and to paint. In March 1918 Bridges wrote to Logan Pearsall Smith, 'it seems that W[illia]m Archer has written a book about India insisting à la Potsdam that the Indians are "savages"—Malih was up here on Sunday and is anxious to publish what his countrymen think "on reading Archer"—I wonder if they wd publish his reply in "the New Statesman"—I am writing to ask.'[60] In September 1918 Bridges was asked to write a poem to be published in the Christmas issue of the *Times of India* as part of an effort to reduce anti-British feeling in India. The government was not keen to have its link with the continent broken during the war or in the period of rebuilding necessary just after it. First Bridges wrote two letters that appeared in the *Times of India* on 12 and 18 November. In these he dealt with a number of the points at dispute. He claimed that the ideas of freedom current in India were Western ideas fostered by the teaching of English literature and history. The history of India, he asserted, was full of internal wrangles, and the present unity came from opposition to the British and would consequently dissolve into disunity if the British were to disappear. Complaints about insufficient provision of education he acknowledged as supported by figures on illiteracy, but he pointed out that mass education in Britain was only recent. On the question of racial prejudice, he said that India had already had a caste system based in part on skin-colour. He attributed prejudice by the British to ignorance and the vulgarity of the minor British officials who were not of good birth and position. The top officials preferred to spend their leisure among their family and friends in as close a re-creation of the 'home atmosphere' as possible. They needed and did not get, he thought, sympathetic understanding for their attempts to do a difficult job in a trying climate. That steps should be taken towards giving Indians a larger share in their government he thought essential, but the problems 'could hardly be more difficult'. He had not, he said, in talking it over with Indians, ever met 'any one of them who had any practical scheme of any sort to propose—and yet the proposals must be practical; there must be some definite first step of constitutional change which will lead on to further advancement'.[61] Although some of the problems of racial prejudice and civil division that Bridges pointed to must equally have been foreseen by Indian leaders (and have indeed proved troublesome to independent India), such letters could not halt the momentum of events leading to independence.

In April Bridges was asked to write two verses for the national anthem to replace the second and third stanzas. He did so, despite disliking both the words and the tune of the anthem. He had earlier suggested that Parry set Blake's 'Jerusalem' as a replacement. The new verses were rejected as 'not simple enough'. In May he delivered the last of his wartime addresses. Given in the Sheldonian Theatre, Oxford, it was on behalf of the Red Cross and was an appeal to the people of Oxford for books for hospitals. The speech shows that he was not quite so unaware of the difficulties faced by soldiers as critics later suggested. He asked people to donate light reading, books that would distract the minds of soldiers and the wounded. He spoke of the 'anxiety, perpetual peril, and strain of the trenches', the 'constant pain and nervous weakness' of the wounded, and the necessity of an 'unlimited supply' of books, regardless of literary merit since the men could exchange among themselves to acquire those that appealed to them.[62] With the increase in the number of students and intellectuals recruited in the later years of the war, there was a growing demand for more serious literature too, for 'such men, when their physical condition does not forbid, are eager to return to their old interests, and make use of their enforced leisure to pursue their studies'. There was, finally, a third group: men used to physical work who, in the tedious time spent recuperating from illness, wanted to learn. These men, with

all their fine qualities, which promise well for stability and betterment, their common sense, patience, good temper, cheerful courage, and devotion . . . yet lack sadly in one important matter, instruction. And no more useful work could possibly be done for the country than to help them to supply this deficiency, of which many of them, as I know, are beginning to be aware.

Bridges, in fact, corresponded with several working men who wrote poetry during the war. Talking of the 'silly scruples' in trying to choose which books to donate led him to speak of 'private property':

I am not myself one of those who think the institution of private property to be a blind injustice, a mere relic of barbarism. If it be a relic of barbarism it is, like some other ancient heirlooms, a most useful relic. I hold property to be a condition of the humanities, the means of progress in culture. But I agree that the private right may lapse where the social duty is neglected; and that no man has a right to hold any property which he cannot or will not make use of—if he is thereby witholding it from another who is willing and able to use it well.

He had gone further in a letter to his conservative friend, Samuel Gee, in 1911,

I have no respect for the hereditary aristocracy, except that some of them seem well-bred—which they may still continue to be—and ever since Henry George's bk on 'Progress and Poverty' I have always held that what he called the 'unearned increment' shd belong to the state. that seems to me the solution of most difficulties, and it is the solid basis and first principle of modern politics or rather economics. Surely Lloyd George has made a very firm step. Anyhow the times are stirring and interesting.[63]

16

The Post-War World

(1918–1922)

Hostilities ceased on 11 November 1918, and Bridges was asked to write a poem on the armistice for *The Times*. He wrote to Muirhead that, as the verses 'have to *rhyme* and be on some old model they have not interested me half as much as they have worried me'.[1] He had also been asked by John Masefield to write a poem for the American Thanksgiving Day since it was to be jointly celebrated by the English and Americans. This was written and revised several times and published on 28 November.

The 'peace' terms appalled Bridges, who feared that the Germans would refuse them and turn to war in a 'Bolshevist' alliance with Russia. Eight years later he had to be persuaded by Edward Thompson to delete the section on it from *The Testament of Beauty* which Thompson felt to be over-emphatic. The draft reads:

> Amid the flimflam of the uproarious city
> my spirit on those first days of jubilant disgrace
> was heavier in me and felt a profounder fear
> then ever it knew in all the War's darkest dismay.
> And round the council-table of that high conference,
> sat to confirm the peace of Europe at Versailles
> Peace had no seat; the voice that drown'd wisdom was his
> who spoke unbending enmity and utmost revenge.[2]

When in July 1919 Bridges was asked to write for *The Times* the ideal peace poem that 'they did not feel they had yet seen', he replied, 'as for peace poem—I cannot know what you feel to be ideal peace in P.H. Square. Poetry will not make much of it. My sole effort has been a short address to General Jan Christian Smuts and it is not good enough to send him . . . He seems to me the only conduit for poetic optimism', an allusion to the League of Nations.[3]

In January Bridges and Monica moved back into Chilswell with one 'very nice' servant. The house was not yet completely restored but part of it was habitable. Bridges was 75. He had, he boasted, become 'a dab hand' at washing up, and could stay on his feet all day, but regretted being unable to 'saw or hew timber for more than 20 or 30 minutes'.[4] In the middle of June, however, with Chilswell not yet completely renovated, they moved back to Postmasters Hall in Oxford. The move was no doubt partly to make arrangements easier for Margaret's wedding on 3 July to Horace Joseph, who was twenty years older than she, the same difference in age as between her parents. Joseph was described by another fellow in the college as 'short and massive, almost square in build, with immensely muscular hands and penetrating glance, to me at least he embodied many of the virtues of the dedicated teacher and scholar. It is true that he was vigorous and uncompromising in debate and probably unaware of the devastating impact of his condemnation of what he thought to be muddled or slovenly.' However, it was also said of him that 'to know him at all well was to become aware of a sensitive, kindly spirit concealed behind the somewhat severe exterior'.[5]

In October 1919, after a holiday on Dartmoor, Bridges wrote to Muirhead,

> we had a most successful 3 weeks holiday in perfect weather. I suppose it must have done one good—I am sure that Monica is the better for it. The house-building is going on—and we really hope to be able to inhabit part of the house by Xmas, the plasterers are to begin their work this week, and a carpenter is now putting in the bedroom doors. Fortunately the weather holds up. Edward is with us now he is awaiting the examination for the All Souls Fellowship, but I think it very doubtful he will be successful. He must be terribly rusty in the ordinary Greek and Latin scholarship. I fancy his history is pretty good. Boar's Hill is becoming a very favourite resort. We have quite a lot of distinguished residents now, but the ruinous state of our house forbids the normal visitations which otherwise really threaten to change our old retirement. Yet some of the happenings are very favourable to us. I am, after 3 weeks at once rather busy, so that I can't settle to write you much of a letter today. Let us meet one day in Oxford, I will come in to meet you, and we can have lunch

together somewhere . . . I wish you had come with us to Devonshire as I proposed.[6]

His doubts about Edward's success were born out, but he was elected the following year.

In the same month the Society for Pure English was finally launched. Once started, the SPE tracts were produced rapidly, two appearing in 1919, one in 1920, which Bridges and Monica prepared while Pearsall Smith was in Armenia, and four more in 1921. In October 1919 Bridges tried to persuade Thomas Hardy to write an article for the SPE, but in vain. The request was made in the rather formal correspondence arising from the gift of an album of forty-three autograph poems. This had been organized by Siegfried Sassoon, Walter de la Mare, and Henry Newbolt, and presented by Sassoon to Hardy that year as an eightieth birthday present. Bridges had entered his poem, 'Trafalgar Square', as the first in the book and written the preface.

In March 1920 the Bridges were invited to one of the King's tea parties and saw there Edmund and Nellie Gosse. Bridges wrote to Gosse that 'I was filled with regret when I found that Kipling had been one of the guests. I have never met him, and you could have introduced me.' With his typical insouciance, he added, 'Monica and I both wanted refreshments, and made straight for the coffee urn—the coffee was regal in quality—and there we sat talking to friends until we had to go back to await summons to be interviewed'.[7]

That same month *October and Other Poems* was published. The volume was in three sections, the first comprised poems written in 1913 in syllabic verse, the second eighteen poems written during the war and published in journals and papers at the time, while the final section contained six poems of various dates. E. G. Twitchett remarked sympathetically that,

even the verbal life in *October*, the last quality which Mr Bridges' poems might be expected to lose, is dimmed and dull, except in the twelve poems which date from 1913 and are in much the mode of the earlier lyrics. It is as if his words had hibernated during the war, and perhaps they did . . . those who stayed at home and heard the proliferated cries of modern patriotism will remember a hoarse, unreal quality in the noise which seemed inseparable from its expression . . . The topical war poems have nothing to commend them but the fascinating improbability that they should have been written by Mr Bridges and the striking certainty that they were.[8]

Bridges included very few of them in subsequent collections. It is where he expresses compassion for the wounded or bereaved that his war poetry is at its most accessible, as for example in 'The West Front' or the opening of 'Trafalgar Square':

> Fool that I was: my heart was sore,
> Yea sick for the myriad wounded men,
> The maim'd in the war: I had grief for each one:

These lines are placed in a context that balances compassion against another set of values—'freedom and honour', 'England's glory', the 'life and glow' of the warrior. Bridges' best poems about the war were written and published after it had ended, when he could freely express the sorrow and despondency he had felt, and was not expected to display only his patriotism. Among these John Sparrow singles out 'Melancholy', written in July 1921:

> 'Twas mid of the moon but the night was dark with rain,
> Drops lashed the pane, the wind howl'd under the door;
> For me, my heart heard nought but the cannon-roar
> On fields of war, where Hell was raging amain: . . .
> As when on an Autumn plain the storm lays low the wheat,
> So fell the flower of England, her golden grain,
> Her harvesting hope trodden under the feet
> Of Moloch, Woden and Thor,
> And the lovingkindness of Christ held in disdain.
> My heart gave way to the strain, renouncing more & more;
> Its bloodstream fainted down to the slothful weary beat
> Of the age-long moment, that swelleth where ages meet,
> Marking time 'twixt dark Hereafter and Long-before;
> Which greet awhile and awhile, again to retreat;
> The Never-the-same repeating again and again,
> Completing itself in monotony incomplete,
> A wash of beauty and horror in shadows that fleet,
> Always the Never-the-same still to repeat,
> The devouring glide of a dream that keepeth no store.
> Meseem'd I stood on the flats of a waveless shore,
> Where MELANCHOLY unrobed of her earthly weeds,
> Haunteth in naked beauty without stain;
> In reconcilement of Death, and Vanity of all needs;

A melting of life in oblivion of all deeds;
No other beauty nor passion nor love nor lore;
No other goddess abideth for man to adore;
All things remaining nowhere with nought to remain;
The consummation of thought in nought to attain.
  I had come myself to that ultimate Ocean-shore,
Like Labourer Love when his life-day is o'er,
Who home returning fatigued is fain to regain
The house where he was unconsciously born of yore;
Stumbling on the threshold he sinketh down on the floor;
Half-hearteth a prayer as he lieth, and nothing heeds,
If only he sleep and sleep and have rest for evermore.

Of this Sparrow says: 'It is difficult to know which to praise most in this wonderful poem, the imaginative power that communicates feeling through vision, or the art that intensifies the emotion by means of word-pattern—a heavily recurring accent and changes rung through the whole length of the piece on three main vowel-sounds, used both as a final and as internal rhymes.'[9]

Characteristically, Bridges' fear that the Treaty of Versailles would cause another war prompted him to act, and in 1920 he initiated what is known as the Oxford Letter to the German professors, which declared a willingness on the part of those who signed to resume communication with German academics, who had been blamed for misleading the people into the war. Although it could only be a gesture, Bridges doubtless hoped that it might lead to a broader movement of reconciliation and he tried to get as many of the Oxford academics to sign as he could. Henry Bradley signed, but in September withdrew his name because he was afraid that the manifesto would be received in Germany as acknowledgement by English academics that Britain had been wrong in fighting. Bridges replied that

> the fear that one's action may be misinterpreted does not seem to me any reason against doing one's duty . . . We have to forgive—as I foresaw when I put Shelley's lines at the end of 'The Spirit of Man' . . . People at home who read the English newspapers forget that the Germans read the German newspapers. I don't see that there is much to choose between them. An Austrian professor came to tea the other day and there was no awkwardness of any sort. My German 'letter' (or manifesto) is an appeal which should bring together the generous minded on both sides.[10]

The letter was printed in *The Times* in October and caused a considerable stir. On 16 December Bridges wrote another letter to the *Poetry Workshop* which explains more fully his statements to Bradley:

When *The Times* (October 18) condemned the Oxford letter to the German and Austrian professors, the denunciation gradually came to be directed against me; and when I replied (October 27), my opponent shuffled off and thought to discredit my arguments by quoting a sonnet I had written against the Germans during the war, alleging that my present attitude was inconsistent with that, and ergo untrustworthy. I could only be gratified to see that I had driven him to such an irrelevant and futile evasion as to find fault with me for being bellicose during the war and peacemaking during peace. It would plainly have suited him so much better if he had been able to accuse me of having been a weak pacifist throughout, who had never felt any patriotic emotion hot as his. None the less the language of the sonnet quoted against me might be held to be inexcusably extravagant, if its history were forgotten or unknown; and I hope that the following explanation may not be too long for your magazine.

The sonnet in question ['Our Prisoners of War in Germany'] . . . was written solely for the purpose of preventing any ill-treatment of the German prisoners in England.

You will remember that, owing to the accounts in the newspapers of the ill-treatment of English prisoners in Germany, there arose a cry in this country for retaliation on our German prisoners. When a minister of the Crown spoke dubiously in the House of Commons on the expediency of such retaliation, *The Times* printed a letter of mine denouncing his hesitancy. The cry subsided, but there was a recrudence of the vendetta feeling later, and it was then that I sent the said sonnet to *The Times*, November 4, 1918.

In those verses I asserted or implied 1) that ill-treatment of prisoners was part of the Prussian war policy; 2) that no-one in Germany protested against it—though, if it were the recognised practice, they must be aware of it; and 3) that they hoped it would provoke us to similar barbarities, that we might thus fall to the level of their own frightfulness: and I believed all that.

It is plain tht the second and third charges fall unless the first be true; and it was not true. Yet I believed it . . . having been misled, as most of us were, by the newspapers. But since the war we have read many narrations written by the prisoners themselves—I need cite only one, the book entitled 'Comrades in Captivity'—from which I learnt that the

Prussian regulations set each prison-camp in charge of a special Commandant, who had a free hand to manage the prisoners as he would, being responsible to headquarters only for their safekeeping. The inevitable result of such a bad system was that where the Commandant was a brute, the treatment was brutal; and the reports of such cases which reached us were absolutely true: but the whole truth was that they were exceptional cases. That book . . . gave me the impression that the prisoners were often, and even generally, treated as well as we could expect; and that, considering their extremely insubordinate conduct they met with more good-natured tolerance than German prisoners would have got from a baited Englishman. I am far from blaming our men for the lightheartedness which kept them alive; it was the insuperable ebullition of the spirit which won the war, and might rather be a theme for national pride and exultation—but it cannot be denied that it made tolerable conditions more difficult to provide, and that the Germans were much 'better' prisoners than our men were.

Now though it still remains true that our countrymen, owing to the personal savagery of their keepers, were sometimes treated with an inhuman cruelty which cannot be condoned, and that there was happily no similar instance of such barbarity in England, yet it is plain that I went too far in my accusation. And that being so, I am not ashamed of retracting my words, and expressing sorrow for having written them: and I can see that as I was misled by the English press, so the Germans probably were by their own; and that they have the same excuse for some of their ill-feeling as I have for mine.

It seems to me that this sonnet is a fair example of the 'animosities' regretted in the Oxford letter. I willingly offer it to the Germans as a discarded animosity in exchange for one of theirs.

By March the following year (1921) Bridges had received what he described as about two-dozen hearty and dignified replies from German and Austrian academics. He also met the German ambassador and found him agreeable.

In November Bridges completed the third edition of his study of Milton's prosody, enlarging the book to include a chapter on accentual verse. As soon as it was finished he turned his attention to writing an introduction to a pamphlet by H. E. Salter urging the restoration of some of Oxford's older street names. Names such as Catte Street and Magpie Lane had been replaced by St Catherine's Street and Grove Street. The pamphlet included a map drawn by Monica of the city as it had been enclosed by medieval walls, showing both old and new street names. Some of the old names were restored, although Seven Deadly Sins, once the name of New Inn Hall Street where Hopkins had lived as an undergraduate, was not.

Bridges also extended his interest in French literature to the essayist and poet Charles Péguy, inquiring of Roger Fry whether Péguy had written anything during the war that he should read; he thought his style queer but good. Fry lent him Daniel Halévy's analysis of Péguy, which he read with interest in December. His admiration of another French poet, Francis Jammes, was to influence his experiments in syllabic verse. He sent Bradley a copy of Jammes' poem 'Juste en face, je vois la maison que Vigny . . .', which he greatly liked but admitted that trying to become friends with the poet was impossible. Jammes, he said, 'has settled down into a Catholic worshipper, and is prouder than ever of beng a countryman'.[11] The Frenchman sent him photographs of his family and their small farm, but the exchange of letters Bridges considered 'unsatisfactory'; Jammes may well not have been as interested in discussing poetic technique as he was. Fry mentioned that he was himself translating Mallarmé. Bridges replied that he considered it such a 'desperate job' that his prime response was curiosity; he admitted finding Mallarmé's French very difficult and suggested that Rimbaud may have influenced his diction. Bridges had chosen five passages from Rimbaud's poetry for *The Spirit of Man*, among them 'Oisive jeunesse' which shares a page in deliberate contrast with Hopkins' 'Spring and Fall'. Like Bridges' other selections from Rimbaud, it comes from *Les Illuminations* of 1872–3, the most heavily annotated section in his copy of *Œuvres de Arthur Rimbaud* (1912).

November 1921 brought Bridges more work with the SPE as Logan Pearsall Smith fell ill. Bridges turned to Bradley for assistance, but again wrote a number of the items himself. Tract no. 4 was, he told Newbolt, closer to what he had in mind than previous ones had been. It contained a 'learned' article on an aspect of language—the tracts occasionally covered languages other than English—followed by miscellaneous notes, some alluding to matters 'in the air' at the time; for instance, he was keen to have a 'good paper on the words that our Tommies invented in the war'.[12] Bridges also hoped to arrange a meeting in mid-January to inform various editors of London newspapers and journals about the SPE and urge them to support and advertise its aims. In the fifth tract, published in May, he had an article on the use of dialect in Edmund Blunden's poems. Bridges chose a number of examples of words that enrich English because they have a specific application, such as 'goistering': 'to behave in a noisy boisterous fashion', used for jackdaws, or 'stolchy' for wet ploughlands. He objected to words that have strong and unwanted overtones, such as 'glinzy' for 'slippery', because it is reminiscent of 'glint', or which he believed had been misused, but overall he praised more as positive and enriching than he criticized. The sixth tract was evidently at one point going to include an article by Robert Graves on Swinburne's rhythms. Bridges wrote to Graves,

> I would like to remind you that in your animadversions on Swinburne's rhythms *you must not bring my name in.* Of course it is only the fact of my having call'd your attention to Hertha that suggested to me the possibility, together with my general sympathy with your views, as you expressed them to me the other day. You belong to a generation that can criticise Tennyson, Browning and Swinburne without incurring suspicion of the jealousy and malevolence which is proverbially attributed to poets—concerning which I have always thought that if it is really a part of the true poet's temper, then, I am not, and cannot be of the clan.[13]

In the end, instead of an article there was a letter by Graves urging that the SPE should not be allowed to degenerate 'into a National Academy or an Eisteddfodd Adjudication Committee' trying to put back the clock. It is an amusing, slightly antagonistic piece of writing. Bridges would have agreed with Graves's stance. When, for instance, his interest in psychology led him to read William MacDougall's book, *The Group Mind*, he considered it 'poor stuff indeed', and thinking that MacDougall should have used the evidence of language, he wrote to Bradley,

> I wish you would . . . write something on the overpowering influence of language in differentiating mankind. Though it might be argued that every 'nation' makes its own language (and this would have to be examined) yet I believe that the final cultured product is very much a matter of chance, at least its final overpowering form and vocabulary is greatly independent of 'human' agency. It seems to me to have a destiny of its own which is in a sense uncontrollable.[14]

Given this belief, the SPE could not in Bridges' view, be didactic; it could only make available information that, if people chose, they could absorb. He was to express similar views in his introduction to the *Chilswell Book of English Poetry*, an anthology designed for use in schools.

Tract VI also contained criticism by George Saintsbury of Henry James's style. Bridges toned down the criticism, explaining: 'Though I suppose I do not admire his later style any more than you do, yet unqualified censure was not admissible nor palatable in our Tract. I [have] read very little and his style has prevented me in spite of my great personal esteem from having a very extensive acquaintance with it.'[15]

In August 1921 Newbolt sent Bridges his *Naval History of the War 1914–18*, written from the British point of view. Bridges considered that

> it is very easy, & it is just, to make out a bad case for the Germans: & it may be useful, because it is well for both sides to have a clear understanding, before reconciliation: but honestly I do not think that just now it is the side of the matter which is in danger of being forgotten by the allies or that it is likely that our side will be too lenient. You probably know that I think the future peace of Europe depends on Germany being conciliated and not ill treated: and ever since the armistice I have felt little but shame because of our attitude—It seems to me at this moment that the Germans are winning the war: which was what I most wished to escape. At least they seem to be legally in the right in most points which are contended, and to be working hard, whereas our folk are wasting and idling. I am not altogether despondent: but as I cannot write more than a few lines I may be giving you a wrong notion of my feelings. The politicians seem very foolish, if indeed they are not mad:—as the French are—and the notion that the French respect us, or are grateful to us, or even like us, is a wild delusion.[16]

Despite this disquiet, however, 1921 was a year in which Bridges felt the desire to write a number of poems. He again used the neo-Miltonic syllabics but made the caesura fall in a far greater variety of places than in the poems of 1913. It has long been realized that this is one of the most striking aspects of Milton's verse—Paull Baum states that 'in the ten thousand lines of *Paradise Lost* there are less than twenty-five instances of the pause coming at the same point for more than two lines consecutively'.[17] Bridges relished such constant versatility, wanting a metre that would enable him to use a wide variety of words and rhythms. This required a longish line where stresses could fall wherever the word-accents dictated, and which could absorb polysyllabic words without forcing them to carry unnatural extra accents. His main interest was in a twelve-syllable line. In the five neo-Miltonic poems using this metre that were published in *New Verse* (1925), Bridges followed Milton's elisions with one main exception: he allowed words ending in 'tion' (sh'n) to be elided, as in 'the nation and all'. Following Milton's practice, Bridges considered that all the elisions were optional but tried to make those he used 'quite natural', speech elisions rather than those which could be spotted only visually. As early as 1891 he had explained to Lowes Dickinson that the effect on speech-rhythm that he envisaged by elision was the partial, not the complete loss of a syllable: 'When two vowels come together the first is more like an appogiatura than anything else . . . [and] "elisions" where a liquid occurs . . . are more like trisyllabic feet.'[18]

A change from the earlier experiments is immediately apparent in 'Poor Poll', dated 3 June 1921, a poem much admired by Auden:

> I saw it all, Polly, how when you had call'd for sop
> and your good friend the cook came & fill'd up your pan
> you yerk'd it out deftly by beakfuls scattering it
> away far as you might upon the sunny lawn
> then summon'd with loud cry the little garden birds
> to take their feast . . .

There is great energy in the line and the tone, linked by relaxed colloquial address, varies from mocking wit to meditative observation. Like T. S. Eliot, as Donald Stanford points out, Bridges was looking for a line in which he could insert other languages and, more importantly, the rhythms natural to them[19]—with evident delight he made use of Greek, German, French, Italian, and Spanish. He had the poem printed separately and showed it to a number of friends to test their reaction to the new metre; and was very proud of the fact that Raleigh was able to read it accurately at sight without any punctuation. 'Poor Poll' showed, he said, in the description of the parrot 'the psychology which Bertrand Russell advocates in the first chapter of *The Analysis of Mind*', a reference to Russell's distinction between 'habit-memory' associated with instinct and the more complex 'knowledge-memory'. The congruence of ideas was, however, Bridges said, coincidental.[20]

New Verse was divided into four sections according to the metres used: syllabic, old styles, accentual, and quantitative. Bridges experimented with the syllabic rhythm for a variety of subjects, from 'Kate's Mother', a description of a visit made when he was a child to his nurse's mother, to philosophical poems meditating on man's evolution and nature. 'Kate's Mother' he described as the 'simplest childish narrative', in which he tried to juxtapose high and low subjects without 'embarrassment or bathos . . . the desideratum in English versification which I wished to supply',[21] and by and large he manages to avoid sentimentality while still conveying wonder and the proportions the world takes on when experienced by a small child. The shadow of the war appears in a number of the poems, such as 'The Widow' and 'The College Garden in 1917', in which he laments the absence of the students but knows that

> life will renew; tho' now none cometh here all day
> but a pensive philosopher from his dark room
> pacing the terrace, slow as his earth-burden'd thought,
> and the agèd gardener with scythe wheelbarrow and broom
> loitering in expert parcimony of skill and time
> while on the grassy slope of the old city-rampart
> I watch his idleness and hearken to the clocks
> in punctual dispute clanging the quarter-hours—

In the spring of 1922 Bridges' 'writing fit' left him. He marked a point ten lines from the end of 'Come se quando', a poem recording a dream about a poet turned prophet who is killed by a crowd, and noted that 'the mood for writing . . . left me suddenly one day at this line. I could not go on and finished the poem with difficulty later.'[22] Of the rest of the volume, one of the most powerful poems is 'Low Barometer', in which he uses the extended metaphor of a storm to describe a man suddenly assailed by his deeply rooted instincts:

> The south-wind strengthens to a gale,
> Across the moon the clouds fly fast,

The house is smitten as with a flail,
The chimney shudders to the blast.

On such a night, when Air has loosed
Its guardian grasp on blood and brain,
Old terrors then of god or ghost
Creep from their caves to life again;

And Reason kens he herits in
A haunted house. Tenants unknown
Assert their squalid lease of sin
With earlier title than his own.

Unbodied presences, the pack'd
Pollution and remorse of Time,
Slipp'd from oblivion reenact
The horrors of unhouseld crime.

Some men would quell the thing with prayer
Whose sightless footsteps pad the floor,
Whose fearful trespass mounts the stair
Or bursts the lock'd forbidden door.

Some have seen corpses long interr'd
Escape from hallowing control,
Pale charnel forms—nay ev'n have heard
The shrilling of a troubled soul,

That wanders till the dawn hath cross'd
The dolorous dark, or Earth hath wound
Closer her storm-spredd cloke, and thrust
The baleful phantoms underground.

Here, in addition to end-rhyme, Bridges uses not only alliteration and alliterating pairs but the more widely spaced repetition of consonants and parallel syntax that he was later to employ in *The Testament of Beauty* to add form and music to a looser metre. The meaning is rich, compactly stated, the tension reinforced by the rhythms. Stanzas 5 and 6 make use of the fearful, almost meaningless images well known to writers of horror stories, but here focused to convey the dread of a civilized man who knows in himself the possibility of committing some deed abhorred by society. Bridges used similar techniques for a passage in *The Testament* that, while alluding to man's evolution, simultaneously acknowledges the power and fundamental nature of instinct. He also conveys the loneliness of each man's struggle with his personality:

> Yet since of all, whatever hath once been, evil or good,
> tho' we can think not of it and remember it not,
> nothing can wholly perish; so ther is no birthright
> so noble or stock so clean, but it transmitteth dregs,
> contamination at core of old brutality;
> inchoate lobes, dumb shapes of ancient terror abide:
> tho' fading still in the oceanic deeps of mind
> their eyeless sorrows haunt the unfathom'd density,
> dulling the crystal lens of prophetic vision,
> crippling the nerve that ministereth to trembling strength,
> distorting the features of our nobility:
> And we, living at prime, what is it now to us
> how our forefathers dream'd, suffer'd, struggled, or wrought?
> how thru' the obliterated aeons of man's ordeal
> unnumber'd personalities separately endured?
>
> (Book II, ll. 661–74)

Much of Bridge's poetry written after the war reflects it indirectly, in statements that show how deeply he had been impressed by man's brutality.

In March 1922 Edward became engaged to Katherine Farrer, the daughter of Lord Farrer, the friends who had provided a home in which he convalesced while Chilswell was uninhabitable. Bridges was very pleased with the news; he and Monica had long been fond of Kitty. Edward had spent part of 1921 working at the League of Nations in Geneva and was now beginning what was to be a very distinguished career as a public servant.[23] In the same month Roger Fry visited Chilswell, after which Bridges wrote to him, 'I enjoyed your visit immensely . . . It is very pleasant to find one's mind so much at ease with a companion'.[24] For much of the year, however, Bridges was concerned with the SPE. He asked Newbolt to advertise it in a lecture he was to give to the Royal Society of Literature in March. He was anxious, too, to increase the number of American subscribers. It was necessary, he thought, to get a consensus of what the best form of the English language was. 'Public school pronunciation', he thought, would provide a good basis but would require widening and improving if it was ever to receive international recognition. There was a proposal for a joint Anglo-American committee to consider relevant issues. Newbolt's account of the proposals agreed by the English members of the committee so differed from Bridges' understanding of the decisions that the relationship between them became decidedly strained. Part of the problem was that Newbolt had not been at a meeting at which the initial proposals were discussed, and had formed his own view of the group's intention. Bridges tried to distance himself and the SPE from the committee that was then set up. After the rumpus the society continued much as before, gathering new members, among them George Bernard Shaw who joined in July.

In June 1922 Raleigh died from typhoid contracted in the Middle East where he had stopped over on his return to England from India. Bridges found this unexpected death 'difficult to realize'. He was, however, preoccupied with Edward's marriage and expressed his feelings more fully later in the introduction that he wrote in 1927 for a selection of Raleigh's letters edited by his widow. Monica, who was doing all the secretarial work for the SPE (whose membership by 1923 numbered nearly 400), was again ill several times during the year and in July she and Bridges took a recuperative holiday. On their return Bridges wrote to Bradley,

> I have been away for about 3 weeks, and got home again last night. I have wandered as far as Inverness-shire and then come down the Caledonian Canal and through Argyleshire to Northumberland where our main headquarters were, near Bamburgh, in some old coast-guard's cottages, not very comfortable, but we spent some of the time with some relatives of my wife, who are plentiful in those parts, and had an enjoyable time on the whole. I am however very glad to be at rest (from motion etc.) and have some rather stiff jobs to attend to here—so I think I am fixed for some time.[25]

One of the 'stiff jobs' he had on hand was an essay, 'Humdrum and Harum-Scarum', which was published in November.[26] It is a reasoned examination of the problems to which free verse is liable. Starting from the conviction that verse differs from prose in that it creates rhythmical expectation, Bridges suggests that 'free verse is good and theoretically defensible only in so far as it can create expectancy without the old metrical devices'. Examining the opening of Dante's Third Canto of *Purgatory*, he points out that 'the diction, rhythm and sonority are carried by the versification without a trace of pomposity or affectation'. Free verse, by contrast, 'must be full of disconsolate patches, for it has no corresponding machinery to carry the subordinate matter'. Trying to overcome the problem of providing appropriate verse for unpoetic material could easily lead, he suggested, to an awareness on the part of readers that the poet was rather desperately improvising, and to an uneasy awareness on the poet's side that 'while pretending honest aesthetic rightness . . . he is only providing ingenious make-shifts which he would have been glad to avoid'. Referring to the French poet Édouard Dujardin's suggestion that the basic units in free verse are grammatical, Bridges objected that

> the grammatical forms of sentences in English are few, and must repeat themselves again and again; and each form has its proper and natural inflection of voice which, however overlaid, will impose its typical intonation on the sentence. Now if the grammatical forms are made coincident with the lines of the verse, they must impose the recurrence of their similar intonations upon the lines . . . one of the difficulties in writing good verse of any kind is to escape from the tyranny of these recurrent speech-forms, and the restrictions imposed by the rules of free verse must make that difficulty immeasurably greater.

Finally, the writer of free verse loses the possibility of playing off the speech rhythm against the metre. He quoted the first two lines of Book II of *Paradise Lost*:

> High on a throne of Royal State, which far
> Outshon the wealth of Ormus and of Ind

and rewrote it to show what was lost:

> High on a throne of Royal State
> Which far outshon the wealth of Ormus and of Ind.

Bridges concluded that, although art requires experiments in order to remain vital, his own conviction was that there remained considerable possibilities of new achievement in metrical prosody and that exploration of such forms as Milton's syllabic verse would be more promising than free verse as he understood it. The argument seems to have been one with which W. B. Yeats was very much in accord, if he was not influenced by it. In 'A General Introduction for my Work' he wrote,

> If I wrote of personal love or sorrow in free verse, or in any rhythm that left it unchanged, amid all its accidence, I would be full of self-contempt because of my egotism and indiscretion, and forsee the boredom of my reader. I must choose a traditional stanza, even what I alter must seem traditional . . . The contrapuntal structure of the verse, to employ a term adopted by Robert Bridges, combines the past and present. If I repeat the first line of *Paradise Lost* so as to emphasize its five feet I am among the folk singers . . . but speak it as I should I cross it with another emphasis, that of passionate prose.[27]

What was later to concern Bridges and make his experiments with syllabic verse controversial was whether syllabics, with their many acceptable and optional elisions and disregard of stress, were a sufficiently firm metrical base to escape the problems he predicted for free verse. His best display of the uses to which syllabics could be put was to be *The Testament of Beauty*.

17

Old Age and *New Verse*

(1923–1926)

In 1923 the SPE brought out another four tracts. These and gathering material for those planned for 1924 gave Bridges plenty to do. The society's membership had been growing, keeping Monica busy with the necessary secretarial work. At the age of 79 Bridges had begun to feel that the job was becoming too much for him, but Logan Pearsall Smith records that frequently, when Bridges had lightened his load by asking someone else to do something, the new worker would find him proceeding 'to perform in the most masterly manner this task himself'.[1]

In February Roger Fry gave two lectures and an informal talk at the University of Oxford, on modern French art and Mallarmé. He stayed at Chilswell and in the mornings worked at three portraits of Bridges. The one Fry chose to give the family made him look melancholy and when it was finished Bridges commented, 'I thought that if I had died without any other later record it would be supposed that I had suffered from acute melancholy, and that my flesh had undergone a visible adipocerous decomposition before death'.[2] He had photographs taken of himself in Oxford to show Fry what he really looked like. Fry had also painted a portrait of Elizabeth but the family did not like this either and relations between him and the Bridges were somewhat strained for several months. In August Monica wrote to him:

> As I see you really wish us to return the portrait of Elizabeth, I have done so. I did not at all like this method of doing it (troubling another to pack it) but not being skilled in packing pictures, I took you at your word and sent it down to 114 Woodstock Road, by the first opportunity, i.e., the day-before-yesterday. It is true that to me this picture does not represent Elizabeth. The portrait of Robert I should like to have and I

thank you for saying that I may. To my thinking it was the most like of the three. Some days when I look at it, it appeals to me more as a likeness than on others. Anyhow, thank you for it very much. As you know, I know nothing whatever about painting. I do know that your landscape on the landing gives me constant and unfeigned pleasure so you are often in Chilswell thoughts.[3]

On 21 May 1923 Henry Bradley suffered a stroke, and died two days later. Bridges began in October but did not complete until 1926 a memoir of his friend, which was published with a collection of Bradley's essays. Bridges clearly liked and respected him; the relationship seems to have been the easy friendship between two family men already firmly committed elsewhere. Bridges divided his memoir into three sections, using, especially in the first part, anecdotes and information from Bradley's friends in order to sketch his life prior to his own acquaintance with him. He achieved a nice balance between accounts of Bradley's philological expertise and humanizing stories of his friend's personality and habits, such as his reluctance to decide, much to the exasperation of fellow examiners, on the class to be awarded to examination candidates, or the hesitations in his speech while he sought the beginning of a sentence that would allow him to express an idea accurately and grammatically. The memoir ends with a statement of Bridges' scepticism about life after death; he could not picture, he said, 'any sort of future existence which should be sufficiently like our present state to continue our mortal sympathies, or, if it should continue them, could continue to satisfy them'.[4] But his memories of Bradley were all, he declared, so pleasant that he could almost imagine 'the delight of his company enduring *in eternum*'. The respect and affection clear in that compliment suffuse the biography, giving it much of its charm.

Bridges' next project was an anthology of poetry for use in schools, but before settling to it he and Monica took a holiday, paying 'a round of visits in Sussex with our "immortal Ford", traversing the county backward and forward obliquely and joining up the ends of our diagonals. We had good weather, and the county was looking its best.'[5] Compiling the *Chilswell Book of English Poetry*, however, he found 'uses me up', though his fatigue is far from evident in the anthology. Bridges sets out in the preface his ideas about the writing and selection of poetry for children, and, as usual, they were strongly felt and expressed. He objected to many of the poems that had been written for children, 'in a technique often as inept as their sentiments'.[6] To give children poems that adults expected them to grow out of was in Bridges' opinion a mistake based on two 'delusions': 'first, that beauty must needs be fully apprehended before it can be felt or admired: secondly, that the young are unimaginative'. Instead, he tried to compile an anthology where there was nothing that a lover of poetry would ever cast aside, and which 'within its proper limitations . . . should be as gratifying to the old as to the young'. The largest number of excerpts is from Shakespeare, with Shelley a close second. Keats, Milton, Wordsworth, and Tennyson are all well represented and, surprisingly, so is Byron, along with Burns and Blake. Bridges included nothing of his own nor of Hopkins', although he chose four of Dixon's poems and two by Yeats. Most of his introduction, which was also printed separately, is devoted to the role he saw poetry and language playing in education. Poetry's 'high imaginative task' is the 'displaying [of] the beauty, solemnity and mystery of man's life on earth . . . the most intimate expression of Man's Spirit'. Bridges links spiritual life with good citizenship but then, moving towards his belief that social morality is temporal and cultural, he notes that 'language has a hidden but commanding influence in directing spiritual life'. Continuing with an idea which he had once tried to persuade Bradley to write about and which is affirmed by anthropologists and structuralist literary critics, he comments: 'In whatever country we may be born, we imbibe the ideas inherent to its speech; nor can we escape from the bias which that accident must give to our minds, unless we learn other languages and study their literatures.' Turning to the national picture he states that dialects 'should be fostered', their 'separate existence as living forces of original character is not incompatible with the preservation of the purity of the main stock, nor with that sense of touch with it which would keep them from eccentricities and distortion. Now if these two desirable things are to be assured, a schooling for all in the main or mother dialect is imperative.' In accomplishing this Bridges recognizes the potential usefulness of radio broadcasts, 'that all, whatever dialect they speak at home, should hear the language of our great literature'. He finishes with a plea that still has force today, that this means of diffusing national culture should not be 'squandered in the selfish interests of commercialism'.

Bridges had complimented A. E. Housman on his *Last Poems* late in June and Housman in return had invited Bridges to spend a night as his guest in Trinity College, Cambridge. The two men discussed the choice of poems for the Chilswell anthology, Housman arguing for the inclusion of Matthew Arnold and Browning. Bridges evidently decided that he wanted some of *A Shropshire Lad* as well, for Housman wrote to his publisher:

> I had better tell you also that I believe he (being Poet Laureate, and an unscrupulous character, and apparently such an admirer of my verse that he thinks its presence or absence will make all the difference to the book) intends to include three poems from *A Shropshire Lad*, though I have not given him my permission, because he thinks he has reason to think that I shall not prosecute him. Well, I shall not; and you will please turn a blind eye too.[7]

It was the only time Housman 'permitted' poems to be reprinted from that volume. He stayed at Chilswell in December when visiting Oxford to give a lecture and wrote about Bridges to his sister, Kate:

> He is an amazing old man: at 79 he gets up at five in the morning, lights his own fire and makes his coffee, and does a lot of work before breakfast. He has a large number of correct opinions, and is delighted when he finds that I have them too, and shakes hands with me when I say that the Nun's Priest's Tale is Chaucer's best poem, and that civilisation without slavery is impossible.[8]

But Housman was notoriously taciturn, a trait which made his visit tiring for Bridges whose 'delight' may have stemmed less from total agreement with Housman's views than from relief at having him contribute anything to conversation. Writing to Monica after Bridges' death in 1930, Housman remarked, 'I do not suppose there is anything I have read oftener than the first four books of *Shorter Poems*.[9] He had not, however, liked his later syllabic verse nor Hopkins' use of sprung rhythm.

In September Bridges lost another of his friends, Francis Jenkinson, who had been University Librarian at Cambridge and with whom he had shared many interests evident in their extensive correspondence. Housman sent Bridges a letter suggesting that he miss the funeral, for which Robert was grateful. He wrote to Housman,

When you put me up that day at Cambridge I was most fortunate in seeing Jenkinson.—He told me just how he stood and we had last words, which I felt might be last words and I should have wept if I had any tears in me. I feared for his fragility, but hoped his courage would pull him through—and it seems to have served him well. The regular bulletins which Stewart kindly sent us were as favourable as possible and I thought that the danger was past. I supposed that after the horrible operation he might have had some years of comfort. He was an old friend of ours and of course everyone loved him. We saw him most years in vacation time, especially because of his relationship with our neighbours the Crums. He used to stay with us at Yattendon.[10]

A month later Bridges received a letter from Stanley Morison, who was interested in printing and in early type, subjects that Bridges had formerly been able to discuss with Jenkinson. Morison had long admired the type and designs used in some of Bridges' volumes of poetry. Bridges invited him to Chilswell and despite the generation's difference in their ages, they became friends. Discussion between them was not limited to typography; Bridges was keen to know Morison's opinion of the 'ethical effect' of *New Verse* and later sent him copies of the private print of *The Testament of Beauty*, asking for advice before publication. Morison was a Catholic convert who had come from a fiercely agnostic family; his father was a commercial traveller and his mother a strong believer in egalitarianism. It has been suggested that their personalities were similar in 'intellect, intolerance and charm'.[11]

By October Bridges had decided to accept an invitation to go to America for three months starting on 22 March 1924. His hosts were to be various universities and educational institutes, beginning with the University of Michigan, where he was given an honorary degree. It was not to be a lecture tour but a series of conversational discussions with students, although in fact while Robert and Monica were staying at Ann Arbor he addressed the medical school with a fascinating lecture on medical practice as he had been taught it in the 1870s. Bridges also received an honorary degree from Harvard. The trip to America gave him his first opportunity of travelling in an ocean liner. He wrote to Muirhead:

This letter shd be posted in a few days at Liverpool. We have had a very good time. but this voyage is the worst part of it, for the ship is crowded with girls going to Wembley. There are some good men on board, but I haven't got at them. Monica & I sit next to the Captain at meals. Fog however has kept him a good deal on the bridge, or whatever corresponds to the bridge in this monstrous hotel. We are now steaming nearly 400 miles a day, with triple screws, over a smooth sea with a N[orth] wind, but are coming into a S[outh] W[est] which will give us different conditions. I hope things have been going well with you. I shall be very busy for a while after I get home, but shall hope to pay you a visit, or perhaps receive one from you, before long—We have the best berths on board—3 rooms with 11 electric lights, & all the luxuries of heating etc, but they do not make life tolerable in the incessant cackle of harsh voices and the hideous accompaniment of banjos and grammophones, or whatever they are called. I must put this letter into an envelope, since there is no means of burning it.—I should put it into the fire if there was one.[12]

In December 1923 Elizabeth married Ali Akbar Daryush in Bombay and spent the next four years with him in Persia, where he worked as a government official. In November Bridges had written to Margaret Woods, 'Elizabeth is off to Persia this month to meet her spouse, and be as much married as the Church of England and the Foreign Office and the Religion of Mahomet will allow of. She is very happy, and Daryush is a very excellent and solid person.'[13] But the bond between Bridges and his elder daughter was close, strengthened by their shared interest in writing poetry, and he missed her badly.

The following month Fry and Bridges made a concerted effort to heal the breach between them. The occasion was Fry's gift of his book, *Vision and Design*. In the letter Bridges wrote expressing his reaction to it he was clearly working through his ideas, with resultant inconsistencies. Fry attributes beauty to the artistic arrangement of planes and lines and, suggesting like Clive Bell that the aesthetic emotion is unlike any other that man experiences, distances it from social or moral function. To Bridges this was too specialized a definition—simply an aid to the artist. Since Bridges did not distinguish between reaction to beauty in the natural world and in art, nor endow the artist with a different type of appreciation from that of other men, he sought a more widely applicable explanation. His theory was heavily influenced by Darwin and therefore linked beauty with sexuality, although he was not altogether happy about the relationship: thus, while acknowledging the scientific theory that our faculty for seeing beauty may depend on the secretions of some gland, Bridges also felt that his own reaction to beauty could most accurately be called 'spiritual mirth' and he suggested that it might be defined as the 'quality in sensible objects which provokes spiritual [religious] emotion'.[14] The attitude grew out of the model of the mind that he had sketched in his talk to the WEA, and is of central concern in *The Testament of Beauty*, although there too he could not reconcile all the implications. In defending his position, Fry said that while he agreed that man's response to artistic beauty was composed of many different emotions, he had come to the conclusion that the fundamental and characteristically artistic response was to artistic form.[15] This was more important than any of the emotions connected with life, and he distinguished between spirituality (a state of mind) and morality (a code for living), a distinction to which Bridges adhered in *The Testament*, calling the first Higher Ethic and the second Lower Ethic, although he considered Higher Ethic religious. Fry visited Chilswell in February, and Bridges' letter thanking him for advice on poems that he had shown him during the visit suggests that, despite genuine appreciation of Fry's comments, some strain remained in their relationship.

The year had its bright spots. Bridges read two of Santayana's books—*American Thought* and *Egotism*—and sent him a letter of appreciation. Santayana's reputation as a writer was growing but, Bridges reported, 'I find the philosophers [at Oxford] are puzzled and reluctant to praise him'.[16] Another friendship of his last years which was started by a letter of admiration was with E. M. Forster, whose *Passage to India* Bridges read and praised when it appeared in 1924. Forster presented him with copies of *The Longest Journey*, *A Room with a View*, *Anonymity: An Enquiry* (1925), and *Aspects of the Novel* which he sent when it was published with a charming and modest note. He stayed at Chilswell in March 1925, writing a somewhat painstaking letter of thanks accompanying an inscribed copy of *Alexandria: A History and a Guide*. Later the relations became easier and warmer, Forster starting his letters 'Dear Bridges'. His sensitivity to nature and ambivalent attitude to the effects on other countries of British civilization are clear in the letters; it is this side of him, that which is evident in the novels, which Forster revealed to Bridges. For example, he described a trip to Africa:

> I have heard the mayors of Johannesburg and Salisbury speak, and have myself addressed a few well chosen words to the Parliament of Uganda. I have seen hundreds of game, all looking alike, and thousands of Africans dressed in the discarded rags of Europe, and every morning of the three months I ate or could have eaten porridge and bacon. Now I come home, bringing nothing with me, not even a cockroach, only a vague and rather painful sense of bewilderment and frustration. Egypt is around me now. I am glad to see it, and the comparative self respect that seems to come from Islam . . .[17]

They are thoughtful letters and good ones, despite being slightly formal. In 1937 Forster defended Bridges to Stephen Spender:

> I suspect you've got that rather interesting and tiresome man (Robert Bridges) wrong. I used to think him not so much noble as naughty, and was very fond of him, and remember how when the war ended he was the first person with any reputation to risk who said we'd better not be vindictive. He was class bound and all that, and oh dear how he lowered his voice before articulating the word 'passion', still he saw science was important—which was more than George Meredith and the rest of them could see—and managed to get broadcasting into The Testament of Beauty, which is a creditable scoop for so old a man. Events moved too quickly for him, yes: now they move far quicker, and if in twenty years there is such a thing as an old man, *he*'ll be infinitely more on the shelf.[18]

Forster was one of the writers who contributed to the purchase of the clavichord which Bridges was given on his eightieth birthday, and in his letter of 8 March 1925 said that he had enjoyed hearing it played. Siegfried Sassoon, who had been secretary of the committee organizing the gift, invited the poet to London for a presentation ceremony before the subscribers, but Bridges, who had seriously overtired himself in completing his memoir of Bradley a few days previously and did not relish the fuss, declined the invitation. He wrote to Margaret Woods, who had sent a note about her pleasure in contributing to the gift:

> I am rather 'overwhelmed' by this Presentation—and having pulled through 3 months solid flattery in America—well, I must leave you to imagine my present distress. Having reason to suspect something of this

kind I had asked one or two friends to prevent it,—and now I learn that it was done with full knowledge of my disapprobation. I am sorry that my friends should have put themselves out on my account, but of course that does not in any way lessen my gratitude or my appreciation of their good will. And I thank you especially for your part in it, and your wish to be present at the 'ceremony.' I am glad today that this is reduced to a visit of Mr and Mrs Dolmetsch here on Saturday. They are to bring his fabrication in a motor car, and he will perform on it. I shall ask a few friends in to greet them. The gift is one that above anything else I should like to have, but if I had had to choose I should never have thought of.[19]

At Christmas Bridges sent a note of thanks to each of the subscribers, accompanied by copies of Lady Ottoline Morrell's photograph of himself seated beside the clavichord. One of the most strikingly handsome of the photographs of Bridges in old age, it shows off his leonine head, with its abundant white hair and neatly barbered beard. His great height is evident from the awkwardly crossed long legs; and his right arm rests negligently on the back of the chair, a pipe tucked into his hand.

In December Bridges had a brief spell of poetic activity and wrote some fourteen lines of verse, which he then abandoned until 1926. When revised, they became the seven opening lines of *The Testament of Beauty*:

> Mortal Prudence, handmaid of divine Providence,
> hath inscrutable reckoning with Fate and Fortune:
> We sail a changeful sea thru' halcyon days and storm
> and when the ship laboureth our stedfast purpose
> trembles like as the compass in a binnacle.
> Our stability is but balance, and wisdom lies
> in masterful administration of the unforseen.
> But little right hav I to flaunt such metaphor
> who never launched my bark upon the perilous seas
> never, you well may say, courted high adventure.
> Truly my life hath been a landsman's pilgrimage
> by earth's historic highways where the desert sands
> are the dust of man's temples, and the vaulted night
> is encumbered with the silence of his extinct fames[20]

In January 1925 Bridges received news that Muirhead was ill. Realizing that at their age any illness might be their last, bringing their long friendship to an end, Bridges wrote,

I wish I could have had a visit from the Muse which wd have allowed me to express something of what I feel of our friendship, now that its long life is so near the end—but I seldom get any sort of lively inspiration now—so I am sending you one of the lyrics that I wrote in 1921 which may possibly be the date of my last poems—in any case it is so far . . . It will recall happy days at Yattendon.[21]

The poem he sent was 'The Sleeping Mansion':

As our car rustled swiftly
  along the village lane,
We caught sight for a moment
  of the old house again, . . .

Muirhead died on 25 January. Bridges was not one of the pallbearers at the funeral, a fact that shows how misjudged was Forster's criticism of him for refusing to act in that capacity at Hardy's funeral in 1928.

The SPE again kept Bridges busy but the summer brought several pleasant events. Gustav Holst wrote in May because he wanted permission to set one of Dolben's poems to music, and Bridges, who was very pleased with the setting, asked him to look at his own poem, 'Awake, my heart to be loved', which he had written for a cello obbligato, but Holst found that he could not supply one. In mid-June Roger Fry visited Chilswell. It seemed to restore much of his old relaxed friendship with Bridges, who wrote to him afterwards, 'Your visit was a great delight and cheered me much—it is sad that you should be so busy as to make such things so rare. I am ordering the books that you praised . . . Do come and lecture again in Oxford as soon as you can.'[22] The summer was particularly beautiful and Bridges wrote to Pearsall Smith,

Enjoying this weather to the full I have little time for work, but have a lot of things on hand which I am luxuriously neglecting. I am bringing out a new volume of poems with Milford as soon as we can get them printed [*New Verse*] and I think a de luxe quarto of some of them (by a London printer who has asked for something) to precede the full book—in which latter, among some classical verse at the end I think of printing that old iambic ode to you—if you do not object. Excuse this horrid steel pen which I should be swearing at if it was not such a lovely summer afternoon. I have been working at embroidery on the lawn all the after lunch hours, and we are just going to have tea.[23]

Among Robert's and Monica's embroideries are beautiful curtains decorated with flowers and birds. Edward Thompson commented on Bridges' love of being outdoors and remembered him frequently lying flat on the ground and talking looking upwards. He used sometimes to prefer to stay at the Thompson's front door rather than sitting inside, lying flat on the stone lintel. 'I have known him do this', said Thompson, 'after heavy rain had made the stone before our front door, which was worn into concavity, into a shallow scoop filled with water.'[24]

Bridges explained that the title of his new volume of poems, *New Verse*, referred to its new versification or metres rather than alluding simply to recent poems. Many of the poems had already been read by his friends, who praised both the 'speed of narrative' allowed by the metre and the freedom to follow 'twists and turns' of thought that came from Bridges' ever-increasing use of run-on lines.[25] The volume contains one of very few love poems in English written in celebration of a long and happy relationship:

How should I be to Love unjust
  Since Love hath been so kind to me?
O how forget thy tender trust
  Or slight the bond that set me free?
How should thy spirit's blithe embrace,
  Thy loyalty, have been given in vain,
From the first beckoning of thy grace
  That made a child of me again,
And since hath still my manhood led
  Through scathe and trouble hour by hour,
And in probation perfected
  The explicit fruit of such a flower?

Not ev'n the Apostles, in the days
  They walked with Christ, lov'd him so well
As we may now, who ken his praise
  Reading the story that they tell,
Writ by them when their vision grew
  And he, who fled and thrice denied
Christ to his face, was proven true
  And gladly for His memory died:

So strong the Vision, there was none
  O'er whom the Fisher's net was cast,
Ev'n of the fearfullest not one
  Who would have left Him at the last.

So 'tis with me; the time hath clear'd
  Not dull'd my loving: I can see
Love's passing ecstasies endear'd
  In aspects of eternity:
I am like a miser—I can say
  That having hoarded all my gold
I must grow richer every day
  And die possess'd of wealth untold.[26]

Morison was keen to print a luxury edition of the syllabic poems using a sixteenth-century calligraphic type designed by Ludovico degli Arrighi. Bridges suggested adding a new letter to the type to distinguish between hard and soft 'g'. Morison had the type cut in France, and the introduction of the additional shape meant that the editing had to be rushed in order to bring out the book before the regular edition. In the hurry one of the poems, 'The West Front', was omitted. The proofs that Bridges saw brought a somewhat stiff letter from him complaining of misprints and that two poems had been confused, so that the first part of one was completed not by its own second half but by the other's. In the end the book appeared in advance of the regular edition only because a printers' strike delayed the Clarendon Press. Although Bridges admired the beauty of Morison's edition, which he called *The Tapestry*, he was not left with much confidence in the printer's efficiency, something which was to affect the arrangements he made for the publication of *The Testament of Beauty*. Of *New Verse*, Vita Sackville-West commented,

Dr Bridges apologizes for the 'distracting variety' of his booklet, but for a book which contains 'Melancholy' and 'Come se Quando' surely no apology is needed. Here is a voice sonorous and noble; though I should prefer to disregard the more sportive pages: it offends me to see Dr. Bridges roguish. But in his old manner this book contains passages as fine as any he has done, and, not to labour the point of the poet's voice, I shall quote in illustration the twelve opening lines of 'Come se Quando', which, as it appears to me, may be set fearlessly against any twelve lines from the great volume of Wordsworth's:

How thickly the far fields of heaven are strewn with stars!
Tho' the open eye of day shendeth them with its glare
yet, if no cloudy wind curtain them nor low mist
of earth blindfold us, soon as Night in grey mantle
wrappeth all else, they appear in their optimacy
from under the ocean or behind the high mountains
climbing in spacious ranks upon the stark-black void:
Ev'n so in our mind's night burn far beacons of thought
and the infinite architecture of our darkness,
the dim essence and being of our mortalities,
is sparkled with fair fire-flecks of eternity
whose measure we know not nor the wealth of their rays.[27]

The variety of forms in *New Verse* prompted Edmund Gosse to write a review that was something of a survey of Bridges' achievement as he saw it. He defended Bridges' right to experiment against those critics who thought he ought to concentrate on the early successful lyrical forms without ranging further afield. Turning then to the question of the Poet Laureateship he said,

The ready answer to objectors who ask why Mr Bridges and not Mr Somebodyelse was appointed to the ancient and honourable office . . . is that he was above every other living Englishman a 'learned' poet, skilled in the complexities of prosodical science, and therefore particularly competent to wear the laurel after a writer who had produced nothing, not a stanza, that was not commonplace or tame in form.

Of *New Verse* he said,

There is, however, nothing revolutionary in the shape given throughout the present exquisite little volume . . . In it we find examples of the four classes of poetic work which a careful reader must distinguish in all Mr Bridges has published since 1873. Here is the orthodox versification which clothes the most popular of his lyrics; here is the neo-Miltonic method which is his latest discovery, and which pretends 'to offer their true desideratum to the advocates of Free Verse'; here is the series of accentual measures which are now . . . very old friends; and here is a mystical fourth body of quantitative verse 'of the most ancient species' composed under the guidance of Mr William Stone, a grammarian in whom (I frankly confess) I detect the Poet Laureate's worst and dearest foe . . . I do not like all these new pieces, and there are some ['Come se Quando' for instance] which I do not even understand, yet there is not one in which I fail to recognise the elasticity of eternal youth.[28]

The generally positive response both in reviews and from his friends to *New Verse* was important in encouraging Bridges to use syllabics for *The Testament of Beauty*.

In July Robert Graves asked Bridges to support his application for an academic post at Cornell. Bridges replied,

> it will give me great pleasure to be of any assistance to you. If you want the letter at once I will send it by return of post—if you tell me. If not, I would wait until I had seen H. S. Canby about it. He is in England and will be coming here, and would probably be able to tell me how your electors would be most successfully approached . . . Walter Raleigh told me of your work with him so that I can say the right thing.[29]

Graves, whose acquaintance with Bridges went back at least to 1921, had to change his plans, and used the reference to obtain a post at the new university in Cairo. When he set off for Egypt, he took with him a copy of *New Verse*, describing the poems as 'fine and fresh, particularly the first group',[30] that is, those in neo-Miltonic syllabics. In return he sent Bridges *Twenty-Three Poems*, a collection of his work that appeared in 1925. Bridges in thanking him wrote, it 'seems to me a good selection on the whole and is persistently entertaining which is more than I have found in some companion sixpennies'.[31] Although Graves thanked Bridges at the time for his help in getting him the academic post, in his autobiography, *Goodbye to All That*, he acknowledged the aid of Arnold Bennett and T. E. Lawrence but omitted any mention of Bridges' assistance; in fact he altogether minimized his account of his relations with Bridges in the book.

By September Bridges was asking friends for samples of handwriting for an SPE tract intended to be 'an exhibition of imitable current cursive handwritings'. Roger Fry and E. A. Lowe contributed 'artistic and paleographic' comments, and no doubt Monica, who was a recognized expert on handwriting, helped considerably. The samples displayed in the tract included examples from Philip Webb, Samuel Butler, and Gerard Manley Hopkins.

The spring of 1926 was a very sad time for the couple. Margaret had an accident which necessitated an operation. She was in the Acland Nursing Home for a while and was then moved to Chilswell where, with the help of a nurse, her parents looked after her but complications finally led to her death on 25 April. The following day, almost in awe of her, Bridges wrote to Rothenstein,

> my daughter Margaret died yesterday morning—She made the most glorious exhibition of human fortitude that can be imagined. I must tell you about it some day—Her fatal complication—which came on suddenly when she seemed to be making a swift recovery from a severe operation—was tubercular meningitis. Through all the racking agony and gradual invasion of her nervous centres, she remained perfectly cheerful, and treated the whole thing, death and all, as a nettle-sting. It was incredible. No doubt it has been done before by others but it cannot have been done better.[32]

Monica collapsed from the strain but, trying to distract her husband from his grief, she urged him to resume the poetic fragment he had started in 1924 and had had to abandon. After cancelling seven of the original lines, he wrote two more and then again found that he could not continue. He and Monica, who had been tied to Chilswell all year and had kept the number of visitors to a minimum, then went away for a change of scene. Bridges returned to the poem on 8 July 1926, regarding it 'merely as a useful distraction',[33] but, becoming absorbed, he then worked increasingly steadily at it for the rest of the year, little thinking that he was to spend the next three years on this testament. It was the best of all possible methods of therapy and seems to mark a transition into the final phase of his life.

18

The Testament of Beauty

(1926–1930)

The Woolfs visited Chilswell early in July 1926, accompanied by Aldous Huxley and Lady Ottoline Morrell. Virginia noted in her diary:

As for Bridges: he sprang from a rhododendron bush, a very lean tall old man, with a curly grey hat, & a reddish ravaged face, smoky fierce eyes, with a hazy look in them; very active; rather hoarse, talking incessantly. We sat in his open room & looked past blue spikes of flowers to hills, which were invisible, but when they show, all this goes out he said—his one poetical saying, or saying that struck me as such. We talked about handwriting, & criticism; how Garrod had written on Keats: & they know a Petrarchan sonnet, but not why one alters it. Because they dont write sonnets, I suggested, & urged him to write criticism. He is direct & spry, very quick in all his movements, racing me down the garden to look at pinks, then into his library, where he showed me the French critics, then said Michelet was his favourite historian; then I asked to see the Hopkins manuscripts; & sat looking at them with that gigantic grasshopper Aldous folded up in a chair close by. Ottoline undulated & vagulated.

He asked me to come again: would read me his poems—not his early ones which want a beautiful voice, & aren't interesting he said: but his later ones, his hexameters. He skipped off & held the gate open. I said how much I liked his poems—true of the short ones: but was mainly pleased & gratified to find him so obliging & easy & interested.[1]

Bridges had praised *Mrs Dalloway* to Forster six months earlier, saying that he liked it, expected that no-one would read it, but that it was beautifully written.

Many of Bridges' friends were now dead or had been widowed. One of these, a friend from his days in London, Sir J. Richard Thursfield, had died in 1923 and his widow now returned to

Bridges his letters to her husband. This brought two responses from Bridges. He told Mrs Thursfield,

> All my life I have successfully avoided the literary mellay: but a P[oet] L[aureate] is fair game, & since my appointment the newspapers have made sporting efforts to draw me in to their vulgar gossip. Altho' the amusement that this can provide to a philosopher is the most irresponsible pleasure & privilege of the office, I am glad to secure any private letters from possible abuse.[2]

His letters to Coventry Patmore had recently been offered for sale without any reference to Bridges' wishes. A couple of weeks later, having read the letters to Thursfield, he wrote to her again: 'they recalled to me even more vividly than I had expected the days when I went off to Yattendon—a retirement which practically put an end to many old friendships—for after those days I very seldom saw Dick at all. in which there is a good deal of food for melancholic reflection—and one is terribly ashamed of oneself when one reads one's old letters.'[3] More friends than Bridges realized kept his letters. Those he could retrieve towards the end of his life he generally destroyed. The fate of his letters to Hopkins, a collection only too neatly gathered together for easy destruction, was probably repeated time and again with other long correspondences.

In March 1926 Humphry Milford, at whose London press the Oxford University Press had its books printed, asked Bridges if he would like to have a series of small volumes of his collected essays published. Bridges was enthusiastic provided the project was undertaken as an experiment in his extended alphabet, with new shapes progressively introduced into successive volumes. This was started in 1927 and, with Monica's guidance, continued after his death. The first few volumes did use unusual shapes and these are initially distracting to the reader. Later volumes use only a few of his spellings, such as 'coud' for 'could', and a cursive 'g' in addition to the printed form, distinguishing hard from soft, but since English uses rather more variants of the sound than these two, the additional shape is probably not by itself a significant improvement.

In the summer Bridges was asked to serve as chairman of the BBC Committee on Pronunciation, whose other members included Sir Johnstone Forbes-Robinson, Professor Daniel Jones,

Mr A. Lloyd James, George Bernard Shaw, and Logan Pearsall Smith. Bridges included in a tract published in 1929 a compilation of the committee's decisions, the vast majority of which are still in use. The combination of work on his poem with the preparation of tracts for the SPE led Bridges to propose that in future the editorship of the tracts should be rotated among the members of the committee. Monica now regularly attended the meetings, taking the minutes. The conflict between his and Newbolt's attitude to the proposed Anglo-American Committee on pronunciation also led Bridges to resign from the Academic Committee of the Royal Society of Literature of which Newbolt was Chairman. As he reminded Newbolt, he had never really been much in sympathy with the society's aims and had joined primarily in the hope of getting to know Rudyard Kipling, whom Newbolt had invited to join but in vain.

There was at this time considerable discussion about the possible future of poetry. Q. D. Leavis asserted in *Fiction and the Reading Public* (1932) that modern preference for fiction suggested that poetry's day was past. In an essay in *Scrutiny* (1925), I. A. Richards said that the atheism among the young would lead either to the demise of poetry or to poetry without spiritual content, a combination, he suggested, that T. S. Eliot had achieved in *The Waste Land* but which Eliot hotly and convincingly denied. Bridges' friend R. C. Trevelyan, acknowledging, like Richards, that modern scientific discoveries were altering fundamentally man's view of the world and hence the subject-matter available for poetry, took a more positive approach. In *Thamyris or Is There a Future for Poetry?* (1925) he concluded that 'though the disappearance of poetry is unlikely, and would be a real disaster, . . . it would be childish and unwise for poets to disregard the fact that our habits of mind are growing continually more scientific'. In his article Trevelyan discussed philosophical poems from the past such as *De Rerum Natura*, asserting that it is unlikely that 'scientific philosophy will ever again inspire an expository treatise'. More likely was the insertion of a philosophy as an 'all-pervading influence'.[4] This is very close to what Bridges did. He had, of course, incorporated philosophical and scientific subjects in his epistles of 1903, but with *The Testament of Beauty* he clearly also had Lucretius, and possibly *Thamyris* in mind for he 'nicknamed' his poem 'De Hominum Natura'. In *De Rerum Natura* Lucretius gives 'scientific' explanations of natural phenomena based on the atomism of Epicurus, lacing a painstaking exposition with keen observation and common sense. Bridges' *Testament* is far more lyrical and personal, although it too follows predominantly one scientific pattern, in his case evolution.

Guérard explains (p. 186),

> Bridges believed that man's instincts are the basis for his intellectual and spiritual achievements; that these instincts are intrinsically good, though the material for vice as well as virtue; that happiness depends upon a harmony of impulses effected through the agency of reason, and that man's ideal aspirations, without which his life is meaningless, find their firmest support in physical beauty.

Bridges was, as well, influenced by A. N. Whitehead's *Science and the Modern World*, the published form of a series of lectures given in 1924 which stress the change in man's understanding of his perception of the world. The importance of the individual's own shaping of his impressions, and the essentially solitary and unique nature of his experience, have found literary expression in Modernist stream-of-consciousness techniques, but Bridges reacted to the ideas in a rather different way. *The Testament* suggests that he fully appreciated the limitations of man's comprehension of the world, but, instead of resorting to recording the experience of particular sensibilities, he sought to place man more firmly within the natural world so that deductions about him could be made by comparison with other species. Hence, instead of presenting a subjectifying view of man, he strove to objectify him. The problem with this, as Bridges had stated ten years earlier, is that the only tool available for understanding man's experience and his mind is that subjective mind itself. Bridges' religious aims further complicated his scientific explanations. In effect, he was doing what he felt the clergy should have been doing—attempting to construct a religion that could be reconciled with modern knowledge and attitudes. Accepting evolutionary theory, he suggested that there are two basic instincts which he termed selfhood and breed, that is, preservation of the self and the species. In man these instincts have evolved respectively into compassion, and a passionate love that has a spiritual element.

Bridges experienced ecstatic reactions to natural beauty that were so powerful he thought they must be attributable to more than was physically evident in nature. This is an ecstasy many adolescents experience, but for most people even the memory of it fades with maturity.[5] However, 'Hurrahing in Harvest' shows that Hopkins continued to feel it into his thirties and Wordsworth clearly retained memories of it. Hopkins used the term 'instress' to express a feeling of communication with God through nature. Bridges' similar experience prompted him to suggest that there was an underlying religious reality to the world which could be perceived through 'essences', qualities in nature that triggered man's innate responsiveness to God. He took the term 'essences' from Santayana but used it in a very different way. For Santayana the term is generally used for the general or 'essential' meaning of words or concepts, for example the idea of a table which is common to a range of actual tables. Asked for comments on the poem, Santayana replied perceptively,

> you charge me to tell you, not what I approve, but what I fall foul of: it is hard to do, because what I approve of, or rather relish and delight in, is clear: it is the episodes, the pictures, the judgements, the wise reflections; whereas what I fall foul of is obscure: it is the system that you say is so much like my own. But before I come to that let me confess that besides the qualities which I expected . . . I lighted on one which I didn't expect at all, and found myself laughing aloud at your wit and naughtiness.[6]

The heart of the difference between Santayana's thought and Bridges' may be seen by examining what each meant by the term 'life of reason'. In his series of books under that title Santayana defined it as 'a name for that part of experience which perceives and pursues ideals—all conduct so controlled and all sense so interpreted as to perfect natural happiness.'[7] This is a description of a moral code arising out of instinct and with that general idea Bridges agreed. However, he had very clear ideas about what the 'ideal' consisted of and they were broadly Christian ideals. Santayana, on the other hand, considered that there could also be many other forms of 'natural happiness' and he therefore found Bridges' scheme too narrow.

Bridges established a routine in which he generally spent two or three hours every morning writing, whenever possible in the garden. Edward suggested that his father normally wrote a page a day. He worked on loose pages in pencil which was erased as they were inked and dated. Of the original 250 sheets, Edward noted that he bound the seventy-eight which he received, except for six which he gave to the British Library. A few of the others were given by his parents to friends after the poem had been printed; the rest were 'torn up Sept. 1929', according to Bridges' note which accompanied the pages he gave to his son. There are numerous revisions, most of which refine or tighten the expression rather than altering the meaning. For example, in talking of the Goths, Bridges wrote 'they neither built nor studied, thought not nor created', then made the line more musical by changing it to 'they neither wrote nor wrought, thought not nor created' (Book I, l. 553). Working in parallel with Bridges, Monica made a fair copy of the poem and, as each book was finished, it was sent to the Clarendon Press and printed in private editions of twenty-five. The private print was suggested by the Press in place of ordinary proofs to ease the job of checking, a task Bridges had always hated. On average ten copies were distributed to friends, who were asked for their 'animadversions'. Some of the copies were seen by more than one person. Bridges was keen to have constructive criticism, and thanks accompanied by brief comment brought, so Edward Thompson records, strong disapproval.[8] The regular recipients were Kenneth Sisam, John Sampson (the Librarian of Liverpool University and a Romany scholar), Percy Withers, Edward Thompson, Stanley Morison, Humphrey Milford, Edward and, after September 1927, R. C. Trevelyan, and Herbert Warren. The most detailed suggestions were made by Trevelyan about the metre.

Bridges completed Book I on 24 December 1926; it was printed by February 1927 and he had copies for distribution by 11 April. It is a general introduction, and probably the most attractive section of the poem. As with later books, he kept two copies for purposes of revision, incorporating into one the suggestions of friends and his own emendations. These were transcribed into the second copy, which was submitted as a corrected proof to the Press. The final section of Book IV is an exception to this practice. It was set from a typed version and there was insufficient time to distribute it before general publication, which was hurried in an attempt to coincide with Bridges' eighty-fifth birthday. A special printing of the final 323 lines was subsequently carried out to complete the sets already distributed.

The advice Bridges received on Book I was of course more important than that for any of the later sections. Edwyn Bevan, the Hellenistic scholar, asked for a clearer skeleton: 'it was the practice of the ancients in long poems to give these indications regularly. They began by stating the subject of the poem as a whole . . . and one finds them before each section, saying what it is going to be about.'[9] The development of Book I from a short fragment may account for its lack of clear organization and Bridges made the structure of the rest of the poem more obvious, afterwards adding titles to the individual books further clarifying his plan.

Although in later books the anecdotal and descriptive passages were made more clearly illustrative of the argument, it was probably a lack of their evident significance in Book I that led Fry to suggest that the description of the clouds (Book I, ll. 277–96), while beautiful and impressive in itself, disrupted the flow of the poem. He likened the problem to his own as an artist when forced to paint out his favourite part of a picture because it was impairing the overall composition. He suggested that Bridges make a collection of such brilliant sections and publish it separately,[10] but Bridges defended what he had done. As Santayana had found, it is these anecdotes and illustrations that are the most enjoyable parts of the *The Testament*.

As well as inviting criticism, Bridges, in subsequent books, made inquiries of several friends and institutions, checking facts that he proposed to use (the pronunciation of 'Giorgione' or the symbolic meaning of the snake with its tail in its mouth, for instance); enquiring about possible sources of information (for example, about the Albigensian crusade); and asking specialists to read through the poem to check the accuracy of his descriptions of agricultural and other matters.

Bridges' writing continued through most of 1927. Despite the cool summer, he spent as much of his time in the garden as he could. Elizabeth and Ali Daryush returned from Persia and settled nearby on Boar's Hill at Stockwell [House], which Monica paid to have built for them. In July Gustav Holst brought some of his pupils to Chilswell so that Bridges and his friends could hear settings he had made of some of Bridges' poems. Bridges wrote to him afterwards,

> you asked me once or twice about the music, whether I liked it: if I did not say much it was because I felt it impertinent in me to pretend to judge of your work, & I thought that the pleasure, which I cd tell you the professionals were feeling was a better compliment than mine would be, because they are accustomed to modern writing, whereas I am oldfashioned. I was relieved to find that they were somewhat in my predicament: which was that I did not understand any piece well on the first hearing, but I liked it at second hearing and came in the end to full pleasure. I liked all the 'Songs' . . . The only piece that I did not take to was 'Assemble all ye maidens' & that cd be accounted for by the great dislike that I have for the *poem*. Its history is queer. I will tell you of it some day . . . Your way of treating the words is so novel, & so unlike anything I cd have imagined, that I think I got on astonishingly well in appreciating your inventions so far as I did. For I really liked them very much: and want to hear them again.[11]

By the end of July Bridges had completed Book II of *The Testament*. This was on 'Selfhood', that is, self-preservation, its operation and evolution. It included the anecdote of Bridges' young chorister at Yattendon, who sat absorbed in the bloody stories of 'Alaric, Tamurlane, Attila and Zingis Khan' while the 'parson's mild discourse pass'd o'er his head unheard' (ll. 576–612), which Bridges used to illustrate man's intrinsically bellicose nature. Bridges concluded the argument of the book with the statement that much of man's inner conflict had arisen from his inability to reconcile his instincts with his reason:

> . . . man's true wisdom were a reason'd harmony
> and correlation of these divergent faculties:
> this wer the bridge which all men who can see the abyss
> hav reasonably and instinctivly desired to build;
> and all their sacraments and mysteries whatsoe'er
> attempt to build it; from devout Pythagoras
> to th' last psychologist of Nancy or of Vienna.
> (ll. 818–24)

By this he does not mean simply the repression of the instincts by reason but a full recognition of innate aggression and passion and an attempt to use and enjoy their less destructive sides. Thus, emotion is not suppressed but channelled into protectiveness and more compassionate and spiritual ecstasy.

In addition to completing Book II in July Bridges was also finishing a second tract on handwriting for the SPE. He wrote to Logan Pearsall Smith that a trip to Sussex had given him the opportunity of meeting Kipling whom he said, 'gave me a kindly welcome at his house'.[12] It was in July too that Lady Raleigh asked Bridges if he would write a memoir of Walter Raleigh to accompany a selection of his letters. Bridges told Saintsbury, 'my interest in it is . . . the pleasure of associating my name with my old friend in this very characteristic presentation of his personality'.[13] Referring to Saintsbury's comparative study of English letter-writers, Bridges asked for a professional opinion of Raleigh's achievement, an assessment of his 'distinct characteristics and excellencies'. Saintsbury's information may have increased the confidence with which Bridges wrote his brief, three-page note, which is placed after a lengthy biographical preface by D. Nichol Smith. In his note Bridges defines the special excellence of the genre of letter-writing as 'spontaneous self-portraiture; any charm of the revealed personality or any mastery of style is subservient to this'.[14] He gently cautions the reader that Raleigh was a spontaneous speaker and writer who 'was almost equally ready to skirmish on either side of a contradiction, perhaps even with a sporting tendency to back the weaker'. Bridges' affection for his friend is clear from his description of what the collection of his letters omits—'the reader will not get an adequate impression of the warm human affection and active consideration for others, the native singlehearted and frank virtue which were the charm of his whole life.' The defect occurs because the family letters, 'which living censorship naturally withholds', are excluded, limiting 'the wave-length of emotion; and it is the hot end of the spectrum that is cut off'. It is clear that Bridges approved of such a 'censorship', and did his best to ensure that it would be imposed on any publication of his own letters, similarly limiting possible comprehension of his personality.

November and December were dull and cold. Monica became ill in November and Bridges contracted a 'villainous cough' that bothered him through most of December, with the result that he was unable to finish Book III of *The Testament of Beauty* before

Christmas as he had hoped to do. The Committee on Pronunciation was stirring up public opinion, not all of it favourable, and Bridges endured an uncomfortable meeting in December. Throughout the life of that particular committee he turned to George Bernard Shaw for his support and help, although Shaw did not always respond to his letters. When either of them was unable to attend meetings Bridges suggested private visits, proposing to see Shaw in London and repeatedly inviting him to Chilswell; 'I hope we should have enough vegetables', he quipped on one occasion, with reference to Shaw's vegetarian diet.[15]

Book III of *The Testament* was complete by the end of March 1928 and appeared in a private print on 25 May. It is on the second principal instinct, 'Breed' or sexuality. In sketching the history of Western ideas about love Bridges included a fanciful metaphor for the rise of the troubadours that is one of the most striking descriptions in Book III:

> As well might be with one who wendeth lone his way
> beside the watchful dykes of the flat Frisian shore,
> what hour the wading tribes, that make their home and breed
> numberless on the marshy polders, creep unseen
> widely dispersed at feed, and silent neath the sun
> the low unfeatured landscape seemeth void of life—
> when without warning suddenly all the legion'd fowl
> rise from their beauties' ambush in the reedy beds,
> and on spredd wings with clamorous ecstasy
> carillioning in the air manoeuvre, and where they wheel
> transport the broken sunlight, shoaling in the sky—
> with like sudden animation the fair fields of France
> gave birth to myriad poets and singers unknown,
> who in a main flight gathering their playful flock
> settled in Languedoc, on either side the Rhone
> within the court and county of Raymond of Toulouse
> (ll. 617–32)

The book ends with a thoughtful passage, too long to quote, on that painting by Titian sometimes called *Sacred and Profane Love*. Bridges saw in it a metaphor for the relationship between sensual and spiritual love and man's indistinct comprehension and desire for both.

Work on the book and growing infirmity meant that Bridges

became increasingly reluctant to leave home. However, he still wrote to friends and read. He noticed in June a critical article on Andrew Lang by Max Beerbohm and, annoyed, wrote to Saintsbury, 'I should like to know what you think should be done about it. It is a pity that duelling has gone out. I don't mean that I should have expected you to cut off M.B's "little ear"—but some one must sharpen his pen'.[16]

The generally positive reaction of his friends to *The Testament* and the satisfaction of the steady battle to express his ideas seem to have created in Bridges a contentment that increased the warmth and charm with which he related to acquaintances, and which is evident in many of his letters from the last years of his life. He wrote, for example, to Trevelyan about Book III:

> I have received your very valuable notes. I don't know whether I wonder most at your kindness or your patience, or your acute sense of disorder, or at my own blundering. I have just pencilled all your animadversions in my copy for correction, and laughed over them very heartily at myself. It is inexcusable in me to send out so careless a draft, and expect my friends to supply my lack of diligence. But really I didn't know there were so many metrical flaws.[17]

In January 1929 he revised his essay on Keats for the *Collected Essays* series and wrote to H. W. Garrod inquiring about conclusions reached in recent work on the manuscripts of 'In a drear-nighted December', which he had noticed. He was disappointed when Garrod could not produce facts that eased or explained his dissatisfaction with the poem's ending. On 28 February Bridges gave the first of the Broadcast National Lectures. He used for his lecture material on which he had been working for the final book of *The Testament*, which attempts to distinguish an ethical, religious system from social convention, suggesting that the former must be based on the evolving instincts while the latter is often limited by the ethos of a particular age. Unfortunately, Bridges caught a heavy cold and could barely deliver the talk. By March the first draft of Book IV was complete. Bridges wrote to Trevelyan, 'I feel as if this year is my last lap in the race'. He was weak with an attack of flu and worried about Elizabeth, who had been seriously ill. He intended to spend the summer doing the corrections to *The Testament* but, unsure of living long enough to complete the task, marked with a cross places where corrections had yet to be made. The Press, he noted, was to take Monica's advice at these places because, having worked so closely with him, she would best know his intentions. He asked Morison if he would like to print a special edition of the entire poem, similar in appearance to *The Tapestry*.

However, there were other tasks to be attended to as well. In May Bridges told Fry that he was going to meet Charles Williams to discuss a second edition of Hopkins' *Poems* that the latter was preparing for Oxford University Press. Fry had encouraged Bridges to investigate the possibility of making the poems available for students at Cambridge and Oxford, who he said were 'clamouring' to read them. Williams's introduction is more prominently placed first in the volume; Bridges had put his at the back, just before the notes. Although Williams' edition was more complete, Bridges had already included all the major poems on which Hopkins' reputation rests today.

In May Bridges was offered the Order of Merit which, after some hesitation, he accepted, and in June he was invited to accept an honorary degree from Cambridge: he already had honorary degrees from Oxford, Harvard, the University of Michigan, and St Andrews. To both parties he explained that he could not attend ceremonies. It was not, he told Lord Stamfordham, the King's private secretary, that he was 'bedridden: indeed I get on very well if I am left quiet, but I am not more moveable than an old "grandfather" clock which you cannot carry about'.[18] Several times in 1929 and 1930 Monica had to take recuperative holidays without him, but he did manage two weeks away in July 1929, for a celebratory holiday after his three years' work on *The Testament*. In mid-July he wrote to Edward, 'it is a red letter day with me as I am sending in the last batch of my poem to the press, and now have only to finish [making a good copy] up to the end of it and that is nearly done'.[19]

The SPE still provided Bridges with work. He wrote to Pearsall Smith in July 1929 urging him to see that someone ensured that the SPE was included in reference books like Whitaker's, with such details as the address, committee, and subscription. He was also keen that Lascelles Abercrombie should be appointed to the committee, since he had been made Professor of English at Bedford

College and might help to propagate the SPE's ideals in London. Holst again visited Chilswell in July, bringing with him girls from St Paul's School to sing his music, and again the occasion was a happy one. In September Bridges wrote to Fry,

> we put our wireless box on the dinner-table last night, and attended to your talk on Fildes and Giotto—I wondered whether you hav redd Joyce's 'Portrait of the Artist as a Young Man'. if not, you will be interested to know of it—the 2nd half of it has some *very* good talk on the essence of art—It rather shocked me when I redd it for the first time a month ago to find how much my lucubrations (in my new poem wh shd be published next month) had been anticipated—I judged that his Jesuit upbringing had rather corroded the rivets in his boiler..yet he seemed to me nearer the truth than any other thinker that I ever came across . . .[20]

In October, in time for his eighty-fifth birthday, *The Testament of Beauty* was published. The success of the poem was totally unexpected: the Clarendon Press had not bound all of the two thousand copies printed for the first day of publication, 24 October 1929. All were sold. The 1,800 ordered on the following day to be printed were sold before they were delivered; the 2,500 ordered six days later lasted scarcely a week; and so it went on. By mid-January 19,300 copies had been ordered and over 18,600 of these sold. By March, after 24,300 copies, the type had to be replaced. Demand gradually dropped, but in 1946 it was calculated that 57,370 copies had been printed in Britain and 10,600 printed and sold in the United States.[21] Printings were so rapidly demanded that all the final corrections were not made until the posthumous 'ninth impression', which is a more accurate text than any of the earlier ones. Bridges said that an editorial in *The Times* (written anonymously by Brodribb) was responsible for the early sales.[22] In common with most of the admiring reviews, it had mentioned Bridges' great age, the length of the poem, and the dedication to the King. *The Testament* was praised as difficult, rich in material, 'a glorified Greats lecture'. Some critics admired the innovation in metre, mentioning Bridges' many experiments of the past and their influence. A view frequently expressed was that it was 'the outpouring of the accumulated wisdom, experience, scholarship, and poetic craftsmanship of one of the richest and mellowest spirits of our time'. The breadth of the subject-matter, the treatment of science and modern inventions such as the wireless and aeroplanes, and the comments on classical writers were cited. Stress was frequently placed on Bridges' treatment of the problems of sex and his faith in the survival of Christian marriage as an institution. The religious belief and Bridges' individualistic, aristocratic philosophy were stated, and the poem called noble and hopeful. Bridges had written to Lord Stamfordham about dedicating the poem to the King. It deals, he said, with 'the present state (critical state) of religious opinions and faiths, and though my attitude is Christian, it is not orthodox'.[23] Lord Stamfordham replied that 'it would seem only natural that an important poem by the King's Poet Laureate should be dedicated to His Majesty',[24] but bearing in mind the rule that 'keeps the Sovereign out of controversial questions and more especially of religious controversy', he suggested that an expert theological opinion should be sought.

The expert chosen was William Temple, recently appointed Archbishop of York, who reported that it was 'for the most part very orthodox. I can only find three places where the thought may be heterodox—and as regards two of these I agree with the poet, so I am bound to regard the aberrations (if there) as respectable.'[25] Temple was of course giving an assessment of the political prudence of publishing the poem, and its popular reception confirmed his judgement. However, to assert that Bridges' attitude is 'very orthodox' is to simplify his position considerably and to ignore his numerous open and oblique attacks on the various churches such as, for example, his description of the Fall as 'the myth of a divine fiasco, on which to assure | the wisdom of God; leading to a foregon conclusion | of illachrymable logic' (Book I, ll. 476–8). Bridges' religious views dispense with eternal damnation as a barbarous anachronism and focus on God's love. E. M. Forster recognized Bridges' dissension when he wrote to him:

> Christ (*as revealed in the Gospels*) has never been loved by me, and this seems to part me not merely from the orthodox but from great companies of the unorthodox, amongst whom I should number yourself. Christ restated, with the name withdrawn and the gestures and accent altered, would seem different, and perhaps it is this restatement that I feel every now and then in your poem, and that moves me so much especially at the end, where you speak of the soul returning the body's loving: though you don't restate openly.[26]

The comment occurs in a letter Forster sent Bridges on 1 February 1930, just before the latter's death. He had, he said,

> been reading in and thinking about The Testament of Beauty a good deal during the last month, indeed I must have read the whole of it more than twice, though not consecutively. My thoughts about it are as unimportant as they must be about any philosophic work, but I wanted to let you know of my pleasure. The metre eases me, flies me along, I find no trouble here, nor with the spelling, and then I get such varied lovelinesses: often a definite phrase—e.g. the one which names the final resting place of the Divine Comedy; but sometimes a beauty on which I can't put and don't want to put my finger—something that is diffused through the depths of an argument—like light through water, and that doubtless implies one of the greater triumphs of the poetic art.—I move pretty blindly through all these countries, but know when I am in them.[27]

Forster's compliment gave Bridges great pleasure and he was one of the last people to whom Bridges sent a letter, no longer written in his own hand but dictated to Monica.

Some reviewers, such as H.B.C. in the *Manchester Guardian* (26 October 1929) and Wallace Nichols (*The Bookman*, June 1930), remarked that Bridges' 'scorn of such material ease as may be attained for all by cheap production and distribution of common needs may enhance the impression of aloofness from contemporary thinking'. The disregard, however, was usually only mildly rebuked. More severe were Herbert Read and F. R. Leavis. Read's article, 'Poet or Pedant' (*Nation and Athenaeum*, 23 November 1929), dealt first with the metre and then with the content of the poem. In the latter he remarked on a 'lack of warmth and humanity. There is no consciousness of that horror of modern civilization, with which the younger generation is afflicted.' He criticized Bridges' attitude to war, concluding that it stemmed from a lack of experience of the 'waste of life without accompanying nobility, life given without strife or effort, nothing but machines and despair'. There is, he added, 'still little else, and this testament of beauty, high and rare though it be, is too remote to comfort us'. Bridges' serious work on *The Testament* began in search for alleviation from sorrow but to give in to despair was to him to make 'a last wisdom of woe' (Book II, l. 525). Like Yeats, he thought that man should face life with courage; like Eliot, he believed that religious faith was needed to make modern life meaningful. He was confident of there being easily perceived codes of right action:

> the duty of mightiness is to protect the weak:
> and since slackness in duty is unto noble minds
> a greater shame and blame than any chance offence
> ensuing on right conduct, this hath my assent,—
> that where ther is any savagery ther will be war:
> (Book II, ll. 562–6)

Although much of the 'philosophy' of *The Testament* is too personal to Bridges and too much of its time, it is important as the attempt of an intelligent man to discover what type of faith was possible after the scientific revolutions that had taken place during his life. It has the timelessly wise and shrewd observations on which his friends commented, and vivid descriptions such that on the discoveries at Ur (Book IV, ll. 284–337) and the episode of St Thomas Aquinas, who, after a vision

> . . . nevermore wrote word
> neither dictated but laid by inkhorn and pen;
> and was as a man out of hearing on thatt day
> when Reynaldus, with all the importunity of zeal
> and intimacy of friendship, would hav recall'd him
> to his incompleted SUMMA; and sighing he reply'd
> *I wil tell thee a secret, my son, constraining thee*
> *lest thou dare impart it to any man while I liv.*
> *My writing is at end. I have seen such things reveal'd*
> *that what I hav written and taught seemeth to me of small worth.*
> *And hence I hope in my God, that, as of doctrin*
> *ther wil be speedily also an end of Life!*
> (Book I, ll. 489–500)

Both these descriptions are used by Bridges to suggest that 'time and clime | conform mind more than body in their environment; | what then and there was Reason, is here and now absurd'. This was his view of social codes and orthodox religion, but he acknowledged too that 'what I now chance to approve, may be or become to others | strange and unpalatable as now appear to me | the weighty sentences of the angelic Doctor' [Aquinas] (Book I, ll. 468–70).

Still actively exploring the literature of the day, Bridges told

Pearsall Smith that he was trying to finish reading Robert Graves's 'disagreeable book "Goodbye to all that"—It seems to me', he said, 'an important book because it is so widely redd: and must set a lot of people thinking of the hell they live in: and make them wish themselves out of it. But not having finished the book I have no decided judgement of it.'[28] 'Have you', he continued, 'redd *Commando*? That is also unique: and differently instructive. Smuts sent me a copy of it.' Smith wanted to publish Bridges' early poem, 'On Receiving Trivia from the Author', but still remembering the scholarly disapproval of Mackail for the metre that he had used, which at the time had made him abandon the experiment, he said that he did not want it published although he gave permission for a private print. Bridges was now ill; the internal haemorrhage that Thompson says he suffered from for the last nine months of his life was taking its toll. He asked Grace Muirhead to lend him Lionel's Italian cape to wrap around him. It was not only a practical comfort while he sat out on the verandah, but it 'consoles my spirit with abundant memories', he said. 'When it is returned to you it will carry memories of me—and who knows who else may be warmed by its historic wrappings.'[29]

One of the last of Bridges' letters, dictated to Monica, was sent to Logan Pearsall Smith:

> Thank you very much for your kind letter. I am really sometimes badly in need of a cordial. My only wish is to have a quiet end, but one can have no experience in dying & I am having more experience than I like. In mere physical inconveniences, I fancy that you cd have given me some hints.
>
> I am glad that you can speak so kindly of my poem [*The Testament of Beauty*] & I think that the lines about the tedious orator will have won your sympathy [Book IV, ll. 1,306–13]. I was very much pleased to find that, when I pieced my thoughts together, they made such a reasonable show.
>
> I am sorry I cannot write you a better letter & in my own hand.[30]

The end came on 21 April. Telegrams and letters of condolence flowed in, many of them recalling Bridges' acts of kindness. He had regarded himself as fortunate, and indeed in terms of his general health and his being comfortably, although not extremely, wealthy, he was. But his attitudes too played a large part in his happiness. He had to face the loss of a number of his closest relatives, a serious and prolonged illness of his own, and the repeated ill-health of his wife and daughters, culminating in Margaret's death. He was not insensitive to these losses but fought against melancholy. In this his good health, his family, and his eagerness to learn were important; photographs of 'R.B.' even as an old man show an interest, a zest for life, that belies the wrinkles. In the obituary of him that Newbolt wrote for *The Times*, he said:

> In presence Bridges was one of the most remarkable figures of his time; there is no company in which he would not have been distinguished. He had great stature and fine proportions, a leonine head, deep eyes, expressive lips, and a full-toned voice, made more effective by a slight occasional hesitation in his speech. His extraordinary personal charm was, however, due to something deeper than these; it lay in the transparent sincerity with which every word and motion expressed the whole of his character, its greatness and its scarcely less memorable littlenesses . . . none would have wished these away; they were not the flaws but the 'grotesque' ornaments of his character. Behind them there was always visible the strength of a towering and many sided nature, at once aristocratic and unconventional, virile and affectionate, fearlessly inquiring and profoundly religious.[31]

NOTES

Unless otherwise stated, the place of publication is London.

Abbreviations

LB	*The Selected Letters of Robert Bridges with the Correspondence of Robert Bridges and Lionel Muirhead*, edited by Donald Stanford, 2 Vols. (Newark, 1983, 1984).
LI	*The letters of Gerard Manley Hopkins to Robert Bridges*, edited by C. C. Abbott, 2nd impression, revised (1955).
LII	*The Correspondence of Gerard Manley Hopkins and Richard Watson Dixon*, edited by C. C. Abbott, 2nd revised impression (1955).
LIII	*The Further Letters of Gerard Manley Hopkins*, edited by C. C. Abbott, 2nd impression, revised and enlarged (1956).
Bridges Family Papers	Those held by the Bridges family.
BP	Bridges Papers, Bodleian Library, Oxford.
DNB	*Dictionary of National Biography*

Introduction

1. Thompson wrote the book during a serious illness which prevented him from completing his checking of it. Knowing that Bridges had expressly asked that a biography not be written, Thompson did not consult the family. As a result the book does contain a number of errors, ranging from ideas that affect assessment of Bridges' work such as 'Bridges rarely if ever went to the theatre' (p. 38) and 'Bridges had never read Rossetti' (p. 81) to carelessness that may affect opinions of his personality, such as the attribution to Bridges of a dismissive speech about a candidate for the Society for Pure English (p. 80). Bridges probably did not go to the theatre when Thompson knew him, but as a young man he saw a lot of French theatre and some

English too, to which he referred in an article of 1909 advocating the construction of a national theatre. About Rossetti he made detailed comments to Dixon, who had been friendly with him. The speech Thompson suggests Bridges made was a typical *jeu d'esprit* by Sir Walter Raleigh, who missed few occasions for disrupting official proceedings.

2. Albert Guérard, *Robert Bridges: A Study of Traditionalism in Poetry* (Cambridge, Mass., 1942, repr. 1965).
3. John Sparrow, *Robert Bridges*, British Council pamphlet, 147 (1962).
4. These include: 'Gerard Manley Hopkins and Robert Bridges', in *Hopkins Among the Poets*, ed. by Richard Giles (Hamilton, Ontario, 1985); 'Robert Bridges and the Free Verse Rebellion', in *Journal of Modern Literature*, 2: 1 (Sept. 1971); 'Robert Bridges on his Poems and Plays: Unpublished Letters by Robert Bridges to Samuel Butler', in *Philological Quarterly*, 50 (Apr. 1971); 'Robert Bridges and Samuel Butler on Shakespeare's Sonnets: An exchange of letters', in *Shakespeare Quarterly*, 22 (Autumn 1971); and 'Robert Bridges, Poet-Typographer', in *Fine Print*, 9 (Jan. 1983).
5. *In the Classic Mode: The Achievement of Robert Bridges* (Newark, 1978).

Chapter 1 Childhood in Roseland

1. Edward Thompson, *Robert Bridges 1844–1930* (1944), 1 (hereafter cited as Thompson); the will of John Thomas Bridges, Public Record Office, Chancery Lane.
2. The house subsequently became the Convent of the Visitation in November 1875, sheltering a Polish order of Catholic nuns escaping from religious persecution, first in Poland and then in Germany. The original house was pulled down in 1975, when the area was turned into a housing estate. Roseland and 'Poet's Walk' are commemorated in the street names. Information about what Roseland was like comes from articles in the *East Kent Mercury* (30 Jan. and 2 Feb. 1975); Ordnance Survey maps and the Tithe Map 1844 (Canterbury Cathedral Library); Census Returns, 1841 and 1851 (Dover Public Library).
3. BP, no. 77.
4. The description of the area comes from *Kelly's Post Office Directory of Essex, Herts, Kent, Middlesex, Surrey and Sussex* for 1845 and 1855; *Bagshaw's Directory of Kent* (1847); C. R. S. Elvin, *Records of Walmer* (n.d.); Stephen Pritchard, *The History of Deal and its Neighbourhood* (Deal, 1864); John Laker, *History of Deal* (Deal, 1917); John Lewis Roget, *Sketches of Deal, Walmer and Sandwich* (1911); Ivan Green, *The Book of Deal and Walmer* (1983); Marquis Curzon, *The Personal History*

of Walmer Castle and its Lords Warden (1927); Elizabeth Longford, *Wellington: Pillar of State* (1972).

5. 'The Necessity of Poetry', *Collected Essays* (1927–36), no. 28, pp. 230–2.
6. Commonplace Book, fo. 3, Bridges Family Papers.
7. 'The Necessity of Poetry', 232.
8. 'Digby Mackworth Dolben', in *Three Friends* (1932), 6–7.
9. John Affleck Bridges, *Victorian Recollections* (1919), 32–41.
10. Information about Molesworth comes from the article in the *DNB* and a biography written by his son, Sir Guilford Molesworth, *John Edward Nassau Molesworth: A Life* (1915).

Chapter 2 Eton

1. The general account of life at Eton is drawn from James Brinsley-Richards, *Seven Years at Eton 1857–1864* (1883) [hereafter cited as *Seven Years*]; Lionel S. Byrne, *Changing Eton* (1937); George Greville, *Memories of an Old Etonian 1860–1912* (n.d.); Sir Henry Churchill Maxwell-Lyte, *History of Eton College, 1440–1910* (1911); Christopher Hollis, *Eton: a History* (1960); P. S. H. Lawrence, *An Eton Camera 1850–1919* (Salisbury, 1980); H. E. C. Staplyton, *Eton School Lists 1853–1892* (1900); and the *Eton College Chronicle*.
2. Henry Guillemard (22 Oct. 1924), BP, no. 109.
3. *Seven Years*, 23, 311, 16.
4. 'Digby Mackworth Dolben', in *Three Friends*, 25–6. Bridges' memoir of his cousin contains most of his published recollections of his schooldays.
5. 'The Reform of Education' (1916), BP, no. 48, fos. 21 and 22. See Chap. 15 below.
6. Examination Papers of Eton College in King's College Library, Cambridge.
7. Henry Guillemard to Robert Bridges (22 Oct. 1924), BP, no. 109.
8. *Three Friends*, 12.
9. 14 August 1879, LI, 85.
10. *Three Friends*, 10–11.
11. Sir Guilford Molesworth, *John Edward Nassau Molesworth*, 75–6.
12. *Three Friends*, 9.
13. Ibid. 7.
14. Ibid. 9.
15. Ibid. 16.
16. Gerard Manley Hopkins to Richard Watson Dixon, 27 Feb. 1879, LII, 24.
17. *Three Friends*, 16.

18. Ibid. 18. Bridges chose several poems as especially exhibiting this fusion: 'Thou liest dead . . .', 'There is a shrine whose golden gate', 'The world is young today', and 'Sing me the men, ere this'.
19. Albert Guérard, *Robert Bridges: A Study of Traditionalism in Poetry* (Cambridge, Mass., 1942), 295. Hereafter cited as Guérard.
20. *Seven Years*, 291–2. The Eton College Rifle Volunteers were 'consolidated' with the First Bucks in March 1875. In May 1878 they were made a separate corps, which was an honour not granted to any other public school (Maxwell-Lyte, 555).
21. *Three Friends*, 31.

Chapter 3 Oxford

1. Much of the information about Corpus Christi at this time comes from two articles by H. A. Strong titled 'Corpus in the Early Sixties' and published in the *Pelican Record*, 7:6 (1905), 178–82 and 8:1 (1905), 8–11, and three articles by Bishop Knox titled 'Memories of Corpus Christi College, 1865–8', published in the *Pelican Record*, 20:2 (Mar. 1931), 86–92, 106–15, 136–42. I have also made extensive use of the *Oxford Calendar* for the years during which Bridges was an undergraduate.
2. Edmund A. Knox wrote later of his fellow students that 'while some to whom I owed most are quite forgotten by the public . . . there were some "who have left a name behind them," Bridges the Poet, [William] Sanday, [Walter] Lock and [John Richardson] Illingworth, theologians; [Francis] Chavasse, [John Eltham] Mylne, [Francis Ambrose] Gregory, Bishops; C. P. Scott, bravest, most competent and most honest of Editors of a great Journal [the Manchester Guardian]; [George Wynne] Jeudwine, Archdeacon of Lincoln; [William Edward] Goschen, the diplomat; [Robert William] Hanbury, Chancellor of the Exchequer; Charles Plummer and Frank Hall, the former historian and saint, the latter—in our days famous as Cox of the 'Varsity Eight for three years, and of the crew that beat Harvard University.' ('Memories of Corpus', 138–9).
3. Ibid. 91.
4. Corpus Christi Archives, E/3/1/1, Oxford.
5. Diaries, vol. 14 (11 May 1866) fos. 31–4, Francis Chavasse Papers, Bodleian Library.
6. 2 Nov. 1865, Bridges Papers, no. 97; LB, 85.
7. Gerard Manley Hopkins to his mother, 4 May 1863, LIII, 77. Sanday eventually became Ireland Professor of Exegesis at Oxford.
8. *Journals and Papers of Gerard Manley Hopkins*, edited by Humphry

House and Graham Storey (1959), 379. Hereafter cited as: Hopkins, *Journals*.

9. Sam Brooke Papers, diary entries for 3 Nov. 1864, 12 May 1864, 2 May 1864, 16 May 1864, Corpus Christi Archives.
10. James Heywood, *The Recommendations of the Oxford University Commissioners with Selections from their Report and a History of the University Subscription Tests, including Notices of the University and Collegiate Visitations* (1853), xxi.
11. Sam Brooke Papers, diary entry for 4 Nov. 1864, Corpus Christi Archives.
12. Knox, 'Memories of Corpus', 141.
13. Tom Zaniello, *Hopkins in the Age of Darwin* (Iowa City, 1988), 12.
14. Janet Howarth, 'Science Education in Late-Victorian Oxford', *The English Historical Review*, 102:403 (Apr. 1987), 334–67.
15. *Catalogue of the Transactions of Societies, Periodicals and Memoirs . . . in the Radcliffe Library at the Oxford Museum* (Oxford, 1871), 9.
16. Knox, 'Memories of Corpus, 93.
17. Francis Chavasse's Oxford Essays (Bodleian Library) and Gerard Manley Hopkins' essays and notebooks (Campion Hall, Oxford) are of interest in this way.
18. H. A. Strong, 'Corpus in the Early Sixties', *Pelican Record*, 180.
19. Chavasse Papers, Essays, p. 105, Bodleian Library.
20. *Academy*, 1 (1870), 117, in Frank M. Turner, *The Greek Heritage in Victorian Britain* (1981), 51.
21. *Oxford University Calendar*, 1865, First Public Examination.
22. 28 Apr. 1865, BP, no. 97; LB, 84.
23. Papers of the Brotherhood of the Most Holy Trinity, Minutes, 22, Pusey House, Oxford.
24. Address of R. M. Benson (14 June 1865), 7, Papers, Pusey House.
25. *Manual of Rules and Prayers for the Use of the Brotherhood of the Most Holy Trinity* (1858), Papers, Pusey House.
26. Minutes, 108, Papers, Pusey House.
27. Robert Bridges, Commonplace Book, fo. 44, Bridges Family Papers.
28. 4 Aug. 1866, LI, 3.
29. George Saintsbury, *A Second Scrap Book* (1923), 35.
30. 25 Nov. 1865, BP, no. 97; LB, i, 85–6.
31. *Three Friends* (1932), 70–1
32. Ibid. 66–7.
33. 26 Feb. 1866, BP, no. 97; LB, i. 86.
34. *Three Friends*, 83.
35. 11 Sept. 1879, BP, no. 109.

36. He was later to become Warden of New College and father of the 'spoonerism'.
37. William Hayter, *W. A. Spooner: A biography* (1977), 42–3.
38. 'The Bible' (23 Mar. 1911), *Collected Essays*, no. 16, p. 100.
39. *Three Friends*, 91.
40. Robert Bridges, Commonplace Book, fo. 44, Bridges Family Papers.
41. J. B. Atlay, *Sir Henry Wentworth Acland, Bart: A Memoir* (1903), 143, 416. In 1871 Wilson became president of the college, a position that had been held by Robert's great uncle, the Revd Thomas Edward Bridges from 1823 to 1843. Unfortunately Wilson's health broke down shortly afterwards, and Bridges was grieved at his death in 1881.
42. *Three Friends*, 102–3.
43. Knox, 'Memories of Corpus', 141.
44. *Three Friends*, 102.
45. 16 Oct. 1866, LIII, 95.
46. 12 Sept. 1867, BP, no. 62; LB, i. 87–8.
47. Gerard Manley Hopkins quoting Bridges in a letter to him, 28 Sept. 1866, LI, 9.
48. *Dover Telegraph* (Nov. 1850).
49. *Three Friends*, 71.
50. Diaries, vol. 15 (18 Oct. 1866), Chavasse Papers, fos. 136–7, Bodleian Library.
51. Rooms Book, Corpus Christi Archives; Bridges to Lionel Muirhead (5 June 1866), BP, no. 97; LB, i. 87.
52. W. F. Rawnsley, 'On Corpus Rowing', *Pelican Record*, 11 (1913–15), 136.
53. Captain's Book, Corpus Christi Archives, E/3/1/1, fos. 79, 80.
54. 17 Nov. 1867, BP, no. 97; LB, i. 89.

Chapter 4 A Period of Uncertainty

1. Gerard Manley Hopkins to Robert Bridges, 9 Jan. 1868, LI, 22.
2. Robert Bridges to Lionel Muirhead, 7 Jan. 1868, BP, no. 97; LB, i. 93. Donald Stanford identifies the books as H. H. Milman, *The History of Latin Christianity* (1854–5); most probably Max Müller's *Science of Languages* (1861, second ser. 1864); F. T. Palgrave, *Golden Treasury of Songs and Lyrics* (1861); Bishop Charles John Ellicott's commentary on the Epistles of St Paul; Arthur Penntryn Stanley, *Sinai and Palestine* (1862).
3. The route and dates are deduced from Lionel Muirhead's sketches, Bridges Family Papers. General information on the area at that time comes from Deborah Bull and Donald Lorimer, *Up the Nile* (New

York, 1979); David Roberts, *The Holy Land, Syria and Egypt after Lithographs by Louis Haghe*, 6 vols. in 3 (1855–6); F. Barham Zincke, *Egypt of the Pharaohs and of the Khedive*, 2nd edn. (1873).

4. Bridges to Muirhead, 24 June 1870, BP, no. 97; LB, i. 110.
5. Muirhead to Bridges, 5 July–2 Aug. 1869, BP, no. 96; LB, i. 101.
6. Muirhead to Bridges, 12 May 1869, BP, no. 96; LB, i. 99. The idea was repeated by Muirhead on 18 Apr. 1870, and Bridges explained that he had decided to become a doctor in a letter to Muirhead of 24 June 1870, BP, nos. 96, 97; LB, i. 109–10.
7. Hopkins, *Journals*, 168.
8. These letters from the Bridges Papers, no. 96, are printed in LB, i. 93–109.
9. *The Times*, 13 Mar. 1868, 12.
10. *The Growth of Love* (1876), no. 9.
11. 29 Apr. 1869, LI, 25.
12. 31 July 1892, Binyon Correspondence, Bridges Family Papers.
13. 20 July 1869, BP, no. 96; LB, i. 104.
14. 20 Feb. 1875, LI, 31.
15. Lecture given by Robert Bridges to medical students at Ann Arbor, Michigan, in 1924: BP, no. 78, fo. 1. Hereafter cited as Medical Lecture.

Chapter 5 Medical Training

1. Helpful accounts of the changes in medicine and medical training can be found in Charles Newman, *The Evolution of Medical Education in the Nineteenth Century* (1957) and E. Ashworth Underwood, 'Medicine, Surgery and their Scientific Development', in *A Century of Science 1851–1951*, edited by Herbert Dingle (1951).
2. Medical Lecture, fo. 2.
3. LIII, 107.
4. *Calendar of St Bartholomew's Hospital and College*, 1871, 42.
5. Thompson, 57.
6. J. P. Cooke, *Elements of Chemical Physics* (Boston, 1860), 9.
7. W. B. Carpenter, *Principles of Physiology* (1842), 54–5.
8. Medical Lecture, fo. 5.
9. Ibid., fo. 2
10. Ibid., fo. 3.
11. [26 July 1870], BP, no. 97; LB, i. 111–12.
12. Bridges to G. Lowes Dickinson, 19 Jan. 1892, BP, no. 108; LB, i. 226. The visit he made in 1876 as part of his medical training would seem to have been too busy to include attendance at lectures on literature.

13. 30 Jan. 1871, BP, no. 97; LB, i. 112–13.
14. Bridges to Lionel Muirhead, [22 Feb. 1871], LB, i. 113.
15. Commonplace Book, fos. 59–60, Bridges Family Papers.
16. Ibid., fo. 60. See also letter to Carry Glover, 22 Aug. [1903], LB, i. 437–8.
17. Bridges to Lionel Muirhead, 11 June 1900, BP, no. 99, fo. 48. Bridges recommended Butler's *Life and Habit, Evolution Old and New*, and *Unconscious Memory*.
18. [15 Apr. 1871], BP. no. 97; LB, i. 114.
19. 18 July 1871, BP, no. 97; LB, i. 114–15.
20. Commonplace Book, fo. 53, Bridges Family Papers.
21. 2 Aug. 1871, LI, 27–8.
22. 2 Apr. 1871, LI, 26–7.
23. 7 Sept. 1888, LI, 282: 'It is not good to be a medical man in the making. It is a fire in which clay splits.'
24. 24 Feb. 1877, LI, 32.
25. P. W. Verco, *Masons, Millers and Medicine: James Crabb Verco and his Sons* (Adelaide, n.d. [?1977]), 60. Hereafter cited as Verco.
26. Medical Lecture, fos. 17–20.
27. 'Harry Ellis Wooldridge', *DNB*, 1912–21 (1927), 594–5. Bridges to Margaret Woods, 23 July [1915], LB, ii. 678.
28. *Memorials of Edward Burne-Jones* (1906), i. 302.
29. Robert Bridges, Commonplace Book, fos. 60–3, Bridges Family Papers.
30. 11 Nov. 1884, LI, 199.
31. Apr., May 1883, LI, 178–9; 1 Jan. 1885, LI, 204.
32. Bridges to his mother, 6 Nov. 1873 and 2 Oct. 1874, Bridges Family Papers; Bridges to Lionel Muirhead, 19 June 1874, BP, no. 97; LB, i. 118.
33. 22 Oct. 1879, LI, 98.
34. *The Savile Club 1868–1923*, printed privately for the Committee of the Club (1923).
35. Guérard, App. C, 293–5.
36. Vol. 43 (Nov. 1880), 51.
37. W. B. Yeats, 'Living Poets. IV, Mr Robert Bridges', in *Bookman* (June 1897), repr. in *The Correspondence of Robert Bridges and W. B. Yeats*, edited by Richard J. Finneran (1977), 56. Hereafter cited as Finneran.
38. Bridges to his mother, 18 Oct. 1874, Bridges Family Papers.
39. Edward Bridges, Notes to 'Letters of Robert Bridges to his Mother', fo. 6, Bridges Family Papers.
40. Bridges to Lionel Muirhead, [Jan. 1874], BP, no. 97; LB, i. 116–17.

41. Bridges to his mother, letters of 28 Jan., 31 Jan., 3 Feb., 24 Mar. 1874, Bridges Family Papers.
42. 19 June 1874, MS Eng poet. c 22, Bodleian Library; LB, i. 117–18.
43. Letters from Hopkins to Bridges of 22 Oct. 1879 and 23 Mar. 1880 (LI, 97, 100) suggest that Bridges tried several times to obtain the invitation for him.
44. Bridges to his mother, 29 June 1874, Bridges Family Papers.
45. Bridges to his mother, 2, 18, 24 Oct. 1874, Bridges Family Papers.
46. Bridges to his mother [Dec. 1874], Bridges Family Papers.

Chapter 6 House Physician

1. Verco, 59.
2. Norman Moore, 'Patrick Black', in *DNB* (1917).
3. Medical Lecture, fo. 8.
4. Ibid., fos. 8–9.
5. Ibid., fo. 11.
6. Ibid., fos. 11–12.
7. *St Bartholomew's Hospital Reports*, 1876.
8. BP, no. 109.
9. 5 Oct. 1875, BP, no. 97; LB, i. 120–1.
10. 4 Jan. 1883, LI, 170.
11. 11 Oct. 1875, BP, no. 97; LB, i. 122.
12. Thompson, 25.
13. Notes lent by Robert Bridges to Kenneth Sisam, quoted in Thompson, 25.
14. Bridges to his mother, 9 Aug. 1875, Bridges Family Papers.
15. John Sparrow, *Robert Bridges*, British Council pamphlet (1962), 30. Hereafter cited as Sparrow.
16. 3 Apr. 1877, LI, 35, 39.
17. Donald Stanford, *In the Classic Mode: The Achievement of Robert Bridges* (Newark, 1978), 56. Hereafter cited as *In the Classic Mode*.
18. 13 Dec. 1875, BP, no. 97; LB, i. 123.
19. 3 Apr. 1878, BP, no. 97; LB, i. 125.
20. 11 Oct. 1875, BP, no. 97; LB, i. 122.
21. Bridges to Lionel Muirhead, 13 Dec. 1875, BP, no. 97; LB, i. 123.
22. Quoted in Oliver Garrod, *The Life of Samuel Jones Gee* (1938), 243.
23. 22 Jan. 1876, Bridges Family Papers.
24. John Potter, 'Robert Bridges (1844–1930): Medicine as a Training for Poetry?', *St Bartholomew's Hospital Journal*, 58:3 (1954), 63. Hereafter cited as Potter.
25. Medical Lecture, fo. 21.
26. 3 Apr. 1877, LI, 33.

Chapter 7 The Casualty Department

1. 'An Account of the Casualty Department', *St. Bartholomew's Hospital Reports*, 14 (1878), 167–82, repr. in *Collected Essays* (1936), no. 30, 265–97. Hereafter cited as 'Casualty Department'.
2. Norman Moore, 'Notes on the Casualty Department', *St. Bartholomew's Hospital Reports*, 14 (1878), 164–5.
3. Medical Lecture, fo. 13.
4. 'Casualty Department', 274.
5. Medical Lecture, fos. 14–15.
6. Potter, 65.
7. Eric C. O. Jewesbury, *The Royal Northern Hospital 1856–1956* (1956), 42–3.
8. Medical Lecture, fo. 15.
9. Ibid., fos. 15–16.
10. John Affleck Bridges, *Reminiscences of a Country Politician* (1906), 105–8. This is confirmed by Julia's will, which makes no mention of her family and in a codicil gives all say in her burial to the Revd William Black of the Mission House.
11. BP, no. 109.
12. The will explains that, in accordance with an agreement at the time of the marriage, neither family of children should be disadvantaged by the union, Dr Molesworth's fortune is to be distributed equally among his own children with a 'token of affection' that is in no way 'a measure of her worth' of £500 for Harriett and all household possessions other than plate, pictures, maps, and so on. The will reads as that of a thoughtful, kind man concerned with being just.
13. 21 Aug. 1877, LI, 46.
14. 25 Feb. [1878], LI, 47.
15. 30 May 1878, LI, 52.
16. 9 June 1878, LI, 55.
17. [8 Aug. 1878], LI, 57.
18. 10 Aug. 1878, BP, no. 97; LB, i. 127.
19. 27 Dec. 1878, BP, no. 97; LB, i. 127–8.
20. 29 Jan. 1879, LI, 62–5.
21. Ann Thwaite, *Edmund Gosse: A Literary Landscape 1849–1928* (1984), 173. Hereafter cited as Thwaite.
22. 15 Feb. 1879, LI, 65–6.
23. Bridges to Edmund Gosse, letters of 2 Mar. and 22 Nov. 1879, LB, 128–30.
24. 9 Apr. 1879, LI, 77.
25. 22 Apr. 1879, LI, 79.

26. Bridges to Mrs Manley Hopkins, 28 Mar. 1909, MSS Eng lett d 143, Bodleian Library; LB, ii, 567.
27. 'Richard Watson Dixon', in *Three Friends*, 121–2.
28. Ibid. 123–4. Dixon asked Robert to investigate such things as the letter of the Council of Wotton of 31 Aug. 1549, giving an account of the suppression of the rebellions in Devonshire, Cornwall, and Norfolk and the capture of Ket, the rebel leader in Norfolk. Dixon wanted the main points from the original letter in the Public Record Office, especially what prisoners were sent to London if mentioned. The handwriting of such documents may well have been difficult to decipher.
29. 5 Apr. 1879, LI, 299.
30. 22 Oct. 1879, LI, 96.
31. 21 Aug. 1877, LI, 46.
32. 29 Oct. 1881, LII, 86.
33. 26 Jan. 1881, LI, 122.

Chapter 8 The Change of Course

1. 27 Apr. 1881, LI, 126.
2. 16 Sept. 1881, LII, 53.
3. 16 Sept. 1881, LI, 135.
4. LII, 53.
5. LI, 137.
6. 'He was so sensitive to physical suffering (more sensitive, I think, than any other man I have met) that he never passed the place in the Broad where Latimer, Ridley, and Cranmer died without shuddering. "That's where they burnt Cranmer", he once observed to me. "Terribly cruel they used to be. *Awfully* cruel, I call it—to burn a man *alive*!" As I set his words down, I am aware that they must seem banal and inadequate; but the real horror which accompanied them was not.' (Thompson, 7).
7. 27 Apr. 1881, LI, 128.
8. 14 May, 16 June 1881, LI, 129–30, 132.
9. Bridges to his mother, letters of 8, 12, 20, 29 Dec. 1881, Bridges Family Papers.
10. Bridges to his mother, letters of 19, 26 Apr. 1882, Bridges Family Papers.
11. 1 Feb. 1882, LI, 142.
12. Bridges to his mother, letters of 24 Mar. and 2, 13 Apr. 1882, Bridges Family Papers.
13. Bridges to his mother, letters of 19, 26 Apr. 1882, Bridges Family Papers.

14. 1 Feb. 1882, LI, 141.
15. 1 July 1882, BP, no. 87/1; LB, i. 132–3.
16. Coventry Patmore to Hopkins, 26 July 1884, LIII, 356.
17. A case in point is 'The Handsome Heart', in which he used a compilation of early versions despite the fact that Hopkins had cancelled this in manuscript and substituted a new version. It needs to be kept in mind, however, that with the edition of 1918 Bridges was trying to present Hopkins at his most attractive.
18. 15 Dec. 1882, LII, 106.
19. 9 Feb. 1883, LII, 107.
20. 3 Feb. 1883, LI, 173–4, 176.
21. Robert Bridges, Commonplace Book, fo. 43, Bridges Family Papers.
22. According to Simon Nowell-Smith, Daniel offered to print some of Robert's work early in 1880 and Bridges suggested including the other writers: 'Bridges, Hopkins and Dr Daniel', *Times Literary Supplement* (13 Dec. 1957), 764. Colin Franklin's book on *Poets of the Daniel Press* (Cambridge, Rampant Lions Press, 1988) is well worth reading for the history of the Daniel Press and accounts of the writers associated with it.
23. Guérard, 157.
24. Ibid. 156.
25. 4 Nov. 1882, LI, 160.
26. 5 June 1882, LI, 145.
27. 26 Sept. 1882, LI, 152.
28. 10 June 1882, LI, 148.
29. On 26 Nov. 1882 Hopkins wrote: 'When I reproached you for treating me as if I were not in earnest I meant, and I mean now, to open up no further question; it was only of the injustice to myself I was thinking then. But "pain" is not the word: it was a mild rebuke to you for being so unreasonable towards me . . .', LI, 163.
30. 4 Aug. 1882, BP, no. 87/1; LB, i. 134.
31. *Pelican Review*, 8 (1905–7), 141.
32. Henry Newbolt, obituary of Bridges in *The Times* (22 Apr. 1930), repeated by, amongst others, Thompson, 6 and Sparrow, 13.
33. Medical Lecture, fo. 19.
34. 27 Sept. 1882, LI, 152.
35. *Three Friends*, 129.
36. 7 Sept. 1882, BP, no. 87/1; LB, i. 141–2.
37. 15 Dec. 1882, LII, 105.
38. 18 Oct. 1882, LI, 154–8.
39. 6 Feb. 1885, LI, 206.

40. 28 Sept. 1883, in Derek Patmore, 'Three Poets Discuss New Verse Forms: The Correspondence of Gerard Manley Hopkins, Robert Bridges, and Coventry Patmore', *Month*, NS 6: 2 (Aug. 1951), 69–78. Hereafter cited as Derek Patmore, 'Three Poets'.
41. 24 Oct. 1883, LI, 189.
42. 15 Dec. 1883, in Derek Patmore, 'Three Poets', 77.
43. 20 Mar. 1884, LIII, 352–3.
44. 4 Nov. 1882, LI, 160.
45. 21 Feb. 1900, British Library Add. MS 44040 fo. 57; LB, i. 364. See too Donald Stanford, 'Robert Bridges on his Poems and Plays: Unpublished Letters by Robert Bridges to Samuel Butler', *Philological Quarterly*, 50 (Apr. 1971), 281–91.
46. Guérard, 139, 133.
47. 6 Feb. 1885, LI, 205.
48. 24 Mar. 1885, LI, 208–9.
49. Guérard, 126.
50. Ibid. 124, 131.
51. Ibid. 130.
52. 23 Sept. 1886, BP, no. 97; LB, i. 158.
53. 17 May 1885, LI, 217.
54. W. B. Yeats, 'Living Poets', *Bookman* (June 1897), repr. in Finneran, 52.
55. 1 Jan. 1885, LI, 203.
56. 15 Apr. 1885, BP, no. 97; LB, i. 151.
57. 25 Aug. 1887, LI, 259–60.
58. 28 Sept. 1887, LI, 261.
59. Bridges to Dixon, 5 July 1897, BP, no. 87/1; LB, i. 320. A copy of the Gregynog Press edition is held by the Bodleian Library.
60. *Spectator*, 12 Nov. 1898.

Chapter 9 Marriage

1. 'Memories of Elizabeth Waterhouse Collected for her Youngest Grandchild by Florence E. Waterhouse' (privately printed, n.d., unpaginated). I am very grateful to Maurice and Rowan Waterhouse for lending me this.
2. These included *A Book of Simple Prayers* (1884), *The Brotherhood of Rest* (1886), *The Island of Anarchy* (1887), *Little Book of Life and Death* (1892), *Companion of the Way* (1908), *Thoughts of a Tertiary* (1909), *Verses* (1897, 1912), and the Introduction to an edition of the Earl of Manchester's *Death and Immortality* (1906), *Little Homilies to Women in Country Places* and *With the Simple-hearted* (both 1904), and *The House by the Cherry Tree* (1911).

3. At Home on 13 Jan. 1878: Thwaite, 173.
4. Edmund Gosse to Monica Waterhouse, 22 May 1884, BP, no. 119.
5. 18 July 1884, LI, 193.
6. Monica Bridges to Lionel Muirhead, 21 Oct. 1884, BP, no. 97.
7. 11 Nov. 1884, LI, 198.
8. Guérard, 93–4.
9. 27 July 1899, BP, no. 99; LB, i. 347.
10. 1 Sept. 1885, LI, 221.
11. 1 June 1886, LI, 225.
12. 2 Nov. 1887, LI, 263–4.
13. 23 Sept. 1886, BP, no. 97; LB, i. 158.
14. 18 Oct. 1886, *The Letters of Roger Fry*, edited by Denys Sutton, 2 vols. (1972), i. 109–10.
15. Bridges to Lionel Muirhead (14 Oct. 1886), BP, no. 97, LB, i. 158–9.
16. 29 Dec. 1886, Royal College of Physicians; LB, i. 162.
17. 5 Aug. 1886, BP, no. 87/1; LB, i. 156–7.
18. 29 Dec. 1886, Royal College of Physicians, LB, i. 161; Oliver Garrod, 'The Life of Samuel Jones Gee', repr. from *St Bartholomew's Hospital Reports*, 71 (1938), 249. See p. 265 below.
19. 18 June 1884, BP, no. 87/1; LB, i. 147–8.
20. Bridges to Lionel Muirhead, 7 Dec. 1886, BP, no. 97; LB, i. 160.
21. Bridges to R. W. Dixon, 22 Jan. 1887, BP, no. 87/1; LB, i. 163. Bridges learnt Spanish in order to read Calderón but found that he had mixed feelings about his plays. He found a full reward for the effort of learning the language in Cervantes' *Don Quixote*, though, which he considered 'as good as Shakespeare but not as various' (Bridges to Margaret Woods, 10 Aug. 1898, MS Don d 113, Bodleian Library.)
22. *Athenaeum*, 16 Jan. (83–4), 23 Jan. (113–4), and 30 Jan. 1904 (147–8).
23. Thompson, 48–9.
24. Bridges to Macmillan and Co., 22 Apr. 1887, BP, no. 112; LB, i. 165.
25. 22 Nov. 1892, MS Eng lett e 30, Bodleian Library; LB, i. 234.
26. Bridges to R. W. Dixon, 19 Apr. 1888, BP, no. 87/1; LB, i. 177.
27. Id., 22 Jan. 1887, BP, no. 87/1; LB, i. 163.
28. Id., 10 Apr. 1886, LB, i. 155.
29. 7 Sept. 1888, LI, 283–4.
30. 24 Dec. 1892, BP, no. 108; LB, i. 235.
31. 7 Jan. 1889, BP, no. 97; LB, i. 182–3.
32. 18 May 1889, BP, no. 62; LB, i. 184.
33. 25 Sept. 1888, LI, 291.
34. 14 June 1889, BP, no. 87/1; LB, i. 185–6.
35. *Three Friends*, 102.

36. 4 Aug. 1890, MSS Eng lett d 143, Bodleian Library; LB, i. 204.
37. Letters of 24 Feb., 8 Mar. 1893, MSS Eng lett d 143, Bodleian Library; LB, i. 238, 239.
38. A. H. Miles, *Robert Bridges and Contemporary Poets* (1906), 179–82.
39. *Edinburgh Review* (Oct. 1893), 491.
40. *Saturday Review* (25 Oct. 1890), 484–5.
41. *Athenaeum* (21 Feb. 1891), 239–40.
42. Bridges to Saintsbury, 13 Oct. 1890, Bridges to Muirhead, 20 Oct. 1890, BP, nos. 103, 97; LB, i. 205–6.
43. 13 Nov. 1890, BP, no. 108; LB, i. 207.
44. Guérard, 133, 134; *In the Classic Mode*, 141.
45. 19 Jan. 1892, BP, no. 108; LB, i. 226.
46. 29 July 1892, BP, no. 87/1; LB, i. 229.
47. 22 Nov. 1892, 10 Feb. 1893, BP, no. 98; LB, i. 234, 237.
48. 5 Jan. 1893, BP, no. 98; LB, i. 236.
49. Bridges to Samuel Gee, 28 Oct. 1893, Royal College of Physicians; LB, i. 249.
50. 27 Dec. 1890, BP, no. 98; LB, i. 209.
51. 9 Jan. 1891, BP, no. 117; LB, i. 211.
52. 14 May 1891, BP, no. 90; LB, i. 218.
53. Bridges to Lionel Muirhead, 10 Feb. 1893, BP, no. 98; LB, i. 236–7.
54. 27 June 1893, BP, no. 90; LB, i. 242–3.
55. George Saintsbury, 'A Nest of Singing Birds', *Illustrated London News* (14 Oct. 1893), 478.
56. Thompson, 65.
57. 17 June 1895, LB, i. 291.
58. 21 Dec. 1893, BP, no. 87/1; LB, i. 253.
59. 18 Apr. 1894, MS Eng lett e 30, Bodleian Library, LB, i. 258.
60. 16 July 1894, Royal College of Physicians; LB, i. 260.
61. 31 July 1894, LB, i. 262–3.
62. BP, no. 37.
63. Ibid., Bridges' copy in BP, no. 37.
64. Thompson, 51.

Chapter 10 Musical Collaborations

1. Commonplace Book, fo.62, Bridges Family Papers.
2. Sir Charles Villiers Stanford, *Pages from an Unwritten Diary* (1914), 273–5.
3. Ibid. 273.
4. Stanford was so impressed with Rockstro's abilities and the new possibilities that modal writing opened up that he induced Grove to appoint him to the Royal College of Music: ibid. 275.

5. Frank Howes, *The English Musical Renaissance* (1966), 153.
6. John F. Porte, *Sir Charles V. Stanford* (1921), 44–5.
7. J. A. Fuller-Maitland, *The Music of Parry and Stanford* (Cambridge, 1934), 58–60.
8. Harry Plunket Greene, *Charles Villiers Stanford* (1935), 251.
9. *Collected Essays*, no. 22, p.65.
10. Ibid., 42, 46.
11. 28 Oct. 1893, Royal College of Physicians; LB, i. 249.
12. W. H. Hadow, *Hymn Tunes*, Occasional Papers, no. 5 (n.d.), 12.
13. 29 July 1892, BP, no. 87/1; LB, i. 229.
14. 10 Oct. 1894, LB, i. 277.
15. 4 Oct. 1895, LB, i. 297.
16. 5 Oct. 1895, LB, i. 298.
17. *Music of Parry and Stanford*, 65.
18. Imogen Holst, *The Music of Gustav Holst* (1968), 122–5, 109.
19. 'On the Musical Setting of Poetry', *Collected Essays*, no. 21, p. 9.
20. BP, no. 18: see Bridges' letter to Arthur Ponsonby, 19 Apr. 1921, LB, i. 774–5 and note, 966–7.
21. John F. Porte, *Sir Charles V. Stanford* (1921), 46.
22. *Music of Parry and Stanford*, 99.
23. Ibid. 98, 100.
24. 29 Jan. 1896, MSS Eng lett d 143; LB, i. 305.
25. John Stevens, 'Gerard Manley Hopkins as Musician', in Hopkins, *Journals*, 463.
26. 30 Mar. 1896, BP, no. 98: LB, i. 307.
27. Commonplace Book, fo. 20, Bridges Family Papers.

Chapter 11 A New Generation of Writers

1. Bridges to Maurice Hewlett, 12 Dec. 1894, BP, no. 110: LB, i. 282.
2. Bridges to R. W. Dixon, 20 Apr. 1895, BP, no. 87/1; LB, i. 288.
3. Henry Newbolt, *My World as in My Time*: *Memoirs* (1932), 184–7. Hereafter cited as Newbolt.
4. Bridges to Henry Newbolt, 25 Nov. 1896, MSS Eng lett c 302, Bodleian Library: LB, i. 311–12.
5. Bridges to Samuel Gee, 27 Jan. 1900, Royal College of Physicians: LB, i. 360.
6. 19 Apr. [1905], MSS Eng lett c 302, Bodleian Library; LB, i. 479.
7. Newbolt, 216–17.
8. Letters of 14 and 19 Apr. 1905, MSS Eng lett c 302, Bodleian Library; LB, i. 478.
9. Commonplace Book, fo. 3, Bridges Family Papers.

10. *The Later Life and Letters of Sir Henry Newbolt*, edited by his wife (1942), 100; quoted in LB, i. 34.
11. Finneran, 3.
12. Ibid. 3–4.
13. Ibid. 6.
14. Newbolt, 192–3.
15. Yeats to Rabindranath Tagore, 1 Aug. 1915, Finneran, 40–1.
16. 15 June 1897, LB, i. 319.
17. 15 Nov. 1907, Finneran, 24.
18. 13 Aug. 1898, BP, no. 87/1; LB, i. 333.
19. Bridges to Muirhead, 21 Mar. 1898, BP, no. 98; LB, i. 328; Bridges to Rothenstein, 2 June 1898, BP, no. 102; LB, i. 331.
20. 29 Dec. 1897, Royal College of Physicians; LB, i. 326.
21. Bridges to Francis Jenkinson, 4 Jan. 1899, Jenkinson Papers, Cambridge University Library.
22. 5 Aug. 1898, BP, no. 98; LB, i. 332.
23. Bridges to Samuel Gee, 29 Dec. 1897, Royal College of Physicians; LB, i. 326.
24. 27 June 1899, BP, no. 99; LB, i. 344.
25. Donald Stanford, 'Robert Bridges, Poet-Typographer', *Fine Print*, 9 (Jan. 1983), 7.
26. Ibid. 7.
27. 31 Dec. 1899, Add MS 44039 fos. 151, 152, British Library; LB, i. 357.
28. 25 Jan. 1900, Add MS 44040, fo. 35, British Library; LB, i. 359.
29. 27 June 1899, BP, no. 99; LB, i. 344.
30. Guérard, 109.
31. *Monthly Review*, 4 (July–Sept. 1901), 114–27.

Chapter 12 In Search of Health

1. Bridges to Lionel Muirhead, 1 June 1900, BP, no. 99; LB, i. 371.
2. 7 Mar. 1900, LB, i. 366–67.
3. 11 Feb. 1901, BP, no. 99; LB, i. 378.
4. 27 Mar. 1901, BP, no. 99.
5. 2 Oct. 1901, in *The Correspondence of Robert Bridges and Henry Bradley, 1900–1923* (1940), 5; also LB, i. 389.
6. 18 July 1901, Royal College of Physicians; LB, i. 384.
7. Bridges to Lionel Muirhead, 16 Dec. [1901], BP, no. 99; LB, i. 393.
8. Ibid.
9. Bridges to Lionel Muirhead, 15 Nov. 1901, BP, no. 99; LB, i.391.
10. William J. Stone, 'Classical Metres in English Verse', in Bridges, *Milton's Prosody* (1901), 115.

11. 23 Dec. 1901, MSS Eng lett c 302; LB, i. 395.
12. Bridges to Henry Newbolt, 6 Jan. 1902, LB, i. 396.
13. W. H. Auden, *A Certain World: A Commonplace Book* (1970), 375–6.
14. Guérard, 27–8.
15. 'Letter to a Musician on English Prosody' (1901), originally printed in *Musical Antiquary*, first number (Oct. 1909), rev. 1914, *Collected Essays*, no. 15, pp. 66–73.
16. *Milton's Prosody* (1921), 86–7.
17. Bridges to Lionel Muirhead, 29 Nov. [1901], BP, no. 99; LB, i. 392.
18. 15 June 1902, Royal College of Physicians; LB, i. 409.
19. 20 Aug. 1902, BP, no. 99; LB, i. 411–2.
20. Commonplace Book, fo. 63, Bridges Family Papers. Chremes and Menedemus had been names of characters in Bridges' comedy *The Feast of Bacchus*.
21. 3 Jan. 1904, BP, no. 90; LB, i. 445.
22. 22 Aug. [1903], BP, no. 109; LB, i. 437–8.
23. 22 Mar. 1902, BP, no. 99; LB, i. 407.
24. 7 Nov. 1902, MS. Don d 131, Bodleian Library; LB, i. 416.
25. 28 Jan. [?1907], MS Don d 131, Bodleian Library; LB, i. 515–17.
26. Bridges to Lionel Muirhead, 11 Aug. 1903. BP, no. 99; LB, i. 436–7.
27. Id., 30 July 1904, BP, no. 99; LB, i. 459.
28. Bridges to Henry Bradley, 17 Mar. 1904, LB, i. 450.
29. 9 Nov. 1904, BP, no. 99; LB, i. 471–2.
30. 11 Jan. 1905, LB, i. 475.
31. 'Bunyan's Pilgrim's Progress', *Collected Essays*, no. 16, p. 129.
32. 5 Aug. [1905], MSS Eng lett c 302, Bodleian Library; LB, i. 490–1.
33. 23 Oct. 1905, BP, no. 99; LB, i. 493.
34. Bridges to Lionel Muirhead, 12 Nov. [1905], LB, i. 496.
35. 23 Dec. [1905], LB, i. 498.
36. Bridges to A. H. Bullen, 15 Jan. 1906, MS Eng lett e 30, Bodleian Library; LB, i. 500.
37. Bridges to Muirhead, 22 Mar. 1906, BP, no. 99; LB, i. 501.
38. Thompson, 73.

Chapter 13 Moving into Prominence

1. Bridges to Lionel Muirhead, 23 Oct. 1905, BP, no. 99; LB, i. 494–5.
2. I am most grateful to Mr David Waterhouse for this information. The first designs date from late May 1905 but were evidently modified before construction began.
3. Bridges to Lionel Muirhead, 26 May 1906, BP, no. 99; LB, i. 504.
4. BP, no. 18.
5. 10 Nov. 1906, BP, no. 99; LB, i. 509.

6. Bridges to Henry Newbolt, 25 Jan. 1907, MSS Eng lett c 302, Bodleian Library; LB, i. 515.
7. 15 Nov. 1907, BP, no. 100; LB, i. 534.
8. 8 Dec. 1906, LB, i. 512–3.
9. Bridges to Lionel Muirhead, 19 Feb. 1907, LB, i. 518–9.
10. Cyril Bailey, *Hugh Percy Allen* (1948), 60.
11. H. C. Maxwell Lyte, *History of Eton College 1440–1910*, 4th edn. (1911), 573–4.
12. Bridges to A. C. Benson, 27 Dec. 1908, LB, ii. 560.
13. 30 Jan. 1908, BP, no. 114; LB, i. 536.
14. 'The Poems of Mary Coleridge', *Cornhill Magazine*, 575: 137 (Nov. 1907), 605.
15. 'Why a National Theatre?', *Daily Chronicle* (22 Oct. 1909), 4.
16. 1 Sep. 1908, LB, ii. 555.
17. Bridges to Samuel Gee, 1 Sep. 1908, Royal College of Physicians; LB, ii. 555.
18. Ibid. 556.
19. Mary Monica Bridges, Preface to *Three Friends* (1932).
20. James Sambrook, *A Poet Hidden: The Life of Richard Watson Dixon* (1962), 111.
21. *Three Friends*, 127–8.
22. Ibid. 139–40.
23. Ibid. 125–6.
24. 15 Dec. 1908, BP, no. 100; LB, ii. 559.
25. *Three Friends*, 88.
26. 7 Nov. 1913, BP, no. 54.
27. 21 Jan. 1909, MSS Eng lett d 143, Bodleian Library; LB, ii. 563.
28. Id., 28 Mar. 1909, LB, ii. 567–8.
29. Id., 11 Oct. 1909, LB, ii. 571–2.
30. 12 Feb. 1910, BP, no. 100; LB, ii. 575.
31. 10 July [1910], BP, no. 100; LB, ii. 577.
32. W. B. Yeats to Bridges, 20 July [1901], Finneran, 21.
33. Bridges to W. B. Yeats, 24 July 1901, Finneran, 23.
34. 28 Jan. 1910, BP, no. 117; LB, ii. 574.
35. [16 Apr.] 1911, BP, no. 100; LB, ii. 585.
36. 11 June [1911], LB, ii. 587–8.
37. 7 Dec. 1911, LB, ii. 598.
38. *The Letters of Sir Walter Raleigh, 1879–1922*, edited by Lady Raleigh, 2 vols. (1926), ii. 390–1.
39. Thompson, 78.
40. G. H. Vallins, *Spelling* (1954), revd. edn. by John W. Clark (1965), 134, 137.

41. [18 Mar. 1912], LB, ii. 602–3.
42. Bradley, 86–7.
43. Reprinted as 'Wordsworth and Kipling' in *Collected Essays*, no. 13, p. 29.
44. SPE Tract no. 1 (1 Oct. 1919), 10–12.
45. Draft of a paper on aesthetics, BP, no. 71.
46. Logan Pearsall Smith, 'Robert Bridges: Recollections', in SPE Tract no. 35 (1931), 483–502. Hereafter cited as Pearsall Smith, 'Recollections'.
47. *Three Friends*, 204.
48. Ibid. 206–7.
49. Thompson, 80; Pearsall Smith, 'Recollections', 489.
50. 30 June [1912], LB, ii. 610.
51. Bridges to Lascelles Abercrombie, 4 Feb. [1913], MS Don d 135, Bodleian Library; LB, ii. 618.
52. BP, no. 71.
53. Sparrow, 5.
54. Bridges to Lionel Muirhead, 13 Mar. 1912, BP, no. 100; LB, ii. 602.
55. Letters of 1 May [1912], 24 May [1912], 4 June 1912, 30 June [1912], LB, ii. 604–5, 607, 610.

Chapter 14 Poet Laureate

1. Bridges to Lionel Muirhead, 25 May 1912, BP, no. 100; LB, ii. 605–6.
2. Bridges to Henry Bradley, 30 June [1912], LB, ii. 611.
3. Thompson, 41.
4. 14 Nov. 1912, BP, no. 100; LB, ii. 612.
5. 22 Nov. [?1912], MSS Eng lett c 303, Bodleian Library; LB, ii. 613.
6. Thompson, 83.
7. Timothy Rogers (ed.), *Georgian Poetry 1911–1922*, Critical Heritage series (1977), 101, 119.
8. Robert H. Ross, *The Georgian Revolt: Rise and Fall of a Poetic Ideal* (1967), 141. Hereafter cited as Ross.
9. Ross, 225.
10. 21 Feb. 1913, MS Don d 131, Bodleian Library; LB, ii. 620.
11. Guérard, 25.
12. J. A. Spender and Cyril Asquith, *Life of Herbert Henry Asquith, Lord Oxford and Asquith* (1932), 68.
13. Lord Birkenhead, *Rudyard Kipling* (1978), 384.
14. Bridges to Herbert Asquith, 15 July 1913, LB, ii. 626.
15. Bridges to J. W. Mackail, 27 Dec. [1913], MS Don c 65, Bodleian Library; LB, ii. 642.
16. *October and Other Poems* (1920), 63.

17. Bridges to Harold Monro, 25 Oct. [1913], BP, no. 112; LB, ii. 632–3.
18. Finneran, 27–8.
19. 2 May [1914], BP, no. 90; LB, ii. 645–6.

Chapter 15 War

1. 19 Apr. 1914, BP, no. 9.
2. Bridges to J. A. Stewart, 2 July [1914], BP, no. 116; LB, ii. 647.
3. 9 Aug. 1914, BP, no. 101; LB, ii. 649.
4. Ibid.
5. 27 Aug. [1914], BP, no. 109; LB, ii. 651. The poem appeared in *The Times* (8 Aug. 1914). When the poem was reprinted in *October and Other Poems*, stanzas 3, 4, and 6 were omitted and the last two lines changed to 'Stand England for honour, | And God guard the Right!'
6. Ibid.
7. Bridges to Pearsall Smith, 17 Dec. [1914], MS Don d 131, Bodleian Library; LB, ii. 655.
8. 27 Jan. [1916], MS Eng lett e 30, Bodleian Library; LB, ii. 699.
9. Raleigh *Letters*, ii. 406.
10. 26 Aug. [1914], MS Eng Poet e 93, Bodleian Library; LB, ii. 650–1.
11. 'George Santayana', *London Mercury* (Aug. 1920), repr. in *Collected Essays*, no. 19, p. 150.
12. 4 Oct. [1914], BP, no. 117; LB, ii. 652–3.
13. On 5 Oct. 1878 Hopkins wrote to Dixon, 'the choruses of *Samson Agonistes* are in my judgment counterpointed throughout; that is, each line (or nearly so) has two different coexisting scansions. But when you reach that point the secondary or 'mounted rhythm', which is necessarily a sprung rhythm, overpowers the original or conventional one and then this becomes superfluous and may be got rid of; by taking that last step you reach simple sprung rhythm. Milton must have known this but had reasons for not taking it.' LII, 15. None of Hopkins' letters to Bridges say this although they may have discussed it. Hopkins may have contributed the idea of two simultaneous rhythms, although he does not call the metre syllabic as Bridges does. Bridges also thought of the superimposed rhythm as accentual rather than more specifically sprung. Consequently, although Bridges did not get his theory from Hopkins, Hopkins' ideas may have suggested in part the direction of his investigation.
14. Donald Stanford, 'Hopkins and Bridges', in *Hopkins Among the Poets*, edited by Richard Giles (Hamilton, Ontario 1985), 5.
15. Bridges to Coventry Patmore, in Derek Patmore, 'Three Poets', 73.
16. I am grateful to Lord Bridges for this information about Bridges' copy.

17. 23 June [1915], Finneran, 33.
18. [12 July 1915], LB, ii. 675–6.
19. I am grateful to Dr John Leigh, who gave me a photocopy of a card written by Elkin Mathews which says, among other interesting things, 'Mr Bridges lunched that day [17 February] with Ezra Pound (a Cork Street poet) and in the evening he dined with the King'.
20. *Ezra Pound and Dorothy Shakespear: Their Letters 1909–1914*, edited by Omar Pound and A. Walton Litz (1985), 310, 316, 330.
21. Card kindly photocopied for me by Dr John Leigh. Mathews writes: 'The Poet Laureate came up from Oxford to attend the King's Levée on Tuesday Feby 24th/[19]14 and called on me at Cork Street in the afternoon. He called again on Thursday the 26th and thrice on Friday Feby 27th when I got him to sign this portrait—having brought it up in the morning from Chorley Wood and removed it from its frame for the purpose . . . W. Strang etched the R.B. Portrait about 1894.'
22. Pound to Felix E. Schelling (9 July 1922) in *The Letters of Ezra Pound*, edited by D. D. Paige (1951), 247. In his essay 'The Glamour of Grammar' Bridges speaks of the desirability of reintroducing words that have been part of our language in the past but have fallen out of fashion. However, he never makes the case for their return on the grounds of antiquarian taste but always for their utility.
23. The poems Bridges liked were: 'Octave', 'Maestro di Tocar', 'Aria', 'L'Art', 'The House of Splendour', and 'The Flame'.
24. Pound to Felix E. Schelling, 8 July 1922, *The Letters of Ezra Pound*, 245.
25. [Aug.] 1915, ibid. 106–7.
26. 'Robert Bridges's New Book', *Poetry* (Oct. 1915–Mar. 1916), 42.
27. 21 July 1934, *The Letters of Ezra Pound*, 336.
28. *Poetry* (Oct. 1915–Mar. 1916), 42. In his biography of Edward Marsh (1959) Christopher Hassall describes a dinner in 1912 during which Pound showed Marsh his version of Sappho's 'Ode to Aphrodite', asking if it contained metrical errors. Marsh, who had learnt quantitative verse from W. Stone's article and from Robert Bridges, pointed out several. Pound blushed but published the poem unaltered. Bridges himself came to disagree with Stone's analysis of many vowel quantities and would have judged the poem on whether or not he liked the rhythms rather than whether they complied with rules.
29. 18 Apr. 1918, BP, no. 101; LB, ii. 730–1.
30. George Santayana, *My Host the World* (1953), 105.
31. Ibid. 124, 104, 107.
32. Meeting of 28 Mar. 1916. The full text of Bridges' speech as printed in the *Times Literary Supplement* (6 Apr. 1916) is in BP, no. 48.
33. BP, no. 48.

34. 'An Address to the Swindon WEA', *Collected Essays*, no. 27, pp. 159–89.
35. 26 Mar. [1917], MSS Eng lett d 143, Bodleian Library; LB, ii. 708.
36. 'Harry Ellis Wooldridge', *DNB 1912–21*, 595.
37. 9 Sept. [1921], MSS Eng lett c 303, Bodleian Library; LB, ii. 778.
38. Edward had become a captain and adjutant. He was awarded the Military Cross in January 1917.
39. Edward Bridges, Appendix to BP, no. 20.
40. J. Arthur Thompson, 'A Biologist's Philosophy', in *Contemporary British Philosophy*, edited by J. H. Muirhead (1926), ii. 323–3.
41. J. C. Smuts, *Holism and Evolution* (1926), 86.
42. BP, no. 48.
43. 'The Necessity of Poetry', *Collected Essays*, no. 28, 203.
44. Ibid. 210.
45. Ibid. 236–7.
46. 'George Santayana', *Collected Essays*, no. 19, pp. 148–9.
47. 7 Sept. 1917, MSS Eng lett d 143, Bodleian Library; LB, ii. 714.
48. Bridges to Kate Hopkins, 18 Feb. [1918], MSS Eng lett d 143, Bodleian Library, LB, ii. 725, and to Logan Pearsall Smith, 16 Feb. [1918], LB, ii. 724.
49. Gerard Manley Hopkins, MS Eng. Poet d 150, Bodleian Library.
50. Bridges to Kate Hopkins, 18 Feb. [1918], MSS Eng lett d 143, Bodleian Library; LB, ii. 725.
51. Dec. 1918, LB, ii. 749.
52. Bridges to G. E. P. Arkwright, 29 Jan. 1918, LB, ii. 722.
53. Cyril Bailey, *Hugh Percy Allen* (1948), 122.
54. 4 Apr. [1918], MSS Eng lett c 303, Bodleian Library; LB, ii. 729.
55. John Buxton and Penry Williams (eds.), *New College, Oxford 1379–1979* (Oxford, 1979), 87. Hereafter cited as *New College*.
56. Bridges to Henry Newbolt, 4 Apr. [1918], MSS Eng lett c 303, Bodleian Library, LB, ii. 729.
57. 28 Apr. [1918], BP, no. 90; LB, ii. 732.
58. 8 Mar. [1919], MSS Eng lett d 143, Bodleian Library; LB, ii. 753.
59. E. J. Molesworth, *The Life of Sir Guilford L. Molesworth* (1922), 66.
60. [18 Mar. 1918], MS Don d 131, Bodleian Library; LB, ii. 726–7.
61. The *Times of India* (18 Nov. 1918).
62. 'Books for Hospitals', printed in *The Times* (24 May 1918), BP, no. 48.
63. 25 July [1911], LB, ii. 593.

Chapter 16 The Post-War World

1. 20 Nov. [1918], BP, no. 101; LB, ii. 744.
2. BP, no. 9. Variant readings have been omitted.

3. BP, no. 20.
4. Bridges to Carry (Glover), 8 Dec. [1918], BP, no. 109; LB, ii. 747.
5. *New College*, 114–5.
6. 12 Oct. 1919, LB, ii. 760.
7. 28 Mar. 1920, LB, ii. 764.
8. E. G. Twitchett, 'The Poetry of Robert Bridges', *London Mercury*, 21 (1929–30), 142.
9. Sparrow, 28.
10. 23 Aug. [1920], LB, ii. 766.
11. Bridges to Roger Fry, 17 Nov. [1920], BP, no. 90; LB, ii. 769.
12. 20 Dec. [1920], MSS Eng lett c 303, Bodleian Library; LB, ii. 772. Tract IV contained an article by John Sargeaunt on 'The Pronunciation of English Words Derived from the Latin'.
13. 11 June [1921], LB, ii. 776.
14. [13 Sept. 1921], LB, ii. 779–80.
15. Bridges to George Saintsbury, 13 Nov. [1921], BP, no. 102; LB, ii. 781.
16. Bridges to Henry Newbolt, 23 Aug. [1921], MSS Eng lett c 303, Bodleian Library; LB, ii. 778.
17. *The Principles of English Versification* (Cambridge, Mass., 1922), 144.
18. 18 Feb. 1891, BP, no. 108; LB, ii. 214.
19. Donald Stanford, 'Robert Bridges and the Free Verse Rebellion', *Journal of Modern Literature*, 2: 1 (Sept. 1971), 26.
20. Bridges' note in a manuscript volume of his poems, BP, no. 18.
21. Bridges to R. C. Trevelyan, 4 Jan. 1926, R. C. Trevelyan Papers, no. 165[1], Wren Library, Trinity College, Cambridge; LB, ii. 860.
22. BP, no. 8.
23. He was to become the first Baron Bridges KG, serving as Secretary to the Cabinet during World War II and then Secretary to the Treasury. One of his most important contributions was the initial reorganizing of the Civil Service for its role after 1945.
24. 6 Mar. [1922], LB, ii. 784.
25. 9 Aug. [1922], LB, ii. 791–2.
26. 'Humdrum and Harum-Scarum', *North American Review* and *London Mercury* (Nov. 1922), repr. in *Collected Essays*, no. 2.
27. Repr. in *Essays and Introductions* (New York, 1961), 522, 524.

Chapter 17 Old Age and New Verse

1. Pearsall Smith, 'Recollections', 500.
2. Bridges to Roger Fry, 10 July 1923, BP, no. 90; LB, i. 805.
3. Monica Bridges to Roger Fry, 17 Aug. [1923], LB, ii. 809.
4. 'Memoir of Henry Bradley', *Three Friends*, 230.
5. Bridges to J. A. Stewart, 19 Aug. [1923], LB, ii. 809.

6. Introduction, *The Chilswell Book of English Poetry* (1924).
7. Richard Perceval Graves, *A. E. Housman* (1979), 237.
8. Ibid. 237.
9. 22 Apr. 1930, BP, no. 119.
10. 25 Sept. [1923], LB, ii. 812.
11. Nicolas Barker, *The Printer and the Poet* (Cambridge, 1970), 9–12.
12. 26 June [1924], BP, no. 101; LB, ii. 825.
13. 2 Nov. 1923, LB, ii. 817.
14. 20 Jan. 1924, BP, no. 90; Fry Papers, King's College, Cambridge; LB, ii. 822.
15. 23 Jan. 1924, *The Letters of Roger Fry*, edited by Denys Sutton, 2 vols. (1972), ii. 547–8.
16. Bridges to Logan Pearsall Smith, 12 Sept. [1924], MS Don d 131, Bodleian Library; LB, ii. 829.
17. BP, no. 109.
18. 10 Jan. 1937, *Selected Letters of E. M. Forster*, edited by Mary Lago and P. N. Furbank, 2 vols. (1983, 1985), ii. 145–6. Thompson provides a different statement about Bridges' prudishness: 'Bridges was not in the least squeamish in private talk and would use the most unexpected words if they were the right words; he never picked about for others more delicate but less expressive. But he disliked coarseness or suggestiveness in literature as signs of mental sickness or poverty of interests.' (Thompson, 74).
19. 21 Oct. 1924, LB, ii. 829.
20. BP, no. 9.
21. [Jan. 1925], BP, no. 101; LB, ii. 840.
22. 17 June [1925], LB, ii. 845.
23. 13 July [1925], LB, ii. 848–9.
24. Thompson, 79.
25. Laurence Binyon to Robert Bridges, 20 Dec. 1925; Roger Fry to Robert Bridges, 18 Dec. 1925, BP, no. 8.
26. 'Vision' (2 November, 1921), in *New Verse*, 65–6.
27. *Nation and the Athenaeum* (29 May 1926); BP, no. 82, fo. 13.
28. *Sunday Times* (3 Jan. 1926): BP, no. 82, fo. 17.
29. 4 July [1925], LB, ii. 847.
30. LB, ii. 972, n. 986.
31. 2 Jan. [1926], LB, ii. 860.
32. 26 Apr. 1926, BP, no. 102.
33. Bridges' note of Nov. 1929, in BP, no. 13.

Chapter 18 The Testament of Beauty

1. *The Diary of Virginia Woolf*, edited by Anne Olivier Bell and Andrew McNeillie, 5 vols. (1980), iii. 92–3, 50.

2. 30 Jan. [1926], LB, ii. 863.
3. 12 Feb. [1926], LB, ii. 866.
4. R. C. Trevelyan, *Thamyris, or Is There a Future for Poetry?* (1925), 87, 62–4.
5. See Michael Pafford, *Inglorious Wordsworths: A Study of Some Transcendental Experiences in Childhood and Adolescence* (1973).
6. 4 Nov. 1929, BP, no. 14, repr. in Daniel Cory (ed.), *The Letters of George Santayana* (1955), 243.
7. George Santayana, *Reason in Common Sense*, vol. 1 of *The Life of Reason; or The Phases of Human Progress*, 2nd edn., 5 vols. (1922), 3.
8. Thompson, 103–4.
9. 5 Apr. 1927, BP, no. 13.
10. 27 Aug. 1927, Fry Papers, No. VIB, King's College, Cambridge.
11. 4 July [1927], LB, ii. 880.
12. 25 July [1927], MS Don d 131, Bodleian Library; LB, ii. 881.
13. 26 July [1927], BP, no. 103; LB, ii. 882.
14. *A Selection of the Letters of Sir Walter Raleigh, 1880–1922*, edited by Lady Raleigh (1928), xxi.
15. [Dec. 1927], LB, ii. 887.
16. 4 June [1928], BP, no. 103; LB, ii. 891.
17. 7 June [1928], Trevelyan Papers, no. 173 [2], Trinity College, Cambridge; LB, ii. 891.
18. 12 June 1929, BP, no. 75; LB, ii. 904–5.
19. 14 July 1929, quoted by Edward Bridges in his introduction to 'The Manuscript of "The Testament"', BP, no. 13.
20. 26 Sept. [1929], BP, no. 90; LB, ii. 909.
21. Simon Nowell Smith, 'A Poet in Walton Street', in *Essays mainly on the Nineteenth Century Presented to Sir Humphrey Milford* (1948), 71.
22. [C. B. Brodribb], *The Times* (24 Oct. 1929), 17. The writer of the editorial was identified by Bruce Richmond in a letter to Robert Bridges of 5 Feb. 1930, BP, no. 14.
23. 12 June 1929, BP, No. 75; LB, ii. 904.
24. 14 June 1929, BP, No. 75.
25. Typed copy, (16 Sept. 1929) William Temple to Lord Stamfordham, BP, No. 75. Of the unorthodox passages he pointed out that a) in Book I, ll. 471–9 Bridges 'repudiates the Augustinian form of the doctrine of the Fall. But he is there in full agreement with the great Greek Fathers, and almost all theologians now repudiate St Augustine at this point. b) In Book IV. ll. 1,253–67 he denies universal, and asserts conditional, immortality. But this I am sure is the prevailing idea of the New Testament and Bishop Gore has probably said the same. c) In Book IV, ll. 1,403–4 he *appears* to deny a physical

Resurrection of Christ. But it is not explicit, and his emphasis is on the reality of His spiritual Resurrection and abiding presence with His disciples: so I do not think there could be any need to boggle at this.'

26. 1 Feb. 1930, BP, no. 13.
27. *Selected Letters of E. M. Forster*, ii. 89.
28. 7 Jan. [1930], MS Don d 131, Bodleian Library; LB, ii. 915.
29. 14 Feb. [1930], BP, no. 101; LB, ii. 916.
30. 4 Apr. 1930, MS Don d 131, Bodleian Library; LB, ii. 917.
31. *The Times* (22 Apr. 1930).

BIBLIOGRAPHY

This bibliography is selective. Place of publication is London, unless otherwise stated.

BOOKS, ARTICLES, AND EDITIONS BY ROBERT BRIDGES

A fuller listing can be found in George L. McKay, *A Bibliography of Robert Bridges* (1933), and Lee Templin Hamilton, *Robert Bridges: An Annotated Bibliography, 1873–1988* (Newark, 1991).

Poems (1873).

The Growth of Love: A Poem in Twenty-Four Sonnets (1876).

Carmen Elegiacum . . . de Nosocomio Sti Bartolomaei Londinensi . . . ad Patricium Black . . . scriptum et dedicatum (1877).

'An Account of the Casualty Department', *St. Bartholomew's Hospital Reports*, 14 (1878), 167–82.

Poems, by the author of The Growth of Love (1879).

Poems, by the author of The Growth of Love, third series (1880).

Prometheus the Firegiver (Oxford, 1883).

Poems (Oxford, 1884).

Eight Plays, 8 vols. (1885–94).

Eros and Psyche. A Poem in twelve measures. The story done into English from the Latin of Apuleius (1885).

On the Elements of Milton's Blank Verse in 'Paradise Lost' (1887).

Milton's Prosody (Oxford 1889, 1893).

The Growth of Love, second edn. (1889).

Shorter Poems, Books 1 to 5, 2 vols. (1890–4).

Eden: An Oratorio, set to music by C. V. Stanford (1891).

'Gerard Manley Hopkins', in *Poets and the Poetry of the Century*, edited by A. H. H. Miles (1893).

Eros and Psyche, revised edn. (1894).

Invocation to Music (1895)

(Editor), *The Yattendon Hymnal*, with Harry Ellis Wooldridge (Oxford 1895–9).

(Editor), *Chants for the Psalter* (Yattendon, 1897).

A Song of Darkness and Light (1898).

(Editor), *The Small Hymn Book* (1899).

A Practical Discourse on Some Principles of Hymn Singing (1901).

Milton's Prosody, including 'Classical Metres in English Verse' by William Johnson Stone (Oxford 1901).

Now in Wintry Delights (Oxford, 1903).

Demeter: A Mask (Oxford 1905).

'Henry Newbolt', in *Poets and the Poetry of the Century*, edited by A. H. H. Miles, second edn. (1906).

Eton Memorial Ode (1908).

Ibant Obscuri: An Experimental Paraphrase of Part of the Sixth Book of the Aeneid in Quantitative Hexameters (1909).

(Editor), *Poems by the late Rev. Dr. Richard Watson Dixon*, with a Memoir (1909).

A Tract on the Present State of English Pronunciation (1910, reprinted Oxford, 1913).

(Editor), *The Poems of Digby Mackworth Dolben*, with a Memoir (1911).

Poetical Works, excluding the eight dramas (1912).

Poems Written in the Year MCMXIII (1914).

(Editor), *The Poems of Digby Mackworth Dolben*, second edn. (1915).

The Chivalry of the Sea (1916).

Ibant Obscuri: An Experiment in the Classical Hexameter, second edn. (Oxford, 1916).

(Editor), *The Spirit of Man: An Anthology in English and French* (1916).

(Editor), *Poems of Gerard Manley Hopkins* (1918).

(Editor), *Tracts*, of the Society for Pure English (1919–30).

October, and other Poems, with occasional verses on the war (1920).

Milton's Prosody, revised final edn. (Oxford, 1921).

Poor Poll (Oxford, 1923)

(Editor), *The Chilswell Book of English Poetry* (1924).

The Tapestry: Poems (Privately printed, 1925).

New Verse, written in 1921 . . . with the other poems of that year and a few earlier pieces (Oxford, 1925).

Collected Essays, Papers, etc., 10 vols. (1927–36).

'Harry Ellis Wooldridge', in *The Dictionary of National Biography, 1912 to 1921* (1927).

A Selection from the Letters of Sir Walter Raleigh, 1880–1922, edited by Lady Raleigh . . . with an Introduction by Robert Bridges (1928).

The Collected Papers of Henry Bradley, with a memoir by Robert Bridges (1928).

The Testament of Beauty: A Poem in Four Books (Oxford, 1929).

On Receiving Trivia from the Author (Stanford Dingley, 1930).

(Editor), *Poems of Gerard Manley Hopkins*, second edn., with an appendix of extra poems and a critical introduction by Charles Williams (1930).

Three Friends: Memoirs of Digby Mackworth Dolben, Richard Watson Dixon, and Henry Bradley (1932).

Eros and Psyche: Specimen Pages (Oxford, 1935).

The Correspondence of Robert Bridges and Henry Bradley, 1900–1923 (Oxford, 1940).

Four Collects (Stanford Dingley, 1947).

Poetical Works, with 'The Testament of Beauty' but excluding the eight dramas, second edn. (1953, 1971).

Twenty-One Letters: A Correspondence between Robert Bridges and R. C. Trevelyan, edited by R. Gathorne-Hardy (Stanford Dingley (1955).

(Editor), *The Spirit of Man,* with an Introduction by W. H Auden (1973).

The Correspondence of Robert Bridges and W. B. Yeats, edited by Richard J. Finneran (1977).

BOOKS BY AUTHORS OTHER THAN ROBERT BRIDGES

Alumni Oxonienses 1715–1886.

ATLAY, J. B., *Sir Henry Wentworth Acland, Bart. KCB, FRS: Regius Professor of Medicine in the University of Oxford: a Memoir* (1903).

Bagshaw's Directory of Kent (1847).

BAILEY, CYRIL, *Hugh Percy Allen* (1948).

BARHAM ZINCKE, F., *Egypt of the Pharaohs and of the Khedive,* 2nd ed., (1873).

BARKER, NICOLAS, *The Printer and the Poet* (Cambridge, 1970).

BEAUFORT, EMILY A., *Egyptian Sepulchres and Syrian Shrines,* 2 vols. (1861).

BELL, CLIVE, *Art* (1914).

BERG, SISTER MARY GRETCHEN, *The Prosodic Structure of Robert Bridges's 'Neo-Miltonic Syllabics'* (Washington, 1962).

BIDDIS, MICHAEL D., *The Age of the Masses: Ideas and Society in Europe since 1870,* Pelican History of European Thought, vol. 6 (Harmondsworth, 1977).

BIRD, GOLDING and CHARLES BROOKE, *The Elements of Natural Philosophy; or An Introduction to the Physical Sciences,* 5th edn. (1860).

BRIDGES, JOHN AFFLECK, *Reminiscences of a Country Politician* (1906).

—— *A Sportsman of Limited Income. Recollections of Fifty Years* (1910).

—— *Victorian Recollections* (1919).

—— *Wet Days* (1879).

BRINSLEY-RICHARDS, JAMES, *Seven Years at Eton 1857–1864* (1883).

BURNE-JONES, G., *Memorials of Edward Burne-Jones,* 2 vols. (1906).

BUXTON, JOHN and PENRY WILLIAMS (eds.), *New College, Oxford 1379–1979* (1979).

Cambridge University Calendars (1863–8).

CARPENTER, WILLIAM B., *Principles of Human Physiology* (1842).

Catalogue of the Transactions of Societies, Periodicals and Memoirs . . . in the Radcliffe Library at the Oxford Museum (1871).

CHAMBERS, ROBERT, *Vestiges of the Natural History of Creation* (Leicester, 1969, repr. from the 1844 ed.).

COLES, V. S. S., *V. S. S. Coles: Letters, Papers, Addresses, Hymns and Verses, with a Memoir by J. F. Briscoe* (1930).

COOKE, J. P., *Elements of Chemical Physics* (Boston, 1860).

CREIGHTON, MANDELL, *Life and Letters of Mandell Creighton, by his Wife*, 2 vols. (1904).

MARQUIS CURZON, *The Personal History of Walmer Castle and its Lords Warden* (1927).

DOLBEN, D. M., *The Poems and Letters of Digby Mackworth Dolben 1848–1867*, edited by Martin Cohen (Avebury Publishing Co., 1981).

ELTON, OLIVER, *Robert Bridges and 'The Testament of Beauty'*, English Association Pamphlet, 83 (Nov. 1932).

ELVIN, C. R. S., *Records of Walmer* (n.d.).

The Eton Observer: A miscellany conducted by present Etonians, 2 vols. (Eton, 1860).

FORSTER, E. M., *Selected Letters of E. M. Forster*, edited by Mary Lago and P. N. Furbank, 2 vols. (1983, 1985).

FOWLER, ROWENA MARY, 'Victorian Lyric Versification' (unpublished doctoral dissertation, University of Cambridge, 1974).

FOWLER, THOMAS *The History of Corpus Christi College* (1893).

FRY, ROGER, *Letters of Roger Fry*, edited by Denys Sutton, 2 vols. (1972).

FULLER-MAITLAND, J. A., *The Music of Parry & Stanford* (Cambridge, 1934).

GATHORNE-HARDY, ROBERT, *Recollections of Logan Pearsall Smith* (1949).

GRAVES, RICHARD PERCEVAL, *A. E. Housman* (1979).

GREEN, IVAN, *The Book of Deal and Walmer* (1983).

GREENE, HARRY PLUNKET, *Charles Villiers Stanford* (1935).

GUÉRARD, ALBERT, *Robert Bridges: A Study of Traditionalism in Poetry* (Cambridge, Mass. 1942).

HAYTER, WILLIAM, *W. A. Spooner: A Biography* (1977).

HEYWOOD, JAMES, *The Recommendations of the Oxford University Commissioners with Selections from their Report and a History of the University Subscription Tests, including Notices of the University and Collegiate Visitations* (1853).

HOLMES, SIR CHARLES and C. H. COLLINS BAKER, *The Making of the National Gallery 1824–1924* (1924).

HOPKINS, G. M., *The Journals and Papers of Gerard Manley Hopkins*, edited by Humphry House and Graham Storey (1959).

HOLST, IMOGEN, *The Music of Gustav Holst* (1968).

HOWES, FRANK, *The English Musical Renaissance* (1966).

HOZIER, H. M., *The Franco-Prussian War* (1870–2).

HUGHES, MABEL, *Everyman's Testament of Beauty* (1932).

JEWESBURY, ERIC C. O., *The Royal Northern Hospital 1856–1956* (1956).

JONES, HENRY FESTING, *Samuel Butler: A Memoir*, 2 vols. (1920).

Kelly's Directory of Kent (1855).

LAKER, JOHN, *History of Deal* (Deal, 1917).

LONGFORD, ELIZABETH, *Wellington: Pillar of State* (1972).

MARWICK, ARTHUR, *Britain in the Century of Total War* (1968).

—— *The Deluge: British Society and the First World War* (1965).

MAXWELL LYTE, H. C., *History of Eton College 1440–1910*, 4th edn. (1911).

MOLESWORTH, E. J., *The Life of Sir Guilford L. Molesworth* (1922).

MOLESWORTH, SIR GUILFORD, *John Edward Nassau Molesworth: A Life* (1915).

MORRAH, HERBERT A., *The Oxford Union 1823–1923* (1923).

MUIRHEAD, J. H. (Ed.), *Contemporary British Philosophy: Personal Statements*, 2 vols. (1924, 1926).

NEWBOLT, SIR HENRY, *My World as in My Time: Memoirs* (1932).

NEWMAN, CHARLES, *The Evolution of Medical Education in the Nineteenth Century* (1957).

NORMAN, CHARLES, *Ezra Pound* (New York, 1960).

Oxford University Calendars (1863–8).

PAFFORD, MICHAEL, *Inglorious Wordsworths: A Study of Some Transcendental Experiences in Childhood and Adolescence* (1973).

Plarr's Lives of the Fellows of the Royal College of Surgeons (1930).

PORTE, JOHN F., *Sir Charles V. Stanford* (1921).

Post Office Directory of the Six Home Counties (1845, 1851).

Post Office Directory of Essex, Herts., Kent, Middlesex, Surrey, and Sussex (1855).

POUND, EZRA, *Ezra Pound and Dorothy Shakespear: Their Letters 1909–1914*, edited by Omar Pound and A. Walton Litz (1985).

—— *The Letters of Ezra Pound 1907–1941*, edited by D. D. Paige (1951).

PRITCHARD, STEPHEN *The History of Deal and its Neighbourhood* (Deal, 1864).

RALEIGH, SIR WALTER, *The Letters of Sir Walter Raleigh, 1879–1922*, edited by Lady Raleigh, 2 vols. (1926).

RITZ, JEAN-GEORGES, *Robert Bridges and Gerard Manley Hopkins 1863–1889: A Literary Friendship* (1960).

ROBERTS, DAVID, *The Holy Land, Syria and Egypt after lithographs by Louis Haghe*, 6 vols. in 3 (1855–6).

ROGERS, TIMOTHY (ed.), *Georgian Poetry 1911–1922* Critical Heritage series (1977).

ROGET, JOHN LEWIS, *Sketches of Deal, Walmer and Sandwich* (1911).
ROSS, ROBERT H., *The Georgian Revolt: Rise and Fall of a Poetic Ideal* (1967).
ROTHENSTEIN, WILLIAM, *Men and Memories*, 2 vols. (1931, 1932).
RUSSELL, BERTRAND, *The Analysis of Mind (1921).*
St. Bartholomew's Hospital and College Calendar (1871).
SAINTSBURY, GEORGE, *A Scrap Book* (1922).
—— *A Second Scrap Book* (1923).
SAMBROOK, JAMES, *A Poet Hidden: The Life of Richard Watson Dixon* (1962).
SANTAYANA, GEORGE, *My Host the World* (1953).
—— *The Letters of George Santayana*, edited by Daniel Cory (New York, 1955).
—— *The Life of Reason; or The Phases of Human Progress*, 2nd edn., 5 vols. (1922).
—— *The Realm of Essence: Book First of Realms of Being* (1928)
—— *Scepticism and Animal Faith* (1923).
—— *Selected Critical Writings of George Santayana*, edited by Norman Henfrey (Cambridge, 1968), vol. i.
SASSOON, SIEGFRIED, *Siegfried's Journey 1916–1920* (1946, repr. 1973).
The Savile Club 1868–1923, printed privately for the Committee of the Club (1923).
SINGER, BETH J., *The Rational Society: A Critical Study of Santayana's Social Thought* (Cleveland, 1970).
SINGER, IRVING, *Santayana's Aesthetics: A Critical Introduction* (Cambridge, Mass., 1957).
SMITH, LOGAN PEARSALL, *Unforgotten Years* (1938).
SMITH, NOWELL CHARLES, *Notes to 'The Testament of Beauty'*, third ed. (1940).
SMUTS, J. C., *Holism and Evolution* (1926).
SPARROW, JOHN, *Robert Bridges* (1955).
—— *Robert Bridges*, British Council pamphlet (1962).
SPRIGGE, TIMOTHY, *Santayana: An Examination of his Philosophy* (1974).
SPROTT, S. ERNEST, *Milton's Art of Prosody* (1953).
STANFORD, DONALD, *In the Classic Mode: The Achievement of Robert Bridges* (Newark, 1978).
STAPLYTON, H. E. C., *Eton School Lists 1853–1892*, 2nd ser. (1900).
STEVENSON, LIONEL, *Darwin Among the Poets* (Chicago, 1932).
STOCK, NOEL, *The Life of Ezra Pound* (1970)
SUTCLIFFE, PETER, *The Oxford University Press: An Informal History* (Oxford, 1978).
THOMPSON, EDWARD, *Robert Bridges 1844–1930* (1944).
THWAITE, ANN, *Edmund Gosse: A Literary Landscape 1849–1928* (1984).

Toynbee, Paget, *The Oxford Dante Society: A Record of Forty-four Years (1876–1920)* (1920).

Trevelyan, Robert C., *Thamyris; or Is There a Future for Poetry?* (1925).

Turner, Frank M., *The Greek Heritage in Victorian Britain* (1981).

Vallins, G. H. *Spelling* (1954), revd. edn. by John W. Clark (1965).

Verco, P. W., *Masons, Millers and Medicine: James Crabb Verco and his Sons* (Adelaide, n.d. [?1977]).

Vernon, H. M. and K. Dorothea Vernon, *A History of the Oxford Museum* (1909).

Whitehead, A. N., *Science and the Modern World*, Lowell Lectures, 1925 (Cambridge, 1926).

Winter, A. Yvor, *Forms of Discovery: Critical and Historical Essays on the Forms of the Short Poem in English* (New York, 1967).

—— *Uncollected Essays and Reviews*, edited by F. Murphy (1974).

Withers, Percy, *A Buried Life: Personal Recollections of A. E. Housman* (1940).

Woolf, Virginia, *Roger Fry: A Biography* (1940).

The Diary of Virginia Woolf, edited by Anne Olivier Bell and Andrew McNeillie (1980).

Wright, Elizabeth Cox, *Metaphor Sound and Meaning in Bridges's 'The Testament of Beauty'* (Philadelphia, 1951).

Young, Francis E. Brett, *Robert Bridges: A Critical Study* (1914).

Zaniello, Tom, *Hopkins in the Age of Darwin* (Iowa City, 1988).

ARTICLES BY AUTHORS OTHER THAN ROBERT BRIDGES

Arnold, Tony, 'The Convent of the Visitation at Upper Walmer', *East Kent Mercury* (30 Jan. 1975), 16.

Binyon, Laurence, Review of W. B. Yeats (ed.), *The Oxford Book of Modern Verse, 1892–1935*, *English*, 1: 4 (1937), 339–400.

Boas, Cicely, 'The Metre of "The Testament of Beauty"', *London Mercury*, 22 (1930), 147–53.

[Brodribb, C. W.], '"The Testament of Beauty"', *The Times* (24 Oct. 1929), 17.

Craigie, W. A., 'Henry Bradley', in *DNB, 1922–1930.* (1937).

[de Selincourt, Basil], '"The Testament of Beauty"', *Hibbert Journal*, 28: 3 (Apr. 1930), 416–35.

Eliot, T. S., 'Reflections on Vers Libre', *New Statesman* (3 Mar. 1917), 518–9.

Endean, Philip SJ., 'The Spirituality of Gerard Manley Hopkins', *Hopkins Quarterly*, 8: 3 (Fall 1981), 107–29.

FOLIGNO, CESARE, 'Bridges and Dante', in *Centenary Essays on Dante* by Members of the Oxford Dante Society (1965), 91–102.

GARROD, OLIVER, 'The Life of Samuel Jones Gee, MD FRCP (1839–1911)' *St. Bartholomew's Hospital Reports*, 71 (1938).

GREW, EVA MARY, 'Music in "The Testament of Beauty"', *Contemporary Review*, 138 (1930), 209–17.

HOWARTH, JANET, 'Science Education in Late-Victorian Oxford', *English Historical Review*, 102: 403 (Apr. 1987), 334–67.

JOHNSON, LIONEL, 'The Poems of Mr Bridges: A Brief and General Consideration', *Century Guild Hobby-horse* (Oct. 1891), repr. as Introduction to *The Growth of Love* (Portland, Maine, 1894).

KELLOG, G. A., 'Bridges's *Milton's Prosody* and Renaissance Metrical Theory', *PMLA*, 68 (Mar. 1953), 268–85.

KNOX, E. A., 'Memories of Corpus Christi College, 1865–8', *Pelican Record*, 20: 2 (1931), 86–92, 106–15, 136–42.

LIPSCOMB, HERBERT, C., 'Lucretius and "The Testament of Beauty"', *Classical Journal*, 31 (1935–6), 77–88.

MAGNUS, LAURIE, '"The Testament of Beauty"', *Cornhill Magazine*, NS 68, (May 1930), 527–38.

MOORE, NORMAN, 'Notes on the Casualty Department', *St Bartholomew's Hospital Reports*, 14 (1878).

—— *'Patrick Black'*, in *DNB* (1886).

NOWELL-SMITH, SIMON, 'Bridges, Hopkins and Dr. Daniel', *Times Literary Supplement* (13 Dec. 1957), 764.

—— 'A Poet in Walton Street', in *Essays mainly on the Nineteenth Century Presented to Sir Humphry Milford* (1948).

—— 'Some Uncollected Authors XXIX: Richard Watson Dixon 1833–1900', *Book Collector* (1961), 322–5.

PATMORE, DEREK, 'Three Poets Discuss New Verse Forms: The Correspondence of Gerard Manley Hopkins, Robert Bridges and Coventry Patmore', *Month* NS 6: 2 (Aug. 1951), 69–78.

PEARSALL SMITH, LOGAN, 'Robert Bridges: Recollections', *SPE* Tract 35 (1931), 483–502.

POTTER, JOHN, 'Robert Bridges (1844–1930): Medicine as a Training for Poetry?', *St Bartholomew's Hospital Journal*, 58: 3 (1954), 62–8.

RAWNSLEY, W. F., 'On Corpus Rowing', *Pelican Record*, 12 (1913–15), 132–7.

SMITH, NOWELL CHARLES, 'Robert Seymour Bridges', in *DNB, 1922–1930* (1937).

SQUIRE, J. C., 'The Laureate's Long Poem', *Observer* (27 Oct. 1929).

STANFORD, CHARLES VILLIERS, *Pages from an Unwritten Diary* (1914).

STANFORD, DONALD, 'Gerard Manley Hopkins and Robert Bridges', in

Hopkins Among the Poets, edited by Richard F. Giles (Hamilton, Ontario, 1985).

—— 'Robert Bridges and the Free Verse Rebellion', *Journal of Modern Literature*, 2:1 (Sept. 1971), 19–31.

—— 'Robert Bridges on his Poems and Plays: Unpublished Letters by Robert Bridges to Samuel Butler', *Philological Quarterly*, 50 (Apr. 1971), 281–91.

—— 'Robert Bridges and Samuel Butler on Shakespeare's Sonnets: an exchange of letters', *Shakespeare Quarterly*, 22 (Autumn 1971), 329–35.

—— 'Robert Bridges, Poet-Typographer', *Fine Print*, 9 (Jan. 1983), 7–9.

STRONG, H. A., 'Corpus in the Early Sixties', *Pelican Record*, 7: 6 (1905), 178–82 and 8: 1 (1905), 8–11.

TURLEY, FRANK, 'The Story of the Harveys of Roselands', *East Kent Mercury* (20 Feb. 1975).

TWITCHETT, E. G., 'The Poetry of Robert Bridges', *London Mercury*, 21: 122 (Dec. 1929), 136–45.

VAN DE POEL, JEAN and S. I. M. DU PLESSIS, 'Jan Christian Smuts', in *Dictionary of South African Biography*, edited by W. J. de Kock (Cape Town, 1968).

WARREN, HERBERT, 'Robert Bridges', *The Poets and the Poetry of the Century*, 8: *Robert Bridges and Contemporary Poets*, edited by A. H. Miles (1898).

WELBY, T. EARLE, 'The Poet Laureate', *Poetry* (9 Nov. 1929), 545–6.

MANUSCRIPTS

Most of the Bridges Papers are in the Bodleian Library, Oxford, although the Bridges family retain a few and six pages from *The Testament of Beauty* are in the British Library. The papers of Francis Chavasse and Gerard Manley Hopkins that I have used here are in the Bodleian Library. The Samuel Brooke papers and Captain's Book of the Corpus Boat Club are in Corpus Christi College, Oxford. The papers of Horace Joseph are in New College and those of C. H. O. Daniel in Worcester College, Oxford. The records of the Brotherhood of the Most Holy Trinity are in Pusey House, Oxford. Some of the papers of Roger Fry and the Eton examination papers are in King's College, and the correspondence of R. C. Trevelyan is in Trinity College, Cambridge. Bridges' correspondence with Francis Jenkinson is in the University Library, Cambridge, and Bridges' letters to Samuel Gee in the Archive of the Royal College of Physicians, London. Tithe maps of 1844 and church records for Kent are in the Cathedral Library, Canterbury, and the census returns in the Public Library, Maidenhead.

INDEX